Protest Politics Today

Protest Politics Today

DEVASHREE GUPTA

polity

First published in 2017 by Polity Press

Polity Press
65 Bridge Street
Cambridge CB2 1UR, UK

Polity Press,
101 Station Landing, Suite 300
Medford, MA 02155, USA

ISBN-13: 978-0-7456-7114-7
ISBN-13: 978-0-7456-7115-4 (paperback)

A catalogue record for this book is available from the British Library.

Library of Congress Cataloging-in-Publication Data

Names: Gupta, Devashree, author.
Title: Protest politics today / Devashree Gupta.
Description: Cambridge, UK : Malden, MA, USA : Polity Press, [2017] |
    Includes bibliographical references and index.
Identifiers: LCCN 2017006634| ISBN 9780745671147 (hardback) | ISBN
    9780745671154 (pbk.)
Subjects: LCSH: Protest movements. | Social action. | Social
    change–Political aspects.
Classification: LCC HM883 .G86 2017 | DDC 303.48/4–dc23 LC record available at
    https://lccn.loc.gov/2017006634

Typeset in 9.5 on 13 pt Swift Light by
Servis Filmsetting Ltd, Stockport, Cheshire
Printed and bound in the UK by Clays Ltd, St Ives PLC

To Bob, for his constant love and support
and Archie, for never leaving my side

Contents

Figures

Tables

CHAPTER 1

The Politics of Protest

Objectives

- To establish how social movements differ from other types of political activity, including institutional and non-institutional forms.
- To examine how modern social movements developed and the political, economic, and social changes that led to their creation.
- To identify how main theoretical approaches used by scholars to study social movement differ in the questions they privilege and the variables they use to explain patterns of protest.
- To determine how scholars use different methodological approaches to answer questions about social movements.

Introduction

One week after the controversial shooting death of Walter Scott, an unarmed black man, by a white police officer in South Carolina, several dozen people gathered in front of North Charleston's city hall on a mild April evening in 2015 to hold a candlelight protest vigil. Carrying signs that said "The World is Watching" and "Black Lives Matter," the protestors demanded accountability for Scott's death, which had been captured on video by a bystander and whose details had intensified an already agonized national conversation about police brutality and institutional racism. It had been almost two years since a Florida jury acquitted George Zimmerman of murder for shooting Trayvon Martin, an unarmed teen who was walking home from a convenience store and who, Zimmerman claimed, had attacked him. The acquittal touched off a wave of protests, while the hashtag #BlackLivesMatter began to circulate on social media sites. Starting out as an online campaign, it made the jump to physical demonstrations one year later to protest the death of Michael Brown at the hands of a white police officer in Ferguson, Missouri. In the months following, Black Lives Matter (BLM) became a national movement, with a network of local chapters and a forceful online presence.

The demonstrations in North Charleston were part of a long list of protests that had taken place all around the United States since Ferguson – in New York, Oakland, Cleveland, Chicago, and Los Angeles, and other cities both large and small. In each case, protestors called attention to issues of institutional racism, police brutality, and unequal treatment meted out by the justice system to communities of color. For several hours, the protestors in North Charleston sang songs, shared personal stories of their own brushes with law enforcement, and observed a moment of silence to honor Scott. They also made demands, including the creation of a citizens' advisory committee with extensive powers to investigate and review police actions. They gave the mayor of North Charleston until 7 p.m. that evening to announce his response. To the protestors' disappointment, the mayor rejected their demands. To those gathered at the vigil, however, this reply was neither satisfactory nor the end of the matter, and organizers promised to step up their campaign of resistance following Scott's funeral the next day to pressure city officials to address their concerns.

On the same day, over 7,000 miles away in the Yemeni capital of Sana'a, a political sect of Zaidi Shia Muslims known as the Houthi took to the streets to protest airstrikes by a coalition of nine Arab states, including Saudi Arabia, Egypt, and Jordan. Several thousand protestors carried Yemeni flags and banners demanding an end to foreign intervention by the Saudi-led coalition in what they argued was a purely domestic conflict between supporters of the ousted President, Abd Rabbuh Mansur Hadi and rebel groups (including the Houthi) who supported his predecessor, Ali Abdullah Saleh. These protests were matched by parallel demonstrations in other Houthi-controlled parts of the country and some even further afield, including an anti-war protest in front of Saudi Arabia's London embassy planned for later that weekend. But the Houthi were not the only ones voicing their discontent in the streets. Even as they marched against coalition airstrikes, in parts of the country controlled by their opponents people marched in support of the coalition and President Hadi, who they claimed had been illegally ousted by rebel forces.

As the Houthi and their opponents were demonstrating in Yemen, activists in Madrid, Spain were carrying out a very different kind of demonstration in front of the Spanish parliament building that same evening: a holographic protest march. The object of their grievance was a controversial Spanish law that sharply restricted when and where people could protest and attached stiff financial penalties – up to €600,000 – for violations. Criticizing the law for severely limiting free speech and assembly rights, activists staged the world's first-ever hologram protest, in which thousands of holographic images of people were projected marching past the parliament building during an hour-long demonstration. Because the parliament was one of several sites subject to the draconian new restrictions, the organizers of the protest wanted to juxtapose the relative freedoms enjoyed by the holograms, which were not limited by the new law, and flesh-and-blood individuals, who were.

While the holograms were marching in Madrid, students at the University of Cape Town were protesting by staying still – in their case, by continuing to occupy an administrative building as part of the Rhodes Must Fall (RMF) movement. The RMF movement started out as a campaign to remove a large statue of Cecil Rhodes, the business magnate and South African politician, who was seen by protestors as a disgraced champion of imperialism and racial subjugation. For nearly three weeks, dozens of students had staged a round-the-clock sit-in to put pressure on the university by disrupting normal administrative operations. As they lived and slept in the building, protestors engaged in discussions about how removing the statue could lead to more extensive reform on campus. Eventually, the University Council yielded to the RMF demands and removed the statue on April 9, 2015. Yet the sit-in continued the next day – despite university orders to vacate the premises – as protestors sought to build on their success to address lingering problems of institutional racism and injustice. For RMF activists, the removal of the statue was not the end, but merely the opening salvo of a longer struggle to "decolonize" the university.

All four of these protests took place on the same day in April, but apart from sharing a moment in time, they seem to have little else in common. The contexts which made it possible for people to protest ranged from the United States' long-established democracy, to Spain's and South Africa's relatively young democracies, to Yemen, which is not, and has never been, fully democratic. Protests happened in rich societies like the United States, where the GDP per capita was over $53,000 in 2013, as well as in the considerably poorer country of Yemen, with a GDP per capita of just $1,473. In addition to sharing the diversity of settings, the protest events themselves differed in focus, target, and tactic. The grievances that motivated protestors to leave the comfort of their everyday routines ranged from police brutality to university culture, and from protests against domestic law to the actions of a neighboring government. The targets included local political elites, the national parliament, a foreign state, and even a university. The protestors sometimes numbered a few dozen, while the demonstrators in Sana'a numbered several thousand, and the Spanish hologram march past parliament – technically speaking – involved no people at all!

The differences among these four examples continue when we consider the outcomes of these various protest events. Over a year after the Sana'a protests, for example, the Saudi coalition continues to bomb Houthi-held areas, while thousands of Houthi continue to protest coalition involvement in the Yemeni civil war. Despite the hologram protest (and others featuring actual people), the Spanish government has yet to repeal its harsh law, and has already levied fines against people in violation of its provisions. Meanwhile, protestors at the University of Cape Town not only succeeded in removing the hated statue of Cecil Rhodes, they also triggered a larger curriculum review and the addition of Black Studies as part of an effort to transform the institution and rid it of institutional vestiges of its colonial past. And back in North Charleston, the protestors eventually did get their citizens' advisory committee after all, though with limited powers and other compromises that left some leaders of the movement doubtful whether it would be of any real use in combating police violence.

Despite these differences in context, characteristics, and outcomes, there are several key commonalities that these four protest events share. In all of the examples, protests were carried out by people who felt deeply about an issue – so much so that they chose to invest their personal time and energies to bring attention to a problem and work for a solution. But participation required more than simple time and energy; it also was costly, as participants had to take time off from work or school, arrange transportation, and perhaps even risk injury or arrest. Yet despite these potential costs, deeply invested individuals in all four cases chose to act in concert with other, like-minded individuals to coordinate their actions and present a united front to their targets. This unity was often expressed through singing songs, telling stories, and sharing experiences – activities that bonded protestors and transformed them from atomistic individuals to a collective working together for a mutually desirable goal. Protests also involved strategies like sit-ins, vigils, and marches – tactics that were public and that demanded attention – in order to achieve their demands.

In addition, the protests themselves were not isolated incidents destined never to be repeated. Rather, in all four cases, protests were part of a larger, sustained effort to bring about social change. The North Charleston protestors planned to carry out their campaign in the days following Walter Scott's funeral, and their association with the national Black Lives Matter movement connected their protests to larger efforts to address issues of systemic racism. Similarly, the April 10 protest against Saudi airstrikes was one of several happening that day in the country, but was also connected to subsequent protests against the coalition's military offensive, in Yemen as well as in London, Toronto, Lebanon, and Iran. The hologram protest may have been the first and only one of its kind, but the organizations that helped to coordinate the demonstration had worked actively to oppose the law since the moment it was passed by the legislature. And RMF protestors continue to challenge the University of Cape Town – and other South African universities – in matters of racial discrimination and injustice. The movement even spread to universities in the United Kingdom and United States, where local students took up the challenge to "decolonize" their institutions and spawned a successor movement – Fees Must Fall – that agitates on the issue of lowering university tuition rates. These similarities – deeply invested participants who shared a sense of purpose and came together as a community, public displays of strength and fortitude, a commitment to ongoing action – suggest that these four protest events are all the handiwork of social movements.

What are Social Movements?

If you were to brainstorm a list of ways in which people could participate in political life, you might name activities like voting in an election, writing a letter to an elected official, donating money to a political party, or answering a pollster's questions about the most pressing issues facing your country today. Perhaps if you had more time to think, you would start to add some activities to your list that are a little less common, like participating in a strike, or taking part in a protest march. You might even think about disruptive activities – such as hunger strikes, sabotage, or riots – that occur far less frequently, but, when they do, have the potential to shake the existing political order. The universe of political activity, in other words, includes a range of actions, some of which might strike you as innocuous, even commonplace, while others might be surprising, threatening, or shocking.

Where do social movements fit into this smorgasbord of political activity? Charles Tilly and Sidney Tarrow suggest that they are examples of *contentious politics*, or politics "in which actors make claims bearing on someone else's interests, leading to coordinated efforts on behalf of shared interests or programs, in which governments are involved as targets, initiators of claims, or third parties" (Tilly and Tarrow 2015: 7). At first, this definition might not seem to be all that helpful since so much of the political world these days seems to involve people acting in combative and antagonistic ways. But what Tilly and Tarrow argue is that contentious politics involve people making demands, such as a shift in policy, or increased funding for an organization, or a change in the way political elites behave. There are many political activities that do not involve demands. Registering to vote, for example, does not involve making demands but following established rules in order to legally fill out a ballot during elections. Likewise, donating money to an interest group like the American Association of Retired Persons or the National Rifle Association does not, by itself, entail making demands on others, though what such groups do with those donations – lobbying for legislative changes, for example – might indeed involve contentious claims.

Not only do contentious actors like social movements make demands, their claims directly affect the interests of other actors in society who may, in turn, resist giving in to those claims. These interests could include holding on to political power, for example, which motivated the autocratic leaders of various Arab states to resist the demands for democratic reforms emerging from the 2011 Arab Spring uprisings. Social movement demands can also affect financial interests, as in the case of protests by North Dakota's Standing Rock Sioux tribe, which objects to a planned oil pipeline that would cross their main source of drinking water and sacred tribal lands. Preventing the pipeline from being built would cost Dakota Access, the company building it, millions of dollars in lost revenue. Contentious demands can also affect other actors' identities and values, as in the case of the 2015 clashes over displaying the Confederate battle flag at the South Carolina capitol building. On one side were protestors who argued for the flag's removal, citing its connection to slavery and racial hatred. On the other side were those who defended the flag, arguing that it was a cherished symbol of Southern heritage and also honored those who lost their lives fighting in the Civil War. As these examples also suggest, the contentious claims that propel social movements can come from all sides of an ideological spectrum; some movements, such as anti-immigration or far-right nationalist movements, are rooted in conservative or even reactionary ideological philosophies, whereas groups like Occupy Wall Street (OWS) or the Lesbian, Gay, Bisexual, and Transgender (LGBT) movement come from a left or progressive stance. Some movements may even contain groups with ideologically conflicting stances. The anti-globalization movement, for example, includes groups that critique neoliberal economic policies from Marxist perspectives as well as groups that oppose globalization as a threat to nationalist identities and conservative values. Regardless, whether it impacts power, money, identity, or some combination of these things, fulfilling social movement demands is rarely a straightforward task.

Defining Social Movements

Contentious politics include a range of phenomena besides social movements, so what are the distinguishing characteristics that set this category apart from other forms of political participation? Sidney Tarrow offers one succinct definition when he argues that movements are "collective challenges, based on common purposes and social solidarities, in a sustained interaction with elites, opponents, and authorities" (Tarrow 2011: 9). While other scholars might define movements slightly differently or emphasize other aspects, Tarrow's formulation is a good place to start because it captures many of the components that reappear in these other definitions.

First, social movements are collective, in that they consist of multiple people working in concert toward a common end. They are, ultimately, *social* spheres that promote interaction among their supporters. These interactions can occur in multiple ways and in multiple locations, ranging from relatively formal movement organizations to less structured and more free-wheeling social media platforms, but still have some kind of organizational structure that can facilitate cooperation across the movement.

Participants in the movement are connected to each other via dynamic and flexible networks that facilitate the flow of ideas and information from one part of the movement to another, as well as help to build a sense of collective identity.

Collective identity, in turn, is important because social movements are about bringing together not just people with common goals, but people who share a sense of solidarity with each other and who identify with others in the movement (Melucci 1995). In turn, people who closely identify with and are invested in the movement will be more likely to be concerned for its well-being and survival and, in turn, to help to sustain movement participation over time (Hunt and Benford 2004). This collective identity may precede a movement's formation, be created as part of social movement activism, or a combination of the two; regardless, this collective sense of belonging and emotional investment that a social movement encourages can be a pleasurable end in itself for activists, whether the movement achieves its demands or not (Jasper 1997: 8).

Duration is also important: one protest event does not a social movement make. It can take time to alter the status quo, and social movements must persist in their demands and work toward them, whether it takes days, weeks, or years. It took the abolitionist movement in the United Kingdom 51 years of work to end slavery in the British empire, from the founding of the first anti-slavery group in 1783 to the final passage of the parliamentary bill. While some movements have shorter life spans than this (and some may last even longer), this capacity to sustain contention is a core feature of social movements and one that differentiates them from riots, which are explosive but short-lived.

Protest Forms and Signaling Credibility

In addition to the above criteria, Charles Tilly and Lesley Wood also argue that social movements use particular types of protest, employing "combinations from among the following forms of political action: creation of special-purpose associations and coalitions, public meetings, solemn processions, vigils, rallies, demonstrations, petition drives, statements to and in public media, and pamphleteering" (Tilly and Wood 2004: 3). Although this seems like a definitive list, social movements are not necessarily bound to just these forms and some can be quite creative in how they articulate their demands. The movement to close down the Vermont Yankee

Nuclear Power Plant, for example, included a group that staged political puppet shows as part of its protest. Students protesting the Chilean government's education policies staged protest kiss-ins and a flash mob with participants dressed in costumes inspired by Michael Jackson's "Thriller" video. And Mexico's Manifesto MX, a street-art collective, organizes graffiti artists to tag buildings with protest murals on topics ranging from neoliberal economic policies to the drug war.

What is noteworthy about these examples is that they are non-institutional. That is, they are activities that occur largely outside formal institutions like courts and legislatures. Social movements do not *always* use non-institutional forms of protest; they also sometimes lobby political parties, testify before Congress, and make use of the courts to advance their causes, as in the case of the LGBT movement, which used the 2015 US Supreme Court case *Obergefell* v. *Hodges* to strike down state-level bans on same-sex marriage. And sometimes institutional actors make use of non-institutional forms of action to make a point or capture the public's attention. For example, following a deadly mass shooting in Florida, 170 members of the Democratic Party staged a one-day sit-in on the floor of the House of Representatives to protest the lack of meaningful gun-control legislation. The tactic infuriated the Republican members of Congress, who argued that it violated the institution's rules and procedures and called it a political stunt.

Via these non-institutional protests, movements must communicate their worthiness (W), unity (U), numbers (N), and commitment (C) in their actions (Tilly and Wood 2004: 4). Combined into the rather inelegant acronym WUNC, such displays are important because they confer credibility and legitimacy on actors who could be seen as threatening or politically marginal, and whose demands could otherwise be easily dismissed. Outsiders who are seen as deserving, moral, upstanding, and respectable might have an easier time than those who display moral licentiousness or reckless behavior. Movements can demonstrate their WUNC-ness in many ways. For example, by featuring respected members of society participating in rallies, they can demonstrate worthiness; by having everyone wear matching shirts or singing common songs, they can signal unity; by having as many people as possible turn out to a rally, they show numbers; and by protesting, despite the ominous presence of riot police nearby, they display commitment to a cause.

Differentiating Movements

The above criteria provide a working definition of social movements and also help us to separate them from other political groups that might seem similar in certain respects. The requirement that movements operate largely outside formal institutions, for example, sets them apart from other collective, goal-oriented, and sustained groups like political parties and interest groups, which operate largely within institutional settings and use much more conventional tactics to get what they want (Johnston 2014: 9–10). This distinction between institutional and non-institutional channels derives from the notion that political parties and interest groups are largely made up of political "insiders" who have privileged access to the levers of power, compared to political "outsiders" like members of social movements (Kornhauser 1959; Tilly 1978; McAdam 1982; Gamson 1990).

While outsiders can still influence politics, it requires more effort than for insiders who have the standing, resources, access, or know-how to wield political influence more easily (Schattschneider 1963; Merton 1972: 11; Lindbeck and Snower 2001). Political parties, for example, can actually pass (or block) legislation, and have a chance to govern the country if they win enough votes (in democracies) or have enough coercive power (in autocracies). Interest groups can also achieve insider status via the resources they have to lobby lawmakers and the possible technical expertise they can offer when bills are being drafted (Maloney et al. 1994). When drafting the 2013 Affordable Care Act (commonly called Obamacare), for example, lawmakers met with a range of interest groups, including those representing hospitals, medical professionals, and the insurance industry, all of which offered technical advice and recommendations to those in charge of writing the bill.

Social movements, by contrast, are relatively disadvantaged when it comes to wielding political power. They lack the deep pockets of powerful interest groups and the institutional standing of political parties. To use Charles Tilly's (1978) terminology, social movements are challengers who seek entry into the privileged political sphere inhabited by insiders. But because insiders have a vested interest in limiting the number of people who influence politics, they may not be willing to permit entry or listen to the demands of outsiders. Being excluded from power, in turn, requires outsiders to work a little harder, bang a little louder, be a little more insistent in their efforts to affect change.

While this distinction between insider and outsider is conceptually helpful, in practice the lines are much blurrier. In Sidney Tarrow's words, social movements are "neither as independent of the polity as they like to portray themselves, nor as ensnared in institutional politics as many later become. They are 'strangers at the gates' who operate on the boundaries of the polity, in an uneasy position that explains much of the ambiguities and contradictions in their strategies, composition and dynamics" (Tarrow 2012: 3). Not all political parties and interest groups, for example, have equivalent access to the levers of power. Marginal political parties usually have little hope of winning seats or having any real influence in policymaking. And not all interest groups and lobbies have equally deep pockets or clout. According to the Center for Responsive Politics, interest groups representing the pharmaceutical industry spent $240 million on lobbying politicians in 2015 – the most of any industry – but the alternative energy sector (wind and solar power companies) spent just 9.6 percent of that amount in the same period. And, as Jack Goldstone (2003) observes, there is no sharp dividing line between movements and institutional actors, as movements can develop deep ties with institutional actors, partner with them strategically, and even turn into them over time, as the African National Congress did when apartheid was abolished in South Africa: as a social movement group, it was banned by the country's government for over three decades, but as a political party, it has won every general election since 1994.

The Rise of Modern Social Movements

Having defined what social movements are, let us now ask: what are their origins? In one sense, protest is old news. The first recorded strike in history, for example, took place over 3,000 years ago in Egypt, near the Valley of the Kings where the ancient pharaohs were entombed. Details of the strike were preserved on papyrus and inform us that it involved the workers who lived in Deir el-Medina, an Egyptian village that supplied the artisans who worked on the royal tombs. Roughly around 1170 BCE, food rations were slow to arrive and, after several lengthy delays, the workers decided to take action. They laid down their tools and left their worksite, demanding their food rations. Government officials gave in to their demands, making this ancient strike a resounding success. In fact, it was so successful that the artisans went on strike several more times in the future when food rations were again delayed (Edgerton 1961).

Though this early strike seems familiar to us in many ways, social movement scholars argue that it does not really constitute a social movement – at least, not in the way we understand it today. In fact, none of the protests that occurred prior to the eighteenth century really had the characteristics that we ascribe to social movements – collective, shared solidarity, with some kind of organizational backing, sustained over time, with displays emphasizing WUNC. As a result, scholars argue that social movements are a relatively modern invention. We can actually date their emergence to the late eighteenth and early nineteenth centuries, and pinpoint their places of origin as Western Europe and North America. But why then, and why there? The answer has to do with the significant social, political, and economic changes that were unfolding at this time – the rise of the national state, the Industrial Revolution, the emergence of democratic principles – that in combination created the social movement that we know today (Tilly and Wood 2004; Jasper 2014).

Protest Then, Protest Now

What were the hallmarks of protest before the rise of the modern social movement? John Archer's detailed historical analysis of protest in eighteenth- and nineteenth-century Britain gives us some inkling. Consider, as an example, protests that developed around the country in response to the criminalization of gathering wood. For many years, rural communities would collect fallen tree limbs, as well as smaller twigs and branches that could be snapped off by hand from woodlands and the Royal Forests, and use this wood for fuel. This custom, however, started to come under attack, and by 1766 was banned outright. Because alternate fuel sources were scarce, wood theft became the most common crime in the UK by the beginning of the nineteenth century (Archer 2000; Briggs et al. 1996).

This conflict generated protests around the country. The details are instructive. In Otmoor, located less than 10 miles from Oxford, "under the guise of pursuing the traditional ritual of beating the bounds, 1,000 locals marched several miles, destroying fences and hedges in the process. In this incident men reportedly dressed as women took a leading part in the destruction . . . [even though] cross dressing in English rural protest was, by this time, unusual" (Archer 2000: 13). In Sussex, 100 miles to the south, the protest took a different form: on St. Andring's Day, people traditionally went squirrel hunting, so, to protest, locals went out on the pretext of hunting squirrels, but "anything that moved was shot and hedges were destroyed and carried home for fuel" (Archer 2000: 13). What makes protests like these different from the strategies and tactics of a modern social movement?

First, these protests tended to be highly localized affairs in which participants were concerned primarily with their immediate sur-roundings and the targets directly in front of them. They lacked a sense of sharing a common grievance with people from elsewhere, and they did not direct their anger at the government that had passed the despised legislation. Even though protests were wide-spread, they were remarkably local in focus (Archer 2000: 19). There is no sense from the accounts of these protests that the villagers in Otmoor knew about or felt common cause with the crowd in Sussex. Moreover, protests were largely aimed at what Sidney Tarrow (2011: 38) calls "the immediate sites of wrongdoing" and the perpetrators associated with them: the tax collector or the grain merchant, and not, for example, the government elites who made the tax laws or set grain prices but who were located many hundreds of miles away in a city that most people would never see.

A second, related point is that these separate protests drew on highly localized cultural forms and practices to shape their pro-tests. The Otmoor protests made use of a locally relevant tradition – beating the bounds – and employed cross dressing, which clearly had some local meaning but was not at all a common practice elsewhere. It seems not to have had sufficient resonance to be employed in the Sussex protest where, again, the local celebration of St. Andring's Day and its custom of squirrel hunting were used to mask the protests that ensued. In Sidney Tarrow's words, the highly localized scale made protest both *parochial*, insofar as "most often the interests and interactions involved were concentrated in a single community," and *segmented*, "because when ordinary people addressed local issues and nearby objects, they took impressively direct action to achieve their ends, but when it came to national issues and objects, they recurrently addressed their demands to a local patron or authority" (2011: 40).

A third feature in these examples is the relatively short-lived nature of these protests; none of them is sustained over time – rather, they come across as impulsive and brief. This is not particularly surprising given our previous discussion: there was no organization, no collective identity, no emotional attachment in evidence – nothing that would help sustain a protest over multiple days or weeks.

Fourth, protests before the late eighteenth century tended to be defensive and reactive moves rather than campaigns to proactively influence political decisions. Take the case of the wood protests: a law passed by Parliament made the long-held custom of gathering wood illegal, but neither protest demanded that Parliament repeal this law. Instead, they were exercises in venting anger and seeking immediate relief for the problem, not long-term political change.

All of these characteristics, however, were about to change. Rather than being "parochial, segmented, and particular" like earlier protests, the modern social movement would be "cosmopolitan, modular, and autonomous" (Tilly 1996; Tarrow 2011: 40–1). The cosmopolitan nature of modern social movements refers to their increased scale and scope; no longer highly localized, the modern social movement connects local, regional, national, and even international action as part of a unified social movement community. The examples that opened this chapter illustrate this point nicely. The North Charleston protest was, in some ways, very localized, insofar as some of its grievances and demands were narrowly focused on policing practices and oversight in a city of under 100,000 residents. At the same time, the protest was self-consciously connected to a much larger national movement – the Black Lives Matter movement – and the tragic death of Walter Scott was given national context when connected with the names of other black victims of police violence. Similarly, although the RMF movement started out highly localized, its focus on confronting racial inequities and discriminatory legacies in education spread to other universities in South Africa and even overseas, to Oxford University, the University of Edinburgh, and the University of California, Berkeley. All of these institutions took inspiration from and identified with the RMF movement. The Spanish protests and the Yemeni protests, too, linked multiple sites of protest in ways that earlier forms of protest simply did not do.

The modularity of protest is also a key feature of modern movements. Modularity, according to Sidney Tarrow, involves easy transferability across settings or contexts (Tarrow 2011: 41). In contrast to earlier forms of protest, which were tied to highly local practices, customs, and understandings, modern movements employ tactics that travel across issue and across space: a sit-in can be used in Toronto by taxi workers protesting the entry of ride-sharing companies like Uber into the city, as well as by Chinese students in Tiananmen Square demanding democratic reforms, as well as by disabled Bolivians protesting the level of benefits they receive from the government. This modular form of protest serves "a variety of sites, on behalf of a variety of goals, and against a variety of targets" (Tarrow 2011: 38). Contrast this with the destruction of hedges while cross dressing in Otmoor or shooting anything that moves on the pretext of squirrel hunting, as in Sussex: not only do these forms of protest travel poorly outside their particular locales, but to use them to protest other issues – bread shortages or increasing mechanization – would seem nonsensical.

Social movements also become autonomous as they increasingly moved from defensive, reactive activity to more proactive, strategic approaches. Whereas Lynne Taylor describes bread rioters as spontaneous and impulsive, apolitical and defensive (Taylor 1996: 483), modern social movements have more control over when, where, and how they make their demands (Tilly 2002: 65). The new autonomous social movements not only initiate protest proactively, but also connect protestors to national centers of power rather than the local faces of their grievances, making it possible to aim for long-term changes addressing root causes rather than seeking temporary relief for the immediate symptoms.

Mechanisms of Change

How and why did the modern social movement emerge? And why did it take on the particular form that it has? Three important transformations lie at the heart of this evolution: the rise of the modern national state, the emergence of industrial capitalism, and the spread of democratic ideals. Each of them shook up the existing political, economic, and social order in ways that had long-lasting effects on popular protest.

The Modern State

In the seventeenth and eighteenth centuries, European countries were undergoing monumental changes in political structure.

In places like Britain and France, feudal structures were being dismantled and, in their place, monarchs were setting up bureaucratic institutions that would make it easier to rule their populations directly rather than relying on intermediaries such as members of the nobility. As they dismantled these feudal structures, they needed a way to carry out the administrative functions that nobles, knights, and their vassals had previously performed. Under a feudal system, for example, the monarch might delegate tax collection to his nobles, who, in turn, would auction off the right to the highest bidder. The winning bidder would then collect taxes from the peasantry, hand it over to the nobleman (keeping some for himself, of course), and the nobleman would, in turn, hand it over to the king (also keeping some for himself, of course). The end result was an inefficient and easily corruptible system of laws and administration that not only diluted the power of the king, but led to discrepancies in enforcement across the country. Under this feudal "tax farming" system, for example, it would not be unusual for two people making the same amount of money to owe completely different amounts in tax, depending on how greedy their respective tax collectors and feudal lords might be. While this system was clearly problematic, monarchs could not simply abolish it without having something to put in its place. Without feudal hierarchies to play that role, state rulers set about developing centralized bureaucracies to carry out these tasks (Tilly 1992).

These bureaucracies were not only centralized, but accountable directly to state leaders. They were also increasingly staffed by people with more specialized knowledge in particular areas. Tax collectors, for example, would no longer be the people who bid the most for that perk, but trained officials who knew the tax code and could administer it fairly and even-handedly. For ordinary people, this shift was significant: the entire population was subject to the same laws, administered in the same way. Moreover, the face of those laws was not the local nobleman or knight, but a representative of the national government itself. These changes fostered not only a sense of horizontal equality and sameness across the population, but also direct connections between individuals and the central government. Now, if there were grievances, it would be more likely that those grievances would be turned toward the national government rather than the purely local, and that individuals would find common cause with others across the country, given that their experiences under the law were far more equal than before.

Industrial Capitalism

In addition to the construction of modern states with their centralized, professional bureaucracies, economic changes also played a role in the evolution of social movements. The first stirrings of industrial capitalism in Britain soon spread throughout Europe, bringing profound social and economic upheavals with them. Industrialization encouraged intensive urbanization as rural populations left their traditional homesteads and moved to cities to work in factories. As a result, by 1850, London had become the largest city in the world – the first European city to achieve this milestone in over 1,000 years (United Nations 1980: 5). It also encouraged greater connectivity to outlying regions of the country, as industries needed reliable and cheap ways to convey raw materials and laborers to manufacturing centers and ship finished goods to consumers. As a result, roads, railways, and canals proliferated across the landscape making it easier to transport goods, but also people and ideas.

Adding to this spread of information were technological innovations in publishing, which made it possible to print cheap books and pamphlets for popular consumption (Anderson 2016). Whereas only the wealthy could afford books before mass printing techniques were perfected, by the middle of the nineteenth century ordinary people could buy books and discover new ideas from far-away places. Together, these forces made it easier for people in one part of a society to learn about, identify with, and potentially support protests happening in other places. Easier travel made it possible to get news about protest tactics and spread those ideas widely. When protest occurred in one place, those towns and villages connected to it by main roads were more susceptible to subsequent outbreaks of protest as the highways served as conduits of information and practice (Archer 2000: 20).

Industrialization also encouraged the development of labor associations, formed to represent the interests of the rapidly growing – and politically marginalized – working classes. These labor associations, in turn, provided an organizational nexus for protests, helping to recruit and mobilize individuals, coordinating activity, and making it possible for episodic bouts of protest to transform into something more sustained and proactive. The collective action that flowed from such organizations became more complex and ambitious, containing explicit programmatic demands and more coherent ideological foundations. Bread rioters did not make sophisticated claims; they just demanded access to bread when it was in short supply. Labor organizations – and the other organized interests that emerged – could make more substantive and systemic policy demands, and frame them as part of a larger ideological agenda. In addition, the organizational structures of such associations made it easier to plan ahead, take advantage of opportunities that presented themselves, and orchestrate protest for the times, places, and targets where it might have the greatest impact.

Spread of Democracy

The final major social change in the eighteenth and nineteenth centuries that affected the evolution of social movements was the spread of democratic ideals and notions of popular sovereignty. Although there were relatively few democracies in the world by the end of the nineteenth century, the idea of democracy was much more widespread. The print revolution had made it easier to circulate the writings of key thinkers like John Locke, and to inform the reading public of developments happening in democracies like Britain, France, and the United States. In a world still dominated by autocratic rulers, the ideals championed by democratic rule – popular sovereignty, freedom, equality, and a government accountable to its own citizens – were enormously appealing to ordinary people.

In addition, the spread of democratic ideas, combined with the development of the national state, also triggered a change in what people believed was the proper relationship between government and those it governs. Whereas earlier monarchical systems justified their authority based on principles like divine right, democracies derived their legitimacy from those they ruled. As a result, government was not seen as separate from and superior to the people; it *was* the people, and subject to their demands. The idea that people were subjects to be ruled over by a remote authority started to give way to the notion that people were citizens, equal members in the polity. This shift in how people thought about the relationship between people and the government, citizens and the state, also affected social movements. Whereas subjects had no right to make demands on a divinely appointed monarch, citizens had every right to make demands of a government that could not be legitimate without their support.

Together, these social transformations also changed social protest in fundamental ways. As state building, industrial capitalism, and democratic ideas spread and affected the social movements that emerged in Europe and the United States, this new idea of what social movements were and what they could do started to spread beyond its point of origin. While not all protest may fit into the cosmopolitan, modular, and autonomous framework, much of it does, regardless of where in the world we look.

It is important, however, not to take this idea too far; protest may generally share certain key features regardless of whether it occurs in Copenhagen or Caracas, but that is not to say that protest is *identical* in different locations. Instead, in this book I argue that social movements are also conditioned by the political and social environments in which they are located, and the nature of their opponents, as well as their past histories and decisions; this makes social movements anything but cookie-cutter versions of each other. Accordingly, in the following chapters, I highlight the similarities among social movements that come from general evolutionary patterns that apply broadly to all social movements, as well as ways that social movements reflect the specific locations in which they operate and histories out of which they emerge.

Studying Social Movements

The last remaining task of this first chapter is to provide a brief overview of some of the main theories and methods that scholars use to study social movements. Each of these approaches contains certain foundational assumptions about human nature, what motivates people to act, and what kinds of variables are particularly important to consider when answering questions about social protest. While people certainly disagree on some of these assumptions or about which variables are particularly important for explaining protest, the study of social movements is, ironically, not nearly as contentious as other fields (Tarrow 2004; Edwards 2014: 3). In part, this stems from a reluctance of scholars to claim any sort of sweeping universal law about social movements; there is recognition that the various theoretical approaches might explain part, but not all, of a particular puzzle, and that theories that emphasize different variables can shed light on distinct aspects of social protest. In the subsequent chapters, I will highlight some of these disagreements and areas of agreement or possible synthesis as they pertain to specific questions about social movements.

Collective Behavior Theories

Collective behavior (CB) theories are the earliest attempts to think systematically about why and under what conditions people turn to social protest. It is a heterogeneous collection of approaches, much of which predates the 1970s. While there are critical differences among different scholars working within the CB tradition, they share certain foundational assumptions about social movements.

First, they argue that social protest is not a part of "normal" society; rather, protest occurs when there is some strain on, or disruption to, existing social structures. When such cracks in the social fabric appear – caused, for example by shocks, tragedies, upheavals, or disasters – people are unable to work out their grievances through conventional political institutions or channels. Protest, in other words, is a symptom of social breakdown and turmoil (Edwards 2014: 10). There are different ideas of where these strains come from. Herbert Blumer argues, for example, that strains are not objective conditions in society, but constructed by individuals when they are unable to cope with change or deal with their grievances (Blumer 1971). Social change can aggravate this sense of grievance, and increases the distance between how good people think their lives are and how good they think they *ought* to be (Gurr 1970). William Kornhauser (1959) builds on this idea by arguing that such breakdowns cause people to feel anxious and alienated from others in society, and that social movements can use this vulnerability to recruit people and offer them a sense of belonging and community. Neil Smelser (1962) argues, by contrast, that it is not individual perceptions of strain but actual, structural strains that generate social breakdowns.

Second, since protest is a manifestation of breakdown when normal institutions are unable to cope, it stands to reason that protest occurs largely outside of institutional structures. Finally, CB theorists emphasize the importance of shared identities and values among movement participants; for them, they are important variables when considering questions about who participates in social movements and why. Individuals who feel adrift in a social order that seems to be breaking down can find a sense of community, purpose, and comfort in a social movement of like-minded individuals (Staggenborg 2011: 12–13).

Resource Mobilization and Political Process Theories

In the 1970s, social movement scholarship took a big step forward with the development of the resource mobilization (RM) school. Dissatisfied with the inability of CB theories to adequately account for empirical patterns of protest and mobilization, early RM theorists like John McCarthy and Mayer Zald proposed an approach based on some different underlying assumptions. RM theory starts from a premise that there is no sharp distinction between social movements and routine political behavior; social movements are not clear-cut outsiders, nor do they employ exclusively non-institutional forms of action. Moreover, participants in social movements are not suffering from any psychological strain but are rational actors capable of making sophisticated cost–benefit calculations about when and how to participate in social movement activities.

RM theorists observe that, if grievances are the key catalyst for social protest, we should have far more protest than we actually do. Everyone is aggrieved about something, but most people do not join protest movements to deal with their grievances. CB theories, in effect, overpredict the amount of protest we would expect to see. Instead of grievances, therefore, RM theorists focus on the variables that facilitate organizing and protest. Their variable of choice is right in the name: resources, both tangible, such as money or physical assets, and intangible, such as reputation and experience (Freeman 1979). Organizations are the main repository for these resources, and, accordingly, have pride of place in RM theories, which point to social movement groups – particularly formal ones – as crucial for initiating and sustaining mobilization (McCarthy and Zald 1977).

Political process theories (PPTs) have similar foundational assumptions to RM theories, but place more emphasis on the interactions between states, social movements, and the larger political context. In trying to account for movement emergence and mobilization, the PPT approach tends to refer back to three core ideas: mobilizing structures (that is, the organizational bases that help to initiate protest), the structure of political opportunity, and framing processes. This approach – and these three ideas – has dominated much of the research on social movements since the 1980s, and there is a great deal of consensus as to their importance (McAdam 2004), though by no means universal acceptance.

One of PPT's central claims is that movements operate within a particular political opportunity structure, loosely understood as dimensions of the political environment that exist within the structures of a given state. Sidney Tarrow further defines political opportunity structures as "consistent – but not necessarily formal or permanent – dimensions of the political environment or of change in that environment that provide incentives for collective action by affecting expectations for success or failure" (Tarrow 2011: 163). A movement that wants to push for stricter gun-control laws might have an easier time achieving its goal when it operates in a place with legislators sympathetic to their aims, but a much harder time if political elites do not support gun control in any way. Partisan control of the executive and legislative branch could, therefore, be an important part of the movement's political opportunity structure. While political opportunity structures are conventionally applied to domestic political arrangements, some scholars also argue that aspects of international politics might constitute transnational opportunity structures that can facilitate (or limit) transnational social movements (Passy 1999).

Some scholars argue, however, that without a precise list of what does or does not constitute a political opportunity, nearly anything could be construed as a political opportunity structure, making it "a sponge that soaks up every aspect of a social movement's environment" (Gamson and Meyer 1996: 275). For critics of PPT, this presents a big problem (Goodwin and Jasper 1999). Defenders of PPT, however, believe the concept can be salvaged and, with more precise description of the causal mechanisms that connect features of the environment with movement strategies, or more exacting definitions, some of the chief concerns about this approach could be mitigated (Meyer and Minkoff 2004).

While PPT was initially seen as highly structural, given its focus on the role that formal organizations play in mobilizing individuals into action (a carry-over from the RM school) and political opportunity structures, it has evolved over time to include certain cultural and ideational factors that contribute to mobilization as well. In particular, PPT focuses on how movements interpret and frame their message in order to appeal to supporters, cultivate allies, and influence their targets. Framing is one of the most important things that social movements do; frames convey particular understandings about the social world, including how the movement sees itself, what the movement believes are the main challenges that need to be addressed, and the best solutions for those problems, as well as why people should join the movement (Benford 1993a). To be effective, frames must resonate with their audience; if they do not, then movements risk being unable to attract enough supporters, persuade key allies to provide support, or outsmart opponents (Benford and Snow 2000).

As with political opportunity structure, the idea of framing processes has its critics as well. For some, framing does not go far enough in acknowledging the important role that identities, culture, and emotion play in social movements (Jasper 1997; Goodwin et al. 2001). Deborah Gould argues, for example, that PPT underestimates the power of emotions and identity, which creates blind spots in its explanations, making it poorly equipped to explain why movements persist, or how they can fracture over internal disagreements, or why they employ particular rituals (Gould 2004). For these critics, the answer requires bringing emotions and culture more centrally into the discussion, rather than including them in what they see as a superficial way.

New Social Movements Theory

While most of the theoretical schools discussed above have emerged out of American social science, New Social Movements (NSM) theory has its roots in Europe. Scholars working there argued that, by the end of the twentieth century, the types of movements that were forming were different in a number of key ways from the movements that were products of the nineteenth and early twentieth centuries. These older movements, they argued, were products of industrial society, and their priorities reflected the conflicts that emerged out of industrial economies. During industrialization, the working classes were vulnerable to exploitation by factory owners and others who had power and resources, and so the social movements that emerged out of industrial economies – such as the labor movement – sought to challenge this domination. Such movements tended to focus on material concerns, like the redistribution of economic resources and protection for workers.

NSM theorists argue that, when manufacturing declines in economic importance relative to the service sector, societies transform into post-industrial economies (Touraine 1971). The kinds of conflicts and forms of exploitation that occur in such economies are different from the ones that emerge out of industrial societies; whereas economic domination of working classes lay at the heart of "old" social movements, "new" social movements focus on how large, anonymous, bureaucratic institutions control and intrude on private lives (Buechler 2011: 159). The environmental movement, LGBT movement, and peace movement, for example, care less about material well-being (though economic issues are not irrelevant for NSMs) and more about quality of life and the values of movement participants (Inglehart 1990). Rather than redistributive goals, NSMs are more likely to work toward increasing individual autonomy and democracy while affirming the collective identities of movement participants (Melucci 1996). What follows from this focus is a tendency to develop movement cultures that are egalitarian, non-hierarchical, consensus-based, and informal. This, in turn, leads to organizational forms that are unconventional and experimental, as well as strategies that may reject conventional forms of protest. Finally, these movements often grow out of identities that are rooted not in class, but in categories such as gender, ethnicity, sexuality, and age. In fact, identity in general is much more central to NSM mobilization, which also reflects a diversity of backgrounds among movement participants, who are no longer drawn narrowly from the working classes (Buechler 2011: 159–61). NSM mobilization can also include lifestyle movements that encourage individual actions to promote broader social change, from contributing to fair trade practices to promoting a religious view of society like the Quiverfull movement (Haenfler et al. 2012). The attention that NSM theory pays to emotions, identity, and culture resonates with many scholars, who bristle at the relatively marginal role they have historically been accorded in American scholarly circles. At the same time, NSM theory has been critiqued as overstating the differences between old, class-based movements and new social movements insofar as movements can combine both material and non-material demands, which makes some critics wonder whether there is anything truly "new" about NSM theory (Staggenborg 2011: 23–2).

Relational Approaches

The relational turn in social movement scholarship starts from the premise that neither structures – like the social networks in which we are embedded – nor cultural variables – like identities and emotions – are static; they are dynamic and constantly changing over time. Moreover, social structures and cultural variables are not autonomous and self-contained; they change via the social interactions we have with others. Relationships, unsurprisingly, are at the heart of this theoretical approach, which holds that the interactions, ties, and exchanges we have with others "constitute the central stuff of social life" (Tilly 2004: 72), and that to make sense of the world around us, we must focus on how our interactions with others shape our understanding of that world.

The relational approach emphasizes the importance of "conversations" (understood broadly, and not just those that occur face-to-face) in shaping our views of the world (Mische 2002, 2011). Our identities, for example, are not given and fixed, but negotiated and reformed in our interactions with others; we might attach different meanings to different parts of our social network, or pull from different parts of our identities as we move through the world and connect with other people. In so doing, we are constantly negotiating, refashioning, and reinterpreting both the structures and the cultural factors around us. Relational approaches pay close attention to the mechanisms by which these changes happen over time (McAdam et al. 2001).

Perhaps this sounds like theoretical quicksand, where nothing is fixed, everything is up for contestation, and meanings shift constantly. Perhaps so, but the relational approach considers both structural variables and ideational or cultural factors and attempts to deepen our understanding of both. For example, political opportunity structures do not simply exist, but must be recognized by movement actors who identify and process whether aspects of the political context will welcome or discourage movement. How do actors recognize and decipher such signals? The relational approach would scrutinize how their interactions with others – movement participants, allies, and elites – inform initial interpretations, as well as how those interpretations change as interactions continue. Similarly, activist identities are not magically created out of thin air; they come about via interactions with others and are also conditioned by contextual factors. How can we understand why activists hold the identities they do? Again, some attention must be paid to the relationships among individuals and how those relationships are also influenced by the environment, all of which can change over time.

Research Tools and Methods

Regardless of the theoretical tradition that informs their work, social movement scholars tend to come from a range of different academic backgrounds, including sociology, political science, history, and law. Because of this, the field is characterized by its strongly interdisciplinary approach to research. One of the practical consequences of this interdisciplinarity is that there is no single, dominant, or preferred research method by which scholars collect and analyze data in order to test their hypotheses and build collective knowledge about social movements. Methodological pluralism, in fact, is seen as an asset by those who study social movements, since a lack of dogmatism about what counts as the "best" tool makes it possible for scholars to approach questions from multiple angles and use the strengths of one technique to offset the possible limitations of another, all without getting tangled up in methodological battles that can polarize other fields of inquiry (Klandermans and Staggenborg 2002: xii; della Porta 2014a). The choice of methodological tool is driven instead by the nature of the question to be answered, since not all methods are equally well suited to answering all questions.

Research methods in social movement research run the gamut from large-N studies, such as statistical analyses with hundreds of cases under examination, to small-N research that examines single case studies in a more detailed and in-depth fashion. In their study of hate crime reporting, for example, Rory McVeigh, Michael R. Welch, and Thoroddur Bjarnson (2003) carried out a statistical analysis of a dataset with over 8,000 observations drawn from across the United States; compare that to Setsuko Matsuzawa's (2011) fine-grained examination of protests against a single hydropower dam in China. These approaches offer different kinds of advantages and limitations: the statistical study can point to large patterns and trends that allow researchers to formulate more generalizable social movement theories – generalizable in that they might be relevant across a range of cases and contexts. However, most movement scholars would probably acknowledge that universal law-like theories are not particularly realistic, given that human behavior is neither mechanistic nor fully predictable; people, unlike molecules and atoms, exercise free will and can act in ways we do not always expect.

While stopping well short of universal laws of social behavior, methods that allow researchers to make more general claims fall short when it comes to the nuances of individual cases; such details get lost when cases are aggregated in large numbers. It is not easy for a researcher working with 2,000 survey responses to know much about the individuals who filled out those surveys; with in-depth interviews, however, a researcher would be able to get a more holistic sense of people's worldviews, their values and beliefs, and the nuances of their political ideologies. Small-N, qualitative methods provide researchers with opportunities to understand their subject in a more minute way – but any conclusions that the researcher might draw from a single case or an ethnographic study might have limited applicability to other cases. After all, a lengthy conversation with a few protestors might shed considerable light on their reasons for joining a social movement; it is not so plausible to extrapolate from five in-depth interviews and apply those insights to explain why the thousands of people who took part in anti-globalization protests, or Black Lives Matter demonstrations, or Tea Party events made similar decisions.

This trade-off between generalizability and idiosyncratic knowledge is a common one, and research methods differ in what type of results they can offer. Figure 1.1 captures this range for a number of methodological approaches used by social movement scholars. While the placement of any of these methods can shift based on the specific details of the research design (e.g., how many people are interviewed, how large the survey sample is, how many protest events are analyzed, etc.), in general, methods like experiments, statistical and formal models, and large-scale surveys aim to produce more general, widely applicable knowledge, while ethnographic methods, in-depth interviews, and highly qualitative methods generate context-sensitive and richly detailed information. When paired together in mixed-methods designs, such approaches can complement each other, offering both nuance and broader applicability of results. Triangulation of this sort can also uncover new information as well as increase overall confidence in research results (Ayoub et al. 2014). It can also help us to develop middle-range theory – arguments that seek to explain classes of empirical phenomena without purporting to create a grand or universal theory that attempts to account for behavior regardless of context (Klandermans et al. 2002).

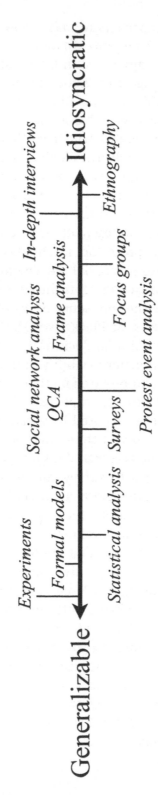

Figure 1.1 *Research methods and type of knowledge generated*

The result of this methodological pluralism is a body of research that uses a diverse set of methodological tools and sources of data. Vincent Roscigno and his co-authors, for example, draw on historical analysis of government archives in their examination of state framing and repression leading up to the Sioux massacre at Wounded Knee in 1890 (Roscigno et al. 2015), while Gabriela Gonzalez Valiant and her collaborators designed an experiment to test theories about online mobilization patterns (2015), and Marco Giugni and Sakura Yamasaki (2009) used qualitative comparative analysis – a medium-N approach pioneered by sociologist Charles Ragin – to analyze the conditions under which anti-nuclear, eco-logical, and peace movements in three countries were able to influence policy outcomes. In addition to a diversity of tools and techniques, scholars can also use different methodologies to focus their explanatory efforts on variables at different levels of aggre-gation. Researchers who are interested in the microfoundations of protest – why, for example, individuals choose to join a social movement – might be drawn to tools that are suited to uncovering individual-level data, such as interviews and surveys. Other meth-ods might lend themselves to isolating and exploring meso-level variables, like attributes of social movement organizations. Still others are best suited to analyzing larger, macro variables, like the nature of political opportunity, or revealing the structure of rela-tionships that are not directly visible to the eye, as social network analysis can do.

In all of this methodological pluralism, however, a number of research methods tend to be used more frequently by scholars. These include statistical methods, single and comparative case studies, surveys and interviews of activists, frame analysis, and protest event analysis. Subsequent chapters delve further into each of these approaches to provide more detail about their uses, limita-tions, and applications.

Concluding Summary

Although social movements are sometimes contrasted with more institutional forms of political activity, at heart, they are one of many channels through which people can voice their political claims and preferences and work together to achieve meaningful change. They are, however, historically specific and co-evolved with the modern state – a relationship that has lasting consequences for what they look like, how they operate, and what kinds of claims they tend to make. This chapter has explored some of the main theories that scholars of social movements have advanced to explain some of the recurring questions about social movements, from why people join them, to whether they have any effect on politics and society. In the chapters that follow, you will find that the theories discussed above will crop up repeatedly. My intent is not to persuade you of the merits of any one approach, but to showcase how they purport to answer common questions that emerge in social movement studies in different ways. Ultimately, however, there is no single, universally suitable, always correct theory that explains every case. Such is life when it comes to studying complex social phenomena.

The remainder of the book examines different dimensions of social movements, with each chapter focusing on one of the key actors, contexts, decisions, or outcomes that are relevant when studying social movements. Collectively, they provide a broad overview of social movement scholarship, covering classic debates as well as new areas of research. Each chapter also outlines a set of learning objectives to orient readers to the main take-aways and conceptual highlights they will encounter in the subsequent text. Chapters all draw on a range of real-life examples, many of them from social movements that are active today, to illustrate key points and themes. These examples represent a wide cross-section of movement issues and settings, which reflects the diversity of social movements to be found in the world. Selected chapters also feature boxed text that highlights specialized methodological approaches that social movement scholars often use to study questions related to that section's core theoretical concerns. These methods spotlights also contain useful internet resources and links for interested readers to explore datasets and analytical tools in a hands-on way. While these periodic methods discussions are not meant to be exhaustive – nor do they cover the full range of methodologies that social movement scholars use – they provide brief introductions to some of the more common ways in which scholars seek to answer questions about how social movements operate. At the end of every chapter, readers will find several discussion questions designed to help them to test their comprehension of key concepts while prompting deeper analysis and evaluation of the material. Finally, each chapter concludes by providing readers with suggested additional readings – usually classic and influential texts – that give those who are interested in delving more deeply into the literature a focused place to start. Together, these features are intended to make this book as useful as possible to those who are relatively new to the study of social movements.

Questions for Discussion

1 How are social movements different from other types of political activity? Why might some people find social protest to be an appealing way to try to influence political outcomes?

2 In what ways are modern social movements different from protests that occurred prior to the nineteenth century? What historical developments triggered the evolution of the modern social movement?

3 What assumptions do scholars representing the main theoretical approaches to studying movements make about why and when people protest? How do these assumptions influence their subsequent claims and conclusions?

4 How can methodological pluralism be beneficial for social movement research?

Additional Readings

Buechler, Steven M. 2011. *Understanding Social Movements: Theories from the Classical Era to the Present*. Boulder, CO, and London: Paradigm. This book provides a good overview of different theoretical approaches to studying social movements and the debates between these approaches.

Johnston, Hank A. 2014. *What is a Social Movement?* Cambridge, and Malden, MA: Polity. This book delves more deeply into how social movements can be defined and distinguished from other types of collective political action, as well as how to differentiate political and cultural movements.

Tilly, Charles, and Lesley J. Wood. 2004. *Social Movements, 1768–2004*. Boulder, CO and London: Paradigm. This book gives an overview of how modern social movements evolved.

CHAPTER 2

The Activist

Objectives

- To examine how views of protestors have evolved over time, from early depictions of irrational groups to contemporary ideas of rational actors.
- To understand how demographic characteristics, including age and socio-economic status, affect how likely particular groups of people are to engage in social protest.
- To determine the role of grievances, social networks, environment, and organizations in mobilizing people to participate in social movements.
- To identify the obstacles to protest and activist retention.

Introduction

Writing in 1897, sociologist Albion Small tells us that "the social movement is, an unfriendly observer might say, a confusion of fussy, fidgety folk, blocking each other and everybody else with their foolishness" (Small 1897: 340). Unfriendly observers certainly were easy to find when it came to social movements of his own era – people who found protests and protestors bewildering, their causes threatening, their motives suspect, their tactics deplorable, and, ultimately, their efforts pointless. The diaries of Kate Frye, a member of the women's suffrage movement in the United Kingdom provides us with a first-hand account of such views. From a middle-class background, Frye first became involved in the suffrage movement in 1906 and eventually became a paid organizer for the New Constitutional Society for Women's Suffrage. Roughly one year after joining the movement, Frye attended a large march through the streets of London. She recounts that, as they moved through the muddy streets of the city, crowds of onlookers gathered to observe the spectacle; she overheard two of them – "quite smart men," she says – remark "I say look at those nice girls – positively disgraceful I call it" (entry for February 9, 1907, in Crawford 2013). Newspaper coverage of these protests also captured many of the antagonistic feelings among the public. In her analysis of stories about the movement in the *Daily Express*, Sadie Clifford noted, for example, that participants were "described as having temperaments of 'folly and fury,'" perhaps crazy or frenzied, and "hooligan[s]. . .who prosecute a 'campaign against society'" (Clifford 2000: 1–4). Fussy, fidgety, and foolish indeed!

Contemporary reactions to social movements in our own day and age would suggest that not much has changed in the century since Small wrote those words. Members of the public still react to protestors – especially people advocating for controversial causes – with confusion and contempt. Take, for example, two social movements that emerged in the United States at roughly similar times: OWS and the Tea Party Movement (TPM).

OWS formed in 2011, following the electrifying pro-democracy movements that had spread throughout the Arab world earlier in the year. Inspired by these Arab Spring uprisings and other grassroots movements against neoliberal economic orthodoxy (Castañeda 2012), the activist magazine *Adbusters* called for a public protest in the same spirit to take place on September 17. Their aim was to call attention to a range of interrelated issues: growing economic inequality (the widely adopted slogan "We are the 99%" stems from this focus), the malfeasance of large Wall Street financial companies, and the harmful influence of corporate interests on democracy. While the OWS movement spawned protests around the country and around the world, the epicenter of the movement was Zuccotti Park in New York City. Here, protestors set up an encampment, organized marches, held working groups, and generally tried to create a miniature society based on the movement's core values.

While OWS had a decidedly left-leaning ideology, the TPM emerged out of popular frustration among conservatives at the political direction the country was taking under a newly elected President Obama and a Democratic-controlled legislature. Not only did the new administration's signature policy proposals, such as health-care reform, worry conservatives, its efforts to help the economy, which had struggled in the wake of the 2008 financial crisis, were seen as exorbitantly expensive and irresponsible. In February, CNBC television reporter Rick Santelli had had enough. Broadcasting from the Chicago Mercantile Exchange, Santelli railed against the administration's plan to provide foreclosure relief to many of the people facing eviction from their homes, shouting that "the government is rewarding bad behavior" and inviting people to a tea party to protest against the bill. The imagery of a tea party, which evoked the Boston Tea Party and its attendant symbolism of resisting tyrannical government, resonated with the public and his outburst quickly went viral. It sparked national interest in a wider movement that prioritized smaller government and sharp cuts in spending to reduce the deficit among other goals. While the TPM never created a public encampment, its members held rallies, protest marches, and disruptive displays to further the movement's agenda.

Both OWS and the TPM captured the attention of national media outlets, which featured them in countless stories analyzing the two movements' scope, goals, clout, and impact. There was also considerable curiosity about their participants and who they were. In keeping with Albion Small's observation, many of the assumptions made by members of the public were uncharitable, especially when characterizing individuals belonging to the movement furthest from their own political beliefs. Individuals commenting on TPM-related stories on alternet.org, an ideologically left-leaning website that appeals to progressive activists described TPM supporters as a "crazy lot," "willfully stupid," "trailer trash," and "racist." Similarly, individuals commenting on OWS-related stories on breitbart.org, an ideologically right-wing website, described the movement's activists as "parasites," "scum," "criminals," and "animals." The stereotypes coalesced quickly: to detractors, the TPM was full of uneducated rubes yearning for a bygone era of white supremacy, while OWS attracted freeloading layabouts looking to live off government handouts and taking no responsibility for their lives.

Empirical studies of OWS and TPM activists, however, challenge these stereotypes. Using in-depth interviews and surveys, researchers show that our assumptions about who activists are – especially activists who support causes with which we disagree – do not always match reality (for more on these research approaches, see this chapter's methods spotlight). Using in-depth interviews and surveys, for example, Ruth Milkman, Stephanie Luce, and Penny Lewis (2013) found that, contrary to stereotypes that OWS was full of unemployed slackers, only 10% were unemployed. A further 6% were retired, 4% were full-time students, and the remaining 80% were employed, mostly in professional occupations like education. Rather than needing government handouts to make ends meet,

Methods Spotlight: Surveys and In-Depth Interviews

Surveys and in-depth interviews are two ways in which social movement scholars can gather information about the people who participate in social movements. Such techniques are particularly well suited to collecting micro-level data about activists: their knowledge, attitudes, experiences, and personal backgrounds (Klandermans and Smith 2002). One of the main differences between surveys and in-depth interviews is their scope; surveys tend to involve a focused set of questions that can be answered quickly and briefly by a range of people. In-depth interviews, on the other hand, involve a more extensive and open-ended conversation with a smaller group of people. A survey might ask respondents whether they had ever signed a petition before, and allow only a "yes" or "no" response; an in-depth interview, on the other hand, might probe for a respondent's reasons for choosing to sign a petition or how signing that petition may have affected their future involvement in social protest. While surveys collect responses from a large number of people in order to find patterns and trends among the respondents and generalize from a sample to a larger population, in-depth interviews aim to produce rich, detailed narratives that capture particular respondents' ideas and worldviews. Surveys tend to convert data for quantitative analysis; in-depth interviews tend to analyze data in more qualitative ways.

In-depth interviews tend to be carried out face-to-face; surveys can be conducted face-to-face as well but do not have to be; respondents can be given paper or online surveys to fill out on their own time. Both surveys and in-depth interviews require careful question formulation in order to achieve meaningful results. For surveys, vague wording, incomplete or confusing answer choices, and other pitfalls of design can produce poor-quality data. For in-depth interviews, question quality is also important, particularly since the questions must be constructed in order to open-up conversation and put the respondent at ease. Such interviews can include closed questions (i.e., ones with a finite list of possible responses, such as last level of school completed), open-ended ones (i.e., questions with no set answer choices), or a combination of the two (Blee and Taylor 2002). Survey questionnaires tend to use primarily closed questions.

In both surveys and in-depth interviews, selecting the right respondents is crucial. Because researchers who use surveys typically wish to make inferences about a larger population of subjects based on the responses of a smaller sample, researchers should recruit a random sample in order to correct for possible biases. Random sampling, however, is not always easy in face-to-face settings; researchers hoping to carry out surveys of activists at demonstrations – especially ones involving people marching or otherwise moving around – must plan well in advance and train survey workers well (Andretta and della Porta 2014: 320-1). Even with well-trained workers, researchers using this method must be aware of the possible bias introduced into the results when some groups of protestors refuse to answer questions more often than others (Walgrave et al. 2016). In-depth interviews usually involve a smaller number of respondents who are purposefully chosen rather than randomized. Such purposeful selection criteria may prioritize specialized knowledge or expertise – leaders of movements, individuals who participated in key events, people who were in the room or took part in a key decision – in addition to capturing representative or typical responses (della Porta 2014b). While these two approaches are somewhat distinct, they can also complement one another. Survey data can, for example, paint a broad picture of general patterns and trends for a particular group; in-depth interviews with selected members of that group can further flesh out key details and insights that brief survey questions cannot uncover on their own.

Explore This Method

There are a number of datasets available online that provide survey data previously collected by scholars. Some datasets, like the World Values Survey (www.world valuessurvey.org) do not focus on social movements, but include questions about civic engagement, including how often people in different countries take part in different types of protest activity, from innocuous actions like signing petitions to more disruptive forms. To get an idea of what kinds of questions you might ask on a survey instrument, explore the questionnaire at Tufts University aimed at measuring the political and civic engagement of young people (http://activecitizen.tufts.edu/wp-content/uploads/questionnaire.pdf). The actual data collected via this instrument are also available online (http://activecitizen.tufts.edu/wp-content/uploads/FinalReport1.pdf). Looking at these questions, what else might you want to ask people to understand their level of involvement with social movements and protest? Which questions might be best answered via another survey? Are there particular questions that would be better if asked in an in-depth interview?

more than a third of OWS activists earned more than $100,000 per year – a proportion higher than in the overall population of New York City, where only 24% of households had income exceeding that amount. On the other side of the ideological spectrum, a survey of TPM members conducted by Gallup and USA Today found that 65% had at least some college education, which is at odds with the idea that its supporters are uneducated. Moreover, 31% had graduated from college, and, of those graduates, half received a postgraduate degree (Saad 2010). Rather than being rubes, the survey found that supporters were, on average, solidly middle-class, with 55% reporting incomes over $50,000. These inconsistencies between the stereotypes about these two movements and the empirical data suggest that people do not always have a good sense of who joins social movements.

Historical Perspectives on Protestors

As discussed in the first chapter, protests prior to the late eighteenth century differed in some key respects compared to the protests associated with modern social movements. They tended to be highly localized, brief, without organizational basis, and focused on violation of community moral norms and customs (Thompson 1971) or addressing momentary grievances without necessarily making political demands about larger, systemic concerns. E. P. Thompson provides one example of this type of protest from 1790, in which Alice Evans, the wife of a local weaver, raised the community's ire by berating him in public, faulting his behavior and lazy disposition. Thompson describes what happened next:

> This conduct (of hers) the neighbouring lords of creation were determined to punish, fearing their own spouses might assume the same authority. They therefore mounted one of their body, dressed in female apparel, on the back of an old donkey, the man holding a spinning wheel on his lap, and his back towards the donkey's head. Two men led the animal through the neighbourhood, followed by scores of boys and idle men, tinkling kettles and frying pans, roaring with cows' horns, and making a most hideous hullabaloo.
>
> (Thompson 1992: 5)

This type of protest, commonly referred to as "rough music" or "charivari," targeted members of the community who had committed some act beyond the pale – adultery, for example – using public mockery and humiliation to make them conform to local standards. Note in this example the lack of larger political claims, the absence of any coordinating organization, the short duration, and the narrowness of the grievance; after all, who outside this immediate community would take an interest in how Alice Evans treated her husband? Note, too, the disorderliness of the display, which was characteristic and intentional. In another incident, Thompson recounts how protestors converged on the target's house, banged on pots and pans, rang bells, threw stones at the doors and windows, dragged the target out of bed, and threw him in the mud (1992: 5). These were not polite demonstrations.

Given the unruliness of rough music or the disruption and violence of food riots, it is perhaps unsurprising that early theories about who protests and why tend to emphasize the chaotic, dangerous, and uncontrolled nature of protesting crowds. They stressed how participants could lose their individual faculties of reason and restraint when swept up in a large group. This was true not just for social miscreants but also for law-abiding citizens, who could also be influenced to act with reckless abandon. French sociologist Gustave Le Bon ([1895] 2001) set the tone for this line of analysis,

claiming that crowds transform people and exert an almost hypnotic effect that overrides critical thinking. Moreover, Le Bon also
argued that crowds could be easily swayed by strong leaders who
could turn these supporters into tools to be manipulated for their
own nefarious ends. The result is that, in crowds, emotions run
high and spread like a contagion, resulting in people who act without thought (Blumer 1951, 1971).

Less spontaneous but far deadlier than a bread riot were the
mass ideological movements of the twentieth century – fascism
and communism – that also seemed to illustrate the principle that
participation in crowds can exert a hypnotic and de-individualizing
effect on people that strips away their capacity to do anything more
than reach simplistic conclusions about cause and effect, right and
wrong. The idea of the madding crowd was an appealing way of
understanding why, for example, so many students in China committed violence against their teachers, strangers on the street, and
even their own family members during the Cultural Revolution,
or why ordinary people living in the Nazi-occupied Polish town of
Jedwabne turned on their Jewish neighbors and executed hundreds
of people in a single day, or the countless other examples of people
who seemed to suspend their individual moral faculties and give in
to the collective madness of the moment.

The people who participate in such movements, collective behavior theorists argued, are highly alienated from the rest of society.
Lacking meaningful bonds with others or a sense of purpose, they
exist on the peripheral edges of social, economic, and political life.
Because of their isolation, such individuals are drawn to join mass
movements because of the sense of community and belonging they
offer. As members, they develop a collective identity that connects
them with others and provides emotional and psychological benefits as well as a sense of purpose (Blumer 1951; Kornhauser 1959).
Participation in nationalist movements provides a good illustration
of this dynamic. The popularity of nationalist ideas across many
European countries in the nineteenth century was in part driven
by major structural transformations that reshaped the social fabric.
The Industrial Revolution, for example, prompted large migrations
from rural to urban areas, and transformed a largely agricultural
workforce into factory workers. Along the way, these changes
meant that people were uprooted from the places in which they
and their families had lived for generations and were suddenly
thrust into anonymous cities, working and living in sometimes

deplorable conditions and without the kind of community bonds that gave them a sense of belonging and identity (Gellner 2009). Moreover, while these social and economic upheavals were taking place, the traditional power and role of organized religion was growing weaker as Enlightenment thinkers promoted secular, scientific values in the public sphere. This erosion of religiosity further weakened the traditional identities on which people could rely, while undermining a long-standing source of group solidarity (Anderson 2016). The result, Ernest Gellner argues, was a population alienated and hungry for a source of community and sense of belonging. Nationalism came along at the right time to fulfill this craving by offering a sense of comradeship and kinship with the members of an extended national "family." In its malignant forms, nationalism has certainly generated the kind of frenzied, destructive behavior that would be familiar to Le Bon and other theorists of the crowd: the genocide of Tutsis by their Hutu neighbors in Rwanda, or the lynching of Muslims suspected of eating beef by right-wing Hindu nationalists.

Compelling as these accounts may be, they also generate important criticisms. For one, scholars dispute the notion that crowds are irrational, emotional, and therefore erratic actors. Anthony Oberschall (1995) suggests that, rather than being simply absorbed into some kind of collective hive mind, crowds are composed of people with different motives, interests, and emotional responses; some of them are more committed to the crowd, and others less so. Some will disappear from the crowd when it starts to rain, others will be slower to abandon the cause. Moreover, individuals do not lose their capacity for rational thought in crowds; they behave with less restraint when surrounded by others because the potential costs of risky behavior are lower in crowds than outside them. Consider the potential costs of participating in a bread riot. If your objective is to voice your displeasure at the cost of bread by destroying the property of the people you feel are responsible for the price hike, you could join a crowd and do so, or you could act alone. If you act alone, the chances that you will get caught are fairly high. But in a crowd, the potential risk is much lower: even if the police turn out in force, it will be difficult for them to catch everyone, so it would be more rational to behave badly when surrounded by other people. Thus, it is not the crowd that generates irrational behavior; it just so happens that bad behavior is more rational in crowds (McPhail 1991; Oberschall 1995: 14–15).

A second line of critique disputes the idea that people who join large protests are somehow the most alienated among us and lack meaningful social connections to others. In fact, empirical studies suggest that those who join movements have strong social connections to others – ties that predate and, in fact, facilitate membership in the movement (Rule 1988; McAdam 1990). Data from OWS seems to point in a similar direction. Ruth Milkman and her collaborators found, for example, that 47 percent of those surveyed also belonged to other organizations, such as anti-war groups, women's groups, and groups working to organize local communities. About a third of respondents were union members, and many had also participated in more mainstream political activities such as donating money to political candidates or working on political campaigns (Milkman et al. 2013). The same could be said for members of the TPM. A CBS / *New York Times* survey found 43 percent reported working actively for political candidates or donating money to political campaigns. This prior experience suggests that "seasoned hands seem to be more common in Tea Party ranks than in the US citizenry as a whole" (Williamson et al. 2011: 27–8).

These figures paint a picture not of people who are isolated from society but of activists who are engaged in their communities, who care deeply about what happens in them, who work to improve them in multiple ways, and whose participation includes both institutional and non-institutional channels. While OWS sympathizers show marked skepticism of mainstream political actors and those who are deeply embedded in existing power structures, many of them have taken an active role in civil society and community institutions (Milkman et al. 2013: 4); the same could be said for many TPM members who, for example, attend church regularly at rates that are at least equal to, and usually far exceeding, those of the general American public (Deckman 2012: 182). These are hardly people who are adrift without ties to anchor them to local culture and society. If anything, it is their community ties that seem to make them more invested in working for change.

Accordingly, critics have questioned the CB argument that crowds are ultimately irrational, or that those who join social movements do so because social breakdowns perpetuate feelings of alienation from others in their community. Other CB theorists have subsequently sought to distance themselves from these two claims, rejecting the idea that crowds are impulsive and irrational, saying that they are instead collections of people whose actions may *seem* impulsive to outsiders, but are actually entirely rational and consistent with the beliefs that emerge from the group as it comes together and confronts challenges collectively (Turner and Killian 1987). To understand how this theory of "emergent norms" works, consider the 2016 Venezuelan food riots, which erupted around the country in the wake of an economic collapse. Writing for the *New York Times*, Nicholas Casey paints a vivid and grim picture of the scene: "With delivery trucks under constant attack, the nation's food is now transported under armed guard. Soldiers stand watch over bakeries. The police fire rubber bullets at desperate mobs storming grocery stores, pharmacies, and butcher shops. A 4-year-old girl was shot to death as street gangs fought over food. Venezuela is convulsing from hunger" (Casey 2016). Le Bon might point out that these riots perfectly illustrate the irrationality of crowds, with all their violent and disruptive tendencies. Emergent norm theory, however, would argue that, 10 years ago, large crowds of Venezuelans were not roaming cities spontaneously looting food supplies; they did not need to when the economy was growing nearly 10 percent per year. What has changed from 2006 to 2016 is not the crowd, but the crisis environment in which Venezuelans now find themselves. Confronted by unexpected or unprecedented challenges, Turner and Killian argue, people may not initially know how to respond, but as they interact with others facing the same situation, they develop shared expectations and new norms that govern their behavior from that point forward. In the case of Venezuela, where the contemporary choice is understood to be "loot or starve," the norm that emerges from the crowd makes looting acceptable and rational, given the circumstances – not the actions of a crazed crowd.

Activist Traits, Activist Motives

Based on the preceding discussion, we cannot simply assume that protestors are anomic individuals at the fringes of society. But then what differentiates people who join movements and those who do not? Demographic factors do not provide much guidance on this question. For any given demographic variables we might select – age, gender, education, socio-economic status, etc. – we could find examples of people matching those characteristics both inside and outside movements. Most movements have gaps between people who are potential members and those who actually participate by turning up to protest events (Klandermans and Oegema 1987, 1994), even though participants and non-participants may share many of the same personal characteristics and traits. In their study of protest participation between 1973 and 2008, Neal Caren, Raj Andrew Ghosal, and Vanesa Ribas (2011) found that people with certain demographic characteristics were more likely to join a protest or sign a petition than those outside those groups. City-dwellers, for example, had a 14.5% probability of joining a protest, compared to 11.7% for suburbanites or 10.3% for rural residents; union members had a 14.4% probability of joining a protest compared to 12.4% probability for non-union members. Those with college degrees had a 70.4% probability of signing a petition at least once, compared to just 38.5% probability for those without a high school diploma. And the richest 25% of respondents had a 63% probability of signing a petition, compared to just 48% probability for those in the lowest income quartile. On one hand, these results – which Caren and his co-authors argue tend to be mostly stable across generational cohorts – seem to suggest that there are demographic variations between participants and non-participants. At the same time, there are people who are college-educated who do not sign petitions as well as high school dropouts who do, just as there are urbanites who will never join a protest and rural dwellers who have joined more than one. Demographics alone are not wholly sufficient as a reason why people participate in social movements.

Grievances and Deprivation

If demographics cannot distinguish activists from bystanders, perhaps what separates activists from those who stand on the sidelines are the grievances they have about the status quo. Certainly, grievances seem like a requirement for participants in social protest; it is hard to imagine people who are content and satisfied with their lot in life taking to the streets to demand change, especially since protesting takes time and energy and sometimes entails serious risks. OWS protestors, for instance, cited a range of grievances they had with the status quo, including income inequality, corporate greed, unemployment, and the corrupting influence of money in politics (Milkman et al. 2013). For their part, TPM members refer repeatedly to their anger over government overreach, ballooning deficits, and specific policies like the Affordable Care Act and bailouts of Wall Street banks and the automobile industry during the Great

Recession (Williamson et al. 2011; Skocpol and Williamson 2012). Note that these grievances are collective in nature; unlike an individual grievance (e.g. a noisy neighbor, a co-worker who hogs all the credit on projects, a classmate who does not contribute to group work), collective grievances are shared among two or more people and are expressed as a shared complaint that requires redress for those affected (Snow and Soule 2010).

Grievances, it should be noted, do not spring fully formed out of thin air. They are *socially constructed* insofar as people must interpret an existing set of conditions as being unfair or problematic and requiring change. Child labor, for example, was common in places like the United States and the UK before the twentieth century since factory owners preferred to hire children because they were cheaper and easier to control than adults. This was considered an unremarkable reality until growing labor movements in the mid nineteenth century started campaigning against the practice. Their efforts to delegitimize child labor helped to alter public attitudes, turning it from a routine and widespread custom to one that was regarded as cruel and unconscionable. Grievances can form in response to all types of conditions, even ones that may not seem objectionable to outsiders. Ted Gurr argues that relative deprivation, or the difference between what people experience and what they believe they *should* experience, produces high levels of frustration and anger (Gurr 1970). A worker who receives a 3 percent pay raise at the end of the year might be satisfied by this increase until she becomes aware that a co-worker received a 5 percent increase for comparable work. All of a sudden, that initial increase is not a cause for celebration but a reason for complaint; despite being objectively better off than she was before, she still feels wronged. Such grievances can be crystallized and amplified in multiple ways and by multiple actors; social movement groups can play a leading role in articulating and spreading grievances. Lance Bennett (2012) further proposes that individuals tied into dense social networks can, via their connection with others, share stories, form solidarities, and convert what might otherwise be idiosyncratic experiences and beliefs into highly personalized motivations to take action. Ultimately, grievances certainly play a role in motivating people to join movements, especially if they are deeply felt (Snow and Soule 2010: 23) and are culturally meaningful (Simmons 2014).

Participation and Differential Engagement

While grievances are important, they are not a complete explanation for why some people join movements and others do not, simply because activists do not have a monopoly on grievances. Think, for example, about the kinds of social problems you would like to fix if you had the power. Child hunger, human trafficking, environmental degradation, government corruption, underfunded public schools – the list of possible issues could potentially go on and on. Unless you think the world is perfect as is, you should be able to think of at least a few things you would change about the status quo. And yet, how many of those problems have moved you to join a social movement? For most people, the grievances they have about the world do not automatically compel them to join movements. Therein lies the problem: grievances are commonplace, but most people do not act on them by engaging in social protest. Table 2.1 shows how frequently people in different countries have participated in various forms of political action, from the fairly tame (signing a petition) to the more risky (participating in a strike).

As the table highlights, with just two exceptions (e.g., signing petitions in the United States and Sweden), the majority of people in these countries have not taken the kinds of action that we commonly associate with social movement participation. Of these different non-institutional political activities, the least intrusive, time-intensive, and costly – signing a petition – is the most popular; even so, only 21.3% of people on average have taken even this small step. While low participation numbers might make sense in repressive autocracies where putting your name on a petition might result in some unpleasant repercussions, even in democratic countries like Chile, Ghana, South Africa, and India, less than one quarter of the population reports ever signing a petition. The survey did not ask about participation in higher-risk forms of participation, but the percentage of people for those activities is likely to be minimal, given low participation in more innocuous forms of protest. Even if collective grievances are widely held in society, collective action does not automatically follow. Instead, as figure 2.1 suggests, subsets of the public have different levels of engagement with an issue, such that protestors form a small subset of all those who care about an issue, which is itself a subset of the overall population. The OWS case bears this out. Popular attitudes toward income inequality in the United States, for example, indicate that a majority of people believe that the current gap between the rich and poor is unfair; a Gallup poll from April 2015 found that 63% of Americans – including 42% of conservatives, 67% of moderates, and 85% of liberals – believe that wealth should be more evenly spread throughout society. And yet most people in the US never took part in OWS protests, marches, or any other event. The grievance might be shared, but the desire to join a movement and protest is not.

Table 2.1 Comparative participation rates (percentages) for different protest forms

	Signed a petition	Joined in boycotts	Attended peaceful demonstration	Joined in a strike	Any other act of protest
Argentina	18.6	2.6	14.1	11.7	5.9
Brazil	44.0	4.6	15.9	13.1	9.0
Chile	21.4	4.0	23.1	16.4	15.7
China	4.5	2.6	1.7	1.4	1.2
Colombia	23.8	13.2	18.3	7.3	5.4
Egypt	1.8	4.6	6.8	1.2	0.5
Germany	42.7	12.9	21.1	11.9	10.9
Ghana	2.1	1.6	4.6	2.3	1.2
Hong Kong	33.9	9.6	16.0	2.9	4.5
India	15.7	14.6	19.7	14.9	14.1
Japan	28.0	1.4	3.6	3.5	1.7
Malaysia	1.9	1.0	2.3	0.5	0.5
Mexico	18.3	2.5	10.2	5.5	4.2
Netherlands	35.4	7.8	11.9	8.8	3.0
Nigeria	8.2	5.7	24.7	40.8	12.1
Pakistan	20.7	4.8	17.0	13.7	11.0
Philippines	10.5	3.2	7.5	2.4	1.7
Rwanda	8.6	0.6	0.9	0.6	1.3
South Africa	11.3	8.3	9.0	7.3	5.1
South Korea	26.4	5.4	9.5	5.3	4.0
Spain	22.1	5.8	24.9	19.5	0.4
Sweden	68.0	21.9	20.8	16.0	14.0
Turkey	9.8	4.5	4.8	3.0	3.3
United States	60.1	15.5	13.7	7.4	5.6
Zimbabwe	13.4	5.0	8.4	5.7	4.2
AVERAGE	*21.3*	*7.4*	*12.4*	*9.2*	*6.2*

Source: World Values Survey, Wave 6.

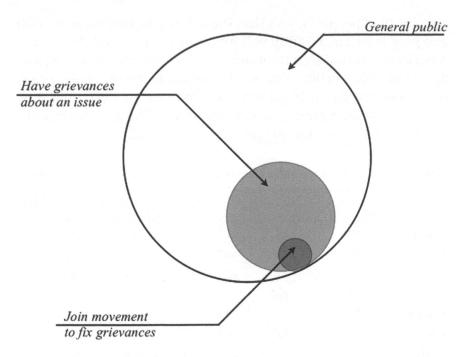

Figure 2.1 *Variation in engagement*

Mobilization Processes

Instead of thinking about static variables that may or may not induce people to protest, scholars have argued that social movement participation is best understood as a dynamic and flexible process of recruitment and mobilization. People rarely wake up one morning and suddenly decide to protest; that decision is the culmination of many steps. Understanding why some people join movements and others – who might look demographically like them and have similar grievances – do not, requires a closer look at these steps. Moreover, since not everyone who starts out caring about an issue takes action on it, there is clearly some attrition that occurs along the way. Therefore, we must also take a closer look at potential obstacles along this process to understand the reasons why otherwise interested individuals may decide not to join movements, and whether this attrition systematically discourages particular types of people from protest. Finally, recruitment into movements is not a simple, one-time event. As Suzanne Staggenborg (2011: 28) notes, it is an ongoing process, in part because movements benefit when they can point to large memberships as proof of their legitimacy and in part because even if people join movements, some

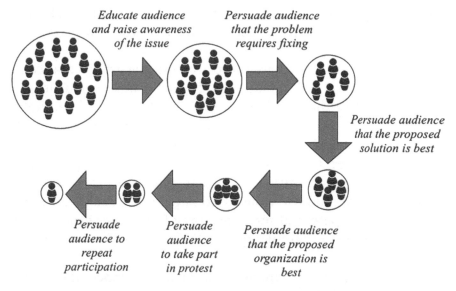

Figure 2.2 *Steps to mobilizing movement participants*

proportion of them drift away and numbers must be replenished (Weiss 1963; Bird and Reimer 1982).

While different scholars may conceptualize the mobilization process in slightly different ways and with more or fewer steps, figure 2.2 provides a general overview of the most crucial parts of the process. At each stage, there is a crucial task that movements must do, whether it involves educating people about a particular issue and crystallizing a sense of collective grievance or persuading individuals who share a grievance that the movement's solution will fix the problem. At each step, movements risk losing potential supporters. To take the case of OWS as an example, movement organizers must first raise awareness of the issues, to inform people about, say, unregulated financial institutions or growing income inequality. Some people will pay attention; they move on to the next step while the rest cease to be potential movement members. Then, OWS must persuade those paying attention that the existence of unregulated financial institutions or growing income inequality is a problem. Some people will agree and move on to the next step; others will disagree and drop out of the process. OWS must next persuade the remaining members of the audience – now holding a collective grievance – that the movement's preferred solution will best address the grievance. Because social problems are complex, there are typically many different ways to solve a problem; movement groups must champion their approach over, say, what elected officials might propose or rival groups argue is the answer. People might disagree with this diagnosis, but those who agree continue the process.

Next, in movements where there are multiple groups that compete for support, individual organizations must persuade the audience to join them instead of their rivals. Take, for example, the case of the Northern Ireland nationalist movement, which advocates for reunifying Northern Ireland with the rest of the Republic of Ireland. In this movement, there are multiple groups that agree on reunification as a goal, but who disagree about whether they should use violence to pursue that goal. They must work to attract potential members away from other groups with similar goals but different organizational identities and tactical preferences.

Once a group has a supportive audience member, they must work to persuade that person to take part in an actual movement activity – to come to a meeting, or attend a rally, or donate money, etc. Again, some people will, but others will decide that the time, cost, or risk is too great. Movements tend to have larger numbers of sympathizers than actual participants; getting these sympathizers over the hurdle to actual involvement is a particularly important step. Finally, because movements are not short, one-time events, they must persuade people who have already participated once to keep doing so. Here, too, there is the possibility for attrition, as dilettantes and the mildly curious will decide that they are uninterested in making a long-term commitment to being an activist.

Structural, Exogenous, and Organizational Influences

The mobilization process as sketched above can be influenced by a variety of factors, some of which can make a movement's job easier by lowering the costs of education or persuasion, while others make those same tasks comparatively more difficult. Political process theorists, for example, argue that changes in the political opportunity structure (POS) can facilitate recruitment by making action seem more urgent or possible. Bursts of mobilization can take place both under expanding opportunity structures, which would make it easier for movements to operate and pursue their goals, and under closing ones, which might move people to action out of alarm and defensiveness (Tarrow 2011: 160).

Two examples will help to illustrate both sides of this relationship. South Africa's anti-apartheid movement was certainly helped by expanding POS when F.W. de Klerk became President in 1989. Whereas his predecessors had instituted severe restrictions on the movement, including banning its leading organizations and imprisoning many of its leaders, de Klerk reversed these policies soon after taking office. Within months of becoming President, he unbanned the African National Congress and other political groups, and released political prisoners, including the ANC's leader, Nelson Mandela. Given that the presence of elite allies is one indicator of an open POS (Tarrow 2011: 163), then South Africa in 1990 would certainly qualify as a country where political opportunities for the anti-apartheid movement suddenly started to open up after decades of closure. After de Klerk's decision, the anti-apartheid movement was able to disseminate its message to potential supporters more widely and without fear of being caught by authorities. It could hold meetings, publish newspapers, and pursue other strategies designed to bring followers into the fold – all of which was made easier by the more permissive POS.

But a closed or closing POS can also be motivating, as the TPM case shows. The Tea Party organized at a time when the Democratic Party had control of the executive and legislative branches, and seemed ready and willing to use that control to pass laws that conservatives deeply disliked. Signature pieces of legislation such as the economic stimulus program that was intended to shore up an economy in crisis were signed into law, while other sweeping reforms like an overhaul of the health-care system were on the horizon. Republicans railed against the Obama administration's policy agenda but, lacking control of both the House and the Senate, were unable to stop many of these bills from passing. For some conservative members of the public, this seemed like an onslaught that had to be resisted before it was too late. It was the threat of closing POS – no longer having a Republican President, losing control in the legislature, facing a protracted economic crisis, etc. – that galvanized the Tea Party Movement into action. Eitan Alimi (1999) similarly points to mobilization under repressive regimes as evidence that a closed POS does not necessarily thwart protest activity.

Short-lived, exogenous events and long-term structural changes can also help or hinder mobilization processes. Urbanization, for example, created a critical mass of people in a concentrated area, which made it possible for movements to communicate with them more efficiently during the mobilization process. The development of media technologies such as the printing press or, more recently, the internet can make it possible for movements to educate and influence larger portions of the public more cheaply. Sudden crises can also make it easier to persuade potential activists of the need to mobilize, as was the case following the nuclear meltdown at Three Mile Island in Pennsylvania. The sudden spotlight on this incident made it easier for anti-nuclear organizations to educate the public and mobilize grievances against nuclear power. Within weeks of the accident, there were large protests organized around the country, including a march with some 65,000 people in Washington, DC, and a mass demonstration numbering 200,000 in attendance (Joppke 1993). But not all crises help movements. When the Irish were seeking independence from the United Kingdom in the early twentieth century, they received a blow when World War I broke out and distracted the attention of both the British government and the general public (Hennessey 1998).

Shocking events can also compel people to take action out of a sense of moral outrage (Jasper 1997). In 2012, for example, the Indian public was horrified by a brutal gang rape of a 23-year-old student on a private bus in Delhi. The story not only made national headlines, it was picked up by the international media and reported all over the world. The horror of the attack triggered protests all around the country and, indeed, across the world, with calls for legal reforms and changes in popular attitudes toward women and gender violence. The Delhi bus incident was certainly not the first instance of gang rape in India, but the sustained media attention (in part owing to the victim's middle-class, educated, and law-abiding profile), the particularly vicious nature of the attack, and the fact that the victim eventually died of her injuries all contributed to the widespread outrage and mobilization that followed.

Structural factors and external events are not the only things that can influence the mobilization process. As we will discuss in more detail in chapter 5, movements themselves have a lot of power to shape public attitudes toward social problems by the choices they make when framing the issue or choosing the best way to address the grievances that people hold. Resource mobilization theorists also argue that groups that have access to financial resources will have an easier time reaching out to potential supporters and converting them into actual supporters. Persuasion requires contact, either in person, via media, or some form of mass communication like mass mailings (Snow et al. 1980: 790). All of these strategies require resources of one sort or another, and movements that have more money, simply put, can mail more letters, hand out more leaflets, knock on more doors, and broadcast more content over the airwaves.

The Microfoundations of Mobilization

The factors described above are macro- and meso-level variables, in that they capture large, structural forces that can affect mobilization as well as intermediate, movement-level forces. But while both types of variables can influence mobilization, making it easier and cheaper or harder and more costly, they still are limited when it comes to explaining why any given protestor commits to social movement activism and her friend or neighbor does not. Not everyone in India who heard about the Delhi gang rape took to the streets to protest about violence against women, for example, and not everyone who is handed a leaflet describing an upcoming protest decides to attend. To get a better understanding of these variations, we need to look at the microfoundations of mobilization: the factors that drive *individual* decisions whether to participate or not.

Whereas early theorists of collective behavior emphasized the seeming irrationality of crowds, describing scenarios where people simply get swept away by the frenzy of those around them, subsequent scholars have instead emphasized that the decision to participate in social protest is ultimately a rational one, based on calculations (implicit or explicit) weighing the cost of joining a movement against the possible benefits of doing so. The benefits certainly include the possible advantages that protestors would enjoy if their campaign were to go well: a successful labor strike might yield more money or better benefits to workers, a successful protest against government censorship might yield more freedom to read and write, a successful rally against a polluting company might result in cleaner air or water.

But against these benefits, potential protestors must weigh the possible costs. All political action is costly, even though the costs might be extremely small in some cases. Voting, for example, does not cost much in established democracies, where it usually requires some expenditure of time and perhaps some expense for transportation to the polling place. These costs may be trivial for many people; I can walk half a block to my polling place, so my cost of voting is very low. But for others, the costs are sufficiently high for voting to be difficult. In the United States, voting takes place during a weekday, which means some people may not be able to take time off from work to cast a ballot. In the 2016 presidential election, people waiting to vote early in Cincinnati, Ohio, formed a line more than half a mile long; for people taking time out from jobs, such a commitment might be simply too much to undertake. Some polling places require a car or a long ride on public transportation, which can exclude other voters. A looming transit strike in Philadelphia, Pennsylvania, during the 2016 presidential election, threatened to make it difficult for those who rely on public transportation to travel to their nearest polling place and to make it too costly to vote. In some places, voting requires individuals to show specific forms of government-issued ID like a driver's license, which itself costs money. Even the innocuous act of voting, therefore, requires people to spend resources if they want to participate.

If we move from mundane forms of participation to those that occur largely outside political institutions, these costs can multiply rapidly. Think, for example, about all the costs that were involved for those who took part in the September 1, 2016 protests against the Venezuelan government of Nicolas Maduro. Organizers of the protest wanted to signal their anger with government policies that have led to massive shortages in food, medications, and vital services over the past few years. During the protest, roughly 1 million people marched through the streets of Caracas, Venezuela's capital, shouting "Venezuela is hungry!" and "This government is going to fall!" People traveled from all over the country to take part, which required them to take time off from work or school, perhaps make arrangements for child care, and spend money on travel, lodging, and food while away from home. Other costs could include purchasing (or making) signs and banners, and risking being arrested (or worse) by police. Compared to voting, this non-violent protest involved considerably more effort, time, and resources for the average participant. High-risk forms of protest – sabotage and other illegal acts, or protest in repressive regimes – carry even more costs and considerably more dangers that rational individuals must weigh against the possible benefits of participation.

This kind of cost–benefit calculation, however, highlights a paradox of participation: if individuals weigh the costs versus benefits of joining a social movement, there would be almost no protest in the world, because joining movements is rarely the rational choice. Mancur Olson (2002) terms this conundrum the "collective action problem." Collective action, such as taking part in a protest, entails a non-zero cost. The benefits of protest, on the other hand, involve the gains that might come if the movement achieves its goals, which is not a certainty. But let us imagine that the movement succeeds in achieving its goals; for most social movements, these successes will also benefit people who chose not to join the movement. Such successes are considered "public goods," which can be enjoyed by anyone in the public, not just those people who fought and risked to achieve them. It makes sense, therefore, to sit back, let others take on the risks and costs, and enjoy the fruits of their victories if they happen. Such "free riders," according to Olson, are more rational than people who choose to engage in most collective action.

The anti-apartheid movement provides a good illustration of the collective action problem at work. The movement achieved its goals when, after decades of work, it succeeded in overturning a racist system of government. It did so at enormous cost to its members. Nelson Mandela, one of the movement's leaders and first President of democratic South Africa, spent 27 years in prison; Thabo Mbeki, another ANC leader and Mandela's successor as President, spent roughly the same amount of time in exile; Steve Biko, the founder of the country's Black Consciousness Movement, died in police custody under mysterious circumstances; ordinary citizens risked being beaten, harassed, imprisoned, or worse if they chose to take part. But when the movement finally succeeded, ushering in democratic elections in 1994, *everyone* in South Africa was able to take part in this new society, not just those who risked their lives and livelihoods. Knowing this, what would you do as a purely rational actor? Olson argues rational people would choose *not* to participate, since they could enjoy all the benefits of success without enduring any of the costs. And if the movement did not succeed, these individuals would be no worse off than before since they had spent neither time nor resources to protest.

Olson's collective action problem suggests that protest should be exceedingly rare. Yet, as figure 2.3 illustrates, clearly there is protest – a lot of it – all over the world. If we look at the

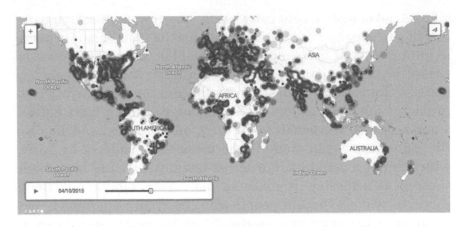

Source: The GDELT (Global Data on Events, Location, and Tone) Project, Database of Protest Events; OpenStreetMap contributors; CARTO.

Figure 2.3 *Protest events around the world on April 10, 2015*

various protest incidents that took place on just one day – April 10, 2015 – we can see events in thousands of places across six continents, in countries both large and small, rich and poor, democratic and autocratic alike. How do we square this inconsistency between Olson's theoretical prediction and the empirical reality?

One way that Olson himself argues that collective action can be made rational is by tipping the balance of costs and benefits toward the latter, either by making participation more attractive (lowering costs, raising benefits) or by making free-riding an unappealing option (raising costs, lowering benefits) (Oliver 1980; Olson 2002). For example, movement groups might entice people to join them by offering them selective incentives that only people who participate can receive. Activists attending a rally might, for example, be treated to a free concert by a well-known musical group, as happened in 1998 when members of the band U2 played in Belfast to generate public support for an upcoming referendum on the Northern Ireland peace accord, or during the 2008 Democratic National Convention in Denver when the band Rage Against the Machine played at a protest event held by Veterans Against the Iraq War. Such benefits are private, not public, goods, enjoyed only by a limited group that excludes non-members. Movement groups can also lower the costs of participation, for example by providing free transportation to demonstrations, which also could make participation more enticing. Labor unions sometimes offer "strike pay" to workers who must forgo their wages while protesting but who still have to make ends meet.

Olson also argues that collective action in small groups lowers the likelihood of free-riding behavior, because in small groups it is easier to monitor (and discipline) people who do not participate but let others carry the burden of collective action. Imagine that you have a group project in which everyone in the group earns a collective grade. Imagine that one member of the group is a free rider who does not contribute to the group but is content to let others do all the work. This individual will receive the same grade as everyone else while contributing a negligible amount. If the group is small, the free rider's lack of participation will be glaringly obvious and everyone will be aware of it and can take potential steps to correct the behavior, including shaming the person or offering incentives to motivate more effort. It would be much more difficult to monitor for free-riding behavior in large groups, which are more impersonal and harder for others to police. As with movements, large groups might have many supporters on paper, but it might be harder to sanction any one person for free-riding. In small groups, however, people can spot and penalize free-riding behavior more effectively.

Scholars have additionally argued that Olson's narrow focus on material costs and benefits excludes some of the more intangible factors that affect whether individuals choose to join movements (Ferree 1992; Friedman and McAdam 1992; Nepstad 2004). James Jasper (1997), for example, points out that joining social movements can provide emotional benefits for people who find joy and opportunities for self-expression in protest, as well as the comforts of building a sense of community with other like-minded individuals. The benefits of solidarity are hard to quantify, so it is little surprise that Olson, an economist, did not factor them into his models. But such emotional benefits can be enormously valuable to movement participants. "It's so empowering to feel the energy of all these people around you," a former student and OWS member told me back in 2011, "everyone is pissed off about what's happening in our society, but there's a sense of hope too, and community, and comfort." A desire to share in the collective identity that movement participants create can be as compelling a reason as calculations of costs and benefits when explaining activist motivations. Jeff Goodwin and Steven Pfaff (2001) argue that people will even join in high-risk activism, where the costs of doing so might seem to

significantly outweigh any possible benefits, if the right commitment mechanisms are in place, like strong identification with the
movement, a belief in the righteousness of the cause, and a deep
connection to other activists. The power of these non-rational reasons for participation suggests that rationality is not always (and
not only) the reason why people join movements. Indeed, Stefan
Stürmer and Bernd Simon found that there are dual pathways – one
more material and one more emotional – that can lead rational
actors into social movement membership (Stürmer et al. 2003;
Stürmer and Simon 2004).

Obstacles and Enablers on the Path to Mobilization

The mobilization process can also be influenced by a range of
individual-level factors that can throw up roadblocks making it
harder to progress from one step to the next, or make it go more
smoothly. David Snow and Sarah Soule (2010) classify these factors into two groups: the social/psychological and the structural/
organizational. While none of these in isolation perfectly predicts
whether someone becomes an activist or remains on the sidelines,
some provide considerable predictive power to the puzzle of
mobilization.

Social and Psychological Factors

Social psychologists have long studied how individual decisions
and behavior might be influenced by a person's social value orientation (SVO). This orientation affects how much empathy and
regard for others an individual might have, and how these feelings
affect an individual's likelihood of cooperating with other people. A
number of experiments have demonstrated that people who have a
highly prosocial psychological orientation are more likely to work
collectively to solve social problems, even when those problems
may not affect them directly (Balliet et al. 2009). This finding is
particularly relevant for social movement participation where the
movements that a person joins may not be working to benefit him
directly, as might be the case with the OWS protestor who might
be concerned about income inequality and unemployment despite
being employed full-time and earning more than $100,000 per
year. People who have weaker prosocial tendencies, on the other
hand, are more likely to prioritize narrow self-interest over all other

considerations. While such people may still join social movements, it would require some kind of personal advantage or gain to overcome the collective action problem.

A person's collective identity prior to joining a movement can also help to move people along the mobilization pathway. While it is not a requirement for participation in the TPM, individuals who self-identify as conservatives are disproportionately likely to follow its mobilization process to its end. Their prior identification with political conservatism might make them more receptive to forming grievances in line with TPM analyses, or make them more accepting of TPM-proposed solutions. Self-identified liberals, on the other hand, are more likely to disagree philosophically that big government is an inherent vice, or that one way of limiting government overreach is to repeal Obamacare. Not all liberals will drop out at such points – one Gallup poll found that 10 percent of moderate and liberal Democrats also identified as Tea Party supporters (Newport 2010) – but many of them will because their prior identities, and the beliefs that are connected to those identities, will make them harder to persuade at each step. Prior collective identity can also make it easier for movements to reach potential supporters at the very beginning of the mobilizational pathway, as people who self-identify as conservative or members of the Republican Party might listen to similar talk-radio hosts, read similar news websites, and belong to similar community organizations, which can make it easier for the TPM to target its message and find people who are open to persuasion.

Another factor is an individual's biographical availability. This concept refers to the biographical details about a person – age, gender, occupation, socio-economic status, and the like – that can make it easier or harder for them to take part in collective action (McAdam 1986, 1990). Since protest involves some expenditure of time and effort, some people are more easily able to make the sacrifices necessary to take part in it. Consider, for example, two individuals who are equally interested in the goals of OWS and who have a similar desire to join an Occupy camp. One of them is a childless college student whose parents pay tuition and cover the costs of rent and food; the other is a single parent who works a full-time job. Which one would have an easier time joining the Occupy camp? The probable answer is the college student because that person has fewer constraints that limit participation. Biographical availability can help to contextualize why, for example, OWS has so many students in its ranks (missing class might be costly, but not as costly as missing work) and the TPM has many retirees. It also explains why both OWS and the TPM have more middle-class members – OWS has many professionals, the TPM has many small-business owners (Skocpol and Williamson 2012; Milkman et al. 2013). Both types of occupations and income levels make it easier to take some time off work without severe financial penalties, compared to workers whose pay would be reduced if they missed their scheduled shifts.

While there are a number of potentially salient biographical categories, most explanations that involve this idea return to age, occupation, employment status, income, and a handful of other variables in their analyses. Research on biographical availability suggests that people who are more secure in their income (middle-class and above) will be more likely to protest compared to the working poor, though the unemployed have perhaps the greatest availability of all. Young people are thought to have more availability than older people, in part because they are less likely to have children and stable careers, though, by the same logic, retirees and people with stable careers might be better positioned financially to take part in protests. The able-bodied, by virtue of their mobility, are more likely to be active in social movements than their disabled counterparts.

Biography is not destiny, however, and the details of who participates can vary across movements and context. Mark Beissinger, Amaney A. Jamal, and Kevin Mazur found, for example, that in the 2011 Arab Spring uprisings, the participants in Tunisia tended to be younger and from a wider variety of occupational backgrounds than their middle-class, middle-aged counterparts in Egypt (Beissinger et al. 2015). The people who participated in the anti-war protests that Stefaan Walgrave, Dieter Rucht, and Peter Van Aelst studied were disproportionately young, female, and highly educated (Walgrave et al. 2010), whereas the average TPM member is also more educated than the general population, but also tends to be middle-aged and male. Outside the developed world, movements that organize around basic human needs might draw disproportionately from the poor and underserved rather than the middle classes, who are unlikely to bear the brunt of such deprivation (for example, see Escobar and Alvarez 1992).

In addition to relatively static biographical details, an individual's past socialization and experiences can also influence likelihood of future participation (Sherkat and Blocker 1994). Individuals who grew up in households with politically engaged parents, for example, are socialized at an early age to care about politics and take an interest in social problems. Many people who attend protests while still young are more likely to continue such activities when they grow older, because they are familiar and are seen as socially acceptable behavior; individuals who lack that early experience can certainly still participate in movements, but may have to work a bit harder for it to feel familiar and comfortable. Milkman and her co-authors discovered that a staggering 82 percent of OWS protestors in their survey reported having participated in their first protest activity before age 22; of those individuals, over half reported their first experience with protest happened when they were still children. Moreover, 42 percent of respondents had participated in 30 or more protest events over the course of their lives, and 26 percent had been arrested for their past participation (Milkman et al. 2013). Participation can give people a sense of personal empowerment as well as the emotional rewards of connecting with other passionate people, which, together with increasing one's familiarity and comfort with protest, increases the likelihood of future participation as well.

Structural and Organizational Factors

In addition to individual psychology and social experiences, scholars have argued that structural and organizational factors can also facilitate or inhibit the mobilization process. One such variable that has received considerable attention is the social network – family, friends, and acquaintances – in which each person is embedded (Snow et al. 1980; McAdam and Paulsen 1993; Passy 2003). Social networks exert their influence in a number of ways. They help to shape individual identities, values, and beliefs via interactions with others. If, for example, most people in my social circle are deeply opposed to fracking as a way of extracting oil, they might influence my position as I talk with them and hear their reactions to the use of fracking by energy companies. But if I am embedded in a different social network – perhaps I have many friends who work for oil companies, or have family members who rarely discuss political issues – my interactions would likely produce a different set of values and beliefs. The first network might pull me toward environmental protest movements; the latter network would be less likely to do the same.

Network effects can also manifest in more impersonal ways too, including on social media where the interactions among people may exist largely in virtual space. A study conducted by the Pew Research Center on conversations about race on social media found, for example, that African Americans reported posting about race in greater numbers than other ethnic groups; some 28% of African American respondents said that "at least some" of their postings on social media involved race, compared to 20% of Hispanics and just 8% of whites (Anderson and Hitlin 2016). More tellingly, not only are African Americans more likely to post such content, but even those who do not post about race are, by virtue of their social media networks, also more likely to encounter such posts from others. A majority (68%) of African American respondents reported that at least some of the posts they see on social media sites covered race or race relations, compared to less than a third (29%) of white respondents; almost a quarter (24%) of African American respondents reported that most of the content they encountered on social media involved race and race relations, compared to just 6% for white respondents. These differences suggest that the different social media networks of these respondents influence the information and conversations they are likely to encounter – differences that, in turn, can shape beliefs, values, and overall orientation to social problems.

Not only do our social networks socialize us and affect how we see and interpret the world around us, but they also provide us with concrete opportunities to become involved in movements. Those people with friends or family members who are involved in protest activity are more likely to participate themselves, in part because these social connections normalize participation in movements ("all my friends are doing it, I should too") and in part because these connections make it easier to find out about issues, organizations, and events. If someone is interested in attending a protest event and has a friend who belongs to the sponsoring organization, it will be easier for that individual to get crucial details about when and where the event will take place; such information may be available to others, but they will have to work a bit harder to find it.

Apart from providing simple information, social networks can also influence whether someone joins a movement by signaling what others in the network are likely to do, which can make participation more or less appealing. If I learn that many of my friends are planning to attend a march, then I might start to think that joining them would be a fun thing to do; my participation would be conditioned not just by my stance on the issue, but also by my desire to be part of the group. Such approaches acknowledge the power of social relations on individual decisions to protest (Marwell and Oliver 1993).

Much of this existing research on social movements focuses on in-person (as opposed to virtual) networks, though scholarly interest in online social networks – especially social media – has grown, particularly in the wake of the Arab Spring uprisings, which made widespread use of Facebook and Twitter to communicate among and connect supporters. Online social networks offer different kinds of interactions compared to in-person networks. They typically involve more frequent contact with a greater number of people, but with each exchange potentially shorter and shallower than in-person interactions among friends and family. Even so, scholars have found they can influence mobilizing effects in similar ways to in-person networks: by helping to construct or reinforce activist identities, by providing information and access to opportunities, and by giving participation social meaning and value (González-Bailón et al. 2011; Castells 2012; Lim 2012).

Finally, one of the most powerful predictors of whether someone will make it to the end of the mobilization process is simply whether they are asked to participate by movement groups (Klandermans and Oegema 1987, 1994; Schussman and Soule 2005). Even if people make it to the very end of the mobilization process, without an explicit invitation to join in protest activities some proportion of sympathizers will stay on the sidelines. Such invitations can be formal, but they can also involve little more than an activist inviting a friend to attend a protest event with her. It is that extra step of extending a welcoming hand that can help to bridge the gap between passive support and active participation. Ziad Munson (2002) even found that this sort of personal invitation can sometimes create a short-cut in the mobilization process. In his study of pro-life activists, he found that the processes of forming grievances and persuading people about the movement and its goals did not have to precede involvement. In fact, some of the most voraciously pro-life activists did not have strong views on the subject before becoming involved with the movement; some were even pro-choice. Their views, grievances, convictions, and identities as pro-life activists were constructed dynamically once they had one foot in the door – and that foot in the door was often the result of someone inviting them to attend a meeting or other event.

While none of the factors described above provide a sure-fire predictor of who will join a movement, they account for some of the key variables that make participation more or less likely. Moreover, these different variables can interact with each other, intensifying or moderating the effects that they ultimately have. Someone who is biographically available, who has been socialized to participate in protest, who has many friends and family members who support the movement, and who is just a stone's throw from the protest site might be a highly likely participant. That same person who is several thousand miles away and who would have to travel at great cost to reach the protest may choose to sit it out. Taken together, these factors help us to account for how people can make it to the end of the mobilization process, and some of the main hurdles that can prevent them from becoming activists.

Retention and Demobilization

As figure 2.2 suggests, once someone decides to take part in protest, the very last step in the mobilization process is the decision to come back and protest again. Retaining activists and encouraging them to stay mobilized is important for movements, since the effort it takes to recruit a brand new member is more burdensome than holding on to a member who has already traversed the length of the mobilization process. Retention is where a movement's ability to foster collective identity and a feeling of solidarity with others becomes crucial. If individuals feel that they are getting some kind of emotional satisfaction from their participation, then they are more likely to stay involved over a long period of time. If the decision to remain engaged is purely one of material costs and benefits, on the other hand, people are more likely to drift away, as the costs of participation are immediate, but the material benefits may take years to achieve. Bert Klandermans argues that demobilization occurs when activists receive insufficient gratification from protest, or when their commitment declines (Klandermans 1997). To this, we might add that demobilization can also occur when activists are sufficiently satisfied with the material and emotional benefits they have received and decide that they no longer need to take part in the protest. In effect, getting what you want can be just as demobilizing as not getting what you want.

Demobilization, though, is inevitable for all but the most determined movement activists. Just as there are degrees of commitment to an issue that separates sympathizers from movement activists, there are also gradations in commitment within the activist community too. Many people are occasional activists, participating in protest when it is convenient for them; a smaller subset are committed activists who take part in movement activities on a regular basis; a still-smaller subset are the true believers, those who have the highest level of commitment and whose identities are deeply intertwined with their work as activists. Demobilization can happen at any of these levels, but it takes more to trigger it as level of dedication to the cause increases. The occasional activists are most likely to stop participating, because they are least involved in the movement and therefore are least likely to enjoy the emotional and solidarity-enhancing benefits that can sustain participation through rocky spells and bruising interactions with authorities. Occasional activists are also more likely to be satiated with small gains compared to the committed activists; true believers are most likely to be unsatisfied with half-measures and will be the ones who vow to continue until all the movement's demands are met.

Concluding Summary

At the heart of all social movements is the activist – the foot soldiers who, when gathered en masse, can exert a powerful influence on politics. There are plenty of caricatures and stereotypes floating around of who protests, often informed by early notions that people who protest are loners, misanthropes, or somehow on the fringes of society. This picture, as this chapter points out, is deeply flawed. But questions remain about why certain individuals become protestors and others do not join social movements. If we think about participation as the result of a series of steps rather than a simple, spontaneous yes-or-no choice, then we can more closely examine who is likely to make it through all the steps and who is likely – for psychological reasons, social reasons, structural reasons, and organizational reasons – to stop short before the end. The picture that emerges of activists is more nuanced than the stereotypes that their opponents casually throw around. Rather than two-dimensional figures, this chapter starts to paint a picture of activists as rational actors, but also people who strive to build a common community with like-minded people, and who derive pleasures from the solidarity that they find in protest.

Even though the mobilization process is presented as a general model that applies across a range of movements and settings, the reality is that activists mobilize around very different sorts of issues, from economic demands to grievances concerning culture and identity. Having gained some purchase on what makes some people more likely to protest, let us now turn to the organizations through which they protest to understand the range and complexity of groups that make up social movements.

Question for Discussion

1   Why did early scholars of social movements think that protestors were alienated and irrational? How did subsequent scholars critique this view of protestors?

2   What role do grievances – individual or collective – play in mobilizing people to join social movements? Why do many scholars argue that grievances are not sufficient to explain protest?

3   How can biographical, social, or environmental conditions increase the chances of an individual being successfully mobilized into activism? Does this suggest anyone can become an activist and participate in protest? Why or why not?

4   How might the challenges of retention be different from those of getting people to join a social movement in the first place?

Additional Readings

Jasper, James. 1997. *The Art of Moral Protest: Culture, Biography, and Creativity in Social Movements*. Chicago: University of Chicago Press. An important book that considers the role of culture, identity, and emotion in movement participation.

McAdam, Doug. 2004. "Revisiting the U.S. Civil Rights Movement: Toward A More Synthetic Understanding of the Origin of Contention." Pp. 201–32 in *Rethinking Social Movement Studies:*

Structure, Meaning, Emotion, ed. Jeff Goodwin and James M. Jasper. Lanham, MD: Rowman & Littlefield. An important treatment, from a political process perspective, of the role that social networks play in mobilization.

Olson, Mancur. 2002. *The Logic of Collective Action*. Cambridge, MA, and London: Harvard University Press. A classic statement of the collective action problem.

CHAPTER 3

The Organization

Objectives

- To examine the range of different entities that make up social movements and recognize the advantages and limitations of these various organizational forms for mounting and sustaining protest.
- To understand key debates about whether social movements benefit from or are harmed by increasing professionalization and formalization.
- To recognize how movement actors can cooperate as well as compete with other like-minded social movement groups.
- To determine the life cycle of movements, from emergence and expansion to decline and dormancy.

Introduction

At first glance, Chile might seem like an odd place for mass protest to break out in early 2011. It was a spring of uprisings all around the world, as one Arab country after another was swept up in headline-grabbing pro-democracy movements that sought to topple autocratic dictators from their entrenched positions in power. It was the spring of tumultuous, occasionally violent anti-austerity protests in Europe, as Greeks and Spaniards took to the streets to vent their anger at government policies that offered little relief from soaring unemployment, deep cuts to social safety nets, and widespread foreclosures that left people homeless and saddled with debt. It was the year when thousands of Israelis erected large tent camps in the middle of major cities to protest skyrocketing housing costs, and hundreds of thousands of people took to the streets of Israel throughout the summer to call attention to the high cost of living and growing inequality in the country. But these were countries grappling with severe economic pressures. Unemployment in Spain was 21 percent, more than double the average in the European Union, while youth unemployment (for those between 15 and 24 years) was approaching nearly 50 percent. The economic forecast in the Arab Spring countries also fueled unrest, as educated young people confronted stagnant economic opportunities and governments that were unresponsive to the demands of their people. In Israel, housing prices had risen 40 percent over the previous six years, while food costs were rising faster than incomes.

Chile, however, was not facing these same sorts of economic pressures or autocratic governments. It was a stable established democracy with competitive, multiparty elections. In 2011, its economic forecast was healthy and expanding (Cummings 2015). Unemployment rates had fallen for three years in a row, and in 2011, settled around 7%, while youth unemployment had also fallen, from 22.7% in 2009 to 17.6% in 2011. The overall economy was growing, as GDP per capita rose from roughly $10,000 in 2009 to $14,500 by 2011. And that same year, according to the UN Development Index – which measures life expectancy, access to education, and other indicators of well-being – Chile was rated the highest-performing country in Latin America and the Caribbean, and among the top 25% in the world. With falling levels of income inequality and modest inflation rates, Chile lacked the dramatic economic and political catastrophes that seemed to trigger the cascade of protests elsewhere in the world.

And yet thousands of students from Chile's universities took to the streets in 2011 in a sustained protest against the government's education policies, which were characterized by a relatively laissez-faire and market-oriented approach consistent with neoliberal economic values (Bellei and Cabalin 2013). These same policies had dramatically expanded the number of people who pursued higher education, rising from 16% of people aged 18–24 in 1990 to nearly 40% by 2010 (Somma 2012). However, the students argued that these very same policies had led to a proliferation of private educational institutions of variable quality that were not adequately regulated by the government. Moreover, these private institutions used discriminatory admissions standards and legal loopholes to enrich their owners. To pay for these private institutions, students and their families had to borrow money from banks at much higher rates than the state-subsidized loans available to students attending traditional universities, but even at traditional universities, tuition rates climbed as institutions sought to cover their own expenses as government support decreased. The net result was an education system that was itself highly segregated by socio-economic status and that, in turn, perpetuated inequalities in society. To fix these problems, students demanded more government funding for state schools, tighter regulation of private, for-profit institutions, and an end to discriminatory admissions standards that contributed to inequalities of access and cost (Bellei and Cabalin 2013).

This student movement did not come together spontaneously; it was organized by dedicated people in student federations that represented all the students enrolled at each university. These university-specific federations, some of which had experience with political engagement and activism dating back decades (Bonilla 1960), represented both public and private universities and, in turn, came together in a national confederation – the Confederación de Estudiantes de Chile (CONFECH) – which took the lead in spearheading the protests and coordinating action among all the different student organizations around the country. CONFECH and its member groups emphasized democratic and participatory norms in their decision-making processes as proposals were discussed and debated by student assemblies around the country, in addition to assemblies held by the individual member federations on their own campuses (Somma 2012: 303).

The protests began in earnest in May 2011 when CONFECH and its members organized a demonstration that drew 15,000–20,000 people to the streets of the capital, Santiago. In the weeks and months that followed, tens of thousands of university students and their allies – high school students, parents, teachers, labor activists, indigenous activists, and even environmental groups – joined in a series of mass public demonstrations around the country, the largest since the pro-democracy movement mobilized against dictator Augusto Pinochet over 30 years earlier. The student protests captured international attention for their use of playful, performative tactics that complemented street demonstrations and marches. People staged a protest flash mob performance of Michael Jackson's "Thriller," held a kiss-in, and organized family-friendly events at local parks, complete with music and other activities that created a festive mood. They also engaged in sit-ins, occupying hundreds of school buildings as well as TV stations and government offices. Some students even went on hunger strike. In addition to these demonstrations, the students' allies also organized parallel protests. Labor unions, for example, called for strikes, including one at El Teniente, the world's largest underground copper mine, and a 48-hour national strike during which some 600,000 people protested around the country.

The government was not indifferent to these mass demonstrations, nor the fact that, in opinion polls, almost 80 percent of the public sympathized with the students. It offered different proposals that fulfilled some of the protestors' demands, but all were rejected by CONFECH as insufficiently addressing their concerns. Not one, but two, different Education Ministers were replaced as the protests went on. All throughout 2011 and 2012, students returned to the streets to continue putting pressure on the government to make bigger, more fundamental changes to the education system. As the months passed, the protests started losing some of their intensity and size, but CONFECH continued to organize for change. The movement dwindled significantly after Chile held a presidential election at the end of 2013 and the winner, Michelle Bachelet, vowed to make sweeping reforms to the education system. While the movement quieted down in the months following Bachelet's election, it did not die out or go away. In fact, it had something of a resurgence in 2015, organizing protests around the country – with marked increases in violence – in response to what it saw as foot-dragging by a government that had yet to follow through on its promises.

The story of Chile's student movement, particularly the level of fierce conviction and creativity demonstrated by the students themselves, is certainly a compelling one. But the case also illustrates a key insight about social movements: even though we may speak about them in the singular – *the* student movement, *the* environmental movement, *the* pro-democracy movement, and so forth – any one movement is actually a complex entity consisting of multiple groups and actors, each with different identities, interests, goals, and tactical preferences that are bound together in a constantly shifting network of relationships. Movements, in other words, are anything but homogeneous, unitary actors. In Chile, the movement had, for example, multiple formal organizations that were involved in protests, including the individual student federations, the central confederation, as well as trade unions, environmental groups, and others. There were also individuals who participated in protest who did not belong to any particular organization at all, including the parents of students. And there were people who did not protest themselves, but aided and abetted the protestors via supportive acts, like the municipal workers in

Santiago's city hall who let a group of about 50 high school students into the building so they could occupy it. To understand movement dynamics requires a closer look at this diversity of actors to better understand their roles and interactions.

Social Movement Organizations

Collective action, especially sustained protests against well-resourced and powerful targets such as governments or corporations, takes time and effort. It also requires resources – namely, money and people – to be carried off successfully. Without a sufficient number of people, movements struggle to be taken seriously and risk being dismissed as nothing more than nuisances. Had the Chilean student movement mobilized 20 people in that first demonstration, rather than 20,000, we might reasonably assume that the government would not have rushed to propose education reforms in response to student demands, nor would they have so readily agreed to meetings between movement representatives and the country's elected officials. Movements also require monetary resources to pay for the sometimes-mundane but necessary costs of coordinating and sustaining protest, which can include all manner of expenses, from renting meeting space to printing banners, to securing protest permits, to arranging for transportation, to maintaining a website. Resources are precious, and they are usually scarce. Movements that are able to muster resources effectively are more likely to initiate and sustain protest over time.

This line of argument stems directly from resource mobilization theory, whose advocates argue that organizations are of particular importance in social movements because they are best able to aggregate resources (McCarthy and Zald 1977). Moreover, such scholars argue that organizations are also better equipped to use those resources for mobilizing people for collective action. Recall from the discussion in chapter 1 that, in RM theory, the individual grievances that people hold are insufficient to generate organized protest because of the collective action problem. Social movement organizations (SMOs), however, can overcome this obstacle by providing selective incentives, lowering the costs, and increasing the benefits of activism. In this argument, SMOs are depicted as relatively formal and often hierarchical organizations (McCarthy and Zald 1977: 1218) that have explicit and established rules and procedures governing group operations, membership criteria, designated processes by which individuals can join or leave the group, clearly defined positions that clarify the roles and responsibilities of their members, and a way to sustain the organization without relying on the participation or leadership of specific individuals.

The resource aggregator advantage that SMOs have can manifest in several ways. Individual supporters of a social movement bring some resources with them – their labor, for example, or access to a car, or knowledge of web design. As individuals, their resources may not add up to much, but if they pool their resources with other like-minded individuals, they can start to make a difference. SMOs can facilitate this pooling process, thereby multiplying the impact that individuals and their separate resources can have. Moreover, organizations can access resources that may not be available to individual activists. The University of Chile's student federation, for example, receives funding from the overall university budget, which underwrites its various operations and initiatives, including its activist work. Formal organizations can also attract resources from sympathetic donors outside the movement, as civil rights groups like the Southern Christian Leadership Conference and the National Association for the Advancement of Colored People (NAACP) did when they received grants from foundations for their work (Jenkins and Eckert 1986: 816). For some movement groups, external funding can even comprise the majority of their funding (Cress and Snow 1996). Formal organizations can also take on fund-raising activities more efficiently by utilizing their administrative structures to target potential donors.

Formal organizations can benefit from having well-developed administrative structures in other ways as well. They can give SMOs an advantage when collecting and disseminating information to their supporters, which can help them to both attract new members from the pool of potential sympathizers and make sure the supporters they already have do not stay on the sidelines but actually take part in collective action. The University of Chile student federation, for example, has a designated Minister of Communication as part of its organizational structure. This individual is in charge of informing the federation's members about the organization's activities and operations on a regular basis. Other federation officers also communicate with members, convene meetings, promote the group's work, and perform additional activities that make it possible for the organization to operate effectively. In addition, formal organizational structures offer clear points of contact for political elites who might want to work with SMOs. Finally, formal organizations are better able to sustain themselves over time compared to ad hoc groups, as their rules provide clear mechanisms by which the organization's reins can be handed over to the next generation of leaders; such groups do not rise or fall with any one charismatic figure but instead are built to sustain themselves – and, in turn, collective action – for longer periods of time. This administrative advantage, combined with its resource advantage, makes the SMO a particularly effective tool for mobilizing people to take part in social movements (Sawyers and Meyer 1999).

There is, however, no single model of SMO that exists across movements; organizations vary considerably in how they structure their operations and, in turn, their operational cultures (Tarrow 2011: 138). Some have a narrow issue focus, while others have more sweeping mandates. Some are local, others are national, and still others have a transnational reach. SMOs can differ in their membership model, with "inclusive" groups prioritizing the number of members, even though those members may play little day-to-day role in operations and little may be asked of them in terms of making a commitment to the organization; "exclusive" groups, on the other hand, prioritize having a smaller number of highly committed members who are expected to participate and further the cause whenever possible (Zald and Ash 1966: 330–1). Groups can be hierarchically organized, with clear chains of command, concentrations of power at the higher levels of the group, and less latitude for autonomous actions among the movement's rank-and-file members. But SMOs can also be horizontal in their structure, giving members relatively equal power and creating an internal culture based on collaboration, reciprocity, and mutual exchange of information (Rucht 1996). The Chilean mobilization featured organizations of both types: the student federations and CONFECH itself were largely horizontal in orientation, stressing participatory norms and giving members ample opportunities to shape the confederation's strategies and tactics; the leaders of the movements served more as the organization's emissaries instead of exerting control over the group (Somma 2012: 303). The students' labor union ally, the Central Unitaria de Trabajadores de Chile (CUT), on the other hand, was far more hierarchically organized, with considerable decision and policy power vested in a small group of people at the head of the organization, and a far more limited, indirect voice for union members (Bensusán 2016).

All of these variations – which are a function of resource avail-ability, general movement environment, and organization-specific histories (Kriesi 1996; Rucht 1996; McAdam 2004) – can exist simul-taneously within the same movement or even within a single SMO as it evolves over time. Although these differences do not prevent dissimilar groups from working with each other, these organiza-tional structures do carry with them distinct strengths and weak-nesses, suggesting that different organizational forms may be better suited to carrying out particular types of movement tasks. Horizontal organizations, thanks to their commitment to broad participation and consultation with members, have more extensive decision-making procedures, which can take considerable time; hierarchical organizations, on the other hand, can reach a consen-sus more swiftly, but since their decisions are made by a relatively small group, can potentially lack broad buy-in from their rank-and-file members. These diversities of form all underscore the point that there is no universal model of a social movement organization, and that different groups can structure their internal operations and relationships with members in various ways while engaging in col-lective action as part of a social movement.

This variety of organizational forms invites questions about why certain organizational structures might emerge at particular times or come to predominate in a particular movement. In her study of women's and minority organizations in the United States, Debra Minkoff (1994) found, for example, that the initial growth of groups specializing in service provision later generated growth in groups that focused more on protest. However, over time, both service providers and protest groups gave way to advocacy organi-zations, which came to overshadow these other groups. To make sense of this pattern, Minkoff and other scholars have drawn on density-dependence theory (Minkoff 1994, 1995, 1997; Carroll and Hannan 2000; Olzak and Ryo 2007). This theory holds that when movements are in their infancy, they may consist of only a small number of organizations; when new organizations emerge in this early period, they tend to be built based on whatever organizational structures already exist and seem to function well. Familiar organi-zational forms dominate because newcomers tend to imitate exist-ing models; groups that survive and thrive – in part because they appeal to external elites, patrons, and possible members – provide a template for others who wish to do the same. By contrast, new and unfamiliar organizational forms will have a harder time being perceived as legitimate and finding their footing and the resources necessary to survive (Pfeffer and Salancik 1978).

While this process can replicate dominant organizational forms and crowd out other types of social movement groups, imitation can also lead to a point of diminishing returns. In early phases of organizational growth, imitating a proven organizational model can confer legitimacy on new groups and lengthen their life span. But, over time, the multiplicity of similar groups can start to increase the intra-movement competition over resources. In time, this competition decreases the rate at which new organizations will be created as well as shortening the life span of the weaker movement groups (Olzak and Ryo 2007). As Minkoff (1994) documented, it can also lead to the diversification of movement organizations, as once-dominant organizational types create space for new organizational types to emerge. Although this process is not the only way in which movement organizations can evolve, it highlights one of the mechanisms by which we can try to understand how groups establish legitimacy, survive (or not), and adapt to changing movement and external circumstances.

Formalization versus Disruption

Given these different types of organizations that are possible, scholars (and activists) disagree on whether a particular type of group is most effective as an agent of change. On one side of this debate are those who observe that, as movement groups persist over time, they tend to become more formalized and more professional. This pattern, Debra Minkoff and John McCarthy (2005) note, is observable among movement groups at the national, state, and even local level. Movement organizations that evolve into more formal and professional entities tend to have full-time paid staff rather than relying on the labor of volunteers. They also tend to shed members, moving away from a mass membership model based on constituents who are themselves beneficiaries to "paper memberships" and resources drawn from those outside the movement (Staggenborg 1988: 587). This combination of formalization and professionalization, in turn, shapes the way that movement organizations operate and their resilience through difficult times. In her work on professionalization in pro-choice movement groups, Suzanne Staggenborg (1988) found that formalized organizations run by experienced, full-time, paid staff tended to prefer more institutionalized tactics and eschewed disruptive, direct-action methods. Having a paid, professional staff also enabled formalized organizations to establish and maintain contacts with other groups, making it possible to forge strategic coalitions with other like-minded entities. And finally, the turn to professional leadership and formal organizations also encouraged the groups in Staggenborg's study to take on tasks aimed at expanding and maintaining organizational influence. Such work as writing grants, cultivating donors, or enlarging the number of people on mailing lists, enabled continuity and stability and, in turn, made it easier for professional-led formal groups to survive the ups and downs of advocacy work. Such structures can pay off in other ways as well. William Gamson (1990) found, for example, that the most successful SMOs in his study were highly centralized and hierarchal, attributes that helped keep organizations united and focused on a common goal.

While formalization and professionalization can be advantageous, some scholars argue that they can ultimately detract from the core mission that animates social movements in the first place. This dynamic, observed by German sociologist Robert Michel and termed "the iron law of oligarchy," unfolds as "the very process of organization implied a separation of leaders from the rank and file, growing self-interest of the organization, and eventually an abandonment of the characteristics of a social movement, including its determination to strive for social change" (Rucht 1999: 152). In other words, as organizations become more professional and formal, energies that would previously be directed toward actual protest, advocacy, or service provision instead become diverted toward organizational-maintenance goals – goals that can de-fang a movement group, make it increasingly status quo-oriented, and ultimately unable (or unwilling) to challenge those in power as it was originally formed to do. The "iron law" predicts that, rather than working to effect change, organizations will increasingly work primarily to sustain themselves while abandoning their original purpose. Fears over this dynamic, in turn, have led some scholars and activists to argue that social movements should be wary of formal organizational structures and professional leaderships. Instead, as Frances Fox Piven and Richard A. Cloward (1974, 1977) argue, movements should embrace structures and tactics that resist institutionalization. Social movements, they argue, gain power from their capacity to disrupt; if formal groups gravitate toward moderate, institutional tactics, then the solution is to avoid formalization and emphasize transgressive, non-institutional methods.

Not all scholars accept this dichotomy of formal-but-toothless versus informal-and-radical. Elisabeth Clemens and Debra Minkoff (2004) argue, for example, that nothing precludes formal organizations from pursuing radical change. Moreover, organizations are not inevitably committed to moderate or radical courses of action; organizations can learn, transform, and adjust their strategies in response to changes in the political environment, choices made by their competitors, allies, and targets, shifts in internal culture and leadership, and other variables that can prompt groups to alter their operations and priorities. Kim Voss and Rachel Sherman (2000) found this to be true for labor unions, which tend to be hierarchical and formal in their structure and operations but can alter their goals and tactics in response to changes in their strategic environment. Debra Minkoff (1999) found similar adaptations among women's and racial minority organizations. That said, the debate over how to balance organization-building activities with advocacy and protest still remains. Resources, time, and energy are all finite, and organizational structure, culture, and type can make some activities both more appealing and easier to execute than others, even though other actors within the movement may disagree about how to prioritize these competing demands.

Other Movement Groups

Social movement organizations have received a disproportionate amount of attention in the scholarly literature but they are by no means the only actors involved in movements (McAdam 1995: 218). Hanspeter Kriesi (1996) argues that other important social movement building blocks include movement associations, supportive organizations, and parties or interest groups. Movement associations, according to Kriesi, include the array of self-help or voluntary groups that movements sometimes create in order to cater for the needs of movement participants, such as the mutual benefit associations of labor unions, which provide members with access to health insurance and social assistance during periods of illness or unemployment. Supportive organizations include friendly outside groups that may sympathize with the movement's goals and provide social support to participants but do not participate in mobilization directly. Examples can include sympathetic media outlets, churches and educational institutions that provide meeting space, restaurants that provide free meals for protestors, and so forth. To this list we might also add informal or ad hoc groups that may lack the structures and stability of the main movement SMOs, but which nonetheless help to mobilize participants, as well as non-affiliated individuals (Oliver 1989) – people who take part in protests without formally belonging to any movement group, like many of the parents and siblings who marched alongside the Chilean students in demonstrations.

Political parties and interest groups can also be part of a larger movement. Even though chapter 1 sought to differentiate them from movements by emphasizing their insider status and use of more institutionalized forms of activity, in reality, these actors are often intertwined and each brings specific strengths to movement politics (Kitschelt 1993). Political parties, for example, can offer access to decision makers and input into legislative processes, while SMOs can deliver mass mobilization to put pressure on political elites and add urgency to movement demands. These kinds of alliances do not always materialize; in 2011, the Chilean student confederation intentionally avoided working with political parties in order to remain free of their influence and ensure control over their strategies and agenda (von Bülow and Ponte 2015). Earlier social movements in Chile, however, did feature such partnerships, as the pro-democracy movement in the late 1970s worked closely with the opposition Communist and Socialist parties to end Augusto Pinochet's autocratic rule.

Together, all of these actors constitute a complex and sometimes crowded social movement terrain, as figure 3.1 illustrates. In this diagram, we start with a movement that has multiple SMOs as well as other organizations and actors in it. Collectively, all these different actors constitute a social movement community. John McCarthy and Mayer Zald (1977) propose two additional aggregate concepts: that the SMOs of any given movement collectively comprise a social movement industry (similar to how all the automakers in a country constitute its automobile industry). In turn, all the social movement industries from this and other movements in a society constitute the social movement sector (akin to how all the industries in a country, including the automobile industry, would constitute its manufacturing sector). We might also include the wider concept of the multi-organizational field (Klandermans 1992), which includes all the other actors and groups connected to a movement organization, including its supporters, rivals, and targets. Empirically, movements vary in terms of the numbers of formal groups and how central those groups are to the operations of the movement as a whole; some movements will have many SMOs, others few, and some may not have any formal organizations at all. Moreover, the internal composition and configuration of groups can also change over time (Staggenborg 1998: 186). Together, the activities and interactions of these different groups contribute to a movement's dynamics.

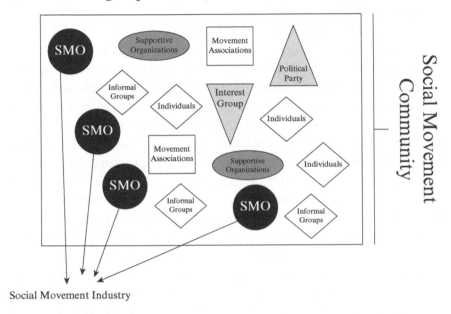

Social Movement Industry

Figure 3.1 *Social movement actors*

From Organizations to Networks

This conventional view of social movements with formal SMOs at their heart has increasingly been called into question by scholars on theoretical and empirical grounds. Theoretically, scholars like Mario Diani have pointed out that focusing on organizations misses much of the important activity within social movements, namely the interactions and exchanges that take place across the many networks connecting individuals and groups (Gerlach and Hine 1970; Diani 2004). Diani argues that movements

> cannot be identified with any specific organization . . . rather, they consist of groups and organizations with various levels of formalization, linked in patterns of interactions which run from the fairly centralized

to the totally decentralized, from the cooperative to the explicitly hostile. Persons promoting and/or supporting their actions do so not as atomized individuals ... but as actors linked to each other through complex webs of exchanges, either direct or mediated. Social movements are in other words, complex and highly heterogeneous network structures.

(Diani 2003b: 1)

In this view, the diagram of movement actors in figure 3.1 is quite limited, in that it treats individuals and groups as static and self-contained entities, ignoring the fact that they are embedded in multiple relationships with others. To understand how movements work, therefore, we must pay closer attention to these relationships – who they connect, how movement actors understand those connections, and what those linkages make possible.

Contemporary examples of social movement also call into question the default emphasis on the importance of formal SMOs in initiating and sustaining collective action. In cases like OWS, formal organizations played a minimal role by design. Lance Bennett and Alexandra Segerberg make this point with respect to the Spanish *indignados* movement, which deliberately eschewed partnerships with the kind of groups that RM theorists would expect to play a leading role, such as political parties and labor unions. Instead, the *indignados* activists reasoned that such organizations were complicit in the economic crisis that had engulfed Spain and therefore should be barred from taking part from their attempt to reform the system. Other civil society groups played a background role at most, which meant that "the most visible organization consisted of the richly layered digital and interpersonal communication networks" (Bennett and Segerberg 2012: 741), which included the movement's website but also many off-line, face-to-face interactions that made it possible to coordinate activity, share information, and build a sense of solidarity, all without formal organizations. In fact, the absence of formal SMOs itself became a point of pride, as participants in the *indignados* movement built a collective identity around having no leaders (Bennett and Segerberg 2012: 741).

Two Views of Networks

It is possible to think about networks as structures that, like highways, connect different sites of movement activity. Just as traffic travels from one place to another on highways, information travels from one site to another. That information, in turn, can help movement actors to exchange ideas, identify opportunities, evaluate strategies, and build a sense of solidarity with one another. James Kitts (2000) argues, for example, that networks facilitate participation since they allow connected groups to share information about opportunities for action; moreover, network structures allow for the circulation and exchange of resources within the network while also transmitting rewards for collaborative behavior or sanctions for actions that might harm the movement. Networks also help to build movement identity among actors via ongoing communication that fosters a sense of interdependence and solidarity. David Strang and Sarah Soule (1998) additionally find that networks promote the diffusion of ideas and tactics from one location to another. This diffusion can even happen across social movements located in very different places if they have the proper network connections. For example, one of the creative tactics that the student protestors used in 2011 was a massive water balloon fight in the streets of Valparaíso, Chile's second-largest city. Members of the student movement subsequently attended a meeting of the World Social Forum, an international gathering of organizations opposed to neoliberal globalization policies, in Porto Alegre, Brazil. There, they encountered members of OWS who heard about, and were inspired by, the students' use of creative protest. These members, in turn, considered using water balloon fights as a tactic themselves (Schneider 2013: 133). This network connected individuals in two different movements on two different continents, but facilitated the transfer of information all the same.

However, not all networks are equivalent conduits; some facilitate movement activity while others constrain it (Wasserman and Faust 1994: 4). To take the metaphor one step farther, some highways are high-speed expressways connecting major cities and some are relatively underused roads that link sparsely populated areas. Movement networks have this same diversity of form and function. Some are strong links that involve regular contact and a significant two-way exchange of meaningful information; they might function akin to our metaphorical expressways, making it possible to transfer large volumes of information between two movement actors. Links that are weaker – because they are newly established, for example, or used sporadically, or only travel in one direction – will transfer far less information between actors, much like the lesser roads of our metaphor.

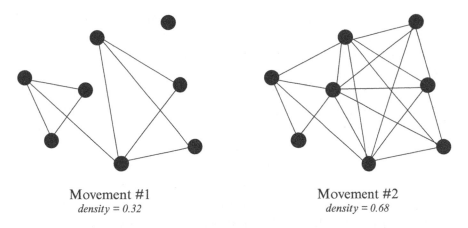

Movement #1
density = 0.32

Movement #2
density = 0.68

Figure 3.2 *Comparing network densities*

This view of networks is an inherently structural one. For scholars who think of networks in this way, the key questions that concern them tend to involve the formal properties of networks as key explanatory variables that can explain patterns of mobilization and movement effectiveness (Marwell and Oliver 1993; Staggenborg 1998). For example, the networks that link actors in the two hypothetical movement communities in figure 3.2 differ in terms of their density; the one on the left has far fewer connections among movement actors (also known as "nodes" in the language of networks); the one on the right has the same number of nodes, but they are embedded in a more interconnected web of ties resulting in a network that is denser (the density measure is calculated by taking the number of actual connections, or "edges," divided by the total number of edges possible between all pairs of nodes).

Given these differences in network structure, we might ask ourselves how these resulting movements might behave. For example, which of these movements would you expect to be more efficient at exchanging information? The movement on the left would certainly have a harder time ensuring information diffuses to all actors equally, since there is one node that is not linked to any other group, and the small cluster of three actors on the left side of the diagram are only linked to the rest via one organization; if anything were to happen to that connection, the cluster of three would be cut off from the remaining four groups. The movement on the right, on the other hand, has multiple pathways connecting all the actors, which would make it easier to diffuse information across the network. On the other hand, there might be unexpected downsides to very densely connected networks as well. Mark Granovetter, for example, argues that actors who are connected by many strong ties risk hearing the same information constantly from other nodes, which can create a kind of "echo chamber" that keeps out new ideas; weak ties to other actors, in contrast, can introduce fresh ideas and thinking that can invigorate a movement (Granovetter 1973). It was a weak, one-off tie, after all, that introduced the OWS activists to the Chilean water balloon tactic.

In addition to the properties of the network as a whole, where groups are located within the network can also matter to overall movement dynamics and the influence that particular organizations might have. Mario Diani (2003a: 107) proposes, for example, that groups with many incoming links from other actors are relatively central within the network and, accordingly, are positioned to play more of a leadership role. Groups that connect many otherwise-isolated nodes are in a position to play movement broker and mediate among different actors, which can make them particularly important for bringing a sense of cohesion and common purpose to the movement community. Figure 3.3 illustrates both of these principles. In the example on the left, the group that is most central to the network – as measured by the number of incoming connections from other groups (i.e., groups that consider it as a partner in the network) – is positioned to play leader. Movement brokers connect otherwise isolated groups which would not have any connections to the rest of the movement community without their links via the broker. For those interested in using this kind of formal network analysis in their study of social movement

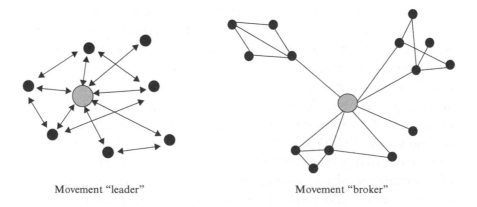

Movement "leader"   Movement "broker"

Figure 3.3 *Network centrality and network brokerage examples*

dynamics, this chapter's methods spotlight provides more details on the technique, and links to web resources to get started.

Scholars who work within a structural tradition acknowledge that movement structures are not fixed; their forms reflect – among other things – organizational resources, breadth of issue focus, and the networks of individual activists within groups (Diani 2003a). But this structural approach has been criticized by those working from within NSM and relational approaches for reifying the formal properties of networks while ignoring questions about how such networks might form, reproduce, change, or disappear (Emirbayer and Goodwin 1994: 1411; Mische 2002). Clare Saunders argues,

Methods Spotlight: Social Network Analysis

Social network analysis is a way for researchers to describe and analyze the relationships between different actors in social movements. These relationships can be portrayed as a collection of nodes and ties. Nodes are the main objects in a relationship and can be individuals, organizations, movements, events, even ideas (Caiani 2014). Ties represent the relationship between nodes. Collectively, the depiction of these nodes and ties creates a visual map of the network, known as a sociogram. Researchers analyze the characteristics of the sociogram to discern features about the network and make inferences about its dynamics. The number of nodes, how densely they are tied together, whether there are some nodes that are isolated or central to the network, all convey information about the relationships that characterize the group. For example, scholars might compare networks that are dense and tightly interconnected with those that are characterized by loose ties and investigate how these differences might shape how quickly information diffuses within each. This kind of analysis can be helpful in understanding the flow of ideas, how alliances and factions form, how learning and adaptation occur in organizations, and other such questions (Diani 2002).

To collect the data necessary to conduct a social network analysis, researchers can use a variety of techniques, including questionnaires, observations of interactions among participants, and written records (Caiani 2014: 376). For example, a researcher interested in how often a social movement organization works with other groups in the movement field might ask a representative of the group to list all the other entities that it works with. A more fine-grained version of the question might differentiate between the groups with which it has a mutual relationship and the groups with which it has a one-way relationship only. This information is then fed into a social network analysis tool that visualizes the sociogram and allows for closer investigation and analysis of the network's structure. Such investigations are often enhanced when scholars complement the technical analysis of sociograms with qualitative data collected by interviews or other more fine-grained techniques to contextualize and give meaning to the ties that connect nodes – information that can go beyond establishing whether a tie exists, to what that connection might signify or mean to the nodes it connects.

Explore this Method

To do social network analysis, you need to have access to software that can help create the necessary sociograms. One relatively accessible tool is the Social Network Visualizer, available at http://socnetv.org/downloads (there are versions for Windows, Mac, and Linux – this is free, open-source software). Once you have the software loaded, you have to load data to generate a sociogram. One easy way to do this is to go to the menu and select Network > Web Crawler. This allows you to type in a URL for a site, and the program will automatically create a social network map based on the links on that website. Try typing in the web address of a well-known social movement organization and see what kind of sociogram is generated by the web crawler. Compare this sociogram with one from a lesser-known organization in the same movement. Are there any differences that you see in their network diagrams? You can also use SocNetV's diagnostic tools to analyze features of the website. Be advised: social network analysis can get quite technical. The manual (http://socnetv.org/docs/index.html) can help you to understand some of the different analytic techniques available to you, and what they measure.

for example, that the mere presence of a network tie between two actors does not inherently or automatically produce the kinds of effects that structuralists claim. Two groups might be officially connected, but that does not mean that the information that might flow across such a link will be useful or have an impact on what movement actors think, how they identify, or what they do (Saunders 2007). What is instead required is closer attention to symbolic and cultural structures that emerge out of interactions among movement actors. Network connections, such an approach holds, are significant not as objective structures, but in how movement participants fashion, negotiate, and find meaning in their connections with each other.

This reorientation also entails a closer focus on the individuals who participate in movements rather than putting formal organizations at the center of network analysis. Individuals are the ones with primary agency in making meaning; moreover, as Lance Bennett (2012) points out, SMOs may be starting to lose their role as mediating between their members and the rest of the movement, as loyalties to formal groups decline and are replaced by more personalized politics. He finds evidence of this pattern in the Spanish *indignados* movement, where individuals used social media and face-to-face communications to create direct relationships with others in the movement. Moreover, these networks were created and sustained not by simple shared interests in movement outcomes or organizational structures, but by sharing of personal experiences and stories (Bennett and Segerberg 2012). Testimonials – an individual's account of going into foreclosure, or being forced to leave the country to find work, or accounts of institutional indifference to the struggles of ordinary people – helped to build trust among members, validated the experiences of others, and contributed to a common conversation about what the movement sought to achieve, ultimately helping to give meaning and emotional intensity to the collective identity that was being constructed. The meanings created *by* these networks of individuals were also meanings created *about* those networks; as these personal expressions were shared, recognized, and passed along by others, such narratives became the engines to connect people and give them a sense of collective identity and membership in the movement (Bennett 2004; Benkler 2006).

The eclipse of SMOs by these personal networks of identity and meaning is facilitated by the widespread use of social media technologies that allows activists to bypass organizations and connect directly with each other and a wider audience outside the movement. The Chilean students' movement, for example, had a multifaceted online media presence, including the now-standard Facebook and Twitter pages. They also set up a separate English-language Twitter account to more effectively communicate with international media outlets and supporters abroad. When they engaged in highly performative protests, especially ones that had a playful air like the "Thriller" flash mob, they uploaded video to YouTube to counter conventional news coverage that emphasized confrontations with the police and episodes of violence. And activists took video everywhere they went, even setting up live video streams on Twitter and Facebook when they occupied the Chilean Senate building. These strategies allowed them unmediated and unfiltered access to the public and total control over their message. New communication technologies also make it possible for people outside formal organizations to aggregate their expertise and resources and access government representatives directly, rather than relying on organizational leaders for such exchanges (Pini et al. 2004).

While the rise of these personal networks does not signal the inevitable demise of traditional SMOs, it does suggest that movements may develop more varied, hybrid forms in the future, some of which will still have formal SMOs playing key organizing and coordinating roles and some of which will have relational networks that take over more of the traditional functions that SMOs were thought to provide. Their different forms suggest that they may have different strengths and weaknesses. For example, the flexibility of interpersonal networks might make it easier to join movements because the number of potential entry points are more numerous than if entry is largely channeled through a smaller number of formal organizations. Flexible networks can also make it harder for authorities to repress movements because there is no single organizational focal point. On the other hand, the flexibility of interpersonal networks might also make it harder for movements to develop coherent ideas and identities, or to act in a concerted fashion (Bennett 2004). Even so, Lance Bennett and Alexandra Segerberg argue that neither has a particular advantage over the other in terms of their ability to sustain long-term participation or, indeed, accomplish the movement's goals (Bennett and Segerberg 2012) – a pronouncement that may change in the future as new movements emerge and negotiate the roles of formal organizations, interpersonal networks, and other movement actors.

Intra-Movement Relations

The heterogeneity of movement actors refers not just to their different types, but to the variety of identities, interests, values, and goals they might hold. Their membership in a movement community implies that they share a common programmatic goal, like reform of education policies, or an end to austerity programs. However, such groups may have little else in common. The anti-globalization protestors who descended on Seattle in 1999 during the ministerial conference of the World Trade Organization (WTO) are a good example. They were a motley crew of labor organizers, human rights activists, environmentalists, consumer advocates, student groups, and even a smattering of anarchists. Some belonged to loose coalitions, such as the Direct Action Network, which brought together a group of anti-corporate activists, or Jubilee 2000, a debt-relief campaign whose members included religious and youth groups. While they shared a common antipathy toward the WTO's neoliberal economic policies, these protestors had distinct priorities of their own – improved protections for workers, or stricter environmental regulations, or opposition to war, or an end to genetically modified foods – and some of these priorities were in tension with those of other protestors. There were also disagreements about the tactics that should be used, with some groups advocating only peaceful protest and others calling for more disruptive approaches and confrontations with authorities. These disagreements became all too apparent during the protests themselves, as some activists engaged in peaceful performances like holding a massive dance party, complete with marching bands, dancers, and cheerleaders, while others, such as the militant anarchists, donned black face masks, smashed shop windows, and threw bottles at police.

With all these diverse organizations, actors, interests, and identities, the relationships they forge among themselves can be highly consequential for overall movement effectiveness; constructive relationships can enhance the work of movement actors and potentially magnify their impact by showing strength in numbers and strategic alliances, while destructive relationships can sap energy and divert attention from the movement's overall collective goals.

Cooperative Relationships

Because social movements frequently operate at a disadvantage vis-à-vis their opponents when it comes to resources or power, cooperating with like-minded groups seems like a natural way to try to tip the scales in their favor. Cooperation, when effective, can increase the number of people that groups mobilize for protest, allow them to pool resources and use them more efficiently, and make it easier to demonstrate unity of purpose. Since members of a common movement community ostensibly share certain underlying goals or grievances, it might seem inescapable that groups would seek out alliances and forge coalitions whenever possible. However, cooperation is not an inevitable by-product of common interests. It requires intentionality and ongoing work to build and maintain the necessary ties. Cooperation among movement actors can be hard work (Staggenborg 1986; Rucht 2004), and disagreements over tactics, priorities, or identities can derail potential partnerships before they have time to take root.

Certain conditions can increase the likelihood that movement groups will cooperate. Suzanne Staggenborg argues that coalitions among movement organizations tend to form under conditions of exceptional threat or opportunity. Moreover, organizations are more amenable to cooperating when there is a material advantage for them to do so, either because partnerships can allow them to tap into jointly held resources (thus allowing them to save their organization-specific assets) or because they lack the ability to take advantage of an opportunity or threat on their own (Staggenborg 1986). Groups that share similar identities will also find cooperation more straightforward. For example, the Standing Rock Sioux were joined in their protests against the Dakota Access Pipeline (DAPL) by hundreds of people from other Native American tribes who may not share the specific grievance against this particular building project but who showed up out of a sense of solidarity and common outrage against recurring patterns of land disenfranchisement and exploitation experienced by Native Americans throughout history. In a similar show of support, the Black Lives Matter website indicates support for the anti-DAPL protestors not because of a shared tribal identity or identity as Native Americans, but out of a common solidarity based on membership in subordinated groups.

On the other hand, groups that have very different types of organizational cultures, or who have distinctive perspectives on an issue due to the experiences and positionality of its members (i.e., groups that are unalike based on class identity, race, religion, etc.), can have a harder time forging long-term partnerships (Beamish and Luebbers 2009), though successful coalitions are still possible across such divides (Bystydzienski and Schacht 2001). When organizations try to partner across national borders in transnational coalitions and networks, additional variables can facilitate or inhibit cooperation, including geographic proximity, cultural similarities among countries, and the capacity for regular communications between alliance partners (Bandy and Smith 2005).

When cooperation does occur, it can take many forms, from ad hoc and episodic partnerships (for example, an informal agreement to show up at another organization's planned rally) to formal coalitions that arrange joint activities over a sustained period (Zald and McCarthy 1980; Rucht 2004). In some cases of long-term cooperation, groups might even form relatively autonomous organizations to coordinate the coalition's work. The case of Chile features multiple examples from different points along this cooperative continuum. CONFECH, for example, was a long-term and relatively formalized (though not autonomous) umbrella group that made it easier for the 29 university-specific federations to work together over a long period of time. The cooperation between CONFECH and the teachers' union, the Colegio de Profesores, on the other hand, was much more informal; it did not spawn separate organizational structures, and cooperation generally only occurred when the groups were coordinating mass demonstrations for particular days.

While there is no ideal form of cooperation (Rucht 2004), different coalitional strategies offer different advantages and disadvantages, usually involving a trade-off between organizational autonomy and joint efficiency. On one hand, combining resources and personnel can help groups to coordinate larger, more frequent protest events, which can further the movement's overall goals. At the same time, while coalitions can help to advance movement and organizational goals, participating in them is not costless (Hathaway and Meyer 1993–4). Some coalitions require a diversion of resources from organizational priorities to activities endorsed by the coalition as a whole. And coalitions may decide on actions with which individual member organizations disagree, which can create potential conflicts between coalition members as well as between a member group's leadership and its rank-and-file members. In Chile, for example, CONFECH encountered some internal tensions among some of its members because its decision-making process awarded each of the confederation's member groups an equal vote, even though some of the member groups were much larger than others. This, in effect, gave disproportionate voting power to a handful of smaller university federations that happened to also be dominated by extreme leftist groups. These federations exercised greater influence relative to their size, and increased resentment among the larger federations (Pousadela 2012).

Conflictual Relationships

In addition to cooperating, movement groups might also find themselves in competitive or conflictual relationships with others in the same movement community. The roots of such conflict stem in part from the harsh reality that, while groups must acquire resources of various kinds in order to mount collective action, resources of all kinds are finite and scarce. Consequently, groups often find themselves competing with others within the movement for those resources (Zald and McCarthy 1980; Rucht 2004). Consider, for example, the environmental movement with its plethora of organizations, which include major international players like Greenpeace, World Wildlife Fund, the Nature Conservancy, and the Sierra Club, as well as thousands of smaller regional and local organizations around the world. All of these organizations need money and labor to wage their campaigns, but their potential pool of supporters does not have endless time for activism, nor does it have endless money to donate. Activists must pick and choose which issues – and which organizations – they will support. If one supporter chooses to donate to, say, Friends of the Honeybees, those resources can no longer go to the Coral Reef Alliance. Competition over scarce resources, in other words, can create a zero-sum environment in which the gains that one group makes can come at the expense of another group.

Intra-movement conflict does not always have to involve resources. Differences in ideology, values, tactical preferences, and priorities can also create tensions within a movement community, provoking internal cleavages and conflict. The Chilean student movement was fortunate to have organizations with highly segmented and non-overlapping memberships: each university had a federation for its own enrolled students; high school students had their own organization; teachers had their union, as did mine workers; the indigenous Mapuche activists had their representatives as well. This kind of membership niche afforded these SMOs some protection from the zero-sum competition described above (Minkoff 1997; Stern 1997). But this lack of competition over membership and resources did not preclude other types of conflictual relationships from developing, like the ideological disputes between radical left-leaning and more moderate groups. High school students had their own internal split between moderate and more radical groups. Finally, CONFECH and the organization representing university deans had a number of strategic disagreements over the students' demands and their protest tactics. The relationship between these organizations, as a result, was frequently antagonistic (Pousadela 2012: 10–11).

Ideological, programmatic, and tactical disputes are not uncommon among social movement groups; they exist even among otherwise friendly organizations. But when deeply rooted, they can create fissures in SMOs. If serious enough, such fissures become fractures, and can eventually spawn new rival organizations that must, in turn, find resources and supporters of their own and further intensify the scramble over scarce goods.

Movement Life Cycles

In chapter 2, we considered how and why individuals might choose to participate in social movements. That discussion took for granted that there were prior movements already in place, ready and eager to receive individuals managing to make it all the way to the end of the mobilization process. However, movements – and the groups that comprise them – are not steady presences just waiting in the background. They have life cycles of their own: they emerge, they grow, they decline, and then they go dormant or disappear (Nepstad 2008). To understand movement dynamics, we must take a closer look at what these different stages entail.

Movement Emergence and Expansion

Movement emergence and mobilization of individual activists present something of a chicken-and-egg problem: if movement organizations and networks help to recruit individuals, then they must exist prior to activists who decide to engage in collective action. But if they exist prior to the activists, who creates the movement organizations in the first place? One possible way out of this riddle is to picture movement groups themselves materializing out of prior organizations that generate community ties and collective identities; these organizations do not magically morph into SMOs, but the personal networks and relationships they foster provide a fertile environment for movements to emerge, like an Oort cloud for collective action instead of comets. Thus, the US Civil Rights movement owes much to the safe spaces and trust built by black churches across the South, which provided an organizational focal point for people to gather, hear sermons about social justice, build a sense of solidarity, and decide to challenge racial segregation (Morris 1996). Because community organizations and social networks do not always engender social movements, leadership may also be necessary to create movements in the first place. John McCarthy and Mayer Zald (1973, 1977) call such individuals who initialize new movement organizations "entrepreneurs," and argue that they are able to mobilize constituencies for such organizations even without sudden shocks to galvanize people into action.

In addition to prior networks and organizations, and the presence of entrepreneurs, scholars also argue that the right political opportunity structure is an important variable that can explain when and why movements emerge in the first place (Tarrow 2011). There is disagreement about what the most appropriate POS actually looks like, however. For some scholars, movements are more likely to emerge when opportunities are open or expanding, which makes new resources available, unlocks new channels for communication, new venues for collective action, and new allies with whom to partner. The outpouring of protest across the Communist world in the late 1980s, for example, was linked to Soviet Premier Mikhail Gorbachev's limited *perestroika* and *glasnost* reforms, which eased repression and opened the door to dissent and critiques of the Soviet system – not to overturn it, but to restructure it. Democratic activists, though, seized on this small opening and pushed through; soon, the floodgates of reform opened in earnest and the old Communist order was never the same.

Others argue that closed or closing POS is more mobilizing and that, in effect, organizations and people are more likely to respond to threats than possible gains (Gould 2004; Johnson and Frickel 2011). The fear/threat motivator seems to fit the details of the Chilean student protests quite well. In 2010, President Michelle Bachelet finished her first term in office. Because the Chilean constitution does not allow the chief executive to serve two consecutive terms, she was not able to run for re-election. Her successor, Sebastián Piñera, took the country to the right of the political spectrum. His political ascendancy suggested that the POS was about to slam shut, helping to explain why the protests erupted when they did.

Of course, neither opening nor closing POS automatically leads to movement formation; individuals must interpret information they receive about their environment to determine whether the POS is opening or closing. Because there seem to be examples that correlate movement emergence with both opening and closing POS, it is also likely that additional variables interact with political structures to create these divergent outcomes; regime type, for example, might be a crucial intervening factor, so that in autocratic regimes (like the Soviet bloc *circa* 1989), openings are more motivating for activists, while in democratic regimes (like Chile *circa* 2011), potentially losing opportunities is what galvanizes people into action (McAdam 2004: 205). Paul Almeida (2003) argues that when POS opens up in authoritarian societies, it makes it easier to build organizational structures, and that these structures, in turn, can be used to sustain protest if the opportunity structure starts to close.

Once movements emerge, they go through a process of expansion as more individuals join SMOs and other actors within the movement community. Expansion might also involve the proliferation of groups as well as increased contention. This expansion is fueled in part by the demonstration effect of early risers: committed individuals and groups who mobilize early and take part in the initial waves of collective action (Tarrow 2011: 167; Castells 2012). Early risers demonstrate in a concrete way the opportunities for protest and the current risks and costs of taking part. In democratic countries with protected rights of speech and protest, such signaling may have less mobilizing value, but in autocratic societies, these signals can help generate a critical mass that might be slow to form on its own. This period of heightened conflict is sometimes described as a protest wave or the beginning of a cycle of contention (Tarrow 2011). In such moments, multiple social movements engage in sustained protest in rapid succession, leading to increased interaction between authorities and activists. Such protest waves can diffuse ideas, tactics, rhetoric, and mobilizing strategies across national boundaries. Initial movement groups can also pave the way for later groups by revealing authorities' potential weaknesses, which can further encourage more protest groups to emerge.

In the Arab Spring protests, for example, smaller, initial protests begat later, larger protests as sympathizers realized that demonstrations were taking place, that activists were able to overcome government efforts to quash that activity, and that sufficient numbers of protestors were taking part, which provided some safety in numbers. On the day that neighboring Tunisia's autocratic ruler, Zine El Abidine Ben Ali, fled from his own country's democratic uprising, a crowd of about 100 people gathered in Cairo's Tahrir Square for a protest. In the days that followed, other small protests, including several cases of self-immolation, occurred all over Egypt. By January 25, the day of the first organized protest, some 50,000 protestors marched to Tahrir Square, and the numbers quickly grew from there: 100,000 four days later, 250,000 just one day after that, and at least 300,000 by early February. Given such large jumps in protest numbers, this period of expansion – for Egypt, but also for movements in general – corresponds to the mobilization of the broadest group of movement participants: not just the deeply committed activists, but the more casual supporters as well.

Movement Decline and Dormancy

As heady as movement expansion can be, it does not last indefinitely. Movement decline corresponds to the period when protest frequency and volume decline: there are fewer protests, they are spaced at longer intervals, they involve smaller numbers of people. Decline can occur for multiple reasons, including a very simple one: exhaustion (Myers 1997). Protest requires resources of all kinds – material ones, physical ones, emotional ones, psychological ones. It can be draining, especially when it involves high-risk forms of collective action. Over time, such activities become increasingly difficult to sustain for most people, and eventually, the less committed will find the costs hard to justify. Exhaustion can also set in earlier or later depending on other kinds of feedback that individuals receive; a thrilling victory could replenish an activist's reserves and renew her desire to stay involved. On the other hand, long periods without objective benefit, in terms of either movement goals or other emotional returns, can intensify the exhaustion spiral (Zald and Ash 1966: 333; Oliver and Myers 2002). External conditions also play a potentially important role here as well: decreasing societal support for a movement, changes in the perceived opportunity structure, and increases (or decreases) in state repression can all diminish the pleasures of protest and the will to stay involved.

A completely different mechanism for movement decline occurs when movement organizations gradually succumb to institutionalization and bureaucratization, which makes them less likely to engage in collective action. Formalization brings a number of advantages: the ability to access resources more effectively, develop partnerships with elites, cultivate areas of expertise, and acquire more sophisticated skills. With this formalization comes continuity and the resources to act more like insiders by cultivating and nurturing relationships with key allies, by developing valuable expertise on an issue, and by lobbying (McCarthy and Zald 1977; Staggenborg 1988: 599). This process, in turn, also can transform social movement groups into more attractive allies for political elites.

But there is a possible downside to this process. Frances Fox Piven and Richard Cloward (1977) argue, for example, that *too much* organization can bog down movements and deprive them of the disruptive power that is their most useful asset. By developing close connections with allies and authorities and developing their own internal structures and processes to resemble theirs, formal SMOs can start to look more like political insiders, with qualities that make institutional forms of action both possible and attractive. Over time, institutionalization can push formal SMOs to become institutional actors themselves that care about their own organizational maintenance as much as (and possibly more than) about their social change agenda (Zald and Ash 1966; Kriesi 1996; Dauvergne and Lebaron 2014). In some cases, movement groups become so institutionalized that they turn into establishment actors like political parties, as happened with several indigenous peoples' movements in places like Bolivia, Colombia, Ecuador, and Venezuela in the 1990s (Van Cott 2005). In the Chilean student movement, the university federations did not become established political parties, but some of the movement's highest-profile leaders ran for political office, including Camila Vallejo – one of the most prominent activists – who won a seat in the legislature as a member of the Communist Party. This raised fears on the part of some activists that the political parties might co-opt the movement and blunt its power (Larrabure and Tochia 2015).

When SMOs become increasingly professionalized and bureaucratized, they also tend to shed supporters, further contributing to a decline in overall collective action. This happens in part because bureaucratic organizations do not require large, mobilized rank-and-file memberships. If an organization works for change via institutional channels, meets with lawmakers, or gives expert testimony before a legislative committee, then it has no real need for large reserves of protestors. A small, specialized, professional staff can do the kind of work that these transformed SMOs are likely to undertake. Moreover, as SMOs change in this way, they are likely to alienate some core supporters who see any turn away from disruption as a betrayal of the movement's goals (Uitermark and Nicholls 2014).

The result of gradual institutionalization, the shedding of most members, and the reaction of the hardcore movement faithful can be unexpected: even as movements decline in frequency and volume of protests, it is also possible for the protests that remain to *increase* in intensity or violence. As Mayer Zald and Roberta Ash explain, as most members drift back to their normal lives and as SMO professionals take some parts of the movement into institutional territory, those who are left in the movement community – those who are still engaged in collective protest – are likely to be the ones with the strongest commitment to movement goals: the ideologues, the purists, the radicals. Without movement professionals and the bulk of members (who, in their less intense commitment, are likely to include larger numbers of moderates and pragmatists), there is little to constrain these radicals from enacting their vision, which can lead to spikes in militant activity even as the movement weakens overall (Zald and Ash 1966: 339).

The final phase in this movement cycle is dormancy, when the movement is in abeyance. When the movement has demobilized, some of the movement's members embed themselves in other institutions and structures, building spaces to sustain the collective identities that the community built during the period of active mobilization. The women's movement after the 1970s, for example, was kept alive in Women's Studies programs where feminist identities could be nurtured and transmitted to new generations of potential movement supporters (Katzenstein 1998; Staggenborg 1998). In this way, movements can bridge periods of activity, and ride out hostile political circumstances. Verta Taylor points out that some movement organizations are better adapted to ride out periods of dormancy, based on their structures and identities; SMOs that are centralized, for example, are more likely to sustain themselves through the ups and downs of movement activity, as are movements that have a more exclusive membership approach (Taylor 1989). Going into dormancy is not, however, without its costs and risks, as the opportunity costs of not mobilizing can weaken member coalitions and resolve while opening the door for radical challengers to take the initiative and crowd out moderate rivals (Sawyers and Meyer 1999).

These four stages of a movement's life cycle are not sacrosanct and not all movements will follow their neat trajectory (Keogh 2013). In addition, the notion of a life cycle has primarily been attached to the fortunes of formal movement organizations. From the preceding discussion, however, it is clear that SMOs are not the only actor in movement communities, and it remains to be seen how ideas about movement life cycles evolve to reflect movements like the Chilean students, the *indignados*, or OWS, where SMOs recede more into the background.

Concluding Summary

When people join social movements, they might participate in any number of groups within a movement community, from formal organizations to informal networks. To understand what movements are and why they behave as they do, it is useful to try to parse some of these key actors and how they are connected together. In so doing, this chapter highlighted a recurring tension within the social movement literature: conflicts between how structuralists might understand movement organizations and how someone more interested in cultural constructions might interpret movements. Neither is right; neither is wrong. Both sensitize us to different facets of movements, from the formal properties of systems to the ways in which meanings are negotiated by those within the systems. While formal SMOs have traditionally occupied pride of place in analyses of movement communities, newer movements like the Chilean student protests, the *indignados*, or OWS suggest that alternative ways of structuring movements are possible. Collectively, such cases provide us with a richer understanding of movement composition and the internal relations among movement actors, both cooperative and competitive.

In addition to examining the internal structure of movements, this chapter also highlighted the importance of movement life cycles, particularly phases of emergence, growth, and decline. These phases do not always move in a neat progression; organizations may traverse the movement life cycle at different rates; some may experience decline that ends in discontinuation while others may simply move into dormancy. These variations depend a great deal on the movement's structure and operations, its members and their level of commitment, as well as larger dynamics in the external environment. All of these variations ultimately underscore the diversity of movement groups and forms that are possible and reinforce the basic truth that movements are neither unitary nor homogeneous actors.

Questions for Discussion

1 In what ways can social movements benefit from developing formal organizational structures and attracting highly trained, professional staff? Why do some scholars argue that such organizations can ultimately be detrimental to the movement's overall political goals? With which perspective do you agree, and why?

2 How might technological developments such as access to the internet and social media limit the role that formal organizations play in decentralized, network-based movements?

3 Under what conditions are social movement groups likely to cooperate with each other? What factors might increase competition among movement groups?

4 How can initial acts of protest encourage more people to mobilize and subsequently form additional social movement groups? Why does this expansion of protest not go on indefinitely?

Additional Readings

McCarthy, John D., and Mayer N. Zald. 1977. "Resource Mobilization and Social Movements: A Partial Theory." *American Journal of Sociology*, 82(6): 1212–41. Highly influential article that emphasizes the centrality of SMOs in the study of movements.

Piven, Frances Fox, and Richard A. Cloward. 1977. *Poor People's Movements: Why They Succeed, How They Fail*. New York: Pantheon. A classic text that makes the case for why movements should avoid tendencies toward institutionalization and professionalization.

Zald, Mayer N. and Roberta Ash. 1966. "Social Movement Organizations: Growth, Decay, Change." *Social Forces*, 44(3): 327–41. Foundational article that provides a good overview of some of the key phases in the life cycle of movements.

CHAPTER 4

The Target

Objectives

- To examine the different criteria that movements use when choosing protest targets, including the potential trade-offs between selecting targets based on culpability, curability, feasibility, vulnerability, and resonance.

- To determine the ways in which globalization and transnational governance affects how movements identify protest targets and broadens the range of available targets.

- To identify why and how movements might decide to influence non-state targets, including for-profit firms, popular norms and attitudes, and underlying social structures.

- To recognize the conditions under which movements might trigger countermovements that mobilize against them.

Introduction

What do cotton, eggplant, corn, and mustard have in common? In India, they have all been the focus of a growing national movement that opposes the introduction of genetically modified (GM) crops into the country. In the past 15 years, this anti-GM movement has taken aim at both the large agribusinesses that produce GM seeds and the Indian government, which activists argue has cut corners when testing the safety of such crops on human health and the environment. Led by a coalition of farmers' unions, environmental groups, consumer advocates, and critics of globalization, this movement has organized protest marches through the streets of New Delhi, held sit-ins in front of the Ministry of Agriculture and the Prime Minister's residence, and even destroyed fields of GM test crops.

It is no surprise that, in some ways, India has become the epicenter of the global anti-GM movement, given the social and economic

Table 4.1 Percentage growth in Indian crop yields, 1980s–2000s

	1980s	1990s	2000s
Rice	3.15	1.21	1.42
Wheat	3.24	1.82	0.73
Corn	2.04	2.22	2.27
Chickpeas	2.48	1.53	1.16
Pigeon Peas	0.07	0.13	0.94
Groundnuts	1.74	1.34	1.76
Mustard	3.00	0.38	2.13
Soybeans	5.27	1.91	1.71
Cotton	4.21	−1.4	10.29
Sugarcane	0.21	0.79	0.59
Fruits	−2.21	1.81	−1.48
Vegetables	−2.46	0.38	1.31

Source: Birthal et al. 2014.

importance of agriculture in the country; according to the World Bank, it represents about 17% of the country's GDP (compared to a worldwide average of just 3.9%), and roughly 50% of all employment (compared to a worldwide average of 13.7%). India is also a major global supplier of agricultural products, with the highest export growth of any country between 2003 and 2013 (USDA-FAS 2014). Today, India is one of the world's largest producers of cotton, beef, wheat, rice, and other staple foodstuffs. Though the manufacturing and service sector together constitute an ever-increasing percentage of the economy, agriculture remains politically important given the sheer number of people whose livelihoods depend on it.

Farmers in India, however, have not had an easy time. Harvests are always vulnerable to environmental shocks, and in India the seasonal monsoons that provide vital rainwater have become more erratic. Both the frequency and severity of droughts have increased since the late 1980s, leading to higher rates of crop failure (Mallya et al. 2016). Declines in global commodity prices have further eroded farmers' incomes. While the government provides subsidies for some crops, such as staple foods, as a cushion in times of hardship, they do not entirely offset losses. India also struggles with declining productivity in agriculture, as table 4.1 highlights.

Apart from cotton, most of the crops listed above have had modest productivity increases at most; half have flat or declining productivity rates. This lack of productivity growth, combined with increasing population growth, also raises questions about India's long-term food security. Finally, with all these economic pressures, farmers have taken on increasing levels of debt as they borrow – often at extortionate rates from unscrupulous local moneylenders – to pay for seeds, fertilizers, and pesticides. The increasing debt burden among farmers has led to a rash of suicides – tens of thousands, according to farmers' groups – across India's rural communities since the early 2000s. These challenges have increased pressure on the central government to come up with a sustainable plan for improving the lives of farmers and the long-term health of the agricultural sector.

Enter GM seeds. Although farmers have for centuries selectively bred plants to encourage certain traits, genetic modification is much newer, and involves introducing changes to plant DNA using biotechnology. Companies like US-based Monsanto and Germany's Bayer have used this technology to develop a range of transgenic seeds promising all manner of benefits, from resistance to common plant diseases to enhanced nutritional benefits. Golden rice, for example, has been genetically modified to produce high levels of beta-carotene in order to address deadly Vitamin A deficiencies in children. Along the way, these big agribusinesses have captured a significant share of the worldwide commercial seed trade. For them, India represents a lucrative market, given the number of farmers and their challenges. GM seeds, such companies argue, give farmers higher crop yields, have greater resistance to common pests, and lower pesticide costs. This pitch proved irresistible, and in 2002, Monsanto licensed the sale of the first GM crop – cotton – in India. In the next decade, this GM variety, known as Bt cotton, was adopted by over 8 million farmers and came to represent nearly 90% of India's cotton crop.

This introduction, however, was not without its fair share of critics. The anti-GM movement swung into action against Bt cotton, arguing that Monsanto's promises fell short of reality. They argued that the cotton crops actually increased toxicity in the environment, as they were not nearly as resistant to pests as the company claimed, which led to farmers using as much, if not more, pesticide to protect their harvests. Moreover, they argued that GM crops harmed biodiversity by crowding out varieties of heritage seeds that farmers had used for generations. Since GM seeds often contain a gene that prevents plants from producing new viable seeds, farmers who used to collect and save seeds to use from one year to the next would now be forced to buy the more expensive GM seeds each year. Finally, they disputed the studies that showed increased crop yields for farmers using Bt cotton, arguing that the methodologies of such studies raised questions about the overall success of the GM experiment, and that production gains (as in table 4.1) reflected increases in the number of acres under cultivation rather than yield.

The widespread protests against Bt cotton did not, however, stop the government from proceeding with new GM seed trials. In 2005, Monsanto introduced Bt brinjal (i.e., eggplant) into India, which was cleared for commercial cultivation after a few years of safety testing. The anti-GM movement, however, mobilized with even greater vigor against this new threat, especially since it introduced transgenic organisms into the food supply for the first time. Its agitations included a blend of traditional marches and demonstrations with creative performances, like the mock funeral processions that carried vegetables (or in some cases, people dressed as vegetables) through the streets of different cities and ended with simulated burial rites. In response, supporters of GM crops mobilized to calm public fears with education campaigns, enlisted the aid of research scientists to address lack of public confidence in GM crop safety, and even offered financial assistance to farmers who bought GM seeds. Both sides accused the other of waging campaigns of misinformation, promoting bad science, colluding with foreign interests, and advocating harmful policies. Ultimately, the anti-GM movement prevailed, as the Indian government called for a moratorium on the introduction of Bt brinjal. Despite this success, the fight over GM crops continues. In 2016, the Indian government's Genetic Engineering Approval Committee cleared GM mustard seeds for commercial use. Though they have yet to get final approval, they also have triggered widespread protests across the country by people who vehemently oppose the introduction of transgenic crops, especially ones meant for human consumption, and who hope that continued protest will sway the government to withhold final approval.

The story of India's anti-GM movement fits the mold set by many of the movements discussed in previous chapters: protestors made demands, those demands impacted the interests of other actors, a variety of organizations helped to crystallize a movement that was able to sustain protest over several years, the movement used a variety of non-institutional techniques to give voice to their members' grievances, and, through these protests, activists from different backgrounds and social groups – students, farmers, scientists, consumers – forged a common identity in their shared opposition to GM foods and the large corporations that seek to profit from their introduction. But there is one key difference between this movement and the examples that this book has raised so far: when it came to the Indian anti-GM movement, the protests were directed not only at the government, but also against a corporation – Monsanto, which has become the face of the GM industry because of its market dominance.

The story of India's anti-GM movement raises an interesting question for students of social movements: when people decide to protest and make demands, *at whom* do they direct their protests and why? In the case of anti-GM protestors, should they target the corporations that create transgenic seeds, the governments that allow them, or both? What about scientists who argue that GM seeds pose no real threat to health? Or the universities who often carry out corporate-sponsored research on GM technologies? Should the anti-GM movement also focus on these groups in their protests?

The issue of targeting is central to this question; in particular, it invites us to consider how movements weigh issues of *culpability* (i.e., targeting those who are at fault for causing the underlying grievances), *curability* (i.e., targeting those who have the power to remedy the underlying grievances), *feasibility* (i.e., targeting those who are available to the protestors), *vulnerability* (i.e., targeting those whose behavior can be changed), and *resonance* (i.e., targeting those who carry particular symbolic or emotional weight).

In an ideal world, social movements would be able to identify a target that is simultaneously culpable, able to fix the problem, easy to target, sensitive to social movement pressure, and a powerful symbol to rouse support from sympathetic publics. But these considerations do not always line up neatly and appropriate targets are not always clear. Consider, for example, the mass protests that erupted in Cochabamba, Bolivia in early 2000 around the privatization of its water supply. The dispute emerged out of a complex set of conditions: Bolivia is a relatively poor country and one of the least developed in Latin America. Plagued by persistent underdevelopment and economic crises, the government applied for loans and other aid from the International Monetary Fund (IMF) and World Bank, which provided assistance but demanded a number of structural reforms that were intended to cut wasteful government spending and corruption. One of these demands involved selling off state-owned businesses, including municipal water services in places like Cochabamba, to private companies who could invest more money, modernize services, and run things more efficiently. Such structural reforms were implemented by the government, but were deeply unpopular among citizens, who resented the control that unaccountable international organizations had over economic policy and who struggled to see benefits in their own quality of life as a result of these new policies.

The water contract in Cochabamba was awarded to Aguas del Tunari (AdT), a subsidiary of the giant US construction company, Bechtel. Upon discovering the water system had been neglected for years, they set about upgrading the infrastructure and, to cover costs, implemented a steep price increase. According to AdT executives, the old water rates were unrealistic and required adjustment to give the utility a reasonable operating budget. From the public's point of view, however, the increases seemed extortionate: for a family living on $100 a month, their monthly water bill could top $20/month – more than they might spend on food. Angered by the price increases, the people of Cochabamba took to the streets en masse to protest. But who should they protest against? Aguas del Tunari actually implemented the price hikes without delivering promised improvements in service and quality. However, it was the Bolivian government that agreed to privatize the water supply and awarded AdT the contract. But even before that, it was the IMF and World Bank that insisted the government privatize utilities in the first place. As the case of Cochabamba highlights, when it comes to targeting, it is not always straightforward who should be in a movement's cross-hairs.

Targeting Considerations

For movements that have multiple potential targets, the process of selecting the right one can be influenced by a number of different factors. One such possibility is a movement's overall purpose and whether it is primarily an expressive movement, which is oriented to transforming culture and developing the identities of its members, or an instrumental movement, which seeks to influence policy outcomes (Rucht 1988, 1990; Van Dyke et al. 2004). Dieter Rucht argues this divide can differentiate movement targets:

expressive movements are more likely to target cultural norms and institutions in order to influence public opinions and social mores. Instrumental movements, on the other hand, will be more likely to focus their attention on the state as both a party to and an arena for policymaking. Ultimately, he argues, "a movement's logic defines a general field of action" (Rucht 1988: 319).

This distinction between instrumental and expressive movements emerges out of the division between PPT and NSM approaches. The former emphasizes the role of states and makes them central to the concerns of movements, which gives rise to an instrumental view of targeting. The latter argues that new social movements are often concerned with the processes of bureaucratization and rationalization that have invaded social life and led to the marginalization of certain identities – marginalization that is often encoded in everyday cultural practices, beliefs, and social norms. Accordingly, movements that have these issues at their heart will be less concerned with shifting policies in the domain of institutional politics and more focused on challenging cultural codes and values (Van Dyke et al. 2004: 30).

The problem with mechanically applying this typology, however, is that movements are rarely so neatly classified, with most movements containing instrumental motives as well as expressive ones. In writing about environmental activists who protested against the construction of California's Diablo Canyon nuclear power plant, for example, James Jasper recognizes their highly instrumental purpose – to stop the plant from opening – but also highlights the identity creation, expression, and affirmation that occurred as part of the mobilization and that were enormously important for the activists taking part in the protests (Jasper 1997). Likewise, classic NSM examples, such as the LGBT movement or the peace movement, often have very strategic and specific policy goals, like increasing funding for HIV/AIDS research or ending involvement in a particular conflict, even as they seek to build and assert the identities of their members. Given these blurred categories, it is useful to consider whether additional criteria might help us to understand a movement's targeting decisions.

Assessing Culpability

An obvious place for movements to start is with culpability: who is responsible for causing the underlying grievances that require remedy? We might expect that movements will want to direct their protest at the actors who are most directly responsible for their core grievances and who, therefore, would seem a fitting target for their demands. When workers demand higher wages, for example, they go on strike to put pressure on the specific employers who set those wages in the first place. But culpability is not always so easy to parse. It may be ambiguous, as Doug Imig and Sidney Tarrow found in their study of protest in the European Union. They argue that policymaking in a complex polity like the EU is often opaque and confusing since policy decisions made in Brussels can feel far removed from the lives of regular people and, accordingly, generate little public interest or awareness. Moreover, when the EU adopts legislation, the member states are the ones who implement and enforce it. As a result, policies that may have originated at the European level become closely associated with national governments instead (della Porta and Kriesi 1999: 15; Imig and Tarrow 1999: 118–19). In addition, as the case of the Cochabamba water wars underscores, multiple actors may contribute to underlying grievances. Globalization intensifies this proliferation of actors, as policymaking shifts from being the sole responsibility of national states to being subject to multilevel governance structures in which national and sub-state governments, international organizations, and even non-state actors are able to play a role (Hooghe and Marks 2003; Sikkink 2005; Harmes 2006; Zürn 2010).

This proliferation of policymaking sites and relevant participants, in turn, multiplies the number of possible targets of protest. This dynamic was evident in the multipronged targeting strategy of South Africa's main labor federation, the Congress of South African Trade Unions (COSATU), when it protested against policies that opened up the country's textile and garment industry to competition from lower-priced goods imported from Asia. Blaming the WTO for dismantling protective tariffs and quotas that protected developing countries from low-cost competition, COSATU organized demonstrations against the WTO during a visit by Pascal Lamy, its Director General. Also blaming the government for dismantling tariffs at a faster pace than the WTO required, COSATU announced nationwide strikes and even formed a human chain in major cities to demand the proposed reductions be delayed for several years. Blaming corporations for helping to drive the demand for cheap goods, they also targeted retailers for stocking imported textiles from China and other foreign sources. COSATU organized pickets of major clothing stores, along with consumer boycotts and protests at retailers' annual shareholder meetings to convince them to stock goods made with domestically sourced textiles.

Assessing Curability

In addition to determining which actors are at fault for generating the underlying grievances, social movements must also weigh the issue of curability: that is, assessing which targets have the ability to fix the problem. In many cases, the same actors that are culpable also have curative power. In India's anti-GM movement, for example, the two main culprits – Monsanto and the Indian government – both contributed to the problem, the former by aggressively marketing transgenic seeds and the latter by permitting access to domestic markets. Both actors also possess the power to reverse the situation and end the use of GM seeds: Monsanto could, for example, pull out of the Indian market and no longer sell its product to farmers, and the Indian government could ban all GM crops, as Germany, Poland, and several other countries have done. In this case, culpability and curability point to the selection of the same targets.

However, curability does not always go hand-in-hand with culpability. In some cases, the parties responsible for the initial grievance or harm are unable or unwilling to make sufficient amends to satisfy protestors. Coal companies in the United States, for example, are required by law to clean up former mining sites and repair any environmental damages left behind, including treating contaminated water and other toxins. When such companies get into economic trouble, however, they may find themselves unable to cover the costs of such a clean-up. In 2016, this scenario came to pass when Peabody Energy, the world's largest coal company, declared bankruptcy. Even though it had over $1 billion in clean-up obligations, its bankruptcy settlement allowed it to pay a fraction of that amount to address its environmental liabilities; the government and taxpayers covered the difference. Curability is also problematic in cases where the original perpetrator of the grievance may no longer exist. Germans who had been forcibly dispossessed of their land by occupying Soviet forces in the 1940s encountered this problem when, decades after the original grievance-causing incident, they attempted to reclaim their property. Ruling in 2005, the European Court of Human Rights determined that the German government could not be held responsible for the actions of either the Soviet Union or East Germany, entities that had ceased to exist some 15 years earlier.

Curability is also a consideration when potential targets have differential power to address a social movement's demands. Local governments, for example, tend to have limited scope for addressing widespread or systemic issues, compared to state or national governments. Municipalities might be able to respond adequately to protests about highly localized matters – like a city ordinance against panhandling – but be unable to take action on matters that involve state or national laws. National and international targets, too, can have limited power over certain matters. In the case of the Cochabamba water wars, the protestors' immediate demand involved rolling back the massive water rate hikes brought about by privatization. While IMF and World Bank policies played an important role in privatizing the water utility in the first place, neither organization had the power to reverse Aguas del Tunari's prices or void the specific contract between the company and the Bolivian government. These international organizations were not a direct target of the protests, despite their partial culpability, because they lacked the power to deliver sought-after change.

Assessing Feasibility

In addition to selecting targets that are culpable and have curative power, protestors must also consider feasibility when deciding which actors should be in the movement's crosshairs. At a minimum, activists must be able to physically access protest sites that are close to their intended target, or that have some other tactical or strategic value, for such protests to have any impact. But physical proximity is not always possible, and, in some cases, achieving it may be prohibitively costly for many movement supporters. It may be easy enough – though not entirely costless – for protestors to attend demonstrations in their own cities; but if protest events involve more significant travel, the cost of transportation, lodging, food, time off from work, and other expenses will start to erode participation rates. Jürgen Gerhards found, for example, that of the 133 SMOs that gathered to protest the IMF during its 1988 summit in Berlin, only 3 traveled from neighboring European countries, and none came from the developing world (in Johnston 2014: 194). Kenneth T. Andrews and Sarah Gaby (2015) similarly found that most protest events in their study of the US Civil Rights movement targeted local actors. Increasing distance, by contrast, can depress mass protests (Marks and McAdam 1999; Walker et al. 2008) and, in turn, harm a movement's ability to call attention to its demands and put pressure on targets.

In such cases, movements will sometimes focus on proxy targets that stand in for their real adversary if the adversary is too remote or costly to access. Protests against international organizations like the IMF and World Bank frequently take this form as their policies affect people living all over the world, but who may not be in a position to protest the institutions directly. In such cases, groups may choose instead to target their own national governments in the hope that doing so will put indirect pressure on the multilateral organizations to which they belong (Johnston 2014: 197; della Porta and Kriesi 1999). Doug Imig and Sidney Tarrow found a similar dynamic in the European Union. In their case study of farmers protesting about EU agricultural policies, they discovered that very few movement groups targeted the EU directly. Instead, movement groups directed their demands toward their own governments because mobilizing on a national level proved to be considerably easier than mobilizing activists in a different country (Imig and Tarrow 1999: 128). Sarah A. Soule (1997) likewise found that universities became proximate targets for students protesting South Africa's apartheid policies in the late 1980s; unable to directly affect either the South African government's policies or the US government's support of the apartheid state, students turned to a close-at-hand target – their universities – and organized divestment campaigns, hoping that the financial pressure from widespread divestment would help to induce change.

Proxies can also include symbolic targets. Take, for example, the case of José Bové, a French sheep farmer who catapulted to international prominence in 1999 when he and other members of a farmers' union destroyed a McDonald's in the small town of Millau. Bové was not angry at McDonald's – at least, not directly. Instead, his anger was fueled by a trade war between the United States and the European Union: the US wanted to export beef that had been treated with growth hormones to the EU, but the EU had banned such products from its market. When the dispute was taken to the WTO for adjudication, it ruled in favor of the United States and ordered the EU to allow the sale of US beef. But the EU continued to oppose US beef exports, prompting the US to retaliate by imposing heavy import duties on European luxury goods including Roquefort cheese. This trade war hurt European producers including Bové, who happened to produce Roquefort on his farm. For Bové, the local McDonald's was not the immediate cause of his woes: it did not produce hormone-laced beef nor did it impose the trade sanctions that reduced his income. It was, however, a potent symbol of US economic interests and the kind of cultural homogenization that critics feared would result from the WTO's promotion of free trade. In absence of WTO or US government targets, the McDonalds became a useful proxy for Bové and other opponents of the emerging global economic order.

Feasibility also involves considerations beyond physical proximity. It requires an assessment of the different opportunity structures that might make it easier to mobilize against some targets and not others. Political process theorists often point to dimensions of opportunity structure, such as the availability of allies, the relative openness of the polity to challengers, and whether political elites are internally divided, to explain mobilization patterns in general (Tarrow 2011: 163–6). But this idea can also be applied to explain mobilization patterns against specific targets: actors whose structures facilitate mobilization could attract more protest than alternatives whose structures dampen mobilization. For example, while organizations are never unitary actors, some are more unified than others. If division among elites facilitates mobilization, then targets that have larger numbers of elites – and thereby greater chances of internal dissent among them – would be a better option than those controlled by a relatively small group of people, where deep rifts are less likely to occur. Governments typically have numerous political elites, multiple levels, and administrative divisions; democracies usually also have rival political parties that vary in their policy preferences. Division among elites would not be so hard to find in such an environment. By contrast, corporations tend to have a much smaller (and more unified) set of elites who control policy (Walker et al. 2008). Divided elites can also make it harder for an organization to coordinate a unified response, which a movement organization can exploit for its own advantage (Jasper and Poulsen 1993).

The relative openness of different targets, the number of channels by which movements can influence decisions, and other structural features can also influence targeting decisions (Weber et al. 2009; Lelieveldt 2014).

Target-specific opportunity structures are not fixed, nor do they automatically encourage or discourage selective mobilization. Like political opportunity structures in general, they must be perceived to be favorable or hostile by movement actors (Meyer and Minkoff 2004). Here, prior reputation, context-specific knowledge, and previous interactions between the movement and the target can inform how activists assess their environment and their potential target's openness to protest. In China, for example, protestors making demands on state officials in the wake of the 1989 Tiananmen Square uprising (and brutal crackdown) exercised considerable restraint in their protests and targeting choices. Although there was no shortage of protest in the 1990s, contentious claims were directed almost entirely toward local governments, as this was viewed as safer than protests targeting the national government. The recent experience of Tiananmen conditioned protestors' views of the political environment and led them to direct their activities toward targets that would be less likely to trigger the wrath of the ruling elite (Tanner 2004).

Assessing Vulnerabilities

In addition to feasibility, movements might also consider how vulnerable a target would be to social movement demands (Walsh 1986). Vulnerability is partly a reflection of how easily a target can resist movement pressure. Targets that are relatively vulnerable will be easier to influence because they are less able to withstand social movement pressure and any costs that protest inflicts on them. Less vulnerable targets, on the other hand, will be better able to weather the potential damage of protest. For example, consumer boycotts may take longer to inflict financial damage on highly profitable companies compared to struggling companies, while strong governments with considerable repressive power will be able to withstand challenges to their authority more easily than weak governments that cannot quell social disturbances. Governments may have more points of entry available to social movement actors compared to a corporation with its hierarchical structure and limited number of decision makers, but governments may also be slow to change because of formal bureaucratic procedures that require buy-in from multiple constituencies, whereas corporations and other private entities can move more swiftly once they make their minds up to act.

Targets can be vulnerable to disruption by movement activities. By engaging in consumer boycotts, for example, activists aim to interrupt business as usual and disturb a corporation's revenue to the point where the target feels it is better off accepting a movement's demands. But, as Joseph Luders (2006) points out, targets must weigh the potential cost of a movement's disruption with the potential costs they might incur by agreeing to concessions, which can also be costly. In the US Civil Rights movement, for example, Luders notes that some targeted businesses were vulnerable to disruption caused by sit-ins or boycotts, but that some of these same businesses were also confronted by white customers who threatened retaliatory boycotts if they gave in to movement demands – boycotts that would create additional concession costs. Other movement targets similarly find themselves between such proverbial rocks and hard places: after grassroots organizations campaigned for toys that did not promote gender stereotypes, Target decided to reorganize its merchandise to reflect category and type of interest as opposed to gender. In other words, toy trucks and dolls would simply be available for purchase – by anyone, for anyone – rather than be sorted into toys for a specific gender. This decision, however, sparked a backlash by people who read ominous intent into Target's action, with some conservative religious groups calling for a boycott of the retailer. Non-corporate actors can also experience the pinch when caught between weighing disruption and concession costs. At Amherst College, an elite private college in Massachusetts, students mobilized to demand an end to Lord Jeff, the school's unofficial mascot and namesake of an eighteenth-century military commander linked to giving smallpox-infested blankets to the Native American population in the area. While protesting students rejoiced, the concession costs became apparent as some alumni opted to withhold donations to the school as a sign of their displeasure. Vulnerability to disruption and vulnerability to concession are two sides of the same coin; Luders argues that how corporations resolve this conundrum depends in part on the nature of the business itself and which type of vulnerability will lead to more losses.

Targets can be vulnerable in other ways as well. Edward Walker and his colleagues suggest that targets vary in how susceptible they are to threats of de-legitimization: governments (particularly democracies) are relatively resilient, whereas other actors might see their stock prices drop, their endowments shrink, and their applicant pools dry up. They also argue that targets are differentially affected by threats of non-participation, which can severely impact some actors while causing modest inconvenience to others (Walker et al. 2008: 41–2). Brayden G. King (2007) argues that groups that have been previously targeted and experienced reputational declines are more vulnerable to future campaigns. Groups that care a great deal about their reputations or are easily influenced by public opinion can also be vulnerable to protest that stigmatizes their business practices (Seidman 2015). The anti-sweatshop movement that was active in the 1990s, for example, targeted companies like Nike and Gap while ignoring other companies that also used low-wage foreign workers, such as Abercrombie and Fitch. Tim Bartley and Curtis Child (2014) argue that this targeting decision was influenced by companies' vulnerability to being shamed: they note that the targeted companies were often recognized by their peers as market leaders or innovators or promoted their philanthropic work and cultivated a reputation of social responsibility – attributes that protestors used to highlight the discrepancies between the companies' lofty goals and the unpleasant realities of using sweatshop labor. Building on this notion, other entities that also care deeply about their public reputation, like universities or health-care companies, would also share this vulnerability and respond to movement demands more quickly to avoid bad publicity (Walker et al. 2008: 43).

Assessing Resonance

While the above criteria suggest that targets are selected for primarily instrumental reasons, movements can also weigh symbolic criteria when deciding whom to designate as their chief opponents. Targets are not simply means to an end, but also carry emotional weight, and some targets are more meaningful or resonant for protestors. This emotional significance, however, is not innate; it is constructed by movement participants operating within particular cultural contexts that shape the meanings attached to particular targets. In other words, targets must be constituted as such by protestors (Bartley and Child 2014). This process of constitution imbues targets with locally specific meanings that may not translate so easily across settings. In the United States, the anti-GM movement tends to construct corporations like Monsanto as profit-seekers that care more about their bottom line than the environment or human health. In India, the anti-GM movement constructs Monsanto as a different kind of target: a modern embodiment of foreign economic control and domination that calls to mind India's colonial past and subjugation at the hands of Western powers. This connection was made explicit during a 2011 protest in New Delhi where protestors chanted "Monsanto Quit India," a reference to the 1942 Quit India movement that fought for independence from British imperial rule. Greenpeace India, one of the participating organizations, noted that the protest was even held on the same day that the original Quit India movement was launched, leaving little doubt that the similarities in slogan were intentional and meant to evoke feelings of patriotism and pride at resisting this agent of foreign economic interests.

Constructing meaningful targets can also point the same movement in entirely different directions, which can only be understood when those targets are put in local context. In examining global justice protests between 1998 and 2001, Lesley J. Wood (2004) found that targeting decisions in different parts of the world follow distinct logics, even though these groups were part of a larger transnational movement opposed to neoliberal globalization. Of the protests that were aimed at specific targets, 27% were aimed at multinational corporations, 19% were aimed at national governments, and 15% were aimed at banks and stock exchanges. Significantly, however, these choices differed by location: protestors in highly developed economies – particularly the United States, Canada, Australia, and New Zealand – tended to direct protest at corporations; protestors in Africa and Asia disproportionately targeted national governments; and banks and stock exchanges were most commonly targeted in Latin America. This variation occurs because "targeting neoliberal globalization" means different things to differently situated actors. Wood argues that in Latin America, for example, neoliberalism was most commonly associated with painful structural adjustment policies implemented at the insistence of the IMF and World Bank; national governments could blame any domestic economic hardship on these policies and point outraged citizens at financial institutions instead. In Africa and Asia, weak states were seen as easily corrupted and made to serve the interests of foreign capital rather than their own citizens (Leander 2004); resisting neoliberal globalization in such contexts, therefore, required targeting state actors and demanding they put citizens ahead of corporations. Since developed countries had neither weak states buffeted by global economic forces nor mandatory structural adjustment programs, the most resonant symbols of globalization in these places were corporations, which were connected to problems of overconsumption, materialism, and waste. Switch these targets around, and they lose some of their mobilizing power, as they lose some of their meaning and emotional significance.

Movement Targets

The factors described above can point to a number of possible targets, but out of all the available options, it turns out that most social movements tend to target states most of the time. This is true for traditional movements (Van Dyke et al. 2004) as well as online protests (Earl and Kimport 2008), and for protests around the world (Ortiz et al. 2013). Moreover, this pattern holds true across multiple decades, as figure 4.1 illustrates. This kind of birds'-eye view of protest requires a large amount of data that allows researchers to aggregate trends across time or space and then analyze those trends using various quantitative techniques. The methods spotlight in this chapter provides more details on such approaches. In the case of figure 4.1, the data come from the Dynamics of Collective Action dataset, which codes newspaper reports of protest activity in the United States between 1960 and 1995, and suggests that, while there are ebbs and flows in the pattern, governments are the most

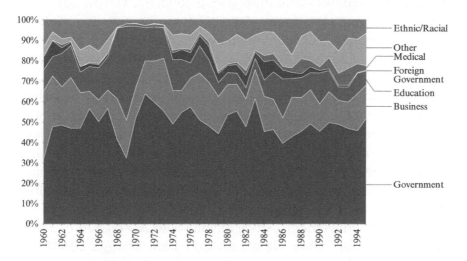

Source: Dynamics of Collective Action dataset.

Figure 4.1 *Common protest targets, 1960–1995*

common protest target across this period. Corporations are also a consistently popular target and usually the second most common focus of protest. Other actors rise and fall in popularity given the particular targeting priorities of movements that are active at different moments in time. Educational institutions were popular targets in the late 1960s and early 1970s, for example, which corresponds to increased agitation against the Vietnam War on university campuses across the country. Medical groups represent a relatively small share of all protest targets, though they were targeted more often in the 1980s as LGBT groups took aim at hospitals, medical associations, and other healthcare providers in an effort to bring attention to the growing HIV/AIDS crisis ravaging their communities.

The prominence of state targets is not particularly surprising. As chapter 1 describes, when social movements evolved from highly localized protests to sustained campaigns, their focus similarly shifted from targets in their immediate vicinity to making claims on the government and its representatives. Given this intertwined and interdependent past, states are indispensable to the study of protest for many theorists, especially those working in the political process tradition. Such scholars do not believe that movements *only* target states; they simply argue that states have been – and continue to be – the main reference point for movements, which can interact with them in multiple ways: as targets, allies, opponents, audiences, mediators, and more (Desai 2002: 67; Tarrow 2011).

States are popular targets for social movements for multiple reasons. They have considerable power to bestow rights upon their citizens or to take them away. This legislative capacity makes them both culpable for many of their citizens' grievances and capable of ameliorative action. States also tend to be relatively accessible targets. They have multiple points of contact with their publics, from local government offices to national government institutions. They also employ many people who could serve as possible allies for movements, including administrators and elected officials, all of whom have their own interests and agendas, some of which might align with movement goals. States also offer the broadest "standing" to movements, since anyone who is a citizen of a state can, in principle, make claims on that state, though admittedly the ability of citizens in autocracies to do so is more limited than in democracies. Nonetheless, citizens are granted standing more easily when pressing claims on states than private individuals

Methods Spotlight: Statistical Analysis

Sophisticated statistical models of the kind found elsewhere in political science and sociology are historically not as widespread in the study of social movements. This is due, in part, to a lack of large datasets that cover multiple movements, multiple contexts, and multiple years. There are no governmental or international organizations that regularly release official statistics about social movement operations, and much of the data that have been compiled have been limited to the particular research interests of the scholars who collect and compile original datasets. Fortunately, these earlier data collection efforts have been made increasingly available to other scholars who can build on these repositories rather than needing to start from scratch. Looking ahead, it is possible complex statistical models will become more common in this area, especially as scholars experiment with more automated ways of collecting data on movement activities.

Statistical methods include a wide variety of approaches, from relatively simple regression models to more intricate techniques. In general, these methods prioritize parsimony – that is, explanatory models that value simplicity over complication and attempt to account for as much variation in social phenomena as possible using relatively few variables. Whereas case studies and other qualitative methodologies revel in rich detail and nuance, statistical models aim for spare and elegant explanations that are easier to apply to a wider variety of cases without getting bogged down in idiosyncratic details. Statistical models also are well suited to analyzing the probabilistic relationship among variables and correlations; they are limited in their ability to uncover causal relationships and mechanisms. Finally, statistical models require a larger number of observations in order to function correctly; if your research interests involve phenomena that are, by their very nature, highly limited (social revolutions, for example, which are few and far between in history), then it may not be possible for you to employ statistical models at all.

Explore this Method

Although statistical methods can get quite technical, even people without much training can use simple descriptive statistics and analytic tools like correlations and contingency tables to start to see correlations in data. If you do not have access to a specialized statistical package like Stata or SPSS, you can still do simple analytics using Microsoft Excel. The University of Texas, Austin, has a basic guide for how to perform some basic commands in Excel (https://www.ischool.utexas.edu/~wyllys/IRLISMaterials/excelnotes.html).

Even if you do not want to carry out full statistical analysis, there are a number of datasets that can still be useful sources of information for research on social movement organizations and dynamics. Jackie Smith and Dawn Wiest have made available their dataset on transnational social movement organizations, covering a 50-year period (www.icpsr.umich.edu/icpsrweb/ICPSR/studies/33863). The Ohio State University hosts a dataset on world political indicators that includes information on over 250,000 episodes of contentious politics from over 230 countries and territories (https://sociology.osu.edu/worldhandbook). The Global Digital Activism Research Project focuses on online activism over the past 20 years (http://digital-activism.org/projects/gdads). And the Dynamics of Collective Action dataset collects information on protest activity from 1960 to 1995 (http://web.stanford.edu/group/collectiveaction/cgi-bin/drupal/node/19). Other sources of information that can be helpful for research include Guidestar, a comprehensive site for information on the non-profit sector (www.guidestar.org/Home.aspx), and Google Trends (https://www.google.com/trends), which collects data on search terms entered into its web browser, providing a peek at the issues, topics, people, and events that are moving people to search for information online.

making demands of non-state actors. Corporations, for example, tend to restrict participation in and access to internal governance structures to owners, employees, investors, and other insiders (Weber et al. 2009). Attending a Monsanto shareholder's meeting requires ownership of company stock, which might be possible for some activists, but out of reach for many.

Some critics counter that this state-centric view no longer reflects reality and that globalization has significantly diminished the power and reach of national states to affect change (Castells 2012). States are no longer unchallenged in their sovereignty as other global actors – international and transnational organizations, multinational corporations, supranational entities – have become increasingly powerful. In the European Union, for example, members of the Eurozone no longer have the power to dictate monetary policy, and countries that joined the Schengen Area, which permits free movement of people among member countries, ceded considerable control over the flow of people across their borders. EU law, moreover, supersedes the national laws of member states and prevails whenever there is a conflict between the two. As a result of globalization, critics argue, states are less likely to be the primary site of governance as crucial decisions, rules, and norms are determined by non-state actors. In turn, states may lose their importance and appeal as primary protest targets.

There is, however, little evidence that there has been a wholesale shift away from state targets. In fact, many scholars point out that, even though globalization may allow international organizations and non-state actors to play a more prominent role in governance, national states still retain considerable power to set and enforce laws, regulate markets, and influence the lives of their citizens. States are also the primary guarantor of rights, which secures their continued relevance for social movements who wish to expand, contract, or change those rights (Moghadam 2013). Globalization, therefore, has not quite knocked the national state off its pedestal.

But it has complicated the issue of targeting by multiplying the number of actors who have the power to influence policy (della Porta and Kriesi 1999), as well as intensifying the impact of the international arena on domestic actors (Meyer 2003).

Globalization increases the level of interdependence and connectedness among actors, including national states, which is one mechanism by which the international and domestic spheres of politics influence each other. Thanks to advances in travel and communications, activists can more easily share ideas, connect with each other across long distances, and develop transnational networks that tap into far-away resources (Ayres 2002). While international connectivity among movements is hardly new, globalization has intensified and accelerated the process, creating new opportunities for mobilization as well as making it easier to coordinate and sustain transnational social movements. Such movements, in turn, can harness larger numbers of activists and coordinate protest across multiple states, which potentially increases the pressure that movements can exert on their targets. The anti-GM movement holds an annual day of action against Monsanto, for example, which involves protests all around the world. In 2016, anti-Monsanto events were held in over 400 cities across 38 countries, including Germany, Argentina, Ghana, and China. This international campaign dramatically multiplies the size of protests focused on the company; while any one city might have anywhere from a few dozen to a few thousand activists in the street, collectively, the anti-GM movement can claim they represented the views of hundreds of thousands of people – a much harder number for a target to dismiss. Similarly, Markus S. Schulz (1998) argues that access to transnational allies and global media made it possible for Mexico's Zapatista movement to persist in its challenge to the state; as an isolated actor with limited domestic resources, the Zapatistas would have been suppressed fairly quickly, but thanks to the movement's transnational connections to other activists and the international media – connections facilitated by globalized communications networks – they were able to mobilize supportive protests in other countries as well as heighten global awareness of their grievances, all of which constrained the Mexican government from harshly repressing the movement.

Transnational networks, in turn, open up new strategies that increase the targeting options for movements that may have limited opportunities to mobilize in their own countries. Movements

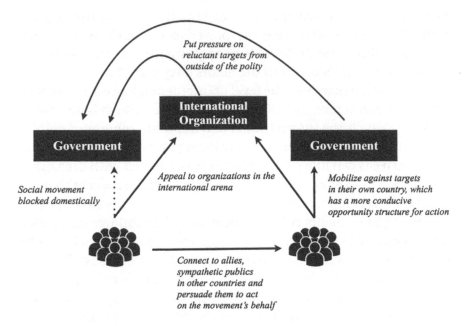

Figure 4.2 *Boomerang model of transnational targeting*

that are constrained by unfavorable political opportunity structures or facing opponents with relatively few vulnerabilities to exploit can, for example, use transnational connections to mobilize allies in other places to target their own governments or international organizations and encourage them to put pressure on reluctant states from above, as figure 4.2 illustrates. Margaret Keck and Kathryn Sikkink (1998) refer to this approach as a "boomerang strategy" in which movements can leverage their transnational connections and the increasing clout of international organizations to target those actors (usually governments) that might otherwise be relatively impervious to social movement demands. "Reverse boomerangs" are also possible, which make it possible for international actors who are unsuccessful at changing state behavior to forge alliances with domestic groups in target countries to mobilize and put pressure on governments from below (Andia 2015; Pallas 2016). In both scenarios, globalization expands the opportunities for movements to mobilize and makes it possible to target actors that would otherwise be out of reach.

The embryonic Greek Macedonian nationalist movement made use of the boomerang strategy when it discovered that its attempts to assert cultural and linguistic rights were summarily blocked by the Greek government, which viewed any such efforts as a dangerous ploy to challenge the unity of the Greek nation (Karakasdou 1993; Roudometof 1996). The movement then attempted to put pressure on the government using its international connections to allies located outside the state: it mobilized members of the European Free Alliance, a group of European regional nationalist political parties, to send letters to the Greek Prime Minister as well as rebuke the government for its actions during a session of the European Parliament (Gupta 2008a). The movement also encouraged sympathizers to mobilize in other countries to persuade their own governments to pressure Greek authorities. In Australia, for example, the Aegean Macedonian Association submitted a petition to the legislature calling on the government to take action, noting that Australia's good standing with the Greek government put it in an excellent position to influence Greece's minority policy.

Non-State Targets

In addition to states, social movements can also target a range of other groups, including international organizations, universities, and religious institutions. International organizations, for example, are particularly common targets for anti-globalization and anti-austerity protestors who see IMF and World Bank policies as eroding state sovereignty and increasing the power of multinational corporations and foreign powers. Universities are also popular targets, particularly as proxies for more distant social issues (Walker et al. 2008: 39). Even religious groups have been targeted by social movements that object to their theological stances or organizational tactics. Businesses, particularly large multinational corporations, are also frequent social movement targets because of their considerable economic power and political clout. As figure 4.1 illustrates, corporate interests are not particularly new targets for movements; even before the 1960s, labor movements typically targeted employers to press for better working conditions and pay. However, protest directed at corporations became more central to a wider variety of movements in the 1990s (Bartley and Child 2014), for both progressive-minded and conservative activists. In fact, given the growing economic and political clout of corporations and the centrality of consumption in advanced economic societies, it is hardly surprising that targeting corporations has become a dominant strategy for many social movement actors.

In many cases, such targeting is intended to push corporate actors to correct certain practices, such as ending their use of sweatshop labor or using greener materials in their products. But sometimes corporations can be targeted not to change their behavior but to enlist their power and influence as allies when confronting a more intractable foe. In response to North Carolina's infamous "bathroom bill" that prevents transgender individuals from using bathrooms that correspond to their gender identity, advocacy groups called on large corporations with ties to the state to put pressure on lawmakers to rescind the measure. Over 42,000 people, for example, signed a petition calling on PepsiCo to not sponsor the 2017 National Basketball Association's All-Star Game as long as it was scheduled to be held in the state, and petitions directly targeting the NBA over the decision generated tens of thousands of signatures. Although it is unclear what role these petitions ultimately played, what is known is that the NBA did ultimately decide to move the 2017 All-Star Game out of North Carolina, and PepsiCo – along with a number of other major corporate entities – came out publicly against the bathroom bill and, in some cases, even withheld their business from the state to push for repeal.

The big difference between corporations and most other social movement targets is that – unlike states, international organizations, universities, churches, and the like – corporations are for-profit entities. As a result, the mechanisms by which movements can induce behavioral changes include some distinct pathways. For example, Sarah Soule (2009) points out that movements can put pressure on a primary corporate target by mobilizing protest directed toward a secondary government target that has regulatory power over industry. While not-for-profit entities are also subject to government rules, corporations are particularly sensitive to changes in their operating environment, as it can affect their future investments and potential risk (Vasi and King 2012). The Indian anti-GM movement has used this approach to good effect: as a result of its protests against Bt cotton – especially its arguments that Bt cotton was not nearly as pest-resistant as Monsanto claimed – the Indian government announced that it would cap the price of Bt cotton seeds. It additionally demanded that Monsanto share its GM technologies with domestic scientists as a condition of market access. Monsanto, for its part, has denounced both actions, halted the introduction of a new transgenic cotton seed, and, given the suddenly uncertain regulatory environment, is re-considering its future investments in the Indian market.

Social movements can also affect business bottom lines with their activities; protests can shrink consumer demand, affect stock prices, shake shareholder confidence in executive leadership, harm corporate reputations, and even weaken credit ratings (Bartley and Child 2011). While such mechanisms are not irrelevant for non-corporate entities, the profit motive that propels corporations makes them particularly vulnerable to campaigns that threaten to inflict economic harm. As an alternative, movements can offer carrots instead of sticks: rather than emphasizing the costs of not giving in to movement demands, activists can offer alternative ways to value corporate products that point to possible financial gains for companies that proactively change their business practices (Dubuisson-Quellier 2013).

Movements can also influence corporations by focusing on secondary stakeholders, like suppliers, or corporate partners. These other actors, while not the primary target for protest, can sometimes be more vulnerable, accessible, or otherwise persuadable. This strategy, in effect, singles out weak links in a corporation's value chain and uses them to put indirect pressure on a company (Baron and Diermeier 2007). Greenpeace used this strategy against Shell Oil in 2014 to protest the company's exploratory drilling in the Arctic. Greenpeace carried out campaigns directly targeted at Shell, including occupying a drilling rig. But it also targeted some of Shell's corporate partners, most notably the Danish toy giant LEGO. The two companies had a decades-long marketing relationship that allowed LEGO to sell Shell-branded toys and distribute its kits at Shell gas stations in 26 countries – an arrangement valued at £68 million. Greenpeace took aim at LEGO and pressured it to cut ties with Shell. Among other tactics, it launched an online campaign in which the song "Everything is Awesome" – made famous by the wildly successful *LEGO Movie* – was repurposed to highlight the effects that Arctic drilling could have on the environment. Sung slowly in a minor key, the song plays as a rising flood of oil engulfs a pristine Arctic scene – including indigenous people, wildlife, and even a Santa Claus – made entirely of LEGO (figure 4.3). Titled "Everything is NOT Awesome," the video quickly went viral, garnering millions of hits on YouTube. The campaign was highly effective and the pressure on LEGO eventually led it to cut its ties with Shell. LEGO was particularly vulnerable to this type of protest, given that Greenpeace highlighted how environmental harms from Arctic drilling might affect the futures of children, the very people

Figure 4.3 *Scenes from Greenpeace's campaign against LEGO*

who play with LEGO toys. As this campaign illustrates, focusing on corporate partners that are perceived as softer targets can be an effective way to signal social disapproval and put pressure on corporate interests.

Finally, movements can affect corporate behavior by targeting specific companies in order to trigger a cascade of other businesses following in their footsteps. This kind of domino effect might occur because companies make changes as a defensive move to avoid becoming targets themselves (McDonnell and King 2013) or because changes made by early adopters send signals to others about new ways of conducting business (Yue et al. 2013). Movements hoping that corporate change diffuses in this way will either focus on the most vulnerable companies, whose behavior is easiest to change, or industry trendsetters, whose behavior carries the most clout. While vulnerable companies may be most likely to yield to movement demands, far-reaching change tends to start with well-respected and prominent companies that may start out less vulnerable, but whose actions tend to reverberate more broadly (Bartley and Child 2014).

Social movement tactics are not only used by activists taking aim at corporate entities; corporations themselves can use social movement tactics to further their own goals, protect their corporate reputations, distract or pre-empt protest that might be aimed their way, or even discredit rivals. Edward Walker and Christopher Rea

(2014) note that firms use a variety of insider and outsider political strategies to achieve their business objectives. Some of these strategies include familiar activities like lobbying or public relations campaigns. But firms can also use non-institutional methods that are more commonly associated with social movement actors, such as joining consumer boycotts of other firms. STA, a global travel organization that caters primarily to young travelers, for example, announced in 2016 it would no longer offer tours of SeaWorld over concerns about the company's record on protecting the welfare of its animals – an announcement that was welcomed by animal rights advocates around the world. Corporations can also fund organizations that can mobilize grassroots constituencies to support their business objectives. As Edward Walker (2014) notes, such professional grassroots lobbying firms recruit individuals selectively and offer them incentives to use tools traditionally associated with non-institutional activism – petitions, letter writing, and other forms of advocacy – in service of their paying clients. One such firm, Arno Petition Consultants, for example, can collect signatures to get legislation on referenda and local initiatives, coordinate get-out-the-vote campaigns for those referenda, and turn out community support at legislative hearings. Such tactics have been effective for movements that target state and non-state actors; in turn, some of those groups have started to embrace the same approaches in their targeting.

Targeting Social Attitudes and Structures

When targeting governments, corporations, universities, religious groups, or other organizations, movements set their sights on tangible, physical opponents. Such targets usually have brick-and-mortar locations, identifiable leaders, and physical sites where movements can stage protests. But what if a movement wants to challenge social attitudes, norms, values, or beliefs, or to change underlying social practices? Such targets may be embodied in certain institutional carriers that reinforce and protect existing social habits, but they are also disembodied and embedded in daily relationships between individuals in a society. How do movements think about targeting when their goal is to challenge gender roles, for example, or received ideas about sexuality?

Apart from targeting organizational actors that contribute to or perpetuate the norms of practices in question, Joshua Gamson

(1989) argues that movements must also confront the processes by which certain ways of thinking or being are classified as "normal," which renders all other behaviors and values that do not fit this standard as deviant or socially undesirable. Such processes tend to be abstract, invisible, and enforced by social sanctions that stigmatize non-conformists and marginalize groups that do not fit the dominant idea of what is acceptable. For Gamson, social norms are a tool of social control that divide individuals into those who "fit" and those who are "other." Challenging that division (and the moral judgments that are attached to it) requires challenging the underlying norm. Movement groups that seek to change social norms and values have a difficult task, as Gamson acknowledges. He writes that, compared to movements that target concrete opponents, the undertaking is particularly challenging "when the struggle is in part against a society rather than a visible oppressor" (Gamson 1989: 363). Taking the HIV/AIDS activist group Act Up! as an example, he points out that part of the organization's approach was to confront broad social stigmas attached to those infected with HIV/AIDS in the early days of the crisis when the disease was not well understood and often dismissed as a problem that emerged out of "deviant" (i.e., homosexual) behaviors.

In the absence of a concrete opponent, movements that hope to change such embedded norms can instead target social practices that reproduce particular notions of "normal" and "abnormal" while developing identities that challenge the idea that those not part of the norm are somehow unusual or aberrant. For example, Act Up! targeted public discourse and challenged the language used to describe and stigmatize those infected with HIV/AIDS. It co-opted symbols that were used to penalize marginal groups – like the inverted pink triangle that was initially used by the Nazis to identify homosexuals – and redeployed them as badges of pride and community (Gamson 1989). Other movement groups have similarly re-appropriated terms like "queer" – once meant to marginalize individuals who did not conform to heterosexual norms – and used them as labels around which communities could build positive identities. Rejecting social norms also involves targeting actors like the media, which play a role in how language is used and constructed. Such approaches are likely to take longer to effect change, but when they do, they can alter fundamental attitudes and social practices on a wide scale.

From Targeting to Target: Countermovements

If social movements are sufficiently threatening to the interests of other actors, they can become protest targets themselves as countermovements form to resist or reverse possible changes to the status quo. Scholars differ on how best to define countermovements. Some focus on the temporal order of emergence: countermovements occur after an initial social movement makes contentious claims (Zald and Useem 1987). If sequencing is the key difference between movements and countermovements, then countermovements can form around all kinds of claims as long as they are oppositional to the initial movement's demands. Clarence Lo (1982) argues that, as a result, countermovements can be progressive as well as conservative in orientation, and may want to preserve the status quo or change it. Other scholars argue that countermovements are limited to movements that resist changes to the status quo; the content of the claims is a more useful criterion, not the order in which movements emerge (Mottl 1980; Dorf and Tarrow 2014). Defining countermovements as status-quo champions may be influenced by empirical realities, since most of the examples that emerged in the twentieth century tended to be conservative or reactionary in nature and to reject changes proposed by more progressive activists (Lo 1982: 118).

For the purposes of this discussion, however, we follow David Meyer and Suzanne Staggenborg (1996: 1632) who combine elements of both content and sequence in their definition: movements and countermovements share similar concerns but "make competing claims on the state in matters of policy and politics . . . and vie for attention from the mass media and the broader public." They add that, when one movement precedes the other, we can call them movement and countermovement; however, if both movements persist over time – as many do – it is easier to simply consider them oppositional movements. Thus, arguing about whether the pro-choice movement initiated mobilization or simply countered the prior mobilization of pro-life activists is not constructive; we can simply think of them as opposing each other over their shared concern about abortion policy.

Not all movements will trigger a corresponding countermovement; the Dynamics of Collective Action dataset suggests that countermovements are actually infrequent, as they are only referenced in about 5 percent of protest-related articles between 1960 and 1995. Of course, that figure might underestimate the number of countermovements, since news coverage of a protest event may not have any reason to mention their opponents unless they, too, were holding a corresponding protest. Even so, it is clear that not all protests generate an opposing backlash. This is not the same as saying movements do not generate enemies; they clearly can and do with some frequency since their claims affect the interests of other social actors. However, these antagonists may not take the form of another social movement. Animal rights activists, for example, routinely alienate researchers who rely on animal testing for drug trials, but such opponents do not tend to form countermovements to protest in the streets.

While the existence of opposition is a necessary, but not sufficient, cause of countermovements, other factors must also be present. David Meyer and Suzanne Staggenborg (1996: 1635) posit that countermovements are more likely to emerge if the original movement shows signs of success. This is not a linear relationship, they argue, but a curvilinear one. If movements are very *unlikely* to achieve their goals, then there is little need for others to mobilize in opposition. If movements are highly *likely* to achieve their goals, opponents may decide that opposition will be futile. It is only when success is possible, but not guaranteed, that countermovements can potentially sway events in their favor. In addition, they argue that the possibility of movement success must threaten someone's interests; if movement goals are uncontroversial and generally acclaimed, then countermovements will have no one to mobilize. Here, mass media can play an important role; when covering social movement demands, journalists often go in search of individuals holding opposing positions in order to provide balanced coverage of different viewpoints. In this way, media can help to manufacture a coherent opposition where one might not otherwise exist (Meyer and Staggenborg 1996).

In addition, allies must be available to support both movements and countermovements. At the very least, supportive allies are helpful in mobilizing movements in the first place and can be instrumental in helping a countermovement get off the ground; this notion of support draws a distinction between elite allies within existing institutional structures and countermovement activists. But Meyer and Staggenborg also acknowledge a more active kind of support: cases where the elite are themselves threatened by a movement and help to form countermovements as a defensive strategy

(1996: 1642–3; Gale 1986; Mottl 1980: 626). At the same time, these countermovements require some minimal amount of autonomy, with their own members, organizational structures, and leaders in order to be distinguishable from the elites that helped to spawn them (Lo 1982: 119). Given that both movements and countermovements need elite supporters, societies with elite divisions – such as countries in which political power is divided among government branches or between federal and state institutions – are more likely to give rise to both movements and countermovements.

Once movements spawn countermovements, the two interact in what Mayer Zald and Bert Useem (1987) describe as a "loose tango." While they may compete for resources, undermine and discredit the other's policies, values, and reputations, and raise the cost of mobilization for their opponents, they develop a level of interdependence in which the actions of one motivate and legitimate the reactions of the other in an ongoing and reciprocal way; in essence, they become part of each other's political opportunity structure (Dorf and Tarrow 2014: 451; Steuter 1992; Andrews 2002; Meyer and Staggenborg 1996). This can even lead to growing similarities between the two movements' tactics and values (Lo 1982), though their competing claims make it unlikely that they would ever fully converge. It is more likely that, if they succeed in blocking a movement's demands, countermovements will disband or their members will be absorbed into existing power structures; on the other hand, if they fail, Tahi Mottl (1980) argues that countermovements go underground and turn to covert resistance against those who seek to implement new changes to the status quo. A third alternative also exists: that movements and countermovements continue as oppositional forces, though this ongoing clash may become more institutionalized as time passes.

Concluding Summary

Although choosing a target might initially seem like a relatively uncomplicated matter for social movements, this chapter has highlighted some of the nuances that movement actors might consider as part of their decision process. As various examples mentioned above underscore, it is not always clear who should be in a movement's crosshairs. The conventional wisdom about social movements tends to pit them against state actors, but states are only one of multiple possible targets, and whether movements focus on states, non-state actors, or some combination of the two depends on how they weigh a number of different considerations. Issues of culpability, curability, vulnerability, feasibility, and resonance guide movement targeting decisions, though these considerations can complicate choices when they do not point in the same direction.

While this chapter has presented the targeting decision as a single choice, it is actually a fluid and constantly shifting commitment. Movements can alter their targets based on their prior experiences, the reactions of their members, the responses of initial targets, and changing external circumstances. Targeting, like so much else about social movements, is a dynamic process, and movements learn and adapt when it comes to selecting the best focus for protests. They must also adapt when their choices sometimes spawn countermovements and other forms of reaction, which in turn condition their future decisions about targeting and other key strategies.

Questions for Discussion

1 How do social movements decide who to protest against? Given the possible trade-offs and considerations that can complicate their targeting decisions, which criteria do you think are most important for social movements to weigh and why?

2 Why do states remain the most popular target for social protest over time? Are there any political, economic, or social developments that you think would make other groups – like corporations, universities, or other non-state actors – more attractive targets in the future?

3 How might a social movement that prioritizes rapid change think about targeting differently from a movement that prioritizes widespread and long-lasting change?

4 Why do some movements generate countermovements? Why don't all movements do so?

Additional Readings

Keck, Margaret and Kathryn Sikkink. 1998. *Activists Beyond Borders: Advocacy Networks in International Politics*. Ithaca, NY: Cornell University Press. A key text that discusses how social movements operate across borders.

Meyer, David S., and Suzanne Staggenborg. 1996. "Movements, Countermovements, and the Structure of Political Opportunity." *The American Journal of Sociology*, 101(6): 1628–60. A good overview of the interactions between movements and counter-movements.

Van Dyke, Nella, Sarah A. Soule, and Verta A. Taylor. 2004. "The Targets of Social Movements: Beyond a Focus on the State." *Research in Social Movements, Conflicts and Change*, 25: 27–51. A useful introduction to how movements might think about a broad range of targets.

CHAPTER 5

The Message

Objectives

- To examine how social movements use frames to create and share meanings in order to define problems, identify culprits, and persuade potential supporters to mobilize in search of solutions.
- To appreciate what distinguishes successful, resonant frames from unsuccessful ones.
- To recognize the consequences of unsuccessful frames and the challenges that face movements when trying to recalibrate frames that are misaligned with their intended audience.
- To understand the ways in which different types of media influence movement messages and how each can enhance or distort a movement's choice of frames.
- To identify the opportunities and limits of the internet for disseminating movement frames to a broad audience.

Introduction

In May 1993, the Supreme Court of Hawaii ruled that denying marriage licenses to same-sex couples might infringe on their civil rights and, as such, be in violation of the state constitution's equal protection clause. Although the landmark *Baehr* v. *Lewin* case did not actually legalize same-sex marriage, it still sent shock waves through the country; for nearly 25 years, gay rights groups had tried to bring similar cases in front of the courts without much success. In 1970, for example, two men sued Minnesota to argue that they should be permitted to marry; that case – *Baker* v. *Nelson* – went all the way to the US Supreme Court without success and was subsequently cited as a precedent in other cases to block same-sex marriage. Since the 1970s, states and municipalities across the country had held referenda to overturn equal rights laws protecting gays and lesbians (Adam 2003). And, as recently as 1986, the US Supreme

Court had upheld state laws that criminalized sodomy, referencing such acts as "infamous crime[s] against nature" (*Bowers* v. *Hardwick*). Little wonder, then, that many gay rights advocates, like William Rubenstein of the American Civil Liberties Union, hailed the *Baehr* ruling as momentous; speaking to the *New York Times*, he described the decision as "a major breakthrough" and "the first court decision to give serious consideration to gay marriage" (Schmalz 1993).

Not everyone was so pleased. Many religious and conservative groups believed that same-sex marriage undermined traditional ideas of marriage being between one man and one woman; moreover, they argued that legalizing same-sex marriage would also threaten families and, in particular, harm children. Though *Baehr*, as already mentioned, did not, in itself, legalize same-sex marriage, its opponents feared that the ruling opened the door to sweeping social change. In short order, driven by what Barry D. Adam describes as a "moral panic," opponents of same-sex marriage organized referenda and pushed legislatures to slam the door shut on marriage equality before it opened any further (Adam 2003; Smith 2007). In 1995, Utah's legislature passed a bill that banned the recognition of same-sex marriages that were performed in other states, which is the customary practice for heterosexual marriages under the US Constitution's full faith and credit clause. In 1996, 14 states passed legislation barring same-sex marriage in addition to the federal government, which passed the Defense of Marriage Act (DOMA), defining marriage as a "legal union between one man and one woman." The following year, an additional 9 states followed suit.

While opponents of same-sex marriage were able to advance their goals in state legislatures, the court system was seen as a potential liability, as judges were more likely than elected officials to reverse same-sex marriage bans. In early 1998, for example, the Alaska Supreme Court ruled that same-sex couples had a constitutional right to marry, overturning a bill barring such marriages that had just been passed the year before. In response, conservative and religious groups organized public referenda to amend state constitutions and define marriage as being between one man and one woman. Just nine months after the Alaska Supreme Court ruled same-sex marriage constitutional, 68 percent of state voters passed a constitutional amendment outlawing it. The same year, 69 percent of voters in Hawaii passed a similar constitutional measure. Both margins reflected public sentiment more broadly, as a Pew

Research Center study found that, in 1996, 65 percent of people across the country opposed gay marriage (Pew Research Center 2012).

The strength of this movement opposing marriage equality, however, also gave rise to its own opposition. Although same-sex marriage had not, up to that time, been a top priority of the gay rights movement, which had focused instead on fighting discrimination issues in employment, housing, and other domains (Moscowitz 2013), the strong movement against same-sex marriage induced gay rights advocates to mobilize as well (Dorf and Tarrow 2014).

Both sides were able to claim victories in the subsequent years. Proponents of marriage equality pointed to legislative and court victories that either passed same-sex marriage bills or overturned bans for violating state constitutions. In 2003, the Massachusetts Supreme Court became the first in the country to fully legalize gay marriage, and the following year, the first fully legal gay marriage was performed in the Cambridge city hall. Supreme Court justices in Connecticut, California, and Iowa followed suit in the following years, and in other states, such as Vermont, New Hampshire, and New York, elected officials passed bills to legalize same-sex marriage. Opponents, however, also made headway in their counterattack. Between 1998, when voters in Alaska and Hawaii approved constitutional amendments barring gay marriage, and 2008, an additional 30 states passed referenda supporting the one-man-one-woman definition of marriage, as Table 5.1 shows.

Over this decade, constitutional bans on same-sex marriage passed in *every* state that held a referendum, effectively blocking sympathetic legislators and courts from mandating marriage equality by law or ruling. In some of the states listed above, the referenda were pre-emptive moves to forestall possible court challenges or legislation; in others – such as California – the referenda passed specifically to overturn prior legislation or court rulings that legalized gay marriage.

The California example was a particularly big blow to marriage equality advocates who had seen it as a bellwether for campaigns in other states (Warren and Bloch 2014). California had passed a bill legalizing same-sex marriage in 2005, becoming the first state to do so via the legislature. In response, opponents collected enough signatures to put a constitutional amendment in front of voters in the 2008 election. This ballot initiative, known as Proposition 8, was a hard-fought campaign, with both sides expending considerable

Table 5.1 States with constitutional amendments barring same-sex marriage

State	Year of referendum	State	Year of referendum
Alaska	1998	Oregon	2004
Hawaii	1998	Utah	2004
Nebraska	2000	Kansas	2005
Nevada	2002	Texas	2005
Arkansas	2004	Alabama	2006
Georgia	2004	Colorado	2006
Kentucky	2004	Idaho	2006
Louisiana	2004	South Carolina	2006
Michigan	2004	South Dakota	2006
Mississippi	2004	Tennessee	2006
Missouri	2004	Virginia	2006
Montana	2004	Wisconsin	2006
North Dakota	2004	Arizona	2008
Ohio	2004	California	2008
Oklahoma	2004	Florida	2008

energy to persuade the public. By this time, the percentage of people supporting gay marriage had risen, from around 27% in 1996 to 39% in 2008 (Pew Research Center 2012); slightly more people in California were in favor of marriage equality than nationally (between 44% and 51% depending on the poll), which made the outcome of the Proposition 8 campaign uncertain.

Supporters of Prop. 8 (i.e., opponents of same-sex marriage) argued that they were defending traditional marriage (and families), and that the constitutional amendment would safeguard the will of the people against activist judges and crusading lawmakers who did not reflect what the public really believed (Khan 2009; Warren and Bloch 2014). For their part, opponents of Prop. 8 (i.e., supporters of same-sex marriage) framed their arguments around the ideas of equal protection under the law and protecting the civil rights of gay and lesbian couples. Indeed, the way in which both sides in California framed their arguments echoed how advocates and opponents of same-sex marriage had tried to sway public opinion in other state referenda campaigns, with advocates stressing the notion of rights and opponents stressing the notion of morality (Hull 2001; Pan et al. 2010; Baunach 2011). Unfortunately for proponents of marriage equality, their arguments did not resonate with enough people, and, on election day, Prop. 8 narrowly passed with 52 percent of the vote. The result was disheartening for same-sex marriage supporters; it seemed that there was no stopping these constitutional amendments from passing.

Then came the Minnesota referendum in 2012. By this point, attitudes toward gay marriage had continued to liberalize – nationally, 46 percent of people were in favor of legalizing same-sex marriage, and 45 percent were opposed (Pew Research Center 2012). Attitudes were sufficiently close for the outcome not to be a sure thing for either side. Under these conditions, both movements swung into action and crafted messages to sway voters to their side. Same-sex marriage opponents returned to their tried-and-true messaging themes: protection of traditional marriage, protection of families, the rights of parents to protect their children, and the need to rein in activist judges and reckless lawmakers. Television ads run by Minnesotans for Marriage, a group opposing same-sex marriage, argued that "marriage is an issue that should be decided by the people," and that "voters should always have the final say" about defining marriage; the ads also included claims that while everyone should be able to love who they want, "we can support gays and lesbians without changing marriage. Marriage is still about children having a mom and dad." One ad featured two concerned-looking parents who argued that, if gay marriage became legal, schools would teach children about gay marriage, and that parents would be unable to object to the inclusion of such content.

Supporters of same-sex marriage, however, had learned lessons from their experiences in California and decided that the traditional civil rights framework they had used to argue – and lose – every prior campaign needed to change. Even though the rights framework had been powerful in the Civil Rights movement 40 years before, it did not seem to move voters to grant same-sex marriage rights in the twenty-first century. Moreover, in the Minnesota context, the rights frame had limited utility: same-sex couples already had a number of rights in the state, including the right to adopt, the right to visit partners in the hospital, bans on housing and employment discrimination based on sexual orientation, and even hate crimes legislation. It would, therefore, be harder to argue that marriage conferred vital civil rights that were otherwise inaccessible. They needed to find something else that would sway the public.

Campaign organizers reasoned that, rather than an abstract and legalistic focus on rights, which did not seem to resonate with many voters, the Minnesota campaign against the marriage amendment should reclaim the emotional ground that same-sex marriage opponents had staked out: emphasizing values, empathy, and morality – particularly the idea that people should treat others the way they would want to be treated themselves. To do so, the campaign should highlight the actual lived experiences of gays and lesbians communicated in one-on-one conversations from the heart that emphasized how the constitutional amendment could hurt real people (Grassroots Solutions 2013). One campaign volunteer, for example, spoke about how, as a little girl, she had fantasized about the wedding dress she would wear and celebrating with her family, and that passing the amendment would deny her the opportunity to realize this deeply felt childhood dream simply because she had fallen in love with a woman. Activists also emphasized that extending the opportunity to marry to all people would strengthen families and, in turn, protect children, which provided a counternarrative to one of the central claims from the pro-amendment camp. One anti-amendment campaign ad argued: "Marriage means love. Marriage means family. Marriage is caring for another person. Minnesotans choose to marry each other to make a vow in front of their family and friends of love, commitment, and responsibility to each other. Love and commitment foster a child's success and happiness, not a parent's sexual orientation." This messaging was also reinforced by other campaign literature, signage, and outreach efforts (figure 5.1).

To counter support from various religious organizations for the amendment, the anti-amendment movement also forged its own religious alliance, complete with a campaign faith director. Moreover, they argued that the amendment actually *undermined* religious freedom by preventing denominations that *did* support marriage equality from presiding over same-sex marriages – a reframing of the rights issue that also sabotaged the religious freedom arguments that gay marriage opponents traditionally used (DeLaet and Caulfield 2009). Above all, the campaign focused on framing the campaign in highly emotional terms, highlighting personal stories and emphasizing to voters what the opportunity to marry meant to the people who lived in their own communities.

As a strategy, it worked. Although it was close – only 110,000 ballots separated the two sides – ultimately, the constitutional

Photo credit: Fibonacci Blue (Creative Commons license).

Figure 5.1 *Marriage equality movement framing, Minnesota*

amendment failed, with 51.2 percent of the public voting against it. Minnesota became the first state in a decade to reject a constitutional amendment barring same-sex marriage by popular referendum. In the campaign post-mortem, the change in message framework and the emphasis on the personal and the emotional aspects of the marriage equality movement were given considerable credit for stopping the amendment's passage in a state where doing so had been anything but certain (Grassroots Solutions 2013). In so doing, the Minnesota anti-amendment example underscores the power that the right message framing can have for the success or failure of a social movement.

Framing and Social Movements

The idea of framing starts from a basic idea: things do not have inherent, automatic meanings. Instead, meanings are constructed by individuals and groups as they interact with each other and attempt to make sense of these interactions using their own experiences and based on the cultural contexts in which they are

Methods Spotlight: Frame Analysis

Frame analysis is a tool that enables researchers to examine how movements, media, and other actors construct and transmit meanings to their intended audiences. Like most concepts in the study of social movements, frames can be treated as both an independent variable (e.g., frames can affect a movement's ability to recruit supporters) and as a dependant variable (e.g., frames can be the product of particular organizational characteristics). Frames are embedded in communication and to get at the data, researchers must distill frames from texts (broadly understood): newspapers, press releases, memoirs, websites, speech acts, visual images, videos, newsletters, posters, and other locations where meanings are constructed, disseminated, and interpreted (Lindekilde 2014). When the relevant texts have been identified and sampled, then researchers must code the texts to identify and categorize the various frames that might be present.

Depending on the particular research question prompting the investigation, researchers may focus on a text's diagnostic, prognostic, or motivational framing; or perhaps the researcher will be particularly attuned to changes in framing over time, or signs of frame alignment (or misalignment) processes among groups in the same movement. These types of goals inform what types of messages will be of particular importance in the data collection phase, since it would be inefficient to try to capture every message and meaning that a text contains. This coding is sometimes carried out via deductive methods, in which the researcher begins examining the relevant texts with particular framing categories in mind. For example, if I were interested in understanding how the Standing Rock Sioux formulated diagnostic frames to support their mobilization against the Dakota Access Pipeline, I might – based on my prior knowledge and research on the case – expect that I would find themes that referenced violation of tribal sovereignty, or perhaps environmental threat. I would therefore generate a list of possible frames and, using this list, identify the number of times and the places where they are found. Coding can also occur inductively, when researchers identify frames as they work with the material. Often, coding involves both inductive and deductive coding: researchers begin with a list of likely frames, and then adapt, supplement, and change that list as they encounter new and different ideas than just the ones they anticipated in advance.

As an example, let us imagine we are interested in how Minnesotans United for All Families framed its campaign in support of marriage equality to promote the idea that it was consistent with religious freedom – a reversal of the conventional messaging that opponents of same-sex marriage had used successfully in early referendum contests. We might examine campaign literature, commercials, and written texts for that explicit message. But we might also find evidence of that frame in more subtle ways: images of same-sex couples in houses of worship, for example, or pledges of support by religious authorities from different faiths. Coding work must be sensitive to the many direct and indirect ways that meanings can be constructed out of words, images, and symbols.

Once texts are coded, then researchers must analyze patterns in the codes. This can be done quantitatively as well as qualitatively. For example, we might count up the number of times particular messages or ideas or symbols appear in texts and compare those numbers to other messages, other groups, other campaigns, or over time. Such techniques can illuminate the relative importance of one frame over another. Researchers can also analyze message patterns in a more qualitative way by exploring not just the number of times particular frames occur, but the relationship between frames, the ways in which messages might reinforce or undercut one another, how nuances in the fashioning of frames affect their resonance, and so forth.

Explore this Method

Frame analysis often begins with researchers identifying what messages or frames are of most interest and the population of texts (broadly understood) to analyze. Researchers then might develop a coding sheet with some initial messages, ideas, words, or symbols that they would expect from the texts. This kind of coding sheet can be fairly simple or extensive. A simple coding sheet might include questions like:

1 What is the source of the news article?
2 What is the primary tone used in the story: positive / neutral / negative?
3 Who does the article suggest is primarily responsible for the problem: government / corporations / international organizations / other countries / other?
4 Does the article suggest the problem will lead to economic difficulties: yes / no?
5 Does the article suggest the problem will lead to social conflict: yes / no?
6 Does the article suggest the problem will lead to environmental damage: yes / no?

By contrast, the following codebook for analyzing how newspapers and online documents frame articles on climate change is far more extensive, with coding categories corresponding to many different levels of analysis: www.ikmb.unibe.ch/ueber_uns/personen/prof_dr_adam_silke/e222290/files222291/Codebook_ClimateChange_SchmidPetrietal_2013_ger.pdf. Another extensive codebook for analyzing news stories about protest events is available at www.ssc.wisc.edu/~oliver/PROTESTS/ArticleCopies/codebook2000.htm. More codebooks – and other resources and suggestions for content and framing analysis – can be located at http://academic.csuohio.edu/neuendorf_ka/content/coding.html.

After exploring some of these resources, you might consider practicing some frame analysis in a simple way. Formulate a simple question that you could answer by examining a social movement organization's diagnostic or prognostic messaging. For example, you could ask: what do animal rights organizations think is the most pressing problem that needs to be solved? You can then develop a sample coding sheet based on the models you explored from above. Then, visit the websites of two or more organizations working on an issue relevant to your topic, read through the messages, and think about how you might use your coding sheet to capture the diagnostic frames being used. If you discover that you need to add or adjust the coding categories as you go – no worries! You are simply using inductive as well as deductive coding process. Just keep in mind that if you add categories after you have coded one or more texts/pages/documents, you should revisit those pages and make sure you apply these new codes to them. Finally, once you have coded your two or more websites, what initial conclusions can you draw about the way the different organizations formulated their frames? What hypotheses can you form to explain any differences between them (or unexpected similarities)?

embedded. "Meanings don't just float in the air around us," James Jasper argues (2014: 42), so, to understand the social world in which we live, we must organize, categorize, and interpret empirical events in order to make them sensible. Clifford Geertz (1973) offers an illustrative example of this interpretative process. Imagine you see two boys rapidly opening and closing the eyelids of their right eyes. This physiological act has no inherent meaning to it; it is observable, but not understandable. If, however, you described what the boys are doing as winking, or involuntarily twitching, you are interpreting what you see, differentiating the observed behavior from other similar kinds of behaviors, and assigning meaning to it. As Geertz posits, "the difference, however unphotographable, between a twitch and a wink is vast . . . the winker is communicating, and indeed communicating in a quite precise and special way" while the involuntarily twitcher is not intentionally communicating at all (1973: 6). Moreover, having differentiated the winker from the twitcher, you might also arrive at other understandings about the boys and their motivations based on the society in which you live and your own individual background. If you are from a Western culture, the wink might signal to you friendliness or flirtatiousness; if you were from China, however, you might interpret that same wink as a rude gesture. A doctor might diagnose the boy with the involuntary twitch as suffering from stress, or dry eye, or some other physiological condition; a superstitious, non-medical professional, on the other hand, might take the same twitch to mean that the boy will soon encounter an unexpected person.

Framing, in other words, is how we construct and negotiate meanings with others in society and attach those meanings to the events, people, and places around us (Tarrow 2011: 142; Gray et al. 2015). Frames are, to use the words of Erving Goffman (1974: 21), "schemata of interpretation" that help us to take disparate facts about the world and weave them into coherent narratives that help us to organize our experiences and navigate how we should respond. Frames provide a way of simplifying and making sense of complex empirical reality. They are, in a sense, cognitive shortcuts that we use to focus attention on some aspects of the world around us (and, by extension, to designate other aspects as irrelevant), tie together discrete events to provide a sense of coherent meaning, and transform how we see or understand the world (Snow et al. 1986). Robert Entman (1993) argues that this simplification occurs via processes of selection and salience. We select some aspects of our perceived reality and make them more noticeable or memorable.

In addition to the way individuals frame their own experiences, groups – such as social movement organizations – can also frame events to articulate common grievances, identify appropriate targets to resolve problems, differentiate themselves from other groups, and mobilize supporters (Benford 1993a; Tarrow 2011). Using a variety of formats, including speeches, visual images, music, costumes, slogans, rituals, and performances, movement actors can propose a particular interpretation of the world and also appeal to the audience's emotions and morality to galvanize people into action (McAdam 1996; Jasper 2014). In so doing, movement actors can also help to build a sense of collective identity among movement participants by clarifying the boundaries between "us" and "them," identifying the movement's heroes, villains, and bystanders, and strengthening the sense of commonalities among members (Hunt et al. 1994; Dimond et al. 2013; Jasper 2014). The activists blocking the construction of the Dakota Access Pipeline, for example, refer to themselves not as "environmental protestors," but as "water protectors," a rhetorical shift that creates a different moral relationship between themselves and the pipeline supporters; the move from protestor to protector paints their actions not as disruptive, but as righteous, which helps to further their narrative around who represents good versus evil in this particular stand-off.

Framing choices are also evident in the controversy over consuming beef in India. The issue is highly controversial and has led to outbreaks of violence, as rumors that certain individuals are involved with beef consumption have led to vigilante groups descending on alleged perpetrators and, in some cases, lynching them. After one such incident in the village of Dadri, an article appeared in *Panchjanya*, a right-wing Hindu nationalist magazine, that pointed fingers at the Muslim community, blaming its leaders for the violence because of their disrespect for the country's (presumed Hindu) traditions. In addition to justifying the lynching by referring to Hindu religious texts that sanction capital punishment for those who kill cows, the article also depicts Indian Muslims as former Hindus who had converted a few generations ago and asks "who has taught the converted Indians to hate their origins, reject the traditions of centuries?" (Bhardwaj 2015).

The framing in this instance makes certain selections and simplifications to further a particular interpretation of the world. It singles out Muslims as the perpetrators of beef consumption even though other religious communities in India, including Christians and Jews, consume it as well. This selection and focus fits with a broader anti-Muslim orientation within Hindu nationalism that paints Muslims, and Pakistan specifically, as the "other" to India's Hindu majority; this article reinforces the notion of Muslims as the villains of the piece and devalues their religious claims by reducing them to lapsed Hindus who ought to adhere to their forgotten traditions rather than following the precepts of a foreign religion. It also frames Hinduism as irrevocably opposed to beef consumption and cites religious texts as support; it paints as heroes those devout Hindus who will kill to protect the cow. Both rhetorical moves elide the fact that the Hindu community is enormously heterogeneous in its views, and that some Hindus eat beef because of personal preference or, in the case of lower-caste individuals, because it is a cheaper protein source than many alternatives. In these ways, the framing choices that the author makes create a particular interpretation of those who eat beef (i.e., foreign, outsiders, disrespectful, blameworthy, apostates) as well as of those who want to impose a ban (i.e., blameless, devout, heroic, pure) and, along the way, glosses over the more complex relationships between religious identity and beef consumption that exist in contemporary India to create what Ann Mische (2008: 233) calls a "provisional homogeneity." All of these choices serve the interests of the Hindu nationalist movement and increase its appeal among its target audience. In fact, movement interests and strategic needs drive framing choices in general. Effective collective action frames can counter the dominant narratives offered up by states and other targets, convert neutral bystanders into supporters, mobilize existing supporters to act, attract media attention, influence authorities, and build coalitions (Benford 1993a; Snow et al. 2014: 30). Frames, in other words, can be highly consequential for movements.

Types of Frames

Social movements use frames to accomplish a number of tasks, including defining and crystallizing grievances, identifying culpable actors to target, proposing solutions that would resolve their members' discontents, and persuading those who support the movement's goals to take action. Each of these tasks is accomplished by a different type of frame. The methods spotlight in this chapter describes how researchers use frame analysis techniques to better understand the various meanings encoded in these messages.

Diagnostic Framing

Diagnostic framing constructs the problem around which movements mobilize. This construction involves the naming of grievances as well as interpreting them in such a way that multiple people who are individually aggrieved begin to see themselves as connected to a common cause and in need of a common solution (Snow and Benford 1992: 136; Tarrow 2011: 144). Neither step – interpreting conditions as grievances and connecting individual grievances to a larger collective grievance – is an automatic one. The experience of Indian Dalits, or lower-caste Hindus, is a case in point. Often deemed "untouchables," they historically have faced considerable discrimination and marginalization in Indian society. They have been subject to segregationist practices in public spaces and schools, denied access to government social services, and are more often the victims of violence (Narula 1999; Thorat and Lee 2008; Ramachandran and Naorem 2013). Because this subordination is typically justified on religious grounds and the "idea that some groups *deserve* less respect and fewer rights than others . . . simply as a result of their birth into a particular social stratum" (Bob 2006: 159), it is conceivable that individual Dalits could interpret their position and its accompanying miseries as inevitable, divinely sanctioned, and therefore immutable. Understanding these experiences as *oppressive* (as opposed to natural) requires a different way of interpreting these events. Perceiving these oppressions as a collective ill and not just the misfortunes of a single individual also requires a frame that connects the experiences of multiple Dalits and emphasizes the commonalities among them. In this way, diagnostic frames help to articulate and shape common identities among movement participants.

Diagnostic framing also involves the attribution of blame, not just identifying who is responsible for the grievance, but also attaching motives and identity to these opponents (Snow and Benford 1988). This step in diagnostic framing is when targets are constructed. In the case of Dalit activists, it would be possible to attribute the blame to different groups, including religious actors, upper-caste Hindus, or the government. If the Dalit movement framed the source of their grievances as outdated religious practices and general social unwillingness to let go of oppressive norms and traditions, it might suggest different targeting strategies than if the movement opted to frame government officials who do not do enough to enforce anti-discrimination laws as the main culprits. Because there might be more than one potential culprit, diagnostic framing can be a contested process with different actors attempting to make their favored frame the dominant one. Such "framing contests" occur at other points in the framing process as well (Benford 1993a). Moreover, diagnostic frames do not remain fixed once they are formed; rather, they are continually negotiated and modified as actors, events, and contexts shift over time.

Prognostic Framing

Once movements have diagnosed the problem and attributed blame, they must also consider what solutions they want to propose. This process involves prognostic framing, in which movement activists specify what should be done and who is responsible for taking that action (Snow and Benford 1988). Prognostic framing is another point where intra-movement disputes can emerge, as different actors may have divergent ideas about appropriate solutions even if they agree on the same diagnostic frame. Splits between radical and moderate movement groups often take place over such disagreements as moderates tend to advocate for solutions within existing institutional and social structures while radicals tend to advocate for more sweeping and systemic change. Feminists might agree on diagnostic frames (for example, identifying sexual violence against women as a core problem and patriarchal institutions as a source of the problem), but differ wildly when it comes to how those problems should be confronted. For mainstream, moderate feminists, the best solution might entail reforming existing institutions, strengthening laws, and challenging social norms around sexual violence. Radical feminists may find all of this inadequate and advocate instead that the only way to combat patriarchy is to escape it completely; some radical feminists did just this by setting up women-only collectives that interact as little as possible with outside groups (Rudy 2001).

Motivational Framing

Together, diagnostic and prognostic framing constitute what Bert Klandermans (1984) calls "consensus mobilization." If movements are able to persuade others of their diagnosis of and solutions for a social problem, then they will generate support for their agenda. However, support does not automatically translate into action; for that, social movements must also employ motivational frames so that passive support becomes active participation. Such action mobilization, Klanderman writes, depends on successful prior consensus mobilization: "[while] consensus mobilization does not necessarily go together with action mobilization . . . action mobilization cannot do without consensus mobilization" (Klandermans 1984: 586). In other words, once a consensus has been built, effective motivational framing can help social movements to overcome potential collective action problems, even in cases where the environment might otherwise make such mobilization difficult (Noonan 1995).

Motivational framing involves cognitive processes that provide rationales for engaging in protest. This rhetorical "call to arms" involves particular types of appeals – what Robert Benford calls "vocabularies of motives" that spur action. These might include language that emphasizes the severity of a particular problem, the urgency of taking action, the efficacy of collective action, and the moral obligation to take part (Benford 1993b). David Snow and Sarah Soule (2010: 138) also suggest that cognitive appeals to costs and benefits (i.e., the greater benefits of action over inaction) and status enhancement (i.e., participation will improve standing, reputation) can be effective ways to mobilize sympathizers to act. Movements will not use all these vocabularies all the time, but even so, these rhetorical strategies are easily found in the messaging of most movement groups. Navsarjan, the largest Dalit rights organization in the Indian state of Gujarat, for example, uses several of these vocabularies when describing its campaign to implement minimum wage protections for day laborers who are disproportionately low-caste. They invoke the idea of severity when they note that Gujarat's minimum wage is one of the lowest in India, and that day laborers make significantly less than even that; they emphasize the tangible benefits of action by pointing out the potential gains from increasing wages; they highlight the efficacy of collective action by describing how the campaign succeeded in getting workers paid the minimum wage in particular villages; and they also acknowledge potential status enhancement when they write: "Because of the diversity within the union, Dalits and non-Dalits are becoming closer; they sit together and drink tea together, and fight for their minimum wages together. This fact has the added benefit of decreasing untouchability practices in the targeted areas" (Navsarjan n.d.). Movements must determine which motivational vocabularies are most appropriate given the issue, the target, the context, and the stakes. The choices that movements make around motivational frames are also contestable and fluid – what might be mobilizing at one point in time may not work later.

While cognitive appeals are important, motivational framing also involves emotions, which can galvanize feelings and make people excited, determined, or passionate about joining a movement. Critics of the PPT approach have argued for the inclusion of emotions in framing analyses overall, since decisions to participate in movements are not just about cognitive worldviews (Benford 1997; Goodwin et al. 2001: 72). Which emotions are particularly effective at motivating – and then sustaining – participation can vary. Negative emotions like fear, anger, and frustration can spur people to action, leading William Gamson (1995) to argue that all successful framing attempts require some reference to injustice. In a similar vein, James Jasper (1997) points out that moral shocks – a sudden, unexpected, intense, and usually negative emotional experience – can move previously uncommitted bystanders to action. On the other hand, more optimistic emotions, such as joy and love, can also play important roles, both in galvanizing action and, perhaps even more importantly, in maintaining activism over time (hooks 1994; Jasper 1997). Motivational framing that emphasizes collective identity can also generate a powerful desire to demonstrate solidarity with others (Hunt et al. 1994). Which frames movements choose is, again, subject to contestation and to considerations like the phase of movement development and the emotional culture of the wider society (Tarrow 2011: 154).

Master Frames

As movements carry out the framing tasks above, certain ideas may be invoked repeatedly across different types of movements and even different social contexts. Movements as varied as the fight against apartheid in South Africa, the Dalit movement in India, the transnational anti-sweatshop movement, and the men's rights movement have all used injustice frames to animate their diagnoses of the problems their members face despite the movements having little else in common. The fact that the injustice frame is applicable to these disparate movements and settings suggests that some interpretative schema are particularly portable; David Snow and Robert Benford call such schema "master frames" (Snow and Benford 1992). Master frames are understood in two somewhat distinct ways. One way is to think of them as generic frames that can move easily across contexts and movement types. For example, notions of injustice, justice, equal opportunity, and rights can have broad applicability to movements across the world (Gerhards and Rucht 1992; Benford 1997). Not all master frames will be relevant and useful to all contexts (Swart 1995) but they will still have fairly broad reach.

Alternatively, the concept of master frames has also been used to describe rhetorical similarities among movements that emerge at similar points in a larger cycle of contention (Snow and Benford 1992). The protest cycle that started with African Americans mobilizing around civil rights, for example, also included the women's liberation movement and the gay rights movement, both of which used a similar rights frame. The takeaway here is that when a particular master frame is successful, then other movements will be more likely to use it as well, since people will be able to make parallel cognitive shortcuts even if the substance of the claims might be different. To put it another way, because the Civil Rights movement achieved many of its goals using a rights frame, it made such a frame more attractive to movements that followed, and when successor movements invoked the rights frame, its familiarity helped to crystallize the movement's demands and legitimated their own claims.

Framing Processes

Prior to the 1980s, scholars of social movements paid little attention to how movements construct meaning; the dominant paradigm at the time – resource mobilization – focused more on material conditions than the impact that culture, identities, and ideas could have. This lack of attention started to change in the 1990s when the idea of framing became incorporated into political process approaches and constructivist theories started gaining more traction across the social sciences. However, much of this initial work on frames tended to treat them as "things" that were relatively static (Benford 1997: 415–16; Snow et al. 2014). Critics of frames-as-things argued that this notion ignored how frames were themselves products of negotiation, contestation, and learning. Instead, as Robert Benford writes, the prevailing view seemed to be that "participant mobilization was simply a matter of movement activists pushing the appropriate rhetorical button" (Benford 1997: 422). To counter this tendency, the critics of this view called for scholars to take seriously the ways in which framing processes are dynamic, ongoing, recurring, and contingent on the web of relations in which activists and groups are embedded. Moreover, framing was not simply a cognitive process but, as discussed above, one that could tap into and mobilize deep emotions as well (Hunt et al. 1994; Goodwin et al. 2001).

Framing is an activity that is not isolated to social movement actors, nor is it restricted to elites; everyone uses frames to simplify and make sense of reality. The frames that we use reflect our own values, goals, cultural inheritances, and experiences (Tarrow 2011: 142). In a sense, we each bring cognitive and emotional maps to make sense of new information and ideas, and our interpretations, in turn, depend on the direction in which our initial maps send us. In addition, the social contexts in which we are located also affect how we frame and how we interpret frames (Noonan 1995). Framing does not happen in a vacuum, and societies have distinct "discursive opportunity structures" (Koopmans and Statham 1999) that condition what ideas are likely to be considered legitimate, realistic, and appropriate. Movement frames that echo and are consistent with these discursive opportunities are more likely to find a receptive home and be effective than ones that are out of step with the way a given society communicates or the principles that are implicit in its conversational landscape (McCammon et al. 2007).

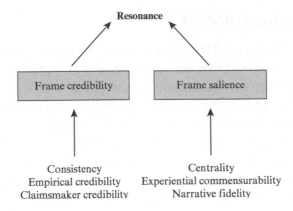

Figure 5.2 *Factors affecting frame resonance*

Rita Noonan (1995), for example, argues that, during the military dictatorship of Augusto Pinochet in Chile, frames that emphasized leftist ideas like working-class radicalism were pushed underground. Such frames could not be effective at mobilizing protest and making contentious claims because they had been expunged from public discourse by the stridently anti-Communist regime. The discursive opportunity structure, therefore, left little room for the types of ideas around which social movements in Chile had traditionally organized. This created an opening for alternatives to emerge, such as feminist and maternal frames, that did not clash with the dominant political discourse but still made it possible for women to mobilize and challenge state policies.

Frame Resonance

In order for frames to be successful, they must resonate with their intended audience, which includes, but is not limited to, adherents and potential sympathizers. Frames that make cognitive sense and that also engage audience emotions will be more likely to connect people to a movement's actions and to mobilize them. To be persuasive in this way, Snow and Benford (1988, 2000) argue that frames must be both credible and salient or, to put it another way, believable and relevant. Each of these two criteria, in turn, depend on additional factors, as figure 5.2 illustrates. Frame credibility has three components. It must be consistent with the other things that a group says it believes or how it behaves. If an organization is seen as hypocritical – saying one thing but doing another or contradicting itself from one moment to the next – its credibility will be undermined. Next, frames must be empirically credible insofar as the claims they make must reflect the audience's perceived reality. Claims need not be objectively factual (Snow and Benford 2000: 620), but there must be evidence available that could be used to support the claim and make it seem believable. For example, the Black Lives Matter movement uses instances of police shooting unarmed people of color as evidence that law enforcement is plagued by institutional racism. Importantly, Snow and Benford note that such empirical evidence does not have to be persuasive to everyone, just to the movement's supporters and potential recruits. This is also the case in the Black Lives Matter movement, as evidence used by BLM to highlight institutional and embedded racism is seen by its detractors as isolated cases of bad cops, not an indictment of law enforcement in general. Finally, those making the claims must also have credibility based on factors like having expertise in the subject matter, experience, or high status in society.

In addition to credibility, resonance also hinges on a frame's salience. This, in turn, depends on centrality of the ideas in the frame to the lives of audience members. If frames appeal to core values or beliefs, or ideas that are particularly important for the audience, they will have higher salience. Experiential commensurability refers to whether the frame makes sense and applies to the daily lived experience of the audience. When same-sex marriage advocates refer to the restricted rights of committed same-sex partners who are unable to marry – not having hospital visiting privileges, or having difficulty accessing insurance benefits, or not being able to adopt – such ideas are likely to ring true for many individuals who have experienced (or know people who have experienced) exactly these situations. Frames that are too far removed from peoples' own experiences will have less salience. Salience also hinges on narrative fidelity, or the idea that frames must be consistent with the cultural meanings and narratives that exist in the audience's society. Mitch Berbrier (1998) found, for example, that when white separatist groups in the United States, which are stigmatized for their racist worldview, framed their promotion of white culture and identity as contributing to cultural pluralism, they were more successful in attracting adherents since diversity and pluralism are typically presented as bedrock values of American society. Finally, for a frame to resonate, it must not only pass these various cognitive tests of credibility and salience, but should also engage audience feelings and emotions as well (Jasper 2014), making resonance an exercise in appealing not simply to the head, but also to the heart.

Frame Alignment

Resonance also implies that movement groups are able to connect with and recruit potential supporters, whom they can subsequently mobilize. This recruitment relies partly on having credible and salient frames, but also requires movements to employ strategies that link their ideas, values, and beliefs to unmobilized individuals and groups, thereby drawing them into activism. Having resonant frames will do little for a movement if it cannot share those frames with potential members who can make the movement stronger and larger. To accomplish this, movements use various frame alignment strategies to connect their work and claims to their target audience, including bridging tactics, amplification, extension, and transformation (Snow et al. 1986).

Bridging tactics connect individuals and groups who might share certain grievances or interests to social movements that are organizing around those very same issues. By linking these previously disparate individuals and organizations together, movements can increase their size and support. Movements use bridging tactics whenever they do organizational outreach like conducting door-to-door canvassing, spreading information through social networks, and using mass media channels to educate the broader public about their issues and goals (Dimond et al. 2013). In this way, they can attract supporters who might share their concerns but who had previously been unaware of the movement or its work. A movement organization that seeks to make puppy mills illegal, for example, might set up an information table at a pedigree dog show on the assumption that the attendees – likely to be small-scale specialty breeders themselves – will already be against the practice and therefore sympathetic to joining the movement. Frame bridging is a common activity for movements and intended to recruit passive sympathizers and convert them into active adherents. In this process, individuals do not change their worldview or beliefs, only act on them with movement prompting (Opp 2009: 238).

Movements can also amplify their frames by building on the pre-existing ideas that people might already have, but that need additional clarification or stimulation to generate mobilization. This might involve more persuasion than is necessary for frame bridging, where the target audience is already presumed to agree with the specific diagnostic and prognostic frames that the movement is offering. With amplification, the pre-existing beliefs or values may need to be reinforced or modified to be congruent with movement frames. For example, an individual who believes that corporations do not care about their workers could be mobilized more easily by a movement like Occupy Wall Street, which can build on that prior belief and amplify it to include a focus on things like income inequality. Similarly, an individual who values personal autonomy and self-reliance might be someone who might be more easily persuaded to join the Tea Party Movement compared to someone who believes that the common good supersedes individual self-interest.

Frame extension requires a movement to expand its own frames and "encompass auxiliary interests not obviously associated with the movement" (Snow et al. 1986: 472). In effect, movements extend frames by trying to make their goals relevant to a wider population of people. The Dalit rights movement, for example, could extend its focus from championing the rights of "Untouchables" to working on behalf of all marginalized people in India. By framing the aggrieved population not as Dalits but as subordinated groups, they might also make their work and demands appealing to others, such as the Adivasis (indigenous tribal populations), who also suffer systemic discrimination. David Snow and his collaborators similarly discovered that in Austin, Texas, largely white and middle-class groups within the peace movement extended their focus to include content on anti-racism, anti-sexism, and other forms of oppression in order to broaden their appeal to minority communities (Snow et al. 1986: 472).

In some cases, movements might find that their frames simply do not resonate with potential supporters who might see little connection between their lives and the movement's work, or might even oppose the movement's claims. In such circumstances, "new values may have to be planted and nurtured, old meanings or understandings jettisoned, and erroneous beliefs or 'misframings' reframed" (Snow et al. 1986: 473). This is particularly challenging to do, because existing ideas and values may be entrenched and the individual resistant to change. However, if people can be persuaded to see their circumstances in a new light or re-examine their assumptions, it is possible to bring them around to a movement's point of view. Ziad W. Munson (2002) notes, for example, that some of the most committed anti-abortion movement activists that he studied admitted to initially having pro-choice views. Their encounters with the movement, however, changed their minds and offered them a different perspective on the issue, and over time, they emerged as especially strident opponents of abortion who engaged the issue with the zeal of the converted.

Framing Dilemmas

Framing processes are strategic and interactive. But they are also contingent and uncertain. There are a number of challenges that movements might encounter as they frame their grievances and proposals, and attempt to mobilize supporters, including constructing frames that are ineffective and having to dispute how others in the movement think something should be framed.

Framing Miscalibration

Despite their best efforts, movements sometimes construct frames that miss the mark and that simply do not resonate with the desired audience. Such frames might reflect the sincere values and beliefs of those in the movement, but without broader appeal, movements can limit their ability to effect change. Movements might also discover that previously effective frames lose their appeal over time and must be adapted to take into consideration changing circumstances, new social values, and emerging identities, in order to stay relevant (Snow et al. 1986). In addition, as the movement engages in contention, its strategies change, as does its leadership. All of these shifts are part of the dynamic movement environment, and all of them make it impossible to develop and then permanently stick with one unvarying set of framing choices. Frames must adapt and evolve to be effective. When circumstances dictate, movement actors may have to shift existing frames to new ones while avoiding perceptions that, in doing so, they are uncommitted or inconsistent in their beliefs.

The anti-death-penalty movement in the United States, for example, has traditionally framed its opposition to capital punishment on moral grounds, critiquing it as a human rights violation or in terms of a religious argument about the sanctity of life. This framing, however, had narrow appeal and was unable to sway most individuals who did not already subscribe to a progressive political outlook (Haines 1996). As a result, the movement then shifted its critique to rationalist and procedural frames that might appeal to a broader audience. It moved from making moral or religious arguments to claims about capital punishment's expensiveness, its ineffectiveness at deterring crime, and how procedural flaws in the legal system might lead to innocent people being executed (Eren 2015).

This dispute within the anti-death-penalty camp points toward another way in which movements might not develop effective frames. While frames have to resonate with a movement's audience, and that resonance is contingent on movements being able to calibrate their ideas and values with the norms and beliefs of society as a whole, if that calibration is *too* good – meaning that the frames simply reflect existing cultural discourse – then it can be hard for movements to challenge entrenched ways of thinking and push for social transformation (Tarrow 2011: 147). This creates something of a paradox for movements: on one hand, movements that want to oppose prevailing customs will want to construct frames that offer an alternative view, but if that alternative strays too far from the existing cultural meanings and attitudes, it will not resonate. This paradox can make it hard for movements to develop frames that sufficiently oppose prevailing ideas and power structures while also not straying too far from what the discursive opportunity structure will support.

Framing Disputes

Recalibrating frames that are misaligned is not always easy, however. If frames are initially articulated in very concrete and explicit ways, any attempt to modify them to reflect changing circumstances or opportunities can risk their consistency and credibility (Jasper 2010b: 75). In addition, shifting frames too often or too much can also alienate existing members who joined movement groups under the old, familiar frame and may not accept new ways of framing the issue. If the disagreements are serious enough, they can lead to schisms and splits within movement organizations. A recalibration-related dispute of this type occurred in the Irish Republican Army (IRA) in 1969 when part of the group's leadership and membership adopted an increasingly Marxist analysis of the conflict between Catholics and Protestants in Northern Ireland. This Marxist diagnostic frame, which pointed fingers at the bourgeois economic elite for fomenting violence and division between the two communities, was rejected by others in the organization who believed the appropriate way to think about the conflict was in more traditional nationalist terms and saw Protestants and the UK government – not class interests – as the real culprits. The disagreement could not be resolved, and the organization split into smaller rival groups.

Such framing disputes can still be damaging even if they do not lead to schisms. Because social movement organizations are not unified actors and are composed of different individuals with their own ideas and interests, they can have sincere disagreements over the diagnostic and prognostic frames that develop. In the anti-death-penalty movement, for example, the shift from a progressive moral/ethical analysis to a more rational/legal view has not gone uncontested. Colleen Eren (2015), for example, argues that while the frame shift has coincided with increased support for anti-death-penalty demands, this should not be interpreted as progress. Instead, she argues for a shift not to the right of the political spectrum but to a stronger commitment to the *left* and support of more radical ideas of economic and social justice. This disagreement underscores the reality that framing disputes can occur not just in movements that run into trouble, but also in movements that seem to be doing well and making gains on their policy goals. While some disagreement can be healthy insofar as it energizes discussion and requires actors to be intentional in their framing choices, too much disagreement can paralyze groups, sapping their energies and diverting focus away from their overarching goals.

In addition to framing disputes *within* movement groups and *among* movement groups, there are also disputes between movements and outsiders, such as oppositional movements, states, and other external actors who develop counterframes to offer a rival interpretation of the world (Benford 2013). These counterframes are not just aimed at these groups' own supporters; they also are part of the crowded discursive field aimed at bystanders and neutral publics to sway general opinion or to stop potential supporters from mobilizing. If movements do not offset them, these counterframes can undermine their support (Klandermans 1992).

When advocates of same-sex marriage initially framed their demands using the idea of equal protection and enjoying the same rights as heterosexual couples, their opponents countered by arguing that rights were not really the issue at all, and if rights were all that were at stake, legislation specifically focusing on those areas of inequity, such as adoption or survivor benefits or hospital visitation, could be enacted without changing the definition of marriage. This counterframe proved to be effective at persuading some people who might have otherwise responded sympathetically toward the rights-based frame offered by marriage equality advocates. A Pew Research Center study illustrates the power of this counterframe by showing the growing support for civil unions that would offer same-sex couples many rights while stopping short of full marriage equality. Between 2003 and 2009, support for same-sex marriage did not appreciably change, with some 53 percent of respondents opposing it. Support for civil unions in that same period increased by 12 percentage points, from 45 percent to 57 percent, suggesting that the idea of granting rights without granting marriage was an effective counterframe (Pew Research Center 2009).

Multiple Audiences

Most analyses of framing start from the assumption that the main audience at which such messages are directed consists of movement supporters, as well as bystanders in the general public who could become supporters. However, social movements operate in a multi-organizational field in which there are more potential audiences than these, including donors, countermovements, governments, other movements that could be allies or opponents, and the media (Evans 1997; Neuhouser 2008; Blee and McDowell 2012). Moreover, movement supporters can be differentiated into distinct groups, including occasional supporters, regular rank-and-file members, and the committed movement faithful. All of these clusters of people will respond in different ways to movement messages based on their identities, interests, cultural contexts, and values, which makes the idea of framing "a" message for "an" audience a nearly impossible task.

Unless movements are able to tailor messages with considerable specificity *and* ensure that only their intended audiences can see them – unlikely in most societies and made increasingly difficult with inexpensive communication technologies – movements will encounter what James Jasper (2010b: 75) calls an "audience segregation dilemma." Because it is hard to direct messages without them also being heard by secondary publics, movements risk contradicting themselves and potentially undermining their credibility.

Pleasing one audience can be hard enough; pleasing multiple audiences – especially when they want to hear different things – can be extremely challenging.

Devashree Gupta (2008b) describes this dynamic with respect to the nationalist movement in Northern Ireland, particularly the challenges that militant groups like the Irish Republican Army and its political wing, Sinn Féin, had to navigate when they started to embrace political participation and contest elections. Up until the 1980s, the republican movement in Northern Ireland had eschewed taking part in elections in order to avoid any sign that they believed in the legitimacy of British political institutions. Instead, they opted for a physical force strategy, using violence against the state. In the 1980s, however, Sinn Féin's leadership made a strategic pivot to pursue a joint strategy of contesting elections alongside armed struggle and framed this change as a better way of taking power than violence alone. To keep their existing members, Sinn Féin could not simply abandon armed struggle at this time without triggering a possible exodus from the organization. As such, its leaders took pains to emphasize their ongoing commitment to physical force republicanism. However, non-Sinn Féin supporters – including moderate nationalists who abhorred violence – could also see this message, which meant that in elections against moderate groups, the party struggled to win over such voters. Members of the Protestant community also heard this message and used it to persuade their members that Sinn Féin and the IRA had not changed and were still dangerous groups, which perpetuated tensions between the two sides. And state officials heard this message as well, which made it more difficult for the IRA and Sinn Féin to argue that they deserved a seat at the negotiating table.

Multiple audiences may also be a challenge for movements that attempt to build transnational coalitions and must, therefore, think about how frames might play across different cultural contexts with different discursive opportunity structures. Because framing processes interact with the existing values, identities, cultural knowledge, and emotions in a society, changing the context can change how problems are diagnosed and the solutions that seem most appropriate. Jackie Smith (2002) demonstrates this tension when talking about the transnational human rights movement, which connects groups working in both Global North and Global South countries. These geographic differences are further compounded by economic differences (between, for example, developed and developing societies) and, together, they limit the shared experiences and cultural touchstones that movement actors have in common. As a result, movement groups diverge on both diagnostic and prognostic frames. Smith describes how movement groups from developed, democratic countries tend to diagnose the problem of human rights violations in narrow, legal terms that suggest the best solutions involve sanctioning governments of developing states that violate international standards. But groups from developing countries often see human rights problems from a different lens, influenced by economic dependence and a colonial experience. They argue that human rights violations are connected to global systems of economic and political exploitation that also implicate even democratic and rich states. Building compelling frames across such cultural differences is not impossible by any stretch, but is made more complicated given the divides that such frames need to cross.

Mediating Frames: The Role of Media

Disseminating ideas is another crucial part of framing; once movements have constructed meanings, they must transmit them to others in order to attract support and generate the enthusiasm and commitment needed for success. Some movement organizations have their own internal channels of communication, like magazines or newspapers, that can help ideas flow among members. But to reach a wider audience, especially the all-important group of prospective members, movements rely on media to provide a bridge to the wider world. This is not a new phenomenon. In early modern Europe, the revolutionary technology of the printing press made it possible for activists of various stripes to print their manifestos and share them across the continent at speeds much faster than had been possible and at a fraction of the cost (Eistenstein 1979; Anderson 2016). Subsequent advances further accelerated and intensified the speed and reach of transmission, making media a crucial element in movement strategy. Vincent Roscigno and William Danaher (2001) found, for example, that in the 1920s and 1930s, labor action against textile factories in the southern United States was more likely to take place in areas close to radio stations – radio stations that were pivotal in building worker solidarity, disseminating information about working conditions, and increasing awareness of opportunities for collective action.

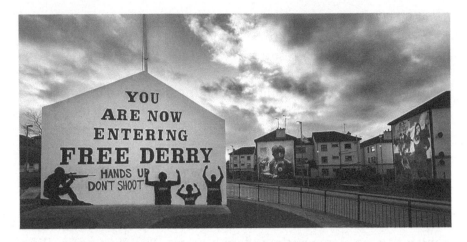

Photo credit: Giuseppe Milo, https://www.flickr.com/photos/giuseppemilo (Creative Commons license).

Figure 5.3 *Black Lives Matter slogan in Northern Ireland*

Once movements release these messages into the world, they have the potential to spread rapidly and widely, especially if they resonate with people. In some cases, the frames spread much further than the movement might have initially expected. The slogan "hands up, don't shoot," which was closely linked to the Black Lives Matter movement, for example, has been invoked by sympathizers far away from the original context. It even cropped up in Northern Ireland, where it was superimposed on a well-known nationalist mural, not only signaling solidarity, but also inviting people to draw parallels between the institutionalized discrimination experienced by African Americans and the historical experience of Catholics in Northern Ireland (figure 5.3)

Though movements can reach more people by using mass media to transmit frames, doing so has consequences. Media have their own framing processes that interact with movement-generated frames in ways that movements cannot entirely control or predict. These media frames, which provide audiences with a central idea or frame of reference, give context and meaning to news stories. Audiences, in turn, rely on media frames to understand issues and make judgments about how important a story or controversy is, who the responsible actors are, who the potential victims are, how to classify events, and how stories relate to broader social patterns or trends (Gamson and Modigliani 1989; Scheufele 1999; Price et al. 2005). While audiences are free to reject media frames based on their own emotional responses and pre-existing values or beliefs (Hull 2001), the way in which media choose to portray a movement's goals or claims can be highly consequential for how the public perceives and feels about them. It can also affect a movement's ability to recruit and mobilize supporters; if media frames reinforce movement frames, it can help the movement, but if movement and media frames diverge, movements can lose support (Cooper 2002).

Media can frame movement ideas and goals in a number of ways. They can select images to highlight particular aspects of a movement or portray its members in particular ways that can elicit sympathy or suspicion from an audience. The choice to label movement activists as "protestors" or "rioters," for example, invites the audience to draw different conclusions about activists' motives and the legitimacy of their claims. Shanto Iyengar (1991) further argues that media can frame movement events as individual occurrences or as part of a larger picture. The former strategy, known as episodic framing, tends to emphasize the distinctive elements about each incident while the latter, known as thematic framing, tends to place issues in a larger political or social context. Iyengar found that when media select episodic frames to depict social issues or movement grievances, the viewing public tends to attribute blame for those problems to the individuals themselves, but when those same events are thematically framed, the audience attributes blame to the government or some external source. Episodically framed stories about living in poverty, for example, are often understood to stem from the choices those individuals made themselves: not working hard enough, or dropping out of school. But when poverty is framed thematically, focusing on things like national poverty rates or unemployment trends, audiences fault government policy. Iyengar notes that episodic frames are far more common, which can make it harder for movements to portray their grievances as widespread, collective, or common.

As in movements, media framing choices are influenced by a number of factors, including social norms and values, their own organizational ideology and culture, available resources, journalistic practices, and the political orientation of the journalists themselves (Scheufele 1999). Moreover, most mass media outlets must also keep in mind how their coverage affects circulation or viewer numbers. Since media groups tend to be for-profit entities, they are more likely to base their coverage on what they think is newsworthy, which often translates into an emphasis on the sensational, the lurid, or the dramatic (Tarrow 2011: 149). Choices to depict rowdy protestors as "rioters," for example, are more likely to grab attention and therefore drive sales.

Comparing Media Platforms: Television, Print, and Internet

Although all forms of media affect the way in which movements are able to transmit their message, they do not exert equivalent effects. Platforms like television, print media, and the internet are all common ways for the general public to receive news and information about the world, but each of these differs considerably when it comes to their costliness, their ability to reach broad audiences, the extent to which they simplify content, and how personalized that content can be. These differences, in turn, shape how easily movements can communicate with potential supporters and how much control they can exert over their message.

Media cost is certainly a concern for movements, which usually operate under varying degrees of resource constraint. Television, for example, requires far more specialized equipment and access to broadcast frequencies. As a result, television offers more limited access, with broadcasting companies acting as gatekeepers for content. Movements that have access to community television (where such options exist) might be able to circumvent this control, though such channels tend to have limited viewership and impact. The accessibility and cost of television are likely to be more of a problem in developing countries, as well as authoritarian ones that limit access as a matter of course. Print media are less costly, especially with the proliferation of computers, printers, and desktop publishing. Movements can more easily publish newspapers or magazines, though getting coverage in non-movement print media – important for drawing in new supporters – is harder. Gatekeeping occurs here too, as journalists and editorial boards make decisions about what stories to cover and how to portray events.

Online platforms, including social media and blogs, are comparatively cheap by comparison. Movements that have access to a computer and a connection to the internet can disseminate ideas with far fewer gatekeepers. Reaching a non-movement audience can still be a problem, but without the cost of materials (e.g., newsprint, ink, postage), content can be disseminated more broadly without increasing expenditure. For these reasons, the internet can function as a counter-hegemonic space that allows for a wider range of voices to be heard (Haas 2005: 388–9; El-Nawaway and Kamis 2013: 34). As a result, it has the potential to give movements the most control over how their frames will be transmitted and provides the fewest opportunities for non-movement actors to intervene and distort those messages. The speed at which online information can be updated, moreover, allows movements to fact-check mass media sources more easily and, when necessary, quickly present correctives to stories that might misrepresent movement claims and beliefs (Drezner and Farrell 2004: 35).

Audience reach is also a consideration for movements hoping to disseminate their message as broadly as possible. All three media platforms have the potential to reach mass audiences, though they do not always do so. The Pew Research Center calculates that, in the United States, 57% of adults often get their news from television; 38% often look to online sources; and only 20% read print media.[1] This pattern had strong generational effects, however; younger people consult "traditional" media sources far less often than those over 50 years who are nearly three times more likely to watch television news and about five times more likely to read a print newspaper than cohorts between 18 and 29 years. This young cohort, however, is the most likely to turn to online sources for news; nearly 50% consult internet sites – nearly double the rate of those over the age of 50 (Mitchell et al. 2016). Around the world, television is notably dominant as a primary news source, as table 5.2 underscores. These results are not disaggregated by age cohort; it is likely that, just as in the United States, younger cohorts use online sources more often. Moreover, the lower numbers for online sources do not mean that most people never turn to the internet for news – only that they did not indicate it as a primary or secondary source. Still, the data are suggestive: in many countries, particularly in the developing world or in autocratic societies, online news is more restricted. As a result, the internet is less likely to yield a broad audience (El-Nawaway and Kamis 2013; Hindman 2008), though the greater reliance on television and newspapers outside highly developed democracies makes it harder for movements to present their frames without encountering media gatekeepers and channeling their messages and ideas through media filters.

---

1 Numbers exceed 100% because respondents could select multiple options.

Table 5.2 Comparing audience reach of different media platforms *(Percentage of respondents who cite each format as their first or second source for news)*

	TV	Print	Online		TV	Print	Online
Argentina	90	37	10	Kuwait	89	63	18
Bangladesh	89	46	1	Lebanon	96	40	14
Bolivia	90	21	6	Malaysia	97	63	9
Brazil	92	51	16	Mali	93	15	6
Britain	83	58	21	Mexico	90	30	4
Bulgaria	96	52	12	Morocco	95	20	4
Chile	88	18	7	Nigeria	77	35	2
China	96	63	9	Pakistan	71	41	1
Côte d'Ivoire	90	36	13	Peru	87	43	10
Czech Republic	82	47	34	Poland	92	45	15
Egypt	87	32	6	Russia	95	51	6
Ethiopia	65	25	5	S. Africa	86	49	3
France	81	53	25	S. Korea	87	47	42
Germany	84	62	19	Senegal	84	17	5
Ghana	73	16	1	Slovakia	90	45	27
India	95	75	2	Spain	88	57	12
Indonesia	99	40	1	Sweden	84	66	25
Israel	80	45	26	Tanzania	44	37	0
Italy	95	53	10	Turkey	97	49	5
Japan	93	75	20	Uganda	12	45	2
Jordan	96	38	9	Ukraine	96	30	6
Kenya	43	41	1	Venezuela	97	73	9
Overall average	*85*	*44*	*11*				
Average, LIC	*58*	*35*	*3*	*Average, F*	*87*	*48*	*16*
Average, MIC	*87*	*34*	*4*	*Average, PF*	*85*	*40*	*6*
Average, HIC	*90*	*50*	*15*	*Average, NF*	*75*	*42*	*6*

Source: Pew Research Center 2007. LIC = low-income country; MIC = middle-income country; HIC = high-income country; F = free; PF = partly free; NF =not free. Income rankings from US Agency for International Development. Freedom rankings from Freedom House.

Media platforms also affect the degree to which movement messages are compressed or simplified before transmission. Television tends to compress messages the most, not only because the time required to delve into nuances may not be available on news programs, but also because it is a highly visual medium (Gamson and Wolfsfeld 1993). Complex messages become reduced to images, and such images can both obscure subtleties of argument and, in their ability to evoke strong emotional reactions from viewers, overwhelm facts (Wischmann 1987: 70; Tarrow 2011). Because they are able to expand on arguments and go into greater depth about activists' position, print media are better equipped to reflect movement frames. Their reliance on the written word over images might make it harder for movements to elicit a visceral, emotional response from an audience, but audience members can learn more about the movement's goals. Online sources combine both the visual strengths of television (e.g., through photographs and streaming video) and the textual depth of newspapers. This makes it possible for movements to both evoke strong emotions from an audience via the dramatic power of images and provide sufficient information to contextualize and explain those images. In this way, the internet has the ability to deliver movement frames without requiring a compromise between nuance and simplicity or emotion and cognition.

Finally, media channels also differ with respect to the degree of personalized content they can deliver. For movements that want to target specific appeals or arouse particular emotions in some audience segments and not others, the ability to personalize communication is an asset. In particular, personalization is helpful for frame alignment processes since some potential members will need only bridging to be mobilized, while others may require more extensive persuasion. Television is highly impersonal in its content. Broadcast media are transmitted to an undifferentiated audience and everyone watching a particular channel sees the same content. Print media can be more specialized. Major daily newspapers, for example, sometimes have regional editions that provide greater coverage of issues germane to a specific area. Online platforms have the greatest potential for personalization since duplicating information and tweaking it for different audiences can be done at relatively low cost. Online communications can also be carried out via both person-to-person and individual-to-masses transmission (Warnick 2007:8), which allows a combination of scale efficiencies as well as customization.

Online Platforms: The Future of Movement Messaging?

Given the ways in which different media platforms affect how movements might communicate with current and potential supporters, it might seem reasonable to conclude that the internet is, overall, the most advantageous channel by which movements can transmit their message to the public. It has low barriers to entry, permits movements to construct frames that are less likely to be altered by other organizations or individuals, and balances the demands of emotion and cognition, personalization and efficiency. It suffers by comparison in terms of audience reach, but with growing access to the internet (Poushter 2016), this may be a temporary limitation. Indeed, the internet has been hailed as a very useful tool for movements hoping to draw attention to their work for many such reasons. Lincoln Dahlberg (2007) argues, for example, that because the internet is low-cost, it allows politically marginalized groups to challenge centers of power more easily and create alternative discursive spaces that are more conducive than the ones in the regular public sphere. Similarly, AbdouMaliq Simone (2006) describes internet platforms as making it possible to form and spread ideas that run counter to dominant narratives without the support of the mass press; over time, such anti-hegemonic notions can even creep into popular consciousness and help to create new opportunities for the movement. This ability to open up discursive space for new and challenging ideas is particularly important in authoritarian societies that more tightly control who can make demands and what they can say. Although internet access in such societies tends to be more limited compared to democracies, such spaces can still promote freer exchange than alternative platforms (Coleman 2005; El-Nawaway and Kamis 2013).

During the Arab Spring uprisings in 2011, such ideas seemed to be validated. In these tightly controlled societies, none of which was open and democratic, there was limited room for dissenting opinions in the mainstream mass media. Freedom House ranked press freedom in this region particularly poorly; in 2010, the countries that were to experience sustained citizen mobilization one year later had an average press freedom score of 71 (out of 100, with 1 being the most free); press freedom scores in the European Union, by contrast, averaged 21 for the same year. In this environment, online forums helped to revitalize a stagnant public sphere and allowed activists to challenge the way governments framed political events (al Malky 2007; El-Nawaway and Kamis 2013). Growing access to the internet also made it an increasingly potent tool; while the proportion of those in Arab countries with access to the internet was still relatively low compared to developed democracies (according to the World Bank, only 29 out of 100 people in the region had access to the internet in 2010, compared to 69 out of 100 in the European Union), that figure had been climbing each year (Howard 2010). Young, highly educated, middle-class, urban-dwelling individuals – precisely the people whose biographical availability makes them prime recruiting targets for movements – had the greatest access (El-Nawaway and Kamis 2013: 60). Moreover, the internet also opened up space for otherwise excluded voices to contribute to discourse. Albrecht Hofheinz (2005: 82) notes, for example, that while mainstream mass media in the Arab world tend to be dominated by men, nearly 50 percent of internet users in the region are women.

Online media, and social media platforms in particular, certainly played a major role in helping movements to spread their message to a broad public, as the photograph in figure 5.4 illustrates. Twitter users in Egypt, for example, sent nearly 1.5 million tweets within the first week of the uprising (Aouragh and Alexander 2011). But more important than the volume of exchange was the content: connected individuals used these forums to discuss current conditions, debate political options, disseminate information, and share videos and pictures (Eltantawy and Wiest 2011). Out of these multiple interactions, grievances were crystallized, prognostic frames formulated, collective identities strengthened, and strong passions aroused. Miriyam Aouragh and Anne Alexander found evidence of these framing processes at work in their interviews with Egyptian activists:

> To have a space, an online space, to write and talk [to] people, to give them messages which will increase their anger, this is my favorite way of online activism. This is the way online activism contributed to the revolution. When you asked people to go and demonstrate against the police, they were ready because you had already provided them with materials which made them angry.
>
> (2011: 1348)

Social media was also a space for activists to engage in motivational framing as well, and to good effect. Christopher Wilson and Alexandra Dunn (2011: 1260) found in their study that of different

Photo credit: Essam Sharaf (Creative Commons license).

Figure 5.4 *Social media and Egyptian protest signs*

mobilizing channels during the Egyptian uprisings, activists rated Facebook and Twitter as most motivating, significantly ahead of print media, radio, television, and even face-to-face contacts. In all of these ways, the internet provided a space for movements to make and share meaning, with not just the individuals they hoped to mobilize but also bystander publics and sympathizers all over the world.

At the same time, the internet poses its own set of problems and constraints for movements hoping to utilize it as an alternative space to make and share meanings. As noted above, the internet's reach is limited, especially in autocratic and developing states. The digital activists in Tunisia's uprising, for example, were primarily affluent and highly educated people living in the capital and surrounding areas. This digital divide can widen the ability of those with resources and status to mobilize in pursuit of contentious claims; those who lack such access, however, have a harder time mounting challenges against authorities, which raises questions about whether internet-aided movement framing democratizes the conversation or narrows it in new ways.

Because online media are relatively costless compared to their physical counterparts, the barriers to entry are few; however, this also can fragment the conversations among activists in ways that encourage divisions among them as opposed to building collective identities. With a proliferation of blogs, Facebook pages, Twitter accounts, and other online spaces where framing conversations take place, it is possible for movement groups to engage *less* with those outside their own immediate network of contacts, which can create echo chambers rather than a productive cross-fertilization of ideas (Coleman 2005: 278; Haas 2005: 389). Moreover, online media have fewer journalistic conventions that govern how information is collected, interpreted, and disseminated. While this opens up space for bottom-up "citizen journalists" to engage in the process of meaning making by sharing their ideas, beliefs, emotions – as well as photos and videos taken with increasingly ubiquitous smart phones – it also potentially makes it harder for audiences to differentiate credible information from red herrings, or to distinguish between those with expertise and experience on a topic and loudmouths with a blog. Fact-checking, which is a standard practice in most credible print and broadcast media outlets, may not occur at all with online media, especially given the speed at which online content is produced and disseminated (Singer 2003: 153). Collectively, this can make it harder for movements to persuade general audiences that their frames are credible.

The epidemic of "fake news" stories that erupted with the 2016 US presidential election, for example, highlights some of the ways in which the internet's speed and lack of conventional gatekeepers can be both a boon and a calamity for movement actors. Stories that have little factual basis can spread quickly via social media postings, and reach thousands of readers in a matter of minutes. In some cases, such stories can effectively rile up a movement's rank-and-file members, fanning their sense of grievance and propelling them to take action. Following the election, stories about individuals being harassed, abused, and attacked for being members of minority communities appeared on many social media sites. While some of these stories were true, not all were; before the fabricated incidents were revealed, however, they generated outrage, calls to protest, and entreaties for donations to anti-hate groups. Fake news can also spread distorted views of social movement actors that can be hard to combat with factual information. One of the most widely disseminated fake news stories of 2016, for example, involved police finding dead bodies with "Black Lives Matter" carved into them – a story that merely cemented perceptions of the movement's tendency to lawlessness and terror among its detractors. Another fake news story purportedly revealed how people protesting the results of the presidential election were being paid to do so, implying that such protests were illegitimate and phony. Even when such stories were fact-checked and shown to be false, the reputational damage had been done (Maheshwari 2016); subsequent protests, in turn, could then be more easily dismissed by opponents as false flag operations orchestrated by corrupt political elites, rather than authentic expressions of public outrage.

Perhaps the most uncertain aspect of the internet for movements that engage in framing work is its vulnerability to surveillance and state coercion. While the internet can seem like an ungoverned space where people can engage more freely in conversation and dissent, governments can still exert considerable influence over it. During the Arab Spring, for example, political blogs critical of the government were frequently censored and their writers arrested (Lim 2013; Ghannam 2011). In countries such as Syria, Yemen, and Saudi Arabia, governments blocked sites to filter content that violated certain political or moral standards. Enterprising activists can sometimes use coded language to avoid such scrutiny, as Chinese dissident bloggers have done by using symbolic speeches and images whose literal meanings allow them to pass Chinese censors intact, but that have subversive hidden and implied meanings (Meng 2011; Tang and Yang 2011), and other scholars argue that the scale of online communications makes it harder for governments to suppress them in the way that they can with broadcast or print sources (Faris 2008). Nonetheless, state surveillance can exert a significant cooling effect on the activists' willingness to engage in risky conversation, let alone take action. Governments still maintain considerable control over communications infrastructure as well, so that when online platforms were implicated as a channel of discontent in Arab Spring uprisings, governments could simply pull the plug, as Egypt did when it shut down nearly all access to the internet and cell-phone service. While analogous forms of surveillance and control exist in print and television as well, the enthusiasm with which online platforms were initially greeted as transformative spaces, offering movements a way to reclaim agency for framing conversations and circumvent channels to avoid more extensive media framing effects, should be somewhat tempered to take into account the more ambiguous ways in which the internet can both facilitate and disrupt the meanings that movements wish to make (Dahlgren 2011).

Concluding Summary

Framing is one of the crucial activities that movement actors perform in order to present various audiences with a coherent idea about why they are engaged in contentious action, why it matters, and why anyone should care. These meanings do not come preformed and fully articulated. Instead, they are constructed and reconstructed continually by movement actors – both elites and rank-and-file members – and affected by the contexts in which they operate, and the beliefs and values of audience members, as well as alternative ways of framing problems and solutions that other allies and adversaries may offer up. Taken together, these shifting inputs and constraints make framing work a dynamic and contingent process. Although frames can miss their mark and have little impact in generating agreement or galvanizing emotion among potential supporters, when movements find frames that resonate, they benefit.

Movements are not the only actors that engage in framing work, however. In disseminating their meanings to the masses, movements must consider the other actors who generate rival meanings, which can include governments and countermovements. Media in particular are relevant to this process since they have their own framing processes and agendas. Some scholars argue that the internet offers a way to circumvent the media's control over the message, though there are additional drawbacks to the internet as well, including new opportunities for the state to monitor and disrupt movement messages. But finding interpretive frames that succeed is only part of the work that movements must do. In addition to making meanings, they must also take action. We turn our attention to strategies and tactics in the next chapter.

Questions for Discussion

1 What role do diagnostic frames, prognostic frames, and motivational frames play in mobilizing potential activists to join social movements? What happens to the mobilization process if any of these frames fails to resonate with their intended audience?

2 What might cause a frame to be misaligned? Why might fixing a misaligned frame be challenging for a social movement organization?

3 How do the media affect a social movement's ability to frame its message? In what ways does this impact vary according to the type of media?

4 Does the internet offer social movements a better way to maintain control of their frames and transmit them to a wider audience? Why or why not?

Additional Readings

Benford, Robert D., and David A. Snow. 2000. "Framing Processes and Social Movements: An Overview and Assessment." *Annual Review of Sociology*, 26: 611–39. Provides a detailed overview of scholarship on framing in social movements.

Scheufele, Dietram A. 1999. "Framing as a Theory of Media Effects." *Journal of Communications*, 49(1): 103–22. A useful introduction to the way in which media can affect the framing processes.

Smith, Jackie. 2002. "Bridging Global Divides? Strategic Framing and Solidarity in Transnational Social Movement Organization." *International Sociology*, 17(4): 505–28. Focuses on the dynamics and challenges of framing in transnational social movements.

CHAPTER 6

The Tactic

Objectives

- To identify the range of tactics that social movements might employ, from contained, routine forms of protest to transgressive and disruptive approaches.
- To recognize the different variables that influence tactical choice, from characteristics of individual protestors, to organizational structures, to environmental conditions.
- To understand the concept of the protest repertoire, how it influences tactical choice, and how it can evolve and change over time.
- To examine how prefigurative politics can be used as a form of social protest.
- To determine the role that online protest plays, both in its ability to complement or transcend physical tactics and in its limitations.

Introduction

It all started with a Twitter hashtag. In 2012, while walking home after purchasing candy at a convenience store, an unarmed black teenager named Trayvon Martin was shot and killed by George Zimmerman. Zimmerman, who pleaded self-defense, was acquitted by a jury in 2013, sparking outrage and a now-famous rallying cry: that black lives matter. Initially launched as a call to action on social media by Alicia Garza, Patrisse Cullors, and Opal Tometi to challenge the ways in which political, social, and economic institutions systematically target black people and deny them their human rights, the movement quickly jumped to physical mobilization and activism after the police shootings of Mike Brown in Ferguson, Missouri, and Eric Garner in New York. The movement quickly spread across the country and around the world, with supportive demonstrations taking place in Australia, South Africa,

Japan, and the United Kingdom, among others. Between July 2013 and March 2016, the hashtags #BlackLivesMatter and #Ferguson were collectively tweeted more than 39 million times, making them the first and third most common Twitter hashtags linked to social movements since the mid 2000s (Sichynsky 2016).

As a movement, it is loosely organized, with a network of local chapters and sympathetic organizations working toward racial justice and addressing how state violence manifests in a number of different policy domains, from prisons to gender. This decentralized and flexible structure has created a fertile laboratory for groups to experiment with a variety of tactics, both creative and conventional, to call attention to their core grievances. Some of these tactics have followed a fairly standard template for social movements: Black Lives Matter (BLM) groups have held rallies in front of government buildings, organized protest marches, and even met with members of Congress to enlist their support for certain legislative reforms. Other tactics display a more theatrical style, like the "die-in" that several dozen ministers held in a cafeteria frequented by many Congressional staffers; the protestors had intended to lie on the floor for 4½ minutes – symbolizing the amount of time that Michael Brown's body lay in the streets after being killed – but after being threatened with arrest, they filed out of the room singing a Civil Rights anthem from the 1960s. Movement supporters have also employed more controversial and confrontational tactics. Activists with Black Lives Matter Cambridge, for example, chained themselves to the Cambridge, Massachusetts city hall for 8 hours to protest the lack of affordable housing before being arrested. Protestors also disrupted campaign events for candidates running for political office, including Maryland Governor Martin O'Malley, Senator Bernie Sanders, and Green Party presidential nominee Jill Stein.

But perhaps the most controversial tactic widely employed by the movement is the roadblock, which has been used to stop traffic on major thoroughfares in cities like Chicago, San Francisco, Atlanta, and even in the UK where, in August 2016, activists obstructed roads leading to Heathrow Airport. In Minnesota, the police shooting of Philando Castille during a routine traffic stop prompted days of protests. On July 9, a contingent of protestors who had been encamped outside the governor's house marched to the nearby interstate highway and halted traffic in both directions for several hours. The standoff between police and protestors turned violent after some demonstrators lobbed fireworks, rocks, and glass bottles at riot police, who returned fire, first using tear gas and non-lethal rounds. By the time the protest ended, over 100 people had been arrested. The public reaction to this and similar protests around the country ranged from confusion to outrage; some self-identified sympathizers wondered whether such tactics did more harm to the cause than good, warning BLM activists that disrupting traffic and inconveniencing people would alienate the public. Others were less judicious in their responses, denouncing the traffic disrupters as criminals, and even threatening to drive over protestors with their cars. Public figures ranging from Atlanta Mayor Kasim Reed to former Arkansas Governor and presidential hopeful Mike Huckabee to television personality Oprah Winfrey contrasted such tactics to those used by the Civil Rights movement several decades earlier and suggested that leaders like Martin Luther King, Jr., would never have used such disruptive methods.

Amid the negative response from many members of the public to such roadblocks, activists and scholars have tried to provide historical context and strategic justification for this approach. Although it currently has a strong association with the BLM movement, it is hardly a new tactic. Traffic was obstructed during the 1965 Civil Rights march – led by Dr. King – from Selma, Alabama to the state capital in Montgomery. In 1989, AIDS activists shut down the Golden Gate Bridge in San Francisco, and, 2 years later, anti-war protestors blocked the city's Bay Bridge. Nor is it a tactic that only US movements have used. Zo Artzeinu, a right-wing nationalist group in Israel, used roadblocks as a way to protest the Oslo peace process in the early 1990s (Shindler 2013: 261), and the same tactic has been used by protestors in Brazil, India, Kyrgyzstan, Cambodia, Nigeria, and elsewhere. In all cases, the roadblock was used intentionally to cause disruption and shock people by upsetting routines. The anger of delayed motorists is not an unfortunate side-effect that could ideally be avoided – it is the point of such tactics. Martin Luther King, Jr., suggested this logic in his famous "Letter from a Birmingham Jail" when he argues that occupation, blockade, and other forms of direct action attempt to "create such a crisis and foster such a tension that a community which has constantly refused to negotiate is forced to confront the issue." BLM activists point out that by disrupting highways – the figurative arteries that sustain urban areas – they can create exactly this kind of vital tension in a way that polite protests cannot do. Along the way, by engaging in high-risk activities such as highway blockages, given the threat of bodily harm that comes from stepping out in front of speeding cars, activists also signal their commitment and seriousness of purpose.

The debate around the BLM movement's use of highway road-blocks throws the question of tactical choice into sharp relief: what should movements do to advance their goals? What are the different factors that influence their choices and how do they weigh their own values, ideologies and appetite for risk, bystander reactions, and other potential inputs when selecting from the range of possible activities that they could use? Tactical choice, as this example suggests, is not a straightforward one; tactics that are symbolically meaningful may not have as much strategic value, and tactics that might be strategically effective may not be practical given the costs and constraints that movement actors face. Tactical selection, in other words, is both highly consequential for movement success and hardly clear-cut.

A Typology of Tactics

Social movements use a range of tactics to accomplish their goals, and tend not to rely on just one method of action. Tactics include those that take advantage of institutional channels as well as more unconventional methods located in non-institutional spaces. Most discussions of movement tactics, however, focus on the non-institutional side, both because movements were historically considered "outsiders" that were limited to non-institutional forms of action, and because such tactics are less routinized and predictable. Lobbying, for example, is often governed by legislation that specifies what types of activities are or are not permitted. In the United States, federal lobbying is governed by the Lobbying Disclosure Act of 1995, which sets out rules around registration and filing quarterly reports with the government; failure to comply carries financial penalties, which encourages organizations to adhere to stated rules. Non-institutional approaches, on the other hand, are more flexible and fluid; their rules are not as formalized and are bound by fewer constraints, which makes it easier for movements to improvise and reinvent tactics as circumstances require. Moreover, while there are relatively few distinctive institutional techniques available to influence policymakers, non-institutional tactics run the gamut from rallies and demonstrations to hunger-strikes, self-immolation, sabotage, and even terrorist attacks, making the choices and trade-offs that movements must consider more complex.

Such non-institutional tactics tend to share some common features, regardless of the specifics that are involved. They are meant to be public: visible to their targets, their supporters, and the larger audience from which future supporters might be recruited. As such, social movement tactics can be understood as performances that are both instrumental, insofar as they are intended to bring about a desired outcome, and expressive, in how they communicate participants' identities, values, and emotions (Taylor et al. 2005; Tilly 2008). Social movements can use tactics to educate as well as to inspire strong emotions like outrage and shock, love and hope. Tactics also have multiple meanings, including the direct message being sent to targets and larger symbolic statements aimed at a broader audience (Ennis 1987: 523). In Iceland, for example, thousands of women left their workplaces at 2:38 p.m. on October 24, 2016, to protest gender-based wage gaps. The action targeted employers, putting direct economic pressure on them to equalize pay between men and women. But the symbolism also mattered: the pay gap meant that, in an 8-hour work day, women were basically working for free after 2:38 p.m. Moreover, the day of the protest also held symbolic meaning: 41 years before, nearly 90 percent of the women in Iceland protested their lack of political and economic power by "taking the day off" – not going to their jobs, attending school, minding children, or taking care of household work – a protest that led to widespread reforms that helped to close the gender gap in politics and started the move toward more equal pay.

Contained, Disruptive, and Violent Tactical Forms

Three specific groups of tactics exist within the broad category of non-institutional strategies: contained, disruptive, and violent (Tarrow 2011: 99). Of these, contained tactics include protest forms that have become fairly conventional and that are often legally protected forms of speech and assembly in most democracies. Peaceful marches, demonstrations, rallies, and consumer boycotts would all be typical examples. Disruptive tactics include many forms of non-violent direct action, some of which may skirt (or cross) the edges of lawfulness. Some of these forms are also familiar and may include sit-ins, tent cities, roadblocks, barricades, and civil disobedience.

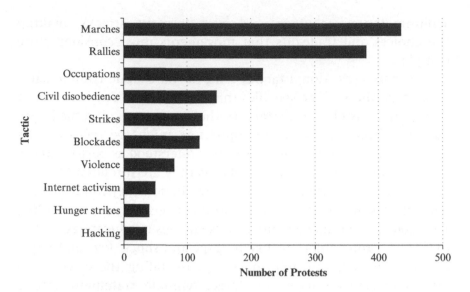

Source: Ortiz et al. 2013.

Figure 6.1   *Selected protest tactics worldwide, 2006–2013*

Disruption is the strategy that the Standing Rock Sioux have employed in their physical obstruction of the Dakota Access oil pipeline being built across their tribal lands and why the residents of Ganjeong village on South Korea's Jeju Island staged sit-ins to delay the construction of a nearby naval base. Violent tactics are the most extreme, are almost always illegal, and include actions targeting property, infrastructure, or other individuals. Contained tactical forms can be contrasted with the idea of transgressive tactics, which include violence and may include some disruptive tactics, depending on their level of social acceptance and familiarity.

The frequency with which these tactics are used varies. Using protest event analysis – a research method described in more detail in this chapter's methods spotlight – Isabella Ortiz and her collaborators studied the details of 843 protest events around the world between 2006 and 2013. They found that marches and political assemblies – classic examples of contained forms of protest – were the most common around the world, with other forms, including both disruptive and violent tactics, used less often (figure 6.1). Although they included more tactics in their assessment than just the ones listed in the figure, these were some of the more common; by contrast, tactics like street theater, self-inflicted violence (e.g., self-immolation), and religious processionals represented fewer than 25 cases apiece in the dataset. They also note that the geographic dispersion of these tactics varies: while marches took place nearly everywhere there were protests, they comprise a higher percentage (73 percent) of protest events in East Asia and the Pacific compared to other regions; rallies and assemblies, by contrast, were proportionally more important in sub-Saharan Africa, found in 71 percent of protests there compared to only 54 percent in South Asia (Ortiz et al. 2013: 32). This suggests that there might be some connection between tactical choice and where social movements are located – an idea explored at greater length later in this chapter.

Although contained tactics are the most common, this does not necessarily mean that they are the most effective. In fact, scholars disagree about which category is likely to yield the most success. Sidney Tarrow (2011: 99) argues that non-violent disruption is a social movement's strongest weapon "because disruption spreads uncertainty and gives weak actors leverage against powerful opponents." Frances Fox Piven and Richard Cloward (1974: 85; 1977) similarly argue that disruptive tactics such as sit-ins, rent strikes, and traffic blockages can effect change by causing "commotion among bureaucrats, excitement in the media, dismay among influential segments of the community, and strain for political leaders." They caution that movements seeking to make incremental change led by strong and highly developed movement organizations will risk becoming mired in bureaucracy and lose the disruptive energy that gives protest its power. At the same time, Tarrow (2011) cautions that disruptive forms of protest are difficult to sustain over time, given the relative cost and time-intensiveness of such tactics. Over time, movements that primarily rely on disruption will move toward more routinized, contained forms of protest; alternatively, they can also radicalize into violence if cost and time pressures induce enough members to exit the movement, leaving behind only the hard-core true believers and militants.

Other scholars argue that contained tactics are precisely the ones that are most likely to be successful because they make it easier for sympathetic elites to work with movements and deliver change (Rojas 2006). Disruption, on the other hand, makes it harder for elites to justify bargaining, and denies them the necessary political cover to make compromises that might be unpopular with some of their constituents. According to this logic, BLM's use of highway blockades makes it less likely that officials will want to negotiate with them because such tactics play poorly with the public (Huff

Methods Spotlight: Protest Event Analysis

Protest event analysis is an increasingly popular tool among scholars who study social movements. It draws on data that capture protest events and allow researchers to ask questions about how often protest happens, how long it lasts, how large it is, where it tends to be located, its targets, the tactics used, the responses of the government, and other features (Koopmans and Rucht 2002). These protest events are captured, described, and sometimes quantified by newspaper reports, police blotters, court documents, and other official organs that compile information about public events and occurrences. From these reports, researchers can construct records of protests and their characteristics in ways that allow them to measure patterns and trends across space and time.

Imagine if we were interested in understanding the relationship between protest size and likelihood of violence breaking out during an event. Protest event analysis might be a useful tool for uncovering such correlations. Using newspaper data, we could compile a dataset of protest events over a specific period of time. For each reference to a protest, we could read the relevant news coverage – supplemented perhaps by other official sources, such as police reports – to collect information about relevant variables of interest: the estimated size of the crowd, whether violence occurred, and, if so, how widespread or intense it was. We could also record other variables that might alternatively explain outbreaks in violence: whether the police used repressive measures toward protestors, whether the protestors were members of formal organizations or relatively decentralized groups, how long the protest lasted, who the target was, and so forth. Once we collected sufficient data, we could then analyze these variables using statistical methods to find correlations among them.

Protest event analysis provides a very useful method for examining protest data, but there are some important caveats to keep in mind. One of the most crucial limitations to this method is that it relies heavily on newspapers and other public records documenting and describing protests that take place. While that might make sense for very large protests, not all protest events get covered, and even those that are may not be described in sufficient detail to meet a researcher's needs (Koopmans and Rucht 2002; Hutter 2014). Newspapers, as chapter 5 highlighted, engage in their own framing work, and their frames (and editorial biases) can lead them to cover certain movements exhaustively while ignoring others entirely. Moreover, characteristics of the protest event or of the movement's main issue can also limit media attention; large, violent protests are more likely to generate coverage, as are issues that are seen as topical and of general interest (Hutter 2014). As a result, researchers may need to draw on multiple news sources rather than relying on the main national newspapers, or to supplement them with other official sources. Still, one of the consequences of this data limitation is that this method may not be appropriate for capturing details about lesser-known or marginal movements; if they are unable to win column inches in a newspaper, they may prove to be difficult to study using this technique.

Explore this Method
Protest event analysis can generate interesting findings about patterns and characteristics of protest, both over time and across space. The National Study of Protest
Events, housed at the University of Notre Dame (http://nspe.nd.edu/index.html) has
a useful visualization tool that allows visitors to see how different protest variables
fit on a map of the United States, and includes clustering of protest by issue type, by
tactic type, and by protest target, among other criteria. A number of other entities
collect event data that can be accessed for your own analysis. The Robert S. Strauss
Center at the University of Texas, Austin, collects protest, strike, and conflict data for
Africa and Latin America (https://www.strausscenter.org/scad.html – requires free
registration). The University of Denver has a protest event dataset on nonviolent and
violent campaigns and outcomes across multiple decades (www.du.edu/korbel/sie/
research/chenow_navco_data.html). The University of Kansas similarly hosts protest
event data for various European countries (http://web.ku.edu/~ronfrand/data). For
those not put off by big data (really, really big data), the GDELT Project culls information about world events from newspapers in over 100 languages and covering
nearly all countries (www.gdeltproject.org/data.html#intro). The GDELT dataset,
which is free, covers over 30 years of news coverage. It requires some patience to
work with (and some technological savvy), but the resources are enormous. There
are many other datasets covering protest events available online. A quick search
will yield dozens more, though some of them can only be opened by a statistical
program like Stata or SPSS.

and Kruszewska 2016). According to this logic, bargaining with
protestors under these conditions can make officials feel weak, and
granting concessions will seem akin to capitulation, which they
will try to avoid. Instead, non-disruptive, contained protest is more
likely to help to persuade officials and the public to act by appealing to their moral principles and demonstrating the movement's
worthiness (della Porta and Diani 1999).

Still other scholars argue that neither disruption nor contained
protest can be as successful as violent protest, which draws more
attention to the protestors and imposes more costs on the target
(Gamson 1990). According to this logic, violence raises the costs
of non-compliance with the movement's demand so high that
any policy concession will seem appealing by comparison. While
not all violent acts of protest are equally coordinated and damaging (Tilly 2003), the idea that, by inflicting sufficient pain, movements can coerce concessions is widespread among groups that
embrace violence or use terrorist acts (Kydd and Walter 2006),
though this approach often fails to produce the desired effect from
governments.

Choosing Tactics

There is, ultimately, no single category of tactic that is best across the board; given the right conditions and contexts, contained, disruptive, or violent approaches can yield positive outcomes or no outcomes at all. Moreover, within each category, there are numerous tactics that are possible. Given this diversity of tactical form, movement organizations and actors must decide how to select the tactics that best suit their needs.

James Ennis (1987) suggests that movement groups weigh both internal considerations and external constraints when assessing their tactical options, including organizational goals, resources, contexts, and more.

Organizational Goals

One way movement groups can start to parse the many tactics that are possible is to clarify what kind of goals they are seeking to advance with their choice, and the mechanisms by which they believe those goals might best be achieved (Bernstein 2003). Groups might want to influence the content of legislation, or influence public opinion, or shame actors into changing their behavior. Some movement members may also value opportunities for personal transformation. Such goals are not isomorphic and point to different kinds of approaches. Groups seeking to weigh in on the content of legislation, for example, are more likely to opt for institutional forms of action, which make it easier to help to shape legislative agendas, persuade lawmakers, share expertise, and be seen as credible partners in the legislative process (Staggenborg 1988; King et al. 2005).

The mechanisms of influence for educating the public or swaying public opinion are different, and might push groups to prioritize tactics that involve more eye-catching and memorable displays to grab the public's attention and interest. The satirical activist troupe The Yes Men, for example, protested Royal Dutch Shell's plan to drill for oil in the Arctic by setting up a booth outside the company's offices in New York and, pretending to be company representatives, handing out free snow cones to passers-by on a hot day. Many people took them up on the offer but were then taken aback when told that the snow cones were made with a chuck of the last iceberg in existence so that people could have "a first taste of the last frontier." Upset people condemned the company and expressed anger at its nonchalant exploitation of nature – only to find out that the whole thing was a stunt. But, by then, The Yes Men had made their point, and got people talking about the company's proposals for the Arctic.

Alternatively, groups that want to put pressure on a chosen target might opt for tactics that mobilize shame, inflict pain, or are otherwise costly. Clothing manufacturer Fruit of the Loom was on the receiving end of such an approach after it closed one of its Honduran factories after a successful unionization drive. In response, United Students against Sweatshops organized a boycott of the company's products that eventually spread to over 100 colleges and universities in the US and UK, costing Fruit of the Loom some $50 million in lost revenue. Eventually, the company caved in and rehired all its Honduran workers and restored full union rights. Pain and pressure can be inflicted via contained, disruptive, and violent tactical forms, which vary in the severity, extent, or type of costs that movements can inflict. Dan J. Wang and Alessandro Piazza (2016) posit that groups pursuing goals that resonate across multiple populations will opt for disruptive tactical forms, while groups that target the government will be more likely to exert pressure using more contained forms. Only those groups with relatively narrow claims that draw support from a limited sector of the public will be attracted to violence because they will be least affected by the potential reputational costs of using such tactics (Giugni 1999).

Movements wanting to employ tactics that encourage processes of self-transformation, by contrast, may prioritize activities that foster a sense of community, allow for participants to experience particular emotions, articulate aspects of their individual and collective identities, and practice different ways of living, working, and being in the world. Many tactics can build a sense of community or generate intense emotions – even violence can have this effect insofar as individuals who use risky tactics can feel tightly bonded with others who are also willing to employ such methods. But movements may also look to additional approaches such as festivals, street parties, or the production of art and music, to strengthen bonds and create space for personal expression. Drag shows and gay pride events, for example, are opportunities to build solidarity and express identity in ways that also heighten positive attachments to the LGBT movement (Britt and Heise 2000; Taylor et al. 2005).

Two caveats should be noted with respect to this idea that tactical choice is conditioned by movement goals. First, movements can and do hold multiple goals simultaneously. And second, tactics can further multiple goals at the same time. As such, the notion that tactical choice is simply a product of the mechanisms by which movements hope to affect change is overly reductive. Moreover, as Jeffrey Juris (2008) notes, sometimes tactics can have contradictory effects, advancing a movement's agenda in one dimension (e.g., strengthening solidarity among activists) while simultaneously undercutting it in some either area (e.g., undermining public support). Tactics, therefore, reflect movement goals, but are not wholly determined by them.

Individual and Organizational Attributes

In addition to movement goals, tactical choice is conditioned by practical considerations, such as the resources required to successfully execute particular strategies (Barkan 1979). Sometimes this expenditure is relatively small – organizing a petition drive, for example, might require only a handful of activists, some paper, and pens. An online petition, by contrast, requires access to the internet and a computer. Tactics like public demonstrations require considerably more investment by groups. A protest march may involve spreading the word among supporters to draw a critical mass of people; filing necessary permits for the gathering; printing banners, signs, T-shirts, and other signals of unity; and arranging for necessary logistical support, from transportation to sanitary facilities. Strikes might involve setting up and managing a strike fund to offset workers' lost wages. Civil disobedience might entail intensive training sessions to teach participants how to resist arrest peacefully and providing legal support to those individuals thrown in jail.

In addition to resources, tactics also require dissimilar organizational structures and members to possess different skills and aptitudes. Little specialized knowledge is required to engage in a sit-in, but groups that want to participate in lobbying or other institutional tactics must have some awareness of established procedures and the professional staff to initiate and nurture contacts with other political stakeholders. Stable, bureaucratic movement organizations that encourage specialized roles, therefore, are more likely to use – and be successful at – tactics that require a base level of expertise and continuity of action (Staggenborg 1988). By contrast, groups that hope to use more transgressive methods, like terrorism or sabotage, require their members to have entirely different skills, and tend to embed those activists in organizational structures that are more decentralized to avoid detection and repression (Dishman 2005; Enders and Su 2007). Participants must also invest personal time and assume some amount of risk to implement tactics. Again, time and risk are variable, ranging from brief, low-risk activities, such as attending a street festival or signing an online petition, to activities that are perilous and require considerable effort over a period of time, such as a hunger strike or civil disobedience. Not all groups cultivate the necessary solidarity and trust among members to carry off some high-risk and time-intensive tactics. As a result, tactics must also be calibrated to appeal to movement members and match their likely level of commitment and appetite for risk – factors that can be shaped via movement culture, but also are influenced by personal biographical availability, values, and beliefs.

In weighing these different factors, organizations may find that tactical choice can pose a number of dilemmas. If movements want to select tactics that demonstrate what Charles Tilly (2006) terms "WUNC" (worthiness, unity, numbers, commitment), they may discover that certain tactics maximize one quality at the expense of another. Risky tactics, for example, can signal commitment, since only the most dedicated activists will put their bodies on the line to protest in the face of threat or danger. Such tactics are effective ways to demonstrate seriousness of purpose since issuing a costly signal indicates that the individual or group is unlikely to be bluffing (Morrow 1999). But many potential activists will be turned off by risky tactics, which can depress the number of people who engage in such protest. Low-risk activism, on the other hand, may appeal to a broader public, but low risk can signal low levels of commitment or unity, and, in turn, deliver low payoffs (Jasper 2010a: 97). These are some of the trade-offs that movements may encounter when trying to select tactics that match their organizational strengths, appeal to their supporters, and also demonstrate the types of qualities that might induce their targets to take them seriously.

Regimes, Development, and Opportunity Structures

In addition to goals and organizational attributes, movements must also select tactics that are appropriate for the particular context in which they are located. Because tactics are not employed in a vacuum, how a movement behaves can be affected by movement actors' perception of the prevailing political opportunity structure they face (Eisinger 1973; D. Meyer 2004; M. Meyer 2004; Tarrow 2011). Open political opportunity structures, in which movements may have elite allies or easier institutional access, might make more conventional or contained tactics more appealing. When such avenues are available to citizens, then risky or high-cost methods of protest will seem less worthwhile and will generate fewer takers. Closed political opportunity structures, on the other hand, might make disruptive or violent tactics seem like better bets because contained politics and institutional approaches may get little traction with political elites or other targets.

Tactics mean different things in different places. Even the distinction between contained, disruptive, and violent is not objective but conditioned by environment. In Cuba, the Damas de Blanco (Ladies in White), who protest the government's human rights abuses, demonstrate every Sunday by attending Mass and then marching silently through the streets of Havana dressed from head to toe in white to symbolize peace. The group adheres to an ethic of non-violence, despite being targeted for harassment by the government, which claims they are a subversive group financed by the United States to sow discord in the country, and has sent security forces to beat and arrest participants as well as to organize counter-demonstrations. In the authoritarian environment of Cuba, this peaceful assembly is anything but contained and conventional; it reads as disruptive and threatening. The same type of protest 250 miles to the north would likely be considered unremarkable and routine in the democratic environs of the United States.

This distinction between protest in authoritarian Cuba and in the democratic US underscores a larger point about how social movements are affected by the locations in which they are embedded – not just by political context, but by economic conditions, cultural norms, and historical memories. Politically, movements tend to have considerably more latitude for action in democratic societies compared to authoritarian ones, which not only offer far more limited space in the public sphere for civil society actors in general, but are more likely to repress those actors that challenge their rule. Not all authoritarian states have equal capacity to repress or enforce their authority (Tilly 1996; Johnston 2011), but, absent a mechanism for citizens to express their displeasure at what the government does, authoritarian states are more likely to resort to repression more willingly than democratic ones in which officials have to face the wrath of voters.

This distinction makes protest of all sorts much more likely in democratic societies than in authoritarian ones. Not only do such societies have a norm of citizens making demands on the state and other actors, but the risks of doing so are less. Michael Bratton and Nicholas van de Walle (1997) find, for example, that democratic societies in Africa experienced comparatively more urban protest than their autocratic neighbors, a finding replicated by other scholars for other movement types, such as ethno-political protest and protest by workers and students (Scarritt et al. 2001), and in non-African contexts (Dalton and van Sickle 2005). But even though democracies experienced *more* protest, Bratton and van de Walle argued that such protest tends to be less violent in form. Part of this difference has to do with government response; autocratic governments are more likely to escalate conflict with movements even if the initial mobilization takes non-violent forms, because small protests can still signal regime weakness to their opponents (Boudreau 2005; Robertson 2009; Kricheli et al. 2011). Once such protests gather steam, there are fewer ways for autocratic governments to channel and manage conflicts, which can lead to relatively quick detours into violence.

As a result of this different environment, movements in repressive regimes consider their tactical choices differently from their democratically situated counterparts. Hank Johnston (2005, 2011) and Carol Mueller (Johnston and Mueller 2001) suggest that movements in autocracies are more likely to test the waters for protest by relying initially on creative, symbolic actions that are relatively brief in duration and that often are couched in coded language to escape regime monitoring. Rita Noonan (1995) found this pattern in her study of women's mobilization in Augusto Pinochet's Chile: unable to make direct complaints about the regime's human rights abuses or repression, the women were able to frame their claims in less contentious forms – invoking ideas of motherhood and domesticity – that masked a more pointed critique of the government. Such tactics can probe the regime's reaction for opportunities to mobilize on a larger scale using more familiar forms of mass protest and contention.

Protests also differ from developing to developed societies and by region of the world, which suggests that economic and cultural factors also can play a role in tactical considerations. Protest certainly

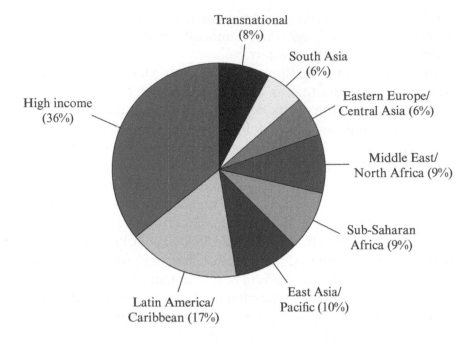

Source: Ortiz et al. 2013.

Figure 6.2 *Protests by region, 2006–2013*

differs in frequency in more developed versus less developed parts of the world, as figure 6.2 highlights. In this chart, all high-income societies[1] are counted together, and all remaining countries (middle- and low-income) in the region are grouped geographically. But, more than that, several authors suggest that protests differ qualitatively too. In less developed countries, grievances tend to focus around threats to physical well-being and crises of consumption – claims that revolve around poverty and deprivation of basic needs such as clean water, access to sanitation, and rising food prices (Noonan 1995: 84; Shigetomi 2009). Such claims, combined with states that are often inefficient, poorly administered, and less accessible to ordinary citizens, make it necessary for movements to focus less on institutionalized forms of protest and more on non-formal methods (Davis 1999; Shigetomi 2009). Moreover, given the urgency of the grievances, contained forms of protest may seem less appropriate than disruption or tactics that put immediate pressure

---

1 Defined by Ortiz et al. (2013) using the World Bank definition of a high-income country: those with a gross national income per capita of $12,476 and above, which includes roughly one-third of World Bank member countries.

on targets to act. Vincent Boudreau (1996) observes that moving in this direction is not without its own dilemmas for movements in less-developed countries; in societies where there may be norms of democratic participation or contained protest, direct action – especially forms that involve seizing land or food – might satisfy members but alienate the middle class and elites, which can limit the movement's influence and reach and, in some cases, trigger a coercive response by those in power. On the other hand, when the grievances involve pressing material needs, such movements may not have the ability to engage in patient protest or persuade their supporters to wait for change, creating what might be a stark choice between issuing "potentially futile calls for reform or potentially disastrous calls to arms" (Boudreau 1996: 184).

Taken together, regime type, developmental level, and political opportunity structure combine in ways that steer movements toward particular tactical combinations, not in any deterministic way, but by making certain forms of action more appealing or viable. In prosperous, open, democratic societies, social movements will be more likely to use institutional forms of action as well as contained forms of non-institutional protest, like demonstrations and marches. In autocratic, closed, and poor societies, social movements will gravitate toward strategies of disruption, violence, even revolution (Boudreau 1996: 183; Tilly 1996). In mixed cases, movement and organizational factors start to play a more influential role: how movement leaders perceive the political opportunities that exist, the extent to which movement organizations respond to democratic decision making or are led by small groups of people, resources, and similar considerations. These mixed cases have the potential for the greatest tactical variety given that there are mixed incentives at work that can conceivably justify a range of strategies.

Protest Repertoires

It is possible to imagine countless tactics that a movement might select, even within the limitations of cost, context, and other factors described above. Yet movements tend to reuse similar tactical forms, both within the same society and across countries. The mass demonstration, for example, can be found in Italy as well as Indonesia; nearly every country in which there is protest has witnessed a protest march or rally. Protestors go on hunger strike in the United States, Turkey, and the Democratic Republic of the Congo.

But other tactical forms are rarely used; the *cacerolazo*, for example, involves people banging on pots and pans to create a hubbub on the streets. Used in certain Latin American countries like Argentina and Chile, it became popular as a low-cost way of voicing discontent: no specialized equipment is needed beyond cookware, yet if sufficient numbers of people take part, the resulting din can be disorienting. Moreover, people can contribute to the clamor by banging on pots and pans while leaning out of the windows of their homes, thus participating without having to physically join a protest march or demonstration – an attribute that made this tactic particularly appealing during protests against repressive Latin American regimes in the 1970s. But movements outside Latin America rarely use the *cacerolazo*. It made a brief appearance in the Quebec student protests of 2012, as well as recent protests in Iceland and Turkey. But apart from these cases, it has not been widely adopted as a tactic by social movements.

This difference between widely used protest forms such as the protest march and more unusual ones like the *cacerolazo* underscores a key point about tactical choice: when activists choose particular tactics, they do not select from the entire universe of theoretically possible options. Even given the limitations of cost, context, and other constraints, movements choose tactics from a relatively small subset of options (Tilly 1995b, 2008). This subset makes up the movement's protest repertoire. In metaphorical terms, if tactics are the tools that a movement uses to accomplish some goal, its repertoire is the toolbox. Only a finite number of tools will fit, so movements must select the most useful tools – the ones that might be most commonly used, or most adaptable to unforeseen circumstances. Tools that may never get used, or that are irrelevant for the circumstances that are likely to arise, will be excluded because space is limited. So it is with tactical repertoires: tactical forms – such as the protest march – that are useful across multiple contexts and lend themselves to different settings and scenarios are part of the repertoire while highly specialized and situation-specific tactics – like the *cacerolazo* – may be excluded.

In the toolbox metaphor, a key selection criterion is usefulness. For protest tactics, a similar principle applies. Tactics that can be deployed across multiple movement types and settings have considerable utility. The *cacerolazo*, by contrast, is not quite so portable. In part, this difference stems from the cultural meanings attached to different forms of protest. Certain tactics are familiar and understood by both protestor and audience. The protest march requires little interpretation for most participants and onlookers, regardless of whether it takes place in Caracas or Copenhagen. The same cannot be said for the *cacerolazo*, which is a familiar and meaningful tactic in some parts of the world, but not others. It is part of a Latin American tactical repertoire, perhaps, but not necessarily part of the repertoire of movements located in the United States or South Korea. Repertoires, therefore, are culturally bounded, or "learned cultural creations" (Tilly 1995a: 42).

Repertoires are also temporally bounded. They can change over time as some tactics lose their cultural significance or power and new ones emerge to take their place. Tarring and feathering or making someone ride backwards on a donkey used to be ways that people in some parts of Europe expressed anger at individuals who had violated some community code, though they have fallen out of use to the point where audiences would have a hard time deciphering what they were witnessing; someone being made to ride backwards on a donkey would not obviously signal "protest" so much as "prank" (or curious performance art) to a modern observer. These kinds of tactics, which were part of the protest repertoire, changed as modern social movements evolved in the late eighteenth century and, with that evolution, created new tactical forms better suited to the national scale, the sustained campaign, the emerging organizational structures, and other features of the new movement landscape (Tilly 1995a, 1995b). Many of these tactics, like the strike, the demonstration, the blockade, or the boycott, are still familiar forms because they are useful and malleable to multiple needs and circumstances.

A movement's protest repertoire is based partly on what resonates, but this idea also presents movements with a potential dilemma. Tactics that are well established, that fit social norms and expectations, and whose meanings and rhythmic beats are understood by all might fit the circumstances, but also risk becoming banal. Protest marches are a fairly familiar sight in most societies, yet such marches can be non-events, failing to arouse much interest from passers-by, let alone authorities or other targets. On the other hand, tactics that are highly innovative can be difficult to pull off if the organization lacks the necessary expertise or skills required (Jasper 2010a: 92). Innovative tactics can also attract a lot of attention, but if movements miscalculate their audience, they can fail to resonate or even potentially alienate onlookers. Violent tactics will generate more attention because they are newsworthy, but could be highly alienating. Movements must therefore navigate a tricky path between appropriateness and novelty: tactics must fit social norms while both challenging them and not overstepping their boundaries.

Not all movement activists accept that tactics must fit social norms and avoid transgression. For members of movements representing historically subordinated groups, including minorities and women, social conventions about what constitutes appropriate behavior and appearance have sharply limited their ability to make contentious claims and be taken seriously. Appropriate behavior, in this instance, means adhering to norms that demonstrate to members of the majority that subordinated groups are capable of acting respectably (Higginbotham 1994). In so doing, such groups would "receive their share of political influence and social standing not because democratic values and law require it, but because they demonstrate their compatibility with the 'mainstream' or non-marginalized class" (Smith 2014).

Individuals who are seen to violate these norms – by wearing the wrong clothes, having the wrong hairstyle, using the wrong words, or behaving in the wrong way – can be dismissed without their demands being addressed. Frederick Harris (2014) gives an example of this type of reasoning from a 2011 speech by Michael Nutter, the Mayor of Philadelphia:

> If you want all of us – black, white, or any other color – if you want us to respect you, if you want us to look at you in a different way, if you want us not to be afraid to walk down the same side of the street with you, if you want folks not to jump out of the elevator when you get on, if you want folks to stop following you around in stores when you're out shopping, if you want somebody to offer you a job or an internship somewhere, if you don't want folks to be looking in or trying to go in a different direction when they see two or twenty of you coming down the street, then stop acting like idiots and fools, out in the streets of the city of Philadelphia.

Those who argue that movement actors must behave in a certain way in order to be taken seriously are usually arguing against disruptive or violent tactical forms, since choosing such strategies, in combination with membership in a subordinated group, can overshadow the actual claims being made.

For opponents of respectability politics, however, such insistence blunts the honest emotional responses of participants and diverts the energies and passions of activists into safe and perhaps toothless channels. For activists who think respectability politics does more to reassure the majority than to help the minority, breaking free of existing repertoires can be desirable, and transgressive tactics can be liberating, even as they are socially polarizing. Many of the BLM tactics can be understood through this lens. Highway roadblocks, while used by other movements in the past, have not become part of the generally accepted repertoire of tactics in the United States; they have been relatively rare and always controversial. Many of the reactions from those opposed to this tactic invoke the idea of respectability: if activists want to be taken seriously, they should not act like hooligans, and that disturbing the routines of others is not what is appropriate for protestors who want to be seen as legitimate and deserving. The response of BLM activists, in turn, echoes the critics. In the words of one protestor who blocked the highway in Saint Paul, "why should I give a damn about your convenience when people in my community are being murdered?"[2] For this activist, breaking free of the repertoire is an advantage, not a mistake.

Emotions, Identity, and Values

While the above discussion has stressed rational and instrumental reasons for picking tactics, ideational factors are also relevant criteria to consider. Movement participants can also favor tactics based on emotional reasons, ideological commitments, personal values, and self-understanding. Activists can derive real pleasure from protest; participating in a movement can generate feelings of love, empowerment, solidarity, and other deeply powerful emotions (Jasper 1997). Such reactions can also derive from selecting tactics that people enjoy carrying out. Movements might also select tactics based on their organization's ideological or moral commitments (M. Meyer 2004), such as when religious organizations opposed to abortion condemn violence as a tactic. In Northern Ireland, internal factionalism that led to an ideological split in the Irish Republican Army produced one splinter group – the Official IRA – that had a Marxist view of the conflict between Protestants and Catholics; true to their class analysis, this group was reluctant to inflict any

---

2 Personal communication with the author, July, 2016.

violence on working-class Protestant communities as they believed that members of the working class should unite across religious lines and confront the real perpetrators of the conflict – the state and the capitalists who profited from ongoing tensions. Tactical choice, in other words, can affirm a group's ideological principles and the identities of its members more broadly (Smithey 2009). Such considerations are no less important than purely instrumental ones and can help to sway organizations toward certain tactics from their overall repertoire of contention.

Space and Place

Tactical choice also involves decisions about where to situate protest in physical space. Proximity to population centers, transportation routes, or symbols of government power can all enhance a movement's mobilization efforts as well as the visibility and power of a particular event. Dingxin Zhao's study of pro-democracy protestors in Beijing's universities, for example, found that the spatial arrangement of student dorms and the proximity in which students were living made it possible for information about the protests to spread quickly and for individuals to become aware of and mobilized into demonstrations and marches (Zhao 1998). Lack of accessible space or the privatization of formerly public spaces can also make protest more difficult (Gieryn 2000: 479). Matching tactics to the best spatial locations, therefore, can be consequential, as some sites will enhance participation, visibility, and impact while others will make it harder for people to take part, be seen, or project power.

Where movements locate protest can also matter for emotional and symbolic reasons. Tactics do not unfold in a vacuum; they are situated in specific places in the world, and those places have meanings that can be constructed by people (Sewell 2001). Physical spaces guide and structure our lives; roadways, for example, shape how we move through cities, and the built environment may influence how we encounter others (Stillerman 2002; Marston 2003). The meanings of those spaces, however, can be interpreted in different ways by various actors. The difference between mere "space" and "place" is that the former is devoid of meaning – map coordinates on a grid. The latter is endowed with "history or utopia, danger or security, identity or memory . . . the meaning or value of the same place is labile – flexible in the hands of different people or cultures, malleable over time, and inevitably contested" (Gieryn 2000: 465). Places, in other words, have significance to us based on our lived experiences in them. They are unique and cannot be substituted for any other place (Agnew 2011). Places also generate attachments – deep emotional ties that can be harnessed by movements or their opponents (Gieryn 2000: 474, 481). Places, in other words, are powerful.

Movements can harness this power by situating tactics in places that convey larger emotional or symbolic meanings (Tilly 2000: 138–9). The BLM movement's use of roadblocks, for example, builds on emotional and symbolic references. Highways were often constructed through black neighborhoods as a way of clearing out those communities and dispersing their populations while providing suburban commuters with fast and easy access to downtown business districts that bypassed and excluded minority neighborhoods (Bayor 1988). None of this was lost on the BLM movement, whose tactic of roadblocks took on an additional layer of significance and meaning when situated in a place that could amplify its impact. Ultimately, choosing tactics is only part of the process; once chosen, tactics also must be put into action in an appropriate location for maximum effect.

Tactical Evolution and Diffusion

Movements can also develop new tactical forms via learning – from each other and from their own experiences. Since social movements engage in sustained activity, they develop a record of successes and failures; by analyzing what worked and what did not, movement actors can alter course, drop tactics that were ineffective, and experiment with new ways to make a difference. Holly J. McCammon (2003) argues that significant defeats are particularly useful opportunities for movements to critically analyze and revise failed strategies. Even in the absence of a crushing defeat, a movement's interactions with opponents can provide valuable feedback that can be used to fuel tactical innovation. As movement targets respond and adapt to movement activities, protestors must constantly experiment with new and improved methods in order to retain an advantage (McAdam 1983).

Movements can also develop new tactical forms via their interactions with other movement groups, both within the same movement (Soule 1997) and from other movements (Meyer and Wittier

1994). Groups that collaborate with each other or participate in joint campaigns can observe the tactics that others use and adopt approaches that might be useful for their own work. Dan Wang and Sarah Soule (2012, 2016) note that such learning can lead to two different forms of innovation: movement groups can invent new tactical forms, or they can combine existing tactics in new and unexpected ways. Reinvention and combination are more likely, they argue, when groups participate in multi-issue protest events that bring together groups with multiple interests and agendas around a common issue. In such a setting, activists can see a diverse array of tactics and be inspired by best practices or new ways of thinking about their own claims. New tactics, on the other hand, are more likely to be introduced by groups that are more peripheral to a movement community. Isolation and disconnectedness from other movement groups reduce the pressure to be conventional and can inspire experimentation that, if successful, can subsequently influence groups who are more centrally located.

Tactical innovations can also diffuse from one movement organization to another absent a common protest experience. Such diffusion can take place via different pathways, including direct personal connections between individuals or among organizations, as well as indirect transmission via mass media (Strang and Soule 1998). Such diffusion processes start from the basic premise that tactics are, to a large extent, modular as, once perfected in one location, they can be transmitted and used in different contexts; their demonstrated success can fuel their subsequent adoption by other actors for other purposes (Tarrow 2011). Such transmission can take place via interpersonal relationships, as individuals share information and experiences with contacts in their social network. Alternatively, movements can also learn about new tactics in a more indirect way when media sources write about them in newspapers or capture them in action on television. The internet further enhances this method of transmission by expanding the number of tactics that can be documented, making them available to more audiences, and accelerating the speed at which this knowledge can be diffused across the world (Ayres 1999).

While diffusion and learning processes can expand the tactical repertoires available to individual movements, not all organizations are equally adept at adopting innovative practices for their own use. Groups that are open to using diversified tactics are more likely to be open to incorporating new practices, though Dan Wang and Sarah Soule argue that at some point, organizations that have a particularly large toolbox of tactics can reach saturation point and no longer be able to adopt new methods. They additionally argue that innovation is more likely to take place when the organizations in a position to learn from each other are already tactically similar – a group that engages in disruptive civil disobedience may have less to learn from a group that stages satirical puppet shows. If groups are *too* similar, however, there may not be sufficient new tactical material to share (Wang and Soule 2012). In addition to tactical similarity, groups that are organizationally similar in terms of size, structure, operational culture, or resources will have an easier time incorporating ideas and practices from each other (Soule 1997). These caveats suggest that there is a limit to modularity. Although learning and diffusion can introduce movements to new approaches that can help them to stay relevant and compelling, not all ideas are equally portable to all places.

Prefigurative Politics

In addition to familiar tactics like marches or rallies or strikes, movements might also engage in prefigurative political practices. Such an approach involves embodying the kinds of social relations, institutions, and culture that movements see as the ultimate goal of their work (Boggs 1977: 100; Epstein 1991). Instead of simply working to change existing practices, movement participants create alternative spaces in which they can build a more idealized version of society. Movement activists can embody (or "prefigure") their desired outcomes even before such practices become routine in wider society, thereby effectively "building the new society in the shell of the old" (Graeber 2013: 190). Groups that advocate for a more egalitarian and democratic society, for example, may adopt organizational practices involving "a minimal division of labor, decentralized authority, and an egalitarian ethos and whose decision making is direct and consensus oriented" (Polletta 2002: 6). In other words, movements live their values and create their version of a better world in miniature.

Occupy Wall Street is one such example. Built around principles of equality, consensus, and democracy, it created a parallel social structure in its Zuccotti Park encampment that allowed movement activists to model a society that renounced neoliberal capitalist principles. Working groups convened around issues like food, public relations, and medical services to manage the logistics of the community. A whole parallel set of social support institutions developed as well: a kitchen that dispensed food (including to the homeless who came asking for help), mental health professionals who provided counseling to those in distress, first-aid posts, and even a lending library complete with Wifi access. It was, in the words of one activist, "a demonstration of what is possible if we think about the world in a different way, free from the domination of capitalist power and state power" (Hammond 2015: 303).

OWS members also rejected hierarchical leadership structures, opting instead for a horizontal and consensus-based style of decision making. Working groups, which were open to anyone, deliberated among themselves and reported back to the general assembly. At this larger meeting, a rotating group of facilitators would lead conversation among hundreds of people. In order for everyone in such a large group to participate in the discussion, OWS used a technique called the "people's microphone" in which an initial speaker's words would be repeated in unison by people nearby, which amplified the sound and let people farther back in the crowd hear what was being said. Participants would use a series of hand signals to communicate with each other during these assemblies (to ask someone to clarify a position, to raise a point of process, to indicate opposition to a proposal, etc.) before trying to reach a consensus position. Although less efficient than more hierarchical forms of decision making, OWS members prioritized principles of participation and inclusiveness. This commitment also meant that OWS had no official leaders but considered all participants equals in building the movement community.

OWS's commitment to prefiguration often confused and frustrated onlookers who did not understand what the movement's activists wanted; unlike more familiar protest organizations, OWS resisted formulating explicit demands. While social movements typically want to rectify specific grievances that their members might hold, Occupy refused to do so, insisting instead that "we are our demands." Setting out specific goals, OWS members argued, would make it easier for existing political actors to co-opt the movement, and also assumed that political elites were willing or able to make changes (Pickerill and Krinsky 2012). As Luke Yates (2015) explains, in the typical social movement, the tactic is the means to achieve some desired end. But the means of prefigurative politics *are* the ends. In other words, the OWS encampment was not a means to achieve some policy outcome; it was itself the outcome that members sought.

Such an approach can have unclear effects, and the impact of prefigurative politics can be hard to assess, especially since prefiguration can have multiple goals that may not be clear, even to movement participants. Francesca Polletta (2002: 7) wonders: "Is building the new society within the shell of the old aimed at persuading people outside the movement of the desirability and viability of radically democratic forms, or is its purpose to transform participants' relationships with each other? Or do activists see themselves as preserving a democratic impulse until a more receptive era?" The mechanism by which prefiguration is meant to produce this new, better society, in other words, is not particularly clear. Marianne Maeckelburgh (2011) offers a more optimistic view, arguing that prefiguration is about helping movement participants to learn how to live and govern, and to think about power in ways that differ from existing institutions. Moreover, the ultimate goal of such approaches is not simply personal transformation, but global transformation, which activists can achieve by building alternative power structures at the grassroots level, not by appealing to political elites or remote international organizations.

New Frontiers: Digital Activism

Not all protest takes place in the physical world. Increasingly, online activism has played a prominent role in movements from the Arab Spring uprisings to the work of hacker collectives like Anonymous. Online, as in the physical world, tactics can be described as contained or transgressive, with the former including activities like online petitions and the latter including disruptive activities like email bombs, as well as tactics that could result in physical violence, such as hacking and taking over a power grid or air-traffic control systems (Constanza-Chock 2003). Jeroen Van Laer and Peter Van Aelst (2010) further divide online protest into two varieties: internet-supported and internet-based forms of activism. Internet-supported forms are cases in which the internet facilitates protest tactics by making traditional tools easier to use, cheaper to employ, or more efficient at mobilizing people. Most movement organizations, for example, have websites with options to donate money to the cause; fundraising, communicating with supporters, and publicizing the group's work can all be done much more cheaply online than with traditional methods. Online tools can also help to coordinate protest activity, a feature that transnational movements have found to be helpful in bringing together activists located in far-flung places. The internet can also supplement the work of movements by automating certain parts of their campaigns or moving them to a virtual environment. Online petitions, for example, are a much more efficient way for many movement groups to collect signatures from the public, which helps to explain their ubiquity (della Porta and Mosca 2005). In all of these cases, online activism either supplements physical protest, or provides an online version of a more familiar tactic. Online protest can also presage protest by helping to form a community of interest before making the leap to mobilization in the physical world (Harlow 2011).

Internet-based forms of protest include new and innovative tools that represent an expansion or shift in the overall repertoire; these are tactics that would be difficult or impossible to pull off without the technological changes since the 1980s. Email bombs, for example, send large volumes of email messages to a user's address and overwhelm the server, effectively shutting down the account and rendering it unusable; genuine email cannot easily be filtered out and hostile mail cannot easily be stopped. Closely related are distributed denial of service (DDoS) attacks, which flood servers with traffic from multiple servers and make it impossible for online services to accept legitimate traffic; from a user's point of view, websites go offline for extended periods of time, but from the target's point of view, this can bring its operations to a standstill. While most DDoS attacks that make the news are associated with criminal enterprises (Arquilla and Ronfeldt 2010), such attacks have increasingly been used by social activists as a form of protest. In 1995, Strano Network, an Italian collective, launched an attack against the French government to protest its nuclear policies. It asked protestors to visit designated government websites at an appointed time to try to knock the sites offline because of the increased traffic; it succeeded in doing so for about an hour. Around the same time, Electronic Disturbance Theater staged virtual sit-ins against politicians' websites and the White House using the same general approach, only, in this instance, participants could select a target from a drop-down menu on the EDT website, click a button, and participate in the attack (Sauter 2014).

More recently, such attacks have increased in scale, size, automation, and duration. DDoS attacks have been used to protest a wide variety of organizations, including the FIFA World Cup website (to protest Brazil's expenditure on building stadiums rather than help-ing the poor); the Westboro Baptist Church (to protest its decision to picket the funerals of people killed in the Sandy Hook elementary school shooting); and even the Estonian government for its decision to remove a Soviet war monument that had been installed in 1946, which angered ethnic Russians. DDoS activities are being used suffi-ciently often in the service of social protest for the hacker collective Anonymous to submit a petition to the White House in 2013 calling for recognition of the tactic as a legitimate form of protest, covered by free-speech protections. For the petition's supporters, DDoS is the modern equivalent of a sit-in, but rather than occupying physi-cal space, it occupies virtual space. The outcome, they argue, is the same: if enough people participate in a sit-in, all business ceases to function; the same could be said of a DDoS attack. While officials have not accepted this argument (and consider DDoS attacks a form of cybercrime, and possibly even cyberterrorism), it is possible that conventions and the legal status of such tactics may change in the future (Li 2013).

Internet-based tactics can also include forms that have a crea-tive or performative aspect. Cybergraffiti, for example, defaces legitimate websites much like physical graffiti defaces buildings; both can also be used to express grievances. During the cyberwar between Georgia and Russia, Russian hackers defaced the website of the National Bank of Georgia, replacing a page with images of twentieth-century dictators, and including the Georgian President alongside them. Organizations can also engage in online culture jamming, which uses existing media and advertising to transmit subversive messages about the very corporations and groups that produced the original content. The satirical activist group The Yes Men purchases website URLs that are similar to the domain names for real organizations. They recreate the look and feel of the target organization so that the aesthetics look similar; however, they change the content to drive home particular messages about the group. To critique the World Trade Organization, they bought the rights to gatt.org (referring to the World Trade Organization's older name, the General Agreement on Tariffs and Trade). They put up a website that looked the same as the WTO's, down to logo, layout, and font. But instead of information about the WTO's poli-cies, the Yes Men version had articles about the perils of unfettered neoliberal economic policy to offer unsuspecting viewers an alternative interpretation of the institution's priorities.

While examples abound of movements using online tools and tactics as part of their protest campaigns, there is considerable debate about how useful the internet is, what it contributes to social movements, and how to assess the quality of the resulting activism. Advocates point out that the internet makes it cheap and easy for movements to disseminate information to a much broader audience than they might have been able to access otherwise, thus magnifying their potential educational impact. It can help to build and strengthen activist solidarities by providing spaces for movement participants and sympathizers to debate, share experiences, and become invested in the group's goals. And several scholars have argued that online participation in movements, even if it involves something as basic as an online petition, can potentially have multiplier effects and make it more likely that individuals will get involved in additional movement activities down the line (Christensen 2011; Lee and Hsieh 2013).

On the other hand, the low cost of most online activism like e-petitions might generate large numbers of participants, but also encourage low-quality participation. Rather than activism, so the argument goes, the internet encourages "slacktivism," not real commitment to movement goals. Moreover, the collective identity that movements might build using online tools is likely to consist of fairly weak ties, since the collective wisdom is that strong ties require in-person contact and interaction. As a result, movement participation that is built largely via online interactions might lead to initial mobilization but have a harder time sustaining participation over time. Finally, the internet can also provide a false sense of security given that many interactions can be made relatively anonymously, which can be appealing to individuals in more restrictive environments. At the same time, surveillance is not absent on the internet, and there can be real-world consequences for online activism, including governments harassing and arresting political bloggers, as happened in places like Tunisia and Bahrain prior to and during the Arab Spring. Government surveillance can also collect the IP addresses of computers participating in online activities that the government deems threatening. Such practices mean that there are risks to online activism just as in physical space. The internet is a quickly evolving space, and while, up until now, it seems to have played a role primarily as a complement to real-world organizing and movement activity, online activism and the norms around it can make it an increasingly autonomous and alternative space for movements to operate.

Concluding Summary

Movements engage in protest, but what that protest looks like, where it takes place, and how it advances a movement's goals can vary significantly. Movements can pick from a wide array of possible tactics, though the specific repertoire available to them and the different considerations that drive choice narrow their options to some extent. Regardless of how and why movements choose the tactics they do, they must try to walk a fine line between picking tactical resonance and familiarity on the one hand, and, on the other, selecting innovative, novel approaches that can grab the public's attention. Tactical choices are a constantly shifting area for movements and change over time as movements learn from their peers, their opponents, from their own past successes and failures, and even the environment in which they operate. Put together, tactical choice is a contested and vital aspect of the work that movements do in order to attain the goals they seek.

These choices reflect organizational identities and values, which can lead movements to intentionally seek out tactics that disrupt or unsettle the public in an effort to reject conventional expectations about how particular groups behave. It can also lead them to eschew tactics that involve specific demands in favor of creating prefigurative communities that embody activist values. And online tactics open up new frontiers of strategic possibilities, both supplementing, and in some cases moving beyond, what is possible in the real world. Given all of these possibilities, tactical choice is a particularly creative area where the performative and public aspects of movements are on full display.

Questions for Discussion

1 How do contained, disruptive, and violent tactics differ from one another? Why do scholars disagree about which type of tactic is most likely to be effective?

2 In what ways do a group's goals, resources, and knowledge affect its choice of tactics? How might these choices vary based on the political context?

3 What determines a movement's protest repertoire? How might protest repertoires evolve over time?

4 Why do some movements engage in prefigurative politics? What are the advantages and limitations of this tactic?

5 In what ways can digital activism complement in-person protest? Do you think digital activism can be as effective as physical protest (or more so)? Why or why not?

Additional Readings

Polletta, Francesca. 2002. *Freedom is an Endless Meeting: Democracy in American Social Movements*. Chicago: University of Chicago Press. Explores the idea of deliberative democracy and prefigurative movements.

Strang, David, and Sarah A. Soule. 1998. "Diffusion in Organizations and Social Movements: From Hybrid Corn to Poison Pills." *Annual Review of Sociology*, 24: 265–90. Describes different mechanisms for the diffusion of ideas and tactics among organizations.

Tilly, Charles. 1996. *Regimes and Repertoires*. Chicago: University of Chicago Press. Lays out the idea of repertoires of contention as well as how repertoires might intersect with regime types.

CHAPTER 7

The Response

Objectives

- To examine how government responses to social movement demands depend on a range of considerations, including the costs and benefits of a particular course of action and how such reactions will be interpreted by potential allies and supporters.

- To recognize the difference between a state's situational and institutional responses to protest.

- To understand how policing tactics evolved from escalated force approaches to strategic incapacitation models and how these strategies compare to policing in other parts of the world.

- To identify what factors influence institutional responses to movements and how these responses can affect movement escalation and radicalization.

Introduction

Each year, Hong Kong residents gather on June 4 to remember the student-led movement that, in 1989, took over Tiananmen Square in Beijing and demanded that the Chinese government implement democratic reforms. Large-scale commemorations of the movement are not permitted anywhere else in China, but for the past 25 years, tens of thousands of people have assembled on that day in Hong Kong's Victoria Park to honor those who participated in protests and lost their lives in the process. In addition to speeches and crowds singing pro-democracy songs by candlelight, the vigils have also featured replicas of the "Goddess of Democracy," a statue erected by the Tiananmen protestors to rally supporters, which has subsequently become an enduring emblem of the movement itself. In 2015, people attending the Victoria Park memorial covered the Goddess of Democracy in umbrella stickers in recognition of the pro-democracy protests that broke out in the city just the year before, in which umbrellas – used by activists as protection against rain and sun and police pepper spray – became the iconic symbol. As a result, the statue became a pastiche honoring not just one, but two, separate pro-democracy movements on Chinese soil.

Observers were quick to point out the parallels between the Tiananmen and umbrella protests. University students played leading roles in both movements, and in each case, organized around democratic demands. The students in Tiananmen, for example, demanded an end to press censorship, the right to protest, and a more transparent and open government. The students in Hong Kong demanded democratic elections in which citizens would have the power to nominate and elect the city's executive leadership, rather than vesting this power in the hands of a committee selected by the Chinese government. Both movements occupied public spaces in important Chinese cities (Beijing, the political capital, and Hong Kong, a major financial hub), creating encampments that lasted weeks. Both employed non-violent protest strategies. The Hong Kong protestors even paid homage to the Tiananmen protestors by building their own version of the Goddess of Democracy – a 12-foot-high statue holding an umbrella placed outside the Hong Kong government headquarters. In neither case did the protestors achieve their core demands: in the wake of the Tiananmen protests, the Communist government tightened its control over society and rolled back tentative reforms that had been championed by moderates within the party, while, in Hong Kong, the method for selecting the city's executive remained in the hands of a pro-Beijing election committee, rather than transferring to the citizens as the protestors had demanded.

Of course, there were limits to these parallels. Separated by 25 years and over 1,000 miles, the two protests took place in very different contexts. The level of economic interdependence between China and the rest of the world had grown considerably since 1989, which arguably made the country more concerned with how its actions might be interpreted by those outside its borders in 2014, compared to two decades earlier. The Tiananmen protestors made their demands while standing in the heart of the capital and at the epicenter of government power, while Hong Kong's entirely distinct legal environment – a remnant of its days as a British territory – provided the umbrella protestors with coveted rights to free speech, free press, and free assembly, and the right to demonstrate, none of which applied to their Tiananmen counterparts. In 1989, the Chinese government was able to strictly limit international press access to and coverage of the protests, while in Hong Kong a free press, uncensored access to the internet, and widespread use of cell phones and cameras coupled with social media meant that the world could watch events unfold in real time in a way that was simply not possible for the Tiananmen demonstrators.

But perhaps the biggest difference of all was the way both protest campaigns ended: one with a bang, one with a whimper. After initially putting up with the Tiananmen protest encampment while government elites fought over whether to open a dialogue with student leaders or to punish them, Chinese hardliners regained political control and swiftly implemented martial law. Soon thereafter, they authorized the military to clear the protestors out of the square – peacefully if possible, but with force if need be. When protestors attempted to halt the progress of troops by blocking streets and surrounding transport vehicles, the army opened fire. Some students in the square fought back by throwing stones and bottles at troops, but they were no match for the superior firepower aimed at them. By the time the protests were finished, hundreds of people had been killed and thousands wounded. The Hong Kong protests were also marred by violence: police used pepper spray and tear gas on activists, wore riot gear and used baton charges to clear streets, erected barricades, and arrested people. Activists reported being assaulted by police and counter-demonstrators at various points throughout the occupation. For their part, the police also accused the demonstrators of engaging in aggressive behavior, throwing objects at officers, kicking and hitting them with umbrellas, and charging at police lines. But, despite the fracas, security forces were relatively restrained in Hong Kong compared to Beijing. There were no incidents of police firing live rounds into crowds of protestors. The military remained on the sidelines and did not take part in crowd control. After some of the movement's leaders called on the protestors to disband the protest sites to avoid escalating violence and, instead carry on pro-democracy work in other ways, many protestors started to demobilize. One week later, police started to dismantle the main occupation site and, while some protestors refused to leave, they were arrested without much fanfare.

This disparity in government response is rooted in several factors. The greater economic interconnectedness, combined with more press coverage, may have made the government reluctant to crack down on protestors for fear of the negative publicity, which could hurt the important financial industry in Hong Kong. The Hong Kong context, with its separate legal environment and its physical distance from Beijing may also have facilitated the more permissive stance toward the umbrella protestors, since their presence was not a direct physical affront to the Chinese central elites. The Hong Kong police also had a reputation for being a well-trained and well-regarded force. The World Economic Forum's annual global competitiveness report for 2013–14, for example, rated Hong Kong's police force fourth out of 148 countries for reliability of police services; mainland China, by contrast, ranked 59 out of 148 in that same study (Schwab and Sala-i-Martín 2013: 426). While this reputation subsequently took a beating in the court of public opinion, Hong Kong had a comparatively elite police force with high educational and training standards for its officers, which may have played some role in how they responded to protestors.

The contrast between the Tiananmen Square protests and Hong Kong's umbrella movement a quarter-century later highlights how movements can elicit different kinds of responses from authorities, ranging from indifference to harsh suppression and every stage in-between. By using comparative case studies – an approach described in more detail in this chapter's methods spotlight – we can better analyze what might prompt governments to vary their responses to even similar-seeming movements. As these paired examples suggest, predicting when and where movements are likely to be tolerated versus crushed is not as simple as differentiating governments according to their repressive tendencies or movements according to how provocative their claims and actions might be. Instead, understanding how movement activity generates responses from their opponents requires an exploration of how multiple factors – those specific to movements, those specific to other actors, those specific to the context in which they interact, and those specific to the interactions themselves – intersect and shape the amount of violence or accommodation that follows when movements make contentious claims and stage public performances.

Situational and Institutional Responses

When movements make claims, they await responses from their targets. Since most protestors target state actors in some capacity, and because the state has considerable power to affect social movement activities, the following discussion will focus primarily on

Methods Spotlight: Case Studies

Qualitative case studies are one of the more common methods used by scholars of social movements. They offer rich, detailed accounts of social movement dynamics, and are particularly useful for asking questions about causal pathways and mechanisms rather than the correlation between variables. Whereas methods that focus on large-N studies, such as inferential statistics, are best suited to uncovering the probability that there is a relationship between a particular independent and dependent variable, case studies are well suited to asking how and why particular relationships might come to be, or how they work or why and under what conditions some factor might cause a given outcome (Ritter 2014). Case studies also make it possible for scholars to consider complex causal relationships when more than one independent variable might influence the dependent variable, or where there may be interactive or recursive causal effects (George and Bennett 2005: 22). Case studies can focus on a single case or multiple cases; when more than one case is involved, this method allows the researcher to compare and contrast across examples, which can increase the analytic leverage and explanatory power of the research design.

Because this method requires researchers to develop considerable familiarity with the nuances and details of the selected cases, this is almost always a small-N research tool; it is rare to find published research that delves into more than a limited handful of cases. Comparative work involving up to three cases is plentiful; the amount of published articles featuring four or more cases starts to drop off, in part because of the amount of time required to achieve mastery of multiple case details. As a result, the choice of cases is almost always deliberate and purposeful, rather than random; researchers might include cases because they are particularly important, or typical, or outliers requiring closer attention. When researchers conduct comparative research, their choice must also consider how comparable the selected case studies are. In such instances, researchers frequently match case studies based on similarities and differences in order to allow them to isolate particular features for closer scrutiny (Przeworski and Teune 1970; Anckar 2008).

The "most-similar systems" approach to matching case studies, for example, tries to find cases that are very alike in as many key respects as possible so that whatever differences do exist can be studied without being muddled by other confounding variables. This approach presumes that cases are matched so that the outcome of interest (the dependent variable – DV) varies between cases. In the hypothetical sample below, imagine that we are interested in trying to understand whether having a decentralized organizational structure plays a causal role in long-term SMO survival. We would try to find two cases that vary in outcomes (one survives, one collapses quickly). We would also want their organizational structures to vary to help us to understand how structure affects organizational life span. But we would want to hold as many other confounding variables constant so as not to muddy the causal relationship of central interest to us. For example, we may want to pick two cases that are both in democracies, since the life span of movement groups in autocracies may be consistently shorter than in democratic states. Similarly, we may want to control for resource level, since rich groups may have an easier time surviving compared to resource-starved groups.

Most-similar systems design

	Case 1	Case 2
Regime type	Democracy	Democracy
Resource endowment	Wealthy	Wealthy
Size of membership	1,000–5,000	1,000–5,000
Movement type	Environmental	Environmental
Organizational structure	Formal, centralized	Informal, de-centralized
DV: Organizational life span	Long	Short

The "most-different systems" approach uses the opposite logic: cases with similar outcomes are matched in order to maximize the differences between them, since variations in these conditions cannot explain their shared outcomes. The researcher can then focus on what the cases have in common to explore how these shared variables might account for common outcomes in otherwise dissimilar circumstances.

Most-different systems design

	Case 1	Case 2
Regime type	Democracy	Autocracy
Resource endowment	Wealthy	Deprived
Size of membership	1,000–5,000	<500
Movement type	Environmental	Human rights
Organizational structure	Formal, centralized	Formal, centralized
DV: Organizational life span	Long	Long

Regardless of whether researchers opt for a single or comparative case study, the material that makes up the case can come from a variety of sources: archival and primary sources, interviews, organization documents, media accounts, quantitative data, and so forth. The aim is generally to provide a detailed account that traces causal processes in a careful and rigorous fashion, specifying how each step in the hypothesized causal sequence operates and providing persuasive evidence for that claim (Collier 2011; Ritter 2014: 101). Such requirements separate analytic case studies from mere description.

Explore this Method

Case studies may seem easy at first, because they may not appear nearly as technical as some of the other research methods that scholars use. However, effective case studies require thoughtful selection and considerable familiarity with their details. To practice the logic of selection and using the most-similar/most-different design criteria, take a look at Swarthmore College's Global Nonviolent Action Database (http://nvdatabase.swarthmore.edu), which contains brief descriptions of dozens of social movement campaigns and protest events around the world and over time. Pick an outcome that interests you – like size of protest, or emergence of a countermovement

– and then try to pick out two cases from the database that you could pair together using either the most-similar or most-different systems design. Keep in mind that, in order to decide what aspects you want to keep similar or different, you will need to think about what potential independent variables might be of most causal interest to you, and what other variables might confound your ability to understand that possible causal relationship. In addition to practicing case selection, you can also practice some of the skills that are useful for process tracing. David Collier, a professor at the University of California, Berkeley, has developed 11 process tracing exercises for case studies (http://polisci.berkeley.edu/sites/default/files/people/u3827/Teaching%20Process%20Tracing.pdf). In each one, he identifies a particular text that you can read, with accompanying questions and prompts to get you to think about the kinds of evidence, connections, and claims that good process tracing involves.

the way that political elites respond to demonstrators and their demands, though many of these dynamics (though not necessarily all the capabilities or tools) are also present in the responses that non-governmental targets make in response to movement actions. Such responses range from bargaining with movements over the type and extent of concessions to stifling the movement with repressive policies; even inaction and letting the movement run its course without interference or acknowledgment is a choice that officials can make, especially if a movement is relatively innocuous (Tilly 1978). Such responses manifest in two distinct but related sites: the places where state officials have physical contact with protestors engaging in public performances (i.e., police interacting with demonstrators), and the places where state officials dictate institutional responses to movement demands (i.e., policymakers determining how to respond to movement claims and organizations). Following Ruud Koopmans (1997), I term the first set of interactions a state's situational response, and the second set of interactions its institutional response.

Though distinct, institutional and situational responses share a number of similarities that are important to keep in mind. First, even though we might talk of a government's response to a social movement, responses are plural, not singular. It is possible for governments to have multiple responses toward a given movement, with some of those responses even contradicting each other. A government might repress a movement's street demonstration while simultaneously offering it some of its demands, or arrest some members of a movement while inviting others to participate in talks with the government. Responses, in other words, need not be consistent, nor must they all point in the same direction. In part, this multiplicity stems from the fact that neither governments nor movements are unitary actors; governments are composed of multiple groups, divisions, branches, political elites, and bureaucratic offices, all of which have their own interests and priorities. It is not outside the realm of possibility to find one part of the government pursuing one response to a movement while a different part follows its own path.

Like governments, movements are not monolithic, which also makes it possible for officials to direct one type of response toward some actors within the movement community while responding to others in an entirely different way (della Porta and Reiter 1986: 6). In her study of British government responses toward the nationalist movement in Northern Ireland, for example, Devashree Gupta (2007) documented the way in which the moderate nationalists who eschewed violence were given preferential access to negotiations while more militant groups within the same movement were targeted for repression. Herbert Haines (1984) and J. Craig Jenkins (1998) similarly found that, in the US Civil Rights movement, external donors were able to distinguish moderate groups from radical groups and reward them differently, channeling resources to bolster the former in an attempt to weaken the latter.

Second, demands and responses are dynamic and interactive; once issued, they shape the way that movements and other actors strategize about future frames, tactics, and responses. Moreover, neither movements nor their opponents are locked into any particular pattern of claim-making or response. Movement organizations that engage in largely non-violent tactics, for example, can shift to more transgressive methods after they see what their initial tactical choices elicit as a response from state officials. In South Africa, the non-violent approach that the African National Congress used to combat the government's apartheid policies in the 1950s generated nothing but harsh repressive measures; at some point, the ANC's leaders determined that peaceful tactics were unable to accomplish anything and accordingly radicalized to embrace more disruptive and transgressive methods, including the use of sabotage and armed struggle against the state (Ellis 2011). Movement groups might also travel in the opposite direction, abandoning transgressive tactics in favor of more contained approaches based on prior responses from officials, just like the Irish Republican Army did when it eventually decommissioned its weapons after many inconclusive clashes with the British government. Governments, too, can alter their approaches at any point, shifting from accommodation to repression and back again, depending on how their prior choices affected movement actions (Moore 2000).

Third, choices that government officials make about how to respond to movements are seen and interpreted not only by activists, but by a range of secondary audiences as well, including the government's own supporters, other potential movements and countermovements, and the general public, all of whom draw conclusions about the identity, values, and strength of the government (for example, see Jefferson and Grimshaw 1984). Governments, therefore, will be sensitive not just to the message they want to convey to challenging movements but to what signals it might send to these other groups. An overly conciliatory gesture might embolden other challengers to make their own demands (Goldstone and Tilly 2001), or anger supporters who prefer that the government not make any concessions at all. An overly harsh response can be equally perilous; for example, worries about the reaction of the international community and possible economic fallout from the financial market may have played a key role in encouraging the Chinese government to exercise restraint with respect to the 2014 umbrella protestors (Lagerkvist and Rühling 2016). Throughout, the media can complicate the government's calculations because they expand the number of potential audiences that might be relevant (Ayoub 2010).

Choosing How to Respond: General Constraints and Considerations

In addition to these general conditions affecting both situational and institutional responses, government officials (and, indeed, any group that movements might target) also make choices about how to react to movement claims that are subject to certain common assumptions and constraints that are worth keeping in mind. First, social movement targets are assumed to be reluctant to make changes to their policies or practices (Samuelson and Zeckhauser 1988). If governments implement changes, they tend to be incremental in nature and gradual in pace; the same could be said for other common movement targets like corporations or universities. Across all of these actors, we can observe a general bias toward the status quo, and opposition to sudden, sweeping changes that can have unknown consequences and unleash destabilizing processes. Large organizations in general, Raquel Fernandez and Dani Rodrik (1991) argue, are presumed to favor moderation and restraint over revolution and spontaneity. This status quo bias will, in general, make targets predisposed to resisting change in general but, if absolutely pushed to do so by a determined movement, to implementing modest adjustments wherever possible.

Movement targets will also prioritize responses that have low costs over responses that have high costs, though each entity will have different ways of defining what costs are most relevant to it. If repression is less costly than bargaining, then officials will opt to repress; if bargaining is less costly than repression, then officials will rein in their security forces. Jack Goldstone and Charles Tilly (2001) argue that these cost assessments also hinge on regime type (also see Johnston 2011). Authoritarian governments, for example, usually regard concessions as more costly than repression because giving in to citizen demands can raise questions about the regime's monopoly on power. However, certain governments might have an "addiction" to particular kinds of responses, favoring them even if doing so may be reflexive and not entirely rational. In any event, the likely costs of particular strategies must also be evaluated alongside their probability of successfully demobilizing the movement. If repression is less costly than bargaining, but highly unlikely to stop movements from protesting, those cost advantages may not be worthwhile in the long run.

At the same time, government officials may not have very accurate knowledge about the true costs of particular responses, or their real likelihood of success. In fact, there is often a high degree of uncertainty around such assessments of cost and risk (Goldstone and Tilly 2001). For instance, governments can only make guesses about the willingness and determination of movement activists to challenge security forces. In the case of the Tiananmen Square demonstration, protestors were willing to risk bodily injury to keep military troops from advancing toward the protest site; in one famous case, a lone individual stepped out in front of a line of tanks and stopped them in their tracks – a moment that became an iconic symbol of citizen resistance. In the Hong Kong movement, by contrast, protestors ultimately dispersed without much commotion, even though the days leading up to the encampment clearance were marked with escalating violence. Not only are governments uncertain about activist intentions and commitment, they may not be entirely persuaded by the commitment of their own security forces. When Tunisia became the Patient Zero of the Arab Spring uprisings, its autocratic leader, Zine el-Abidine Ben Ali, ordered the military to help quell the disturbances but, instead, they turned against the regime and sided with the protestors, effectively bringing Ben Ali's rule to an end. These examples underscore the difficulty facing political elites when formulating responses to movement demands.

Taking political risks and failing can result in serious consequences for a ruling elite, as the Tunisia case suggests, but even if miscalculations stop well short of regime collapse, governments will try to avoid them for fear of appearing weak to their enemies as well as supporters. Weakness opens the door to other challengers (both social movement challengers and rivals for political power) and can make supporters question their allegiance. For democratic leaders, weakness from bad policy gambles can be punished in elections, though the fallout at the polls also depends in part on the government's strength and overall store of political capital, which affects how willing it is to take policy risks (Gupta 2007). Selim Erden Aytaç and his collaborators found this pattern to be true in newer democracies as well; regimes that were relatively secure politically could take greater risks in repressing protestors because they had some "cushion" in case such tactics backfired; democratic rulers who had unstable levels of electoral support, on the other hand, trod much more carefully when it came to repression, given its inherent risks (Aytaç et al. 2017). For autocrats, both concessions and failed repression can demonstrate a tenuous hold on power and an opening for others to challenge the existing regime.

Taken together, these considerations shape the way in which targets respond to movement activity. While the argument outlined above is admittedly rationalist in nature, the organizational logic of larger, bureaucratic entities such as governments, corporations, universities, or other common movement targets makes it more likely that rationality, rather than emotional responses, is a fruitful starting point for analyzing target reactions. At the same time, as the discussion below suggests, there is plenty of latitude for emotions, culture, identity, and values to also shape the way actors react to movements, particularly when it comes to situational responses in which movement actors confront state representatives while protesting.

Situational Responses: Public Order and Policing

When protestors hold protest events, it creates an opportunity for state actors to respond right away. Not all protests will generate this kind of contact; many events are sufficiently innocuous for authorities to be unaware of them or to decide to keep their distance, and protests targeting private actors may not involve state authorities at all. In fact, in a study of protest in New York between 1968 and 1973 – a period of considerable activist agitation – Jennifer Earl, Sarah A. Soule, and John D. McCarthy (2003) found that police only attended about 31 percent of the 1,901 events in their dataset. But when security forces are involved, how the government's representatives react to movement tactics creates useful signals about how the state views the movement's actions and demands. These reactions are primarily directed toward non-institutional methods that movements use to advance their cause. Institutional methods are governed by well-defined rules and norms, which creates less uncertainty about how either side will behave during their interactions, unlike non-institutional channels that are more flexible and permissive. Given state officials' vested interest in maintaining public order and stability, the unpredictability of non-institutional movement activity can be a source of concern and a point of friction. How to respond to protestors, therefore, is a crucial question for governments and their agents.

In setting policing policy, political elites can set general expectations for officer behavior, and state policies can shape the training and operational practices of police forces. But as Donatella della Porta and Herbert Reiter (1986) observe, police officers have a relatively high level of discretion in their actions compared to other government agents given their involvement in situations that can be highly volatile. As a result, police reactions to protestors are influenced not only by state-level policies and elite attitudes but also by a range of other inputs, including departmental culture and leadership, their knowledge of protestor identities and motives, the characteristics of the protestors and protest tactics, and the overall dynamics at the point of contact (Earl and Soule 2006). This, in turn, helps to explain the considerable variation in how police might respond to protestors within the same country, or even within the same police department. On July 7, 2016, for example, one group of activists marched through the

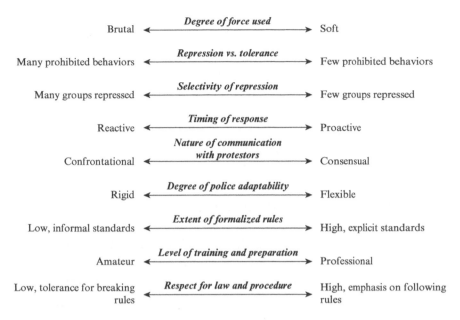

Figure 7.1 *Variable dimensions in policing practices*

streets of Manhattan to protest deadly police shootings of African Americans; the event resulted in occasional clashes, including one incident where a woman was tackled to the ground by several police officers, and at least 40 were arrested; one week later, another march – also through the streets of Manhattan and also to protest deadly police shootings of African Americans – unfolded without incident, injury, or detentions.

Police responses can vary along a number of key dimensions, as figure 7.1 (adapted from della Porta and Reiter 1986: 4) illustrates. While police in particular places might exhibit clusters of behaviors that reinforce each other (for example, being overly brutal, reactive, and confrontational), these different dimensions are distinct and officers can locate themselves at different places on each continuum – locations that can potentially even change from one protest event to the next. At the same time, certain behavioral tendencies and inclinations have historically been grouped together into distinctive policing philosophies that have shaped how security forces in multiple places have thought about how to interact with protestors and maintain public order. In the United States, three distinct policing styles have risen to prominence over the past century: the escalated force approach, the negotiated management approach, and the strategic incapacitation approach.

Escalated Force Approach to Protest Policing

The escalated force approach characterized the prevailing attitude to public order policing for much of the twentieth century.
Characterized by a confrontational stance toward protestors, this
strategy sought to control public spaces by force and did not tolerate movement groups attempting to lay claim to those spaces, even
temporarily or symbolically (Noakes et al. 2005). If initial attempts
to restore order did not work, this approach dictated systematically
escalating the amount of force applied until protestors complied
with police demands. Police frequently turned out in large numbers to potentially problematic sites with the assumption that a
dramatic show of force could limit trouble; if that failed, they also
employed riot control techniques and tools – tear gas, fire hoses,
police dogs – to confront activists and limit their actions. In so
doing, police using an escalated force strategy tended to ignore or
disregard the rights of protestors and sometimes viewed claims to
free speech and assembly as smokescreens for criminal behavior,
which they could set aside in order to remove agitators and agent
provocateurs for the greater social good. Communication between
the police and protestors was minimal and antagonistic, and police
had little knowledge or understanding of protestors' motives and
goals. Police tended to respond swiftly to any perceived breaking of
rules or flouting of social conventions; moreover, these responses
often involved policing meting out punishments on the spot (i.e.,
physical violence) in lieu of arresting protestors and letting the
courts sort out how to handle infractions of the law (McPhail et al.
1986).

   Not all protest was handled in this way. Clark McPhail, David
Schwingruber, and John McCarthy observe that police were often
willing to tolerate protest that took on familiar, contained forms.
When they recognized and felt comfortable with the type of tactics
that protestors used – the peaceful rally or the polite picket – police
allowed demonstrations to take place unmolested. But there was no
tolerance for protest that hinted at innovative tactics or employed
disruption, even if such tactics were non-violent in nature. Under
an escalated force paradigm, "civil disobedience was equated with
anarchy" (McPhail, et al. 1986: 52). Police also had little tolerance
for protesting groups that themselves violated social norms; middle-class members of the majority community were much more
likely to receive the benefit of the doubt compared to individuals

who were from subordinated groups or who represented "deviant" lifestyles or ideologies. As a result, policing through the 1960s and 1970s could include relatively orderly protests, such as the 1970 postal workers' strike that resulted in no arrests and no police crackdowns, as well as the 1968 Democratic National Convention protests in Chicago where an overwhelming police presence and heavy-handed tactics resulted in widespread violence and brutality.

The escalated force approach had its share of critics who argued that this style of policing was counterproductive and did more to create social disturbances than suppress them. Some argued that the idea of turning up at protests with a show of overwhelming force might be appropriate for riots or militant labor disputes of the early twentieth century, but that the strategy was poorly matched to the kind of civic protests happening in the 1960s and 1970s; the diversity of protests simply required a more flexible approach (McPhail et al. 1986). As protest crowds increased in size and sophistication during this period of heightened unrest, a simple show of force became increasingly provocative rather than overpowering (Redekop and Paré 2010). The failure of escalated force to contain violence also raised questions about its effectiveness at the federal level. Four different presidential commissions examined policing issues and made recommendations to revise major aspects of the existing heavy-handed policing model. In 1965, for example, the President's Commission on Law Enforcement and Administration of Justice noted that preserving order and constitutional rights would be far easier if "the leaders of protesting or demonstrating groups discussed, in advance with the police, the appropriate times and places for demonstrations and the methods of demonstrating" (quoted in Maguire 2015:76). Taken together, these critiques and pressures pushed police to adopt a new model for dealing with protestors: negotiated management.

Negotiated Management

Advocates of the negotiated management style of policing argued that, instead of repressing protestors, officers should instead work with activists ahead of time and negotiate the contours of demonstrations in advance. This way, police could accomplish two crucial objectives at once: they could minimize public disorder and increase the predictability of protest events. Allowing protests to take place would give social movements temporary control of public space, as John Noakes, Brian Klocke, and Patrick F. Gillham acknowledge, but doing so would potentially yield greater benefits for public order:

> Police would under-enforce the law and negotiate with protest groups prior to a demonstration in an effort to establish mutually agreeable terms and conditions under which the demonstrations would be held. To reach such an agreement, police would help protest groups cut through legal red tape, protect permit-holding protest groups from counter-demonstrators and ignore minor violations of the law during demonstrations in exchange for compromises from protestors on the route of the protest march or the location of a rally.
>
> (Noakes et al. 2005: 239)

With negotiated management, police deviated in some key ways from the underlying assumptions of escalated force (McPhail et al. 1986: 51–3). Instead of disregarding activists' First Amendment rights, police instead took steps to safeguard them and considered this an important component of their duties, alongside protecting property or lives. This did not give protestors *carte blanche* to cause chaos, but, with this new turn in policing, there was greater tolerance for some amount of disruption as a necessary and acceptable by-product of protest. Instead of trying to prevent it outright, police instead worked to limit and channel it to places and times where it could be contained and minimized. They also helped to arrange the logistics of protests and, in so doing, shaped the contours of events. For example, if a group's proposed venue or protest route was at odds with police preferences, officers could point out the problems with the initial plan and suggest alternatives more in keeping with their own priorities (Redekop and Paré 2010).

Key to this channeling effort was the development of public order management systems – policies, practices, and procedures designed to regularize and routinize protest to make it as predictable as possible (McPhail et al. 1986). One way police achieved this was by designing detailed permitting systems that required protestors to meet with department liaisons and work out details of staging and routing in advance. The US National Park Police, for example, requires demonstrators who want to stage a protest in highly symbolic Washington, DC locations, such as the monuments along the National Mall or the White House, to fill out an extensive form at least five days before an event to receive the necessary permits. The current 2017 form is seven pages long (including instructions and

notices), imposes an application fee of $120, and requires move-
ment groups to specify event start and stop times; locations; estimated number of participants; the equipment required (including
amplification, tents, stages, and props); plans for providing sanitation services, clean-up, and recycling; how participants will get to
and from the event; and names and contact information for event
marshals. It also requires a designated contact person who assumes
responsibility for the event.

This negotiated style deviated from the escalated force approach
in a number of other key respects. It put a premium on extensive
communication with protest groups as part of the planning process. Through these interactions, police and protest organizers
would come to know each other, set rules and expectations around
protest behavior, and pre-arrange ways to combat violations. Social
movement groups, for example, designated marshals from their
own organizations to help police their own people, and if civil
disobedience was part of the day's tactics, the police might even
pre-arrange arrests to estimate how many detainees there might
be and to get an initial sense of whether they should expect passive or active resistance (McPhail et al. 1986: 53). Vern Redekop and
Shirley Paré (2010: 14) recount how police in Alberta even set up a
storefront office prior to the 2002 G8 Summit to meet with movement organizers and work out details of the protests in advance.
Such tactics also relied on force or arrest as a last option, with police
taking up a less visible presence at protest events.

The negotiated management approach did seem to dramatically
reduce the frequency and the level of violence associated with
police/protestor interactions in the 1980s and 1990s (Noakes and
Gillham 2007; Gillham et al. 2013; Maguire 2015). In part, this
reduction was due to the amount of communication and negotiation, but also because many of the prominent movement groups
that had emerged out of the 1960s had subsequently developed
more extensive organizational structures and professional staff.
In keeping with Suzanne Staggenborg's (1988) expectations, such
groups were more inclined to leave behind disruptive street protests
in favor of institutional political activities for which they were well
equipped. Any protests that they organized were "well-planned,
carefully arranged, and fully permitted" (Noakes et al. 2005: 240;
also see Johnston 2011). Moreover, such groups were able to work
easily with police, designate people to liaise with the department,
and enforce pre-arranged details during their events because of

their formal organizational structures, which facilitated communication between leaders and members. But not all groups had the wherewithal or desire to engage with police in this controlled way.

Although negotiated management appeared to be a compromise solution that worked for everyone, not all protestors were pleased with the results. More confrontational grassroots groups rejected the idea of pre-arranging protest details with state officials, arguing that doing so undermined their ability to use disruption to call attention to their cause and put pressure on authorities. For more radical groups, the turn toward professional and moderate social movement organizations – which were a key feature of making negotiated management work as a strategy – de-fanged them and denied them of the very power that made them a force with which to be reckoned (Noakes et al. 2005). They also argued that, while negotiated management seemed to lessen police repression at protest events, this was an illusion and merely substituted overt forms of coercion (i.e., riot police, tear gas, use of violence) with more insidious and hidden forms of coercion and channeling that resulted in less physical violence but limited the actions of social movements just the same. Because negotiated management required the cooperation of protest groups to be effective, these radicals' refusal to agree ahead of time to protest restrictions revealed the limits of the policing strategy (Noakes et al. 2005; Gillham and Noakes 2007; Gillham et al. 2013; Maguire 2015).

Strategic Incapacitation

Negotiated management started to fall out of favor as the dominant mode of public order policing after the 1999 World Trade Organization protests in Seattle, which a number of scholars point to as a watershed moment (Noakes et al. 2005; Gillham and Noakes 2007; Noakes and Gillham 2007). The protests featured a wide assortment of activists broadly opposed to neoliberal economic policies, including labor unions, environmental groups, human rights organizations, and a fair smattering of anarchists. While the police, following the negotiated management handbook, worked out protest details with many of the formal organizations that planned to show up to the WTO meetings, not all groups agreed to prior limits on their actions and the "choreographed demonstrations" that would result (Maguire 2015). These grassroots radicals were relatively unknown entities to the police; in many cases, they lacked formal organizations or designated points of contact with whom police could negotiate, and their operational culture, which relied extensively on consensual decision making, made it hard for the police to predict their actions ahead of time. This decentralized structure, moreover, made it nearly impossible for organizations to develop and enforce any kind of prior demonstration plan, as members were able to improvise and alter their protest tactics on the fly (Gillham and Noakes 2007). Meanwhile, social media and mobile technology made it possible to share information among different activists, and counteract police more effectively than before (Earl et al. 2013). When the protests spiraled out of control, resulting in injuries and millions of dollars' worth of damage, the police were caught off guard, and the limits of negotiated management were made evident to officers in other cities who vowed not to make the same mistakes. In the following year, John Noakes and Patrick Gillham (2007: 335) write, police forces spent millions of dollars to acquire riot gear, attend specialty training, and prepare to "control a new breed of protestor" – one that was neither willing nor able to negotiate restraint ahead of time. The events of 9/11, just two years later, further intensified the turn away from negotiated management as police became more militarized and incorporated into an overarching homeland security paradigm (Gillham 2011; Maguire 2015).

In some ways, the strategic incapacitation model harkens back to the escalated force model. The new approach, Alex S. Vitale (2007) notes, has a zero-tolerance attitude toward disruption, seeing even minor disturbances as opening up opportunities for more widespread upheaval. In this reasoning, strategic incapacitation resembles the idea of "broken windows policing," which holds that, by preventing small crimes (e.g., vandalism, littering, graffiti, loitering), police can prevent a general climate of lawlessness that permits more serious crimes to occur (Kelling and Wilson 2015). In its public order analogue, by preventing even small disturbances during protests, police can stop violence, riots, and other social ills from unfolding. By prioritizing public order over free expression, strategic incapacitation resembles escalated force; but this new approach attempts to head off problems before they can begin and is generally more proactive in channeling movement activity than escalated force, which is at heart a more reactive approach.

Strategic incapacitation has two variants, the so-called "soft hat" or command-and-control approach, and the "hard hat" or Miami method (Vitale 2007). Soft hat approaches to incapacitation aim to micromanage all aspects of protest to leave nothing to chance or serendipity. This includes not just a highly restrictive permitting process, but also tight control over physical spaces as well: extensive use of barricades, police lines, and other techniques to divide, surround, and control the flow of people at protest events (Vitale 2007; Maguire 2015). Soft hat techniques also include extensive surveillance of protestors and contingency planning to prevent protests from getting out of hand. For groups that are likely to be more aggressive and hard to control, police can also employ hard hat methods, which involve the overwhelming show of force, a militarized approach to protest control (borrowing tools and techniques from riot police), creation of no-protest zones, pre-emptive arrests and detentions, and heavy use of less-lethal weapons (Vitale 2007; Maguire 2015). Strategic incapacitation shares a preference with negotiated management for *proactive* policing (compared to reactive policing with escalated force), but whereas negotiated management *underenforces* the law (letting minor offenses slide in the name of preserving order), strategic incapacitation *overenforces* the law to accomplish the same ends (Gillham and Noakes 2007). This approach also includes impression management insofar as officials also try to de-legitimate protestors by framing them as dangerous to public order. In the case of Occupy Wall Street, demonstrators were described as outsiders, violent, unsanitary, dangerous, a threat to the middle class, and "the very embodiment of just about every negative stereotype known to inspire public antipathy" (Gillham et al. 2013).

While not all contemporary protest events feature strategic incapacitation practices, many of the headline-grabbing incidents do, including many Black Lives Matter protests and the standoff between police and protestors blocking the Dakota Access pipeline in North Dakota. Contained protest is still likely to be met with negotiated management (Waddington 2007), but for more unfamiliar protest styles and transgressive tactics, police are likely to exert as much control as possible. In the New York Occupy encampment, for example, police created hard zones to prevent protestors from getting close to the financial institutions that were among their targets; when activists wanted to camp at Chase Manhattan Plaza, police encircled the space with barricades and officers. As Patrick F. Gillham, Bob Edwards, and John A. Noakes (2013) describe, even the bronze bull statue by the New York Stock Exchange had a round-the-clock armed guard to prevent vandalism or symbolic repurposing by protestors. Moreover, the tight control of space extended to adjacent "soft zones," where First Amendment rights were suspended, even for journalists covering the protests, who were also cordoned off far away from protestors. Police use of tear gas, less-lethal beanbag rounds, pepper spray, and other forms of crowd control contributed to the repressive environment.

Alternative Policing Styles and Comparative Models

The above discussion is admittedly focused on policing philosophies in the United States, though these techniques have also diffused to other countries around the world (Vitale 2007). But other countries have developed distinctive policing philosophies influenced by their own political histories and current contexts. In Europe, some law enforcement agencies advocate a strategic facilitation or liaison-based model that bears some resemblance to the negotiated management approach. As Clifford Stott, Martin Scothern, and Hugo Gorringe (2013) argue, this approach is strongly influenced by the European context in which national policies must be congruent with general principles set out in the European Convention of Human Rights, which create a legal framework whereby interference with free expression can only be allowed if clear and stringent criteria are met; undue restrictions on protest at the national level can, in turn, be struck down at the European level (Stott et al. 2013).

The liaison model advocates that police maintain clear lines of communication with protestors. These channels are used not only to coordinate the details of protests but to establish a level of trust with activists in order to help with decision making during the event. This knowledge, in turn, allows officers to be more fine-grained in their assessments about how to target force when needs arise, so that arrests or other coercive responses are not applied indiscriminately but only to those elements responsible for the disturbance. During protest events, police integrate themselves into crowds rather than holding themselves separate and apart; unlike the unobtrusive and minimal presence in the negotiated management approach, however, police liaisons wear distinctive uniforms to help them to facilitate crowd control but in a non-threatening manner (Scott, et al. 2013). Some of these features echo recommendations put forth in the interim report from President Obama's Task Force on Twenty-First Century Policing (2014), which suggests that, instead of strategic incapacitation, police adopt a more "layered response to mass demonstrations . . . [and] prioritize de-escalation and a guardian mindset." Moreover, the report echoes ideas about disaggregating movements and not treating protesting crowds as homogeneous actors when only some subset of them may be involved in transgressive protest (Maguire 2015: 104).

In addition to the liaison model, European security forces must also contend with how to respond to transnational protest events given the unique multi-level governance structure of the European Union, an issue that is of increasing interest to governments outside the EU context as well. Herbert Reiter and Olivier Fillieule (2006) note, however, that this is an area where practice has not evolved as far as theory. They argue that, in the EU context, national practices and standards still have considerable weight, and an absence of European norms or standards around issues such as data privacy and protection can hamper cross-border security efforts. They argue that, to date, most transnational policing has involved information exchange, which is a useful area of cooperation, but also one that supports a focus on pre-empting problematic protests rather than facilitating the broad exercise of free speech and assembly.

This orientation also leaves open room for more militaristic styles of policing (reminiscent of strategic incapacitation policies) against transnational movements like the groups working for global justice that protest meetings of large international organizations or meetings among heads of state. Such protests have frequently been framed as threats to national and international security, which, in combination with the information-sharing/pre-emption tendencies and still-developing cooperative norms among states open the door to a more restrictive, aggressive policing style, with emphasis on deterrence and control, and escalated use of force. Moreover, as Donatella della Porta and Sidney Tarrow note (2012), these policing strategies also evolve and adapt over time as protestors experiment with different tactics and as police seek to learn and share ways of handling public order used by their peers in other countries, for example via training in principles of strategic incapacitation employed by US law enforcement. The result, they note, is that policing tactics also diffuse in ways akin to tactical diffusion among movement organizations.

Outside the United States and Europe, policing styles can be significantly shaped by political and economic contexts, particularly the extent to which a country is democratic or autocratic, as well as its level of economic development. We know comparatively less about policing practices in such settings, and whether there are stable philosophies that guide training and police tactics (della Porta and Reiter 2006: 175). In some authoritarian regimes, police forces have less institutional autonomy and fewer standards of professionalism than in economically developed democracies; writing about sub-Saharan African countries, Otwin Marenin (2014) argues that the security services, including the police, tend to be heavily politicized and employed for partisan or particularistic goals rather than maintaining public order. As a result, police forces in such countries are likely to take a heavy-handed approach toward protestors, given that their political masters are unlikely to tolerate dissent, seeing it as a threat to their own legitimacy (Chang and Vitale 2013). Economically underdeveloped states, in turn, also tend to use repression more often than developed states, though the mechanisms for why this might be the case are undertheorized (Davenport 2007b). One hypothesis is that they are more likely to have a decentralized security apparatus with non-state actors and non-governmental groups helping to police and keep public order as part of an overall outsourcing or privatization of the state's traditional security function (Leander 2004; Baker 2010; Marenin 2014). Police in these circumstances are unlikely to develop much autonomy from their economic masters, on whom they are dependent for their very existence; as a result, they will be more likely to serve the interests of those who control the purse strings rather than the public good. In both authoritarian and economically underdeveloped states, it is unlikely that security forces will face much scrutiny of their methods or public accountability for their actions, which can further encourage heavy-handed tactics.

At the same time, weak states and authoritarian states both rest on shaky political foundations with shallow and easily disrupted claims to legitimacy. If such states attempt to repress challengers and fail, their hold on power can be significantly undermined in a way that consolidated democracies or wealthy states need not fear nearly as much. As a result, Paul Chang and Alex Vitale (2013) argue, governments in these types of positions are more likely to target relatively weak movements – those that are low-status (for example, lacking significant international support) or unable to impose significant costs on the regime (for example, consisting of largely subordinated groups). Confronted with challengers that both can threaten the state's hold on power and have sufficient resources or support to make repression both costly and risky, Chang and Vitale propose that authoritarian states (and, perhaps, weak and poor states as well) might seek to co-opt them as a safer way to avoid damaging confrontations.

Accounting for Variations in Protest Policing

Even when there is a discernable policing philosophy in place, as the discussion above has suggested, there are still occasions where police might opt to use more or less aggressive tactics to maintain public order. Because policing is often decentralized to local-level officials and has considerable room for impromptu changes in strategy based on developing dynamics on the ground, there is considerable discretion left in the hands of front-line officers about when they ought to allow protest to take place with little interference and where more restrictive practices should be employed. Because policing is selective toward groups – and this is a pattern evident all over the world, regardless of setting – it is worth investigating why police sometimes let certain protestors use certain tactics, while leaving little room for others.

Scholars suggest there are several broad sets of factors to consider when thinking about variability in policing: macro-level factors, including whether the state is democratic or authoritarian, whether the culture places much weight on citizen rights and free speech, and amount of transparency or public accountability for officials (della Porta and Reiter 1986; Davenport 2007a). There are also meso-level factors that involve the nature of policing organizations themselves: their level of funding, access to training, standards of professionalism, self-image (that is, whether they see themselves as guardians or warriors), and level of centralization within departments (Jaime-Jiménez and Reinares 1986; Rahr and Rice 2015). Particularly important are the protest features themselves. David Waddington (2007) argues that police are more likely to favor negotiated management strategies when protests are carried out by more institutionalized and well-known movement organizations and when the activists themselves are older, middle-class, and familiar (either personally or as a demographic) to officers (also see Redekop and Paré 2010). Jennifer Earl, Sarah A. Soule, and John D. McCarthy (2003) add that, as protests grow in size, officers are likely to shift from using more negotiated approaches to more coercive ones.

In a similar vein, the tactical choices that movements use during protest events can also matter: when police encounter unfamiliar tactics or more disruptive, transgressive tactics, they will turn toward strategic incapacitation in response for fear of protests spiraling out of control, but familiar, contained forms of protest are more likely to elicit negotiated management (Noakes et al. 2005). Cody Warner and John D. McCarthy (2014) point out that not just the particular tactical choice but the tactical *mix* might also play a role in policing calculations: movements that have a diverse repertoire (and that have many arrows to select from their tactical quiver) will make police more cautious and likely to err on the side of strategic incapacitation compared to movement groups that use both contained and limited forms of contention (also see Davenport 1995). Finally, David Waddington (2007) argues that not just the tactics but the setting and target of protests can also matter. When protests occur in highly symbolic settings or are directed at high-value targets (for example, visiting foreign dignitaries), the policing stakes are perceived to be higher, with institutional/social reputations on the line. As a result, police will want to maintain more control over such events, which might push them to more restrictive approaches.

These different factors can combine in various ways to intensify or moderate the effect on police choices. When protestors are well known, represent highly institutionalized and moderate organizations, use a few contained and familiar protest tactics, and are located in a democratic country, we might predict that police are likely to use negotiated management; change some of these variables – say, move the same protest to a more autocratic regime, or make the protest about an explosive political issue, or site it in a particularly sensitive place, and the policing calculations can shift to more of an incapacitation model. In all of these calculations, static variables like demographics, setting, and tactic are also interpreted by police through the lens of their previous experiences and expectations about what protestors might do in this particular round of protests. Past actions as well as beliefs about the future matter (and are interpreted in subjective ways), which makes this more about likelihoods and tendencies rather than a strict predictive formula.

That said, scholars have posited that these different inputs can point to two scenarios in which protests are more likely to be repressed: cases in which they are perceived to be a threat, and cases in which protesting groups are perceived to be weak. Police might gravitate toward repressing weak movement organizations because such groups are less likely to fight back effectively. In effect, targeting repression at the weak is a low-cost and low-risk strategy: police will have a higher success rate and can employ force without as much fear of harm or political or social repercussions. William Gamson (1990) argues this point when he notes that security forces are not as likely to challenge groups that can inflict costs on them. Targeting weak groups can happen in any setting, but we might hypothesize that in democracies where there is a norm of allowing protests and free speech (within limits), groups that are weak pose little harm and allowing them to protest is the easiest way for governments to demonstrate that they allow space for dissenting voices (see Davenport 2007b). In autocratic societies, on the other hand, weak protestors might be a tempting target to demonstrate the regime's intolerance for opposition. What counts as "weakness" can vary, though it can be linked to movement characteristics (size, demographics, resources) as well as external factors (level of support from outside actors). Jennifer Earl and her collaborators note, for example, that movements representing disadvantaged groups – the poor or ethnic/racial minorities – are often at a disadvantage vis-à-vis well-financed groups representing majority populations (Earl et al. 2003).

On the other hand, police might be harsher toward more threatening groups (McAdam 1982; Ayoub 2010). Groups that are less institutionalized, that use unfamiliar tactics, that are known to favor disruptive forms of protest, or that make radical demands will be seen as more harmful (see Chang and Vitale 2013). According to this logic, groups that represent subordinated or marginalized groups might also be disproportionately targeted for aggressive policing due to being perceived as dangerous while also occupying a structurally weak position in society. Christian Davenport, Sarah A. Soule, and David A. Armstrong (2011) found this to be the case in the United States for police interactions with African American protestors across three decades, which created a different dynamic for those "protesting while black" compared to movement groups representing primarily members of the demographic majority. In this assessment, front-line officers are also influenced by institutional assessments of harm and threat, which can affect their own perceptions, though protest dynamics on the ground generate their own, separate input.

Institutional Responses: Repression, Co-optation, Deflection, and Concession

While police are the front-line officials tasked with maintaining public order, political elites can also formulate strategies to respond to movement demands at an institutional level. Institutional responses tend to target underlying mobilizing structures rather than protest directly and, as such, tend to be more general in their focus, to use legal processes and mechanisms to respond to movement demands, and to be direct in their effects (Koopmans 1997). While state-level responses can vary from repressing movements to acquiescing to their demands, state actors tend to steer clear of giving movements everything they want, since such concessions can be costly and open the door to other claimants. That is not to say that movements never get what they want; they do – but such outcomes are rarely the first move states make. Clear and decisive victories are uncommon, absent weak states that cannot resist social pressure, or the presence of elite allies who embrace the movement's goals as their own. Instead, most governments will experiment with some mixture of repression, co-optation, and incremental concession as part of a broader strategy to de-mobilize movements by making mobilization difficult, making movement demands less oppositional to state interests, and providing sufficient benefits so that movements lose steam and their potential for disruption.

The particular mix of repression, co-optation, and concession depends in part on whether a state leans toward more coercive or facilitative responses to challengers (Johnston 2011). In this, we might expect that authoritarians are more likely to reach for repressive tools while democratic elites – given their concern for public opinion, winning elections, and support for human rights norms – reach for alternatives (Davenport and Armstrong 2004; Davenport 2007b). While this general association is broadly accepted, there are nuances in the way regime type affects the likelihood of harsh repression being used, as opposed to softer tools of control. Helen Fein (1995) argues, for example, that both well-established democracies and well-established autocracies are less likely to employ violence compared to states in the middle of the spectrum (also see Regan and Henderson 2002). It might also be the case that stable countries of any regime type are less likely to resort to repression compared to countries that have a more shifting political environment; democratizing states, in other words, might be less benign in their reactions than countries not undergoing transition, and until a country reaches a particular threshold of "democratic-ness," their allegiance to free speech and assembly norms is not certain. Regime type, in other words, is not quite as clear-cut a variable as might initially appear and countries might develop different mixes depending not only on whether they are democratic or not, but also on how stable they are and how deeply entrenched the regime type is.

Regardless of regime type, when reacting to movement demands, governments will want to minimize the amount of change they have to deliver, keeping policy concessions incremental and gradual. Reducing the pressure from movements that push for greater, faster change is thus a key priority. States have many different ways they could potentially weaken a movement's momentum, including encouraging an unfavorable public image, restricting the resources it needs to operate, thwarting activist recruitment, fueling internal rivalries and schisms, and delegitimizing leaders (Marx 1979; Davenport 2014). These different mechanisms can affect the supply of movements by making it harder for them to form or to function, as well as the demand for movements by reducing their public support.

Overt forms of repression are certainly one way to accomplish this by depriving movements the space in which to operate. The South African government followed this path when it outlawed the African National Congress and many other groups working to end apartheid in 1960. Similarly, Saudi Arabia banned the Muslim Brotherhood, whose brand of populist Islam is seen as a threat to the ruling royal family. Even democracies will restrict movements it sees as threatening, as both the United Kingdom and India do with armed separatist groups operating within their borders. Blatant repression, however, can be a risky strategy. It may not actually demobilize movements as much as move them underground, making their activities harder to track and control. Repression can also generate a public backlash, both at home and, potentially, abroad. If the movement is seen as sympathetic, then this backlash can undermine the regime's support and even legitimacy. And if repression is unsuccessful, it can also make the regime seem weak.

For these reasons, regimes may employ less obvious forms of control, including co-optation, channeling, and deflection, all of which minimize a movement's ability to challenge government authority. Christian Davenport (2014) argues that states can address the grievances that fuel the movement and "deplete" the problem. This strategy removes the movement's *raison d'être* and makes their claims irrelevant. Crucially, governments need not actually fix the underlying problems or grievances to deflect movement activities; they only need to distract people from those problems in some fashion. Patrick F. Gillham, Bob Edwards, and John A. Noakes (2013) suggest that governments can employ counterframing to shift public perceptions, and malign the movement to turn off its pipeline of support. For example, after a sniper killed five police officers at a peaceful Black Lives Matter protest in Dallas, the lieutenant governor of Texas called the members of the BLM movement hypocrites and cowards, and said during a television interview that, when shots were fired, the same activists who criticized the police "ran the other way, expecting the men and women in blue to turn around and protect them." Other lawmakers similarly condemned the movement, arguing on social media that the movement's central claims were lies and reframing the movement as the perpetrators of violence, not its victims. This rhetoric may not have dissuaded the movement's members, but the idea of the BLM movement itself being the instigators of violence is a frame that has gained some purchase in some quarters and can be used to challenge the legitimacy of the movement's goals and activities. Myra Marx Ferree (2005) notes analogous forms of "soft" coercion can be used by non-state actors to exert social control over movements; such groups often use strategies of ridiculing, stigmatizing, and silencing movements to limit their ability to challenge social norms and conventions.

Governments can also deprive movements of resources, which in turn limits their ability to carry out mobilization and protest activities. Here, overt bans are possible, but subtler forms of control can also be effective. Governments can create "front" organizations that appear to champion the same issues as the targeted groups and that compete for resources, siphoning off support from the initial SMOs (Davenport 2014). Governments can also use regulatory mechanisms and legal procedures to restrict activists' ability to generate resources. Funds can also be used to channel movement groups into less threatening positions. J. Craig Jenkins (1998) documented this dynamic among civil rights organizations in the United States; he found that funding from external donors tended to be channeled toward more moderate organizations, which strengthened their position vis-à-vis more radical organizations and rewarded groups that developed more centralized, professional organizational structures. Over time, such resource flows helped to build up groups that advocated less radical policy changes, and marginalized those whose positions were less palatable to policy elites.

In addition to these strategies, government officials can also attempt to co-opt movements and weaken their position by incorporating elements of their strategies or structures into the state apparatus, which, over time, blunts their desire for disruption or weakens their appeal to movement supporters. As Patrick Coy and Timothy Hedeen (2005) argue, co-option is rarely a grand plan, but can unfold in many incremental steps that, collectively, redirect movements to more institutionalized, less ambitious goals. For example, governments can offer movement leaders opportunities to influence policy by joining government commissions or task forces; by enlisting their services, officials can tie movement actors to their own goals and objectives and bring them into the system rather than have them standing in opposition to it (Uitermark and Nicholls 2014). In so doing, elites can reduce activists' ability to serve as regime critics, given their own participation in making policies. This co-optation both limits what movements can push for and distances those movement actors who are given preferential access or status from others in the movement, which can contribute to internal disputes and schisms. Such strategies can be double-edged for movement leaders: on one hand, co-optation can lead to positions of some (limited) influence and a chance to advance some of their policy goals. Co-optation, in other words, might give the movement some of what it wants. But it can also make it harder for the movement to push for bigger reforms, leading to what Marcus McGee and Karen Kampwirth (2015) term "visibility without rights." As Coy and Hedeen write:

> determining whether the inclusion/participation is a positive step forward for the movement's long-range goals is a difficult and delicate task. The movement representative's seat at the table and the voice that comes with it may partially transform the prevailing system and may modify power relations, but not always for very long or deeply . . . and not without other costs to the movement or movement organizations . . . One cost is the loss of the movement's relative autonomy to create

and maintain independent social and political spaces where critiques of status quo norms and policies may be nourished and articulated free from the conceptual constraints and boundaries of established thinking and existing policies.

(2005: 417)

In addition to these potential trade-offs of working with state actors, movement elites can also face a backlash from their own supporters who might interpret the decision to collaborate as a betrayal. Changing the system from within is not always a popular sell as leaders of the Inkatha Freedom Party discovered when they argued that the best way to end South Africa's apartheid system was not to oppose it with force of arms (as the ANC argued) but to work with allies in the government to reform it peacefully. This proved to be a controversial stance, and the party's leader, Chief Mangosuthu Buthelezi, was accused by some regime opponents of being a turncoat or government puppet. Such attitudes are more likely if the decision to work with the government yields few tangible benefits; the longer co-optation goes on without meaningful results, the harder it will be for leaders to justify the strategy or disentangle themselves.

The Consequences of Government Choices

Regardless of how government representatives respond to movement claims and protest events, their choices form part of the larger strategic environment that informs subsequent movement dynamics. Just as governments react to what movements are doing and have done in the past (along with interpreting the reasons why prior government choices worked or failed), movements observe how officials respond to their activities and adjust their future demands, mobilizing strategies, frames, tactics, targets, and event organizational structures accordingly. In this way, movements and their opponents both influence how each other behaves, and react to the behavior that they helped to shape. Movement and government choices, in other words, are highly interdependent and recursive (Tilly 1995a: 39). But government responses to movement tactics can have some specific consequences that are worth noting, particularly in the relationship between repression, subsequent levels of protest activity, and the likelihood of movement radicalization.

Repression and Mobilization

If one of the government's chief goals is to minimize movement activity and curtail demands for change, it would want to avoid any responses that might increase a movement's size or strength. Unfortunately, it is not always clear which combination of responses might accomplish this goal. One area of uncertainty is the effect that government repression has on subsequent social movement activity, sometimes called the "repression–mobilization nexus." Some scholars argue that higher levels of repression increase costs sufficiently to dampen the level of mobilization we might see: the more states repress, the less protest there will be (Olzak et al. 2002), and what protest does take place might be more moderate and modest in its claims in order to avoid state targeting (Vairel 2011: 36). On the other hand, increasing levels of repression might also *increase* protest if the state's coerciveness makes people angry. As Christian Davenport writes, "fear [of repression] can be provocative as well as paralytic" (2014: 30–1). Still others argue that repression does not have a simple linear relationship to mobilization; at very high levels or very low levels, there is no appreciable effect on mobilization, but in some middle zone, repression can increase mobilization (the inverted-U model). This logic can itself be inverted: at very high and very low levels of repression, mobilization increases (at high levels, because of increased grievances from the repression itself; at low levels, because of the reduced cost of protesting), and in some middle zone, repression can decrease mobilization. As Hank Johnston (2011: 108–13) illustrates, these are just four possible relationships between these two variables – there are still more combinations that are possible (figure 7.2)! Complicating matters even more, there is empirical proof for all of these proposed relationships so that, as Ekkart Zimmerman claims, there are "arguments for all conceivable basic relationships between government coercion and group protest and rebellion" (quoted in Koopmans 1997: 151; Earl 2011).

To parse this puzzle and the conflicting evidence, Ruud Koopmans (1997) suggests that thinking about institutional and situational responses as two distinct dimensions helps clarify the repression–mobilization nexus. He argues that institutional forms of coercion depress protest while repression at the point of police–protestor contact tends to increase it. Another way to parse the data is to

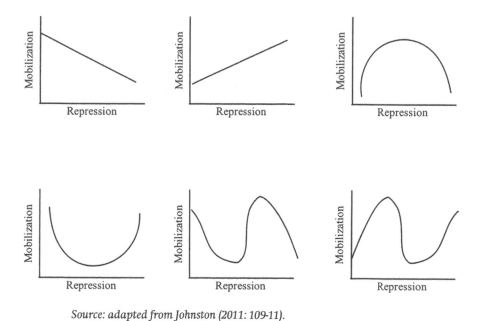

Source: adapted from Johnston (2011: 109-11).

Figure 7.2 *Possible relationships between repression and mobilization*

think about short-term and long-term effects of repression. Looking at the 1979 Iranian Revolution, Karen Rasler (1996) argues that repression can lead to short-term declines in protest mobilization, but that, over a period of time, as activists regroup and rethink their approach, it can spawn a more powerful movement. Thinking about repression and sequencing in a different way, Christopher M. Sullivan, Cyanne E. Loyle, and Christian Davenport (2012) argue that when protest activity is already declining, repression can revitalize mobilization, but when protest activity is increasing, repression can dampen it. For other scholars, it is not the timing or sequencing of repression as much as the quantity and perceived proportionality that counts. David Hess and Brian Martin (2006) argue this point, noting that if the repression is perceived to be unjust, then it can elicit widespread outrage against the state; here is where a combination of hard tactics and "soft control" methods like counterframing a movement in an unsympathetic way can be used to complement one another. Finally, Mark Lichbach (1987) suggests that a key aspect of the repression–mobilization nexus is the consistency of response: governments that have a coherent and steady approach to either tolerance or repression will generate less mobilization as a result than governments that apply coercion in an erratic manner.

The lesson here is that the repression–mobilization nexus is ambiguous if we treat all forms of repression and all forms of mobilization as interchangeable. If, however, we disaggregate the timing, the type, the intensity, or other key characteristics of a repressive policy (and, similarly, disaggregate what we might mean by "mobilization") it might be easier to find clear relationships between such variables (Earl 2011). It is also worth noting that such disaggregation might also make it easier to identify the conditions under which repression has no appreciable effect on mobilization, which is also a possible outcome.

Radicalization and Escalation

In addition to affecting the amount of mobilization, government reactions can also influence the nature of movement claims and tactics, particularly the extent to which they remain moderate or become more extreme, or, in the case of tactics, the extent to which they remain contained or become more transgressive. These processes of radicalization and escalation can be triggered by repression, though other government responses can produce them as well. When governments engage in repression – particularly when that repression is perceived to be unfair and heavy-handed – it can encourage movement groups to consider more costly tactics in order to compel the government to listen. Movements tend not to start with fully transgressive tactics from the very beginning; such tactics are costly and risky, so organizations will move to them gradually, when more contained forms seem ineffective.

Not all movement actors will agree that the ineffectiveness of contained tactics in the face of repression warrants tactical escalation; if such disagreements arise in movements, they can produce schisms. In extreme cases, these schisms can spawn rival breakaway groups that then compete with the parent organization for support, resources, and legitimacy (Gupta 2014). Such splits tend to occur along moderate–radical lines – divisions that are often echoed by a parallel split over whether to pursue moderate, incremental goals or insist on more radical, transformative goals. These disagreements over what a movement should demand can occur not only because of state repression but also because of co-optation.

When some members of a movement are co-opted and advocate for working with state officials to reform the system, the hardliners, purists, and ideologues may reject the idea of compromise and changing institutions from within. The rejection of this approach can independently produce schism. Combined with disagreements over tactical responses to repression, it can produce potentially debilitating internal disputes that divert attention away from the target and focus it on intra-movement dramas.

When radical–moderate splits take place, they offer states additional strategic options for dealing with movements and limiting their power. When movements have multiple, rival groups, states can pit them against each other by using selective incentives to strengthen the least threatening while repressing the most troublesome (Gupta 2007). This strategy can produce a so-called "positive radical flank effect" (Haines 1984, 1988), in which the presence of a radical challenger helps rival moderates to gain support from external allies who want to avoid the more intractable group gaining ground and supporters. By promoting moderate groups over radicals, in turn, government elites can channel protest into more contained, institutionalized, predictable, and unthreatening forms. Moreover, by elevating the moderates and working with them, the government can hope to satisfy a sufficient number of movement supporters for them to decide active participation is no longer necessary. Once such individuals demobilize and allow moderates to work within institutions, the only people likely to remain in the movement are the ideologues and purists who, unfettered by the moderates, can radicalize without fear or constraint (Tarrow 2011). However, such groups are also more vulnerable to counterframing by elites, who can more easily portray them as zealots, extremists, fanatics, or – if they use violence – terrorists. Once such labels stick in the public mind, then the state has considerable latitude to employ force against the remaining activists without much fear of pushback or censure.

This dynamic can be seen in the evolution of the nationalist movement in Northern Ireland, which has been internally divided between relatively moderate and more militant organizations (Gupta 2007). Throughout the three decades of violence known as the Troubles, the British government (as well as the Irish government) made explicit choices to bolster the position of moderates in order to marginalize and weaken the more threatening organizations such as the Irish Republican Army. When the IRA eventually disbanded and its political wing, Sinn Féin, decided to work within existing political institutions, it carried most of its supporters with it, but those who disagreed with this strategy – the self-styled "true republicans" – defected and reaffirmed their support for armed opposition to the British state. But this choice also made it easy for the British government to present the dissident republicans as terrorists and extremists; indeed, all of those dissident groups have been placed on multiple international terrorist watch lists while Sinn Féin has gone on to become one of the largest political parties in Northern Ireland.

Concluding Summary

Social movements protest to call attention to their demands and to elicit a reaction from authorities. While this chapter has focused primarily on the reactions of state authorities – both those in charge of situational responses at protest sites and those who shape institutional and policy responses to movements – many of the ideas and dynamics discussed here also apply to non-state actors as well. While corporations, universities, and other potential opponents of movements may not possess the same personnel or power as a national state, the distinction between situational response and institutional response remains a useful one. Protests in universities, for example, feature interactions between student demonstrators and campus security staff, just as protests at corporations feature clashes between activists and private security forces. In such instances, there are also individuals at higher levels of the institution who can shape policies, offer carrots (and threaten with sticks) to try to control, manage, channel, and minimize the changes that movements demand.

In all of these interactions, the choices that states (or other targets) make are informed by a number of variables, including past experiences with protesting groups and expectations about their future behavior. Protestors, in turn, respond to government reactions by calibrating their future strategies to maximize their impact. Together, these actions–reactions–adjustments–readjustments constitute an intricate and variable set of interactions that shape and are shaped by what others are doing. It is what makes movements so dynamic, but also can make it harder to pin down the effects of particular choices – as in the repression–mobilization nexus – because so many outcomes are highly contingent. As the next chapter discusses, this contingency is also a feature of movement outcomes in general.

Questions for Discussion

1 In what ways do governmental preferences for incremental change, minimizing cost, and limiting risk affect how they are likely to react to social movement demands? Why might authoritarian and democratic regimes reach different conclusions about how to best respond to social protest?

2 How does the dynamic interaction between police and protestors, in which each side learns from and adapts to the actions of the other, help to explain the evolution of policing from escalated force strategies to strategic incapacitation? How can we explain the difference between public order policing in the United States and in other countries?

3 How do attributes of individual police departments and movement protest tactics affect the way that police choose to maintain public order?

4 Why might states prioritize coercive or facilitative approaches when deciding on an institutional response to movement demands? What factors might shape this decision?

5 Why might repression be a counterproductive response for governments hoping to curtail protest? Why might governments nonetheless believe repression is a rational response to social movements?

Additional Readings

Earl, Jennifer. 2011. "Political Repression: Iron Fists, Velvet Gloves, and Diffuse Control." *Annual Review of Sociology*, 37: 261–84. Provides a good overview of a number of topics related to repression, policing, and social control.

Jenkins, J. Craig. 1998. "Channeling Social Protest: Foundation Patronage of Contemporary Social Movements." Pp. 20–35 in

Private Action and the Public Good, ed. Walter W. Powell and Elisabeth S. Clemens. New Haven, CT: Yale University Press. Examines how grants from external donors can co-opt and moderate social movements.

Noakes, John A., and Patrick F. Gillham. 2007. "Police and Protestor Innovation since Seattle." *Mobilization*, 12(4): 335–40. Provides an overview of some key developments in public order policing.

CHAPTER 8

The Aftermath

Objectives

- To recognize the different ways that movement success can be defined and assessed.
- To determine what variables might affect movement success and the difficulties involved in determining how and when movements make a difference.
- To understand the role social movements play in larger macro-social processes and structures, including democratization and globalization.

Introduction

Under Polish law, groups that wish to propose legislation to the country's parliament may do so if they are able to gather 100,000 signatures from citizens within a three-month span. In early July, a group of pro-life organizations did just that, collecting over 450,000 signatures in support of a bill that outlawed abortion in virtually all cases. Poland's existing law bans abortion aside from instances involving rape, incest, and cases in which the mother's life or fetal health are at stake; the proposed measure would have ended those exceptions and added penalties for women who sought to end their pregnancies and physicians who aided them in doing so. The bill was received enthusiastically by the Catholic Church, which wields enormous social influence in the country, as well as the ruling Law and Justice Party, whose members voted overwhelmingly to send the proposal to a parliamentary committee for consideration. Its top officials also signaled support for the measure; Beata Szydło, the Polish Prime Minister, indicated during a radio interview that she backed the idea of tightening the country's already strict abortion laws.

But not everyone in the country was so enthusiastic. A few days before parliament was to hold a vote on the bill, pro-choice groups organized massive protests to voice their opposition to the proposed legislation. Across the country, thousands of women and men dressed in black and took to the streets carrying protest signs and coat hangers to send the message that the bill would not end abortion, but drive it underground, making it more dangerous. The participation in this "Black Monday" demonstration was larger than even organizers expected. Despite bad weather, 30,000 people gathered in the rain and cold in Warsaw's Castle Square while thousands more protested in nearly 100 other Polish cities. Tens of thousands of people went on strike, missing work and classes, as part of the campaign. The protests also took to social media where individuals posted pictures of themselves dressed in black and holding signs as a show of support. People in other countries even held protests in solidarity, with parallel demonstrations taking place in Prague, Oslo, Reykjavik, Dublin, Brussels, and other cities around the world.

The impact of these demonstrations was striking. Although the Law and Justice Party had previously endorsed the bill and indicated its strong support for the measure, it backtracked following the protests. At the start of the week, some members of the government had dismissed the protestors as trivial or worse; Witold Waszczykowski, the Foreign Minister, had remarked that opponents were merely "dressing up, screaming silly slogans and vulgarities" and "making a mockery of very important issues," while Krystyna Pawłowicz, one of the Law and Justice parliamentarians, said that the bill's opponents were "fans of killing babies." But as public opinion shifted in support of the demonstrators – and in favor not just of vetoing the proposed measure, but possibly even of liberalizing the laws currently on the books – government officials started to sing a different tune. Two days after the strike and street protests, the government's Minister of Science and Education said that the protests had "caused [the government] to think and taught us humility," while the leader of the Law and Justice Party, Jaroslaw Kaczynski noted that "observing the social developments, we have come to a conclusion that this legislation will have an opposite effect to the one that was intended . . . this is not the right way to proceed." Meanwhile, the Prime Minister and other lawmakers distanced themselves from their previous statements on the proposed bill. Lawmakers eventually defeated the measure in a 352–76 vote, angering the bill's supporters and surprising its opponents (Davies 2016; Lyman and Berendt 2016).

The Polish pro-choice protests seem to point to the ability of social movements to effect real social change. Prior to the mass outpouring of opposition, the abortion ban seemed certain to pass; shortly after the demonstrations, however, the bill failed decisively, with government officials admitting that their stance shifted as a result of the protests. This example seems to affirm what political scientists Gabriel Almond and Sidney Verba found when studying civic culture in democracies. They argue that when confronted with a political problem, many citizens turn not to formal groups like political parties for help, but to informal associations, "arousing their neighbors, getting friends and acquaintances to support their position, circulating a petition," and that cooperating "with one's fellow citizens in attempting to influence the government . . . is an effective means of increasing one's own influence" (Almond and Verba 1965: 150, 151). It is an alluring idea, and given the Polish example, one that is empowering for citizens who might otherwise feel relatively powerless when confronting vast and impersonal political institutions and those who wield more political and economic influence. But is this optimism warranted? Is the Polish case a representative example of what social movements can accomplish, or is it an outlier?

A quick review of some of the main movement examples from previous chapters reveals a decidedly mixed picture. There are movements that can point to significant policy gains: the marriage equality movement was able to defeat the Minnesota constitutional amendment that would have enshrined the one-man-one-woman definition of marriage; Greenpeace's campaign against LEGO led to the company breaking off a decades-long partnership with Shell; anti-GM groups in India were able to halt the distribution of Bt brinjal seeds; and the Chilean government elected in 2013 promised to deliver on some of the key demands of the student movement, including making higher education more accessible and affordable to all. On the other hand, some movements experienced little or no progress in advancing their goals. Hong Kong's umbrella protestors were unable to compel the government to institute democratic election rules, Occupy Wall Street failed to reform the neoliberal economic order or eradicate income inequality, and Black Lives Matter continues to fight systemic racism in public institutions. In some cases, social protest actually left participants *worse* off than before, as in the case of the pro-democracy protestors in Tiananmen Square who not only failed to bring about political reforms, but whose protest ushered in a reversal of more liberal policies that had been put in place prior to 1989.

These examples highlight the futility of asking whether movements are effective at delivering social change. The answer is yes. And also no. It is clear that movements *can* sometimes accomplish meaningful, even dramatic, results, but they can also flail around ineffectively and fail to deliver on the outcomes that their supporters seek. Even cases of success can be ambiguous. The marriage equality movement managed to beat back the Minnesota constitutional amendment in 2012, but, in that same election year, it failed to defeat a similar amendment in North Carolina. Greenpeace was able to sever the ties between LEGO and Shell, but doing so did not prevent Shell from pursuing its plans to drill for oil in the Arctic. And while Indian activists were able to prevent the introduction of GM eggplant seeds, that success did not carry over to other possible GM crops, such as mustard, that might be approved in the future. The Arab Spring uprisings are a particularly vivid example of this ambiguity of outcome: the pro-democracy protests that swept through the region led some countries to switch from autocracy to democracy (Tunisia), others to make some democratic reforms without committing to full democracy (Morocco), some to move to democracy only to revert back to authoritarian rule (Egypt), others to use the protests as a reason to increase repression against their citizens (Bahrain), and in a few countries, protests ushered in political unrest and collapse (Libya, Syria).

As such variation suggests, the issue is not *whether* movements matter, but *how* they matter: when they might be successful, what the consequences of their mobilization might be, and the extent to which those consequences affect the lives of people in those societies. There is little scholarly consensus on these questions, with some arguing that movements have considerable influence on public policy (Baumgartner and Mahoney 2005), while others counter that they have very little (Giugni 2007). Edwin Amenta and his co-authors (2010: 293) attempted to uncover patterns across movements to give some concreteness to such questions by analyzing 54 movement case studies from top sociology journals. They found that 93 percent of the cases had demonstrated at least some weak influence on policy outcomes (a third of the cases had strong influence), but ultimately noted that this analysis was limited in the conclusions that could be drawn as their sample was not representative and focused mostly on larger movements that tend to be more successful in general. As a result, the issue of when and where and how movements matter is still an unsettled one.

Defining Movement Outcomes

One of the key difficulties that face scholars trying to untangle these questions is a definitional one: what counts as movement success? At first glance, this may seem like a straightforward question insofar as movements are presumably successful when they get what they want. But what is it that movements want? In the case of the Polish pro-choice movement, the answer is relatively simple: it wanted to defeat the specific abortion legislation that was introduced in spring 2016. But not all movements have such a specific and concrete goal. The student movement in Chile, for example, had a long list of demands that all pertained to education reform but included provisions ranging from making higher education more affordable, to regulating private, for-profit institutions, to overhauling admissions policies and standards, to increasing wages for educators. Even so, the Chilean students have fairly concrete demands. The protestors in Tiananmen Square wanted democratic reforms – but what, specifically, such reforms should entail were never fully clarified or universally agreed upon among movement participants. And as a prefigurative movement, Occupy Wall Street shied away from making any explicit demands at all, preferring instead to embody the kind of egalitarian and democratic society it wanted to inspire. Measuring movement success by the ability to achieve some specific menu of policy requests, therefore, is not at all straightforward.

Further complicating the issue are cases of partial gains and hollow victories. When movements are able to further some of their policy goals, but not all, does that count as a success or a failure? The anti-GM movement blocked transgenic eggplant, but not cotton, and its fight against GM mustard may not succeed; does it count as a success because it achieved some victories, or a failure because it did not accomplish everything on its list of demands? Hollow victories also complicate coding movement outcomes insofar as they might count as technical victories but be rendered impotent because of later reversals or imperfect implementation. The BLM protestors in North Charleston who convened after the shooting death of Walter Scott, for example, pushed for the formation of a citizens' advisory committee with powers to oversee the police department. They got their wish – technically speaking. But when the details of this new group were finally revealed, many BLM activists criticized the proposal for not going far enough and doing too little to promote the kind of transparency and accountability they were seeking. These definitional difficulties are what prompt many scholars to conclude that defining "success" is not as simple as determining whether a movement has achieved its stated demands (Tarrow 2011: 215).

Broadening the Definition I: What is Success?

Since achieving stated policy goals is an overly limited and problematic standard of success, scholars have proposed alternative ways of defining and assessing movement outcomes. In a particularly influential formulation, William Gamson (1990) argued that movements succeed when they can win new advantages for their constituency and/or gain recognition from elites. New advantages can include policy gains like changes in laws, practices, or benefits. Workers who go on strike for better compensation might get a salary increase, or more flexible sick leave, or a more generous pension plan. They might also obtain benefits like the right to form a labor union, which involves changing a group's institutional access and power. The other dimension – gaining recognition – makes it possible for challenging groups to be seen as legitimate by those in positions of power. For example, when the South African government finally legalized the African National Congress in 1990 after banning the group for 30 years, it gave the organization legal standing, which made it possible for the ANC to bring an end to apartheid through overt methods. Legalization was seen as a victory for the group since it no longer had to remain in the shadows but could advocate openly and enter into negotiations with the government as a lawful group with valid political demands.

Focusing on policy outcomes and legitimacy, however, still strikes some scholars as being an overly broad definition (Giugni 1998). The concept of "new advantages," for example, can be further refined into different types of advantages, such as procedural, structural, or substantive. Herbert Kitschelt (1986) distinguishes among these three types of advantages with examples drawn from the anti-nuclear movement, with procedural gains coming from getting greater access to formal institutions and arenas of decision making (e.g., getting anti-nuclear referenda placed on electoral ballots), substantive gains coming from policy decisions (e.g., persuading lawmakers to increase research funding for green energy alternatives), and structural gains coming in the form of a reorganization of the political system (e.g., the formation of Green parties to contest elections). The idea of a movement's constituency has also been challenged as overly narrow, with calls to broaden the idea to one of collective goods (Amenta and Young 1999) such that movements can affect more than just the individuals who belong to movement groups. Labor movements that agitate for a 40-hour working week, for example, stand to benefit all workers, not just those who currently belong to labor unions.

These types of success can be further complicated by considering not just whether movements can gain an advantage but also the degree of responsiveness to movement claims demonstrated by those in power (Burstein et al. 1995). Thinking of outcomes in this way reorients us from looking only to see whether there has been a formal change in policy to asking about the effects of that policy when assessing movement outcomes. Paul Schumaker (1975) argues that political elites can respond to movement demands in different ways, all of which might be subsumed under Gamson's notion of winning new advantages, but that have distinct repercussions for a movement's goals. He differentiates access responsiveness (i.e., elites being willing to hear a movement's concerns) from agenda responsiveness (i.e., willingness to place demands on the agenda) from policy responsiveness (i.e., adoption of new policies). This is where Gamson's typology ends; but Schumaker goes further, distinguishing between achieving policy gains and achieving social change. He argues that movements might achieve output responsiveness (i.e., the effective implementation of new policies) as well as impact responsiveness (i.e., the degree to which grievances are alleviated).

In this way, Schumaker invites us to consider whether "success" should primarily capture policy shifts or whether it should also take into consideration the degree to which the underlying complaint that generated social movement mobilization in the first place has been addressed. These two things do not always go hand in hand; groups might successfully push to pass desired policies only to discover they do not affect the underlying problem in the intended way or to the intended extent. One of the goals of groups that worked to pass abstinence-only sex education programs in US high schools, for example, was to lower teen pregnancy rates. Such

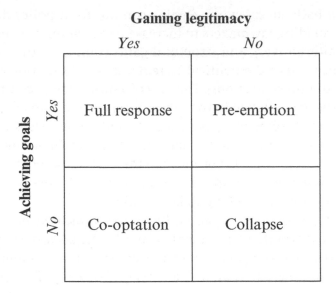

Source: Gamson (1990).

Figure 8.1 *Typology of movement outcomes*

groups were successful in getting some state legislatures to adopt this curriculum, which suggests a clear victory; but if the metric is not about the policy but the underlying problem – teen pregnancy – then the victory is far more ambiguous, as some studies show teen pregnancy rates in abstinence-only states as higher than in places with comprehensive sex education programs (Kohler, et al. 2008; Stanger-Hall and Hall 2011), while advocates of abstinence-only programs point to countervailing evidence (Jemmott III et al. 2010).

In addition to broadening the range of outcomes and making nuanced distinctions between winning an advantage and the potential impact of that gain, scholars also argue that definitions of success should acknowledge that outcomes are not binary. That is, policies are not simply present or absent but can manifest to different degrees, which invites questions about whether a success needs to meet a particular threshold in order to count. Gamson, for example, offers four different ways in which movements might win advantages and gain access (figure 8.1). The resulting typology makes it clear that Gamson's two dimensions of success can operate independently; a movement organization might gain legitimacy without policy gains and vice versa. But it raises questions of whether the mixed-success cells should count as primarily successes or failures. Co-optation, as chapter 7 suggested, can result in meaningful advantages for movement groups, even though it also typically reduces their ability to push for more extensive or radical change; still, some change is usually better than no change from the perspective of most challenging groups. Similarly, pre-emption might undercut a movement group's purpose by incorporating its agenda into existing organizations and institutions (also see Tarrow 2012). Far-right political groups in Europe, for example, have seen their anti-immigrant stance incorporated into some mainstream political party platforms, which puts their issues on the agenda while disassociating those policies from groups that mainstream political actors might find distasteful (van Spanje 2010). The problem becomes even more acute when we move from a four-cell typology to arguments that there are more gradations between success and failure, or incorporate outcomes that do not just involve failure to change policy, but include possible back-lashes that actually worsen the initial grievance condition (Amenta and Young 1999: 26) or unintended consequences that might contradict the original goals (Giugni 1998: 386). Most movements do not have unambiguous and decisive victories; they sometimes gain some advantages but might experience setbacks in other ways, so that their overall trajectory is one of continual incremental victories and losses (Snyder and Kelly 1979; Gupta 2009).

Ultimately, there is no objective way to solve this question of what counts as success. There is a basic subjectivity at play here insofar as different actors bring various definitions of success to the table, and perceptions of success may matter more than objective criteria (Burstein et al. 1995; Giugni 1998: 383). Doowon Suh (2014: 5) argues this point when he claims that "it is not *objective consequences* but *perceived and interpreted subjective outcomes* that are causal to movement dynamics" (emphasis in original). Moreover, these perceptions can be influenced by framing choices so that "subjective outcomes do not always mirror objective ones but the two can diverge" (Suh 2014: 5). This opens the door to movement actors and their opponents providing alternative interpretations to advance their own interests. Governments, for example, might frame particular concessions as significant wins for a movement organization in the hope that doing so will encourage some activists to demobilize, even if the concessions in question might stop short of delivering what the movement demands. Movement elites, on the other hand, are likely to frame outcomes that encourage ongoing mobilization and new recruitment by appealing to positive emotions of efficacy and empowerment (i.e., framing outcomes as successes that vindicate the group's ability to effect change) or, alternatively, by appealing to emotions of fear and anxiety (i.e., framing outcomes as failures to persuade the group it must step up its efforts) (Gupta 2009). What counts as success, in other words, depends a great deal on how we choose to interpret it.

Broadening the Definition II: Which Successes?

The various definitions and examples discussed above all focus on policy outcomes: concrete policy gains, the impact of those policies, or a group's standing to pursue policy changes. But this narrow focus on policy excludes a range of other impacts that movements can have. Movements can also matter for culture, identity, emotion, discourse, and other less tangible domains that are not easily reduced (if at all) to a piece of legislation or institutional processes. Such effects have historically been underexplored (Giugni 1998; Tarrow 2011), though this gap has been increasingly filled with new scholarly work since the late 1990s. Some of this work addresses the way that social movements can influence the personal lives and identities of individuals, both through the experience of participation itself and in the way that movements can shape social understandings about particular identities. Doug McAdam (1999) observes that activists who helped to register black voters during the 1964 Freedom Summer campaign displayed different biographical trajectories from their counterparts who did not participate; some of these differences could be framed as net positives (e.g., an overall higher level of political and civic engagement, including participation in other activist opportunities), while others could be seen as more ambiguous (e.g., such activists were less likely than others in their age cohort to marry and have children). Movements can also affect individual identities and ideologies by strengthening an individual's sense of belonging to a community or her support for a particular worldview (Melucci 1996; Munson 2002).

In addition to individual biographical and identity effects, movements can also shape the way that society at large thinks about and talks about particular identity groups. The Dalit movement in India, for example, has concrete policy goals around dismantling discrimination, but it also wants to challenge social preconceptions and prejudices around the Dalit identity and to associate it with demands for dignity and equality. Through their efforts, the movement's members hope to influence both state and society. Such goals are intertwined; the advances that they make in one domain can influence the other: "States provide authoritative communications that can greatly influence identities and are often in the vanguard of recognizing new identity claims through changes in policy . . . these results can range from a challenger's constituency gaining more respectful labels in official government representations, to having the group formally recognized in state policies and regulations . . . to defining racial categories" (Amenta et al. 2010: 291). And just as state practice can carry over into the way society talks (and thinks) about social categories like "Dalit," so too can changing social practices influence government policy.

Similarly, movements can affect social discourse, mores, and norms more broadly (della Porta 1999). Because meanings and social understandings are constructed, movements can offer alternative framings. Through their demands and their actions, they can present alternative narratives about particular groups or social ills. In this way, HIV/AIDS activists sought to de-stigmatize those who carried the illness (Gamson 1989) and LGBT activists reclaimed the word "queer" and turned it from a slur to an identity that people can celebrate (Rand 2014). As Marc Steinberg notes, by "artfully transforming the meanings of the discourses used to dominate them, challengers both provide their claims with credibility and cast doubts on the assumed truths power holders voice through these words" (2002: 224). Movement claims and rhetorical strategies can also take on lives of their own and enter mainstream consciousness where they can shape broader conversations and influence the way that people interpret the world around them. Occupy Wall Street's slogan, "We are the 99 percent," for example, arguably has entered into public discourse in this way; variants of this idea of haves and have-nots have subsequently surfaced in contexts ranging from soundtracks (e.g., a Woody Guthrie album marketed as a "soundtrack for the 99 percent") to real-estate listings (e.g., "live like the 1 percent") to political rhetoric completely unconnected with the Occupy focus on income inequality and neoliberal capitalism; Democrats in Congress, for example, used the phrase in connection with legislation on mine safety, among other issues (Stelter 2011).

Movements can also influence the emotions of those who participate, which is another type of outcome that is rarely referenced. As James Jasper (1997) argues, movement members can feel very deeply when part of a movement community, and while some of these feelings might be instrumental (for example, anger or frustration fueling a desire to take action), other emotions can be pursued as ends in themselves. To put it another way, sometimes movement participants join in order to experience and reinforce particular feelings. Among these, Jasper names loyalty and solidarity toward others, pride, compassion, joy, hope, love for – and sometimes erotic attachments to – other members of the movement community. A related outcome can be the social capital and trust that participation can create among those who join movements (Diani 1997). Such experiences are not simply a by-product of participation – for some, they are significant features of becoming part of a movement community. They constitute outcomes on their own.

Finally, movement outcomes can also include the ways in which they shape the landscape for other movements. If we think about the relationship between movements and other actors as a series of interactions in which each group makes choices that, in combination with the choices of other actors, produce some kind of effect, those outcomes then become part of the environment and the historical record and shape subsequent choices. When the marriage equality movement squared off against proponents of the one-man-one-woman definition in places like California or Hawaii, the consequences of those battles subsequently shaped the tactics, frames, and other strategic choices of other movements and their adversaries. As Doowon Suh (2014: 5) summarizes, "movement outcomes become a critical factor in the subsequent rounds of collective action and the future dynamics of social movements." In this sense, even abject failures and reversals can pave the way for subsequent successes if those future actors are able to learn from the past and make necessary adjustments to their operations and priorities or to pave the way for others (Staggenborg 1995). This learning, however, is not only limited to groups within the same movement. As David Meyer and Nancy Whittier (1994) point out, this learning can also happen across movements, as the effects and choices of one movement can be imitated or adapted by entirely unconnected groups who look to the experiences and outcomes of other movements to emulate successes and avoid failures.

Broadening the Definition III: When and Where Should We Look?

Movement outcomes happen in many different venues, and can manifest not just as policy outcomes, but also as discursive outcomes, identity outcomes, emotional outcomes, and more. This wealth of domains broadens our idea of where to look for evidence of movement impact, but can also magnify other analytical difficulties. Movement outcomes are difficult to assess not only because mixed outcomes are possible, but also because the impacts that movements can have need not move in the same direction across different domains. To put it another way, movements might have a positive impact according to one criterion but have that impact undermined by outcomes in a separate domain. Rory McVeigh, Daniel J. Myers, and David Sikkink (2004) found this contradictory effect in their study of the Ku Klux Klan and its framing strategy. The same strategies that served the organization well in terms of recruiting and mobilizing supporters and making them feel deeply connected to others – positive results in terms of collective identity, solidarity, and emotion – also worked to alienate the general public and limited the Klan's ability to make progress on its political goals and blunted its broader impact. Here, success in one domain directly undercut the group's success in another; more broadly, it suggests that movements sometimes have to strategize about the trade-offs they may face and how they should prioritize the different kinds of outcomes they might be seeking (Bernstein 2003).

Mixed outcomes are also possible when targets respond in variable ways to protest. Because government targets are not unitary actors but composed of multiple departments and individuals, heterogeneous responses are not unusual. This heterogeneity is further accentuated when movements have differential effects at local, regional, national, and international levels (Pastor, Jr., et al. 2009). This dynamic can occur in any political system, but in states that are large and federal, the multiplicity of government officials and levels can significantly magnify the range of outcomes that movements might experience at the same time. In the US, the move to limit the resettlement of Syrian refugees, for example, has received support from some state governors, including the ones from North Carolina, Illinois, and Ohio. At the same time, the mayors of key cities within those three states, including Chapel Hill, Chicago, and Dayton, have explicitly stated they would welcome refugees.

These simultaneous and oppositional outcomes can make it more complicated to assess how a movement might matter in general or at a national level without disaggregating the political environment in some way. The same could be said for non-government targets when, for example, protests against corporations might change the behavior of some, but not all, of the businesses in a given industry.

Timing and sequencing also create their own analytical complications. It is not clear at what temporal point we should assess movements to determine what, if any, impact they might have had. Unless movements are able to influence some kind of policy or other domain in a clear, decisive, and short time span – like the Polish pro-choice movement, which protested on a Monday and defeated the intended legislation on the Thursday of the same week – the appropriate amount of time required to capture the impact is uncertain. Look too soon and impacts may not be visible; wait too long, and any effect may be hard to attribute causally to movement actions. Such effects may not even be visible until after the movement loses steam and goes into dormancy. As Kenneth Andrews (1997: 801) writes: "the impact of movements may lag behind the peaks of mobilization, so that effects are seen only after the movement has declined." It is also possible for movements to have different effects in the short and long terms (Rasler 1996), or that initial gains erode over time. All of these scenarios can complicate the analysis of what "counts" as a movement success or effect.

Assessing Causality and Explanatory Variables

Apart from the definitional difficulties, social movement scholars must also confront the thorny problem of causality when assessing how movements might matter. Even if we fix a concrete and bounded definition of the outcomes in which we are interested, it is not at all easy to attribute responsibility for such outcomes, since the number of factors that might influence policy change, or implementation, or social norms, or discursive practices are many. In the case of the Polish pro-choice movement, such attribution is not as difficult because the temporal sequencing limits the number of other factors that might have intruded to change the minds of elected officials. Moreover, there is first-hand testimony from a number of different legislators connecting their change of mind to the protests; drawing a conclusion that the protests "caused" the change, therefore, is not such a large leap. But for many movements, this causal connection is much harder to demonstrate convincingly. If the government increases fuel efficiency standards for automobiles, for example, is that a result of environmental groups mobilizing to reduce fossil fuel use? Or does that decision also reflect lobbying efforts by companies pioneering hybrid and electric engines or public opinion polls supporting higher fuel efficiency standards? If all three influenced the decision, how important was the social movement's actions versus lobbying and public opinion? It should quickly become apparent that parsing out shares of responsibility is no easy task (Burstein et al. 1995; Tarrow 2011).

Part of the difficulty is that the outcomes to which movements contribute involve many other actors. Public policy is shaped not just by movement organizations, but by political parties, lobbyists, countermovements, public opinion, the media, and perhaps other governments and international organizations. Otto von Bismarck once quipped that laws are like sausages; it is better not to see them being made. Perhaps this is true, but because legislative processes are often complex, lengthy, and opaque, it is hard to differentiate causal contributions even when watching them from start to finish. Other types of outcomes similarly involve multiple actors. Cultural effects, for example, are shaped not just by the movement, but by countermovements, government responses, and the media. In fact, in their study of movement case studies in top journals, Edwin Amenta and his collaborators found that, of the 50 cases in which a positive outcome or effect was reported, the overwhelming majority – 47 – were mediated by other actors and conditions (Amenta et al. 2010). Purely internal effects, like emotions or feelings of collective identity, are comparatively easy to attribute to the work of movements. Here, too, other actors are also relevant since movement dynamics are intimately shaped by what other actors do in response to its claims; still, movements can affect their internal environments more directly than outcomes in the external environment.

Explaining Outcomes: Key Variables

Even though it might be difficult to fully disentangle movement actions from the other inputs that might influence outcomes, social movement scholars have still attempted to identify the factors that might increase a movement's likely impact. If not all movements are successful (however we might define success), then what differentiates the successful movements from the ones that have little or no positive impact? Although research does not point to a single "magic bullet" that, when present, guarantees movement success, there are clusters of variables that recur as significant predictors of positive outcomes. The most frequently invoked come from the political process tradition that, given its dominance in existing theories of mobilization, has carried over to studies of movement outcomes as well.

First, a number of scholars have proposed that one key determinant of a movement's effectiveness is whether it is situated in a favorable political opportunity structure (Jenkins and Perrow 1977; Kitschelt 1986; Amenta et al. 1992; Amenta and Young 1999; Cress and Snow 2000; Soule and Olzak 2004). For most studies of political opportunity structure and outcomes, the focus is primarily on policy success, or whether a movement is able to enact at least some of its legislative priorities. But the same idea could be applied to outcomes in non-policy domains and the opportunity structures that might apply. A movement's ability to affect public discourse, for example, might hinge on operating within a favorable discursive opportunity structure (McCammon et al. 2007). A movement's emotional impact, in turn, might hinge on the prior emotion cultures present in the organization, as well as broader emotional opportunity structures, or what Katja Guenther (2009: 341) describes as the "expectations governing what emotions are considered appropriate, or feeling rules." The idea of change being facilitated by certain macro-structural rules or institutional arrangements thus can translate to settings beyond the strictly political. In all cases, movements must match their strategies to their existing environment in order to maximize their impact (Giugni 1998: 379).

Certain dimensions of the opportunity structure are more frequently invoked as being crucial to a movement's chance of success. First, movements can have more of an impact when they operate in an environment going through a period of flux or upheaval. Jack Goldstone (1980) argues that movements can achieve their goals more often during periods of crisis, and Sidney Tarrow (2011: 215) similarly argues that when the political system is unstable – perhaps during increased periods of contestation or the height of a protest cycle – "claims become so broad and elites so besieged that profound changes are forced onto the agenda." But crisis moments and periods of heightened protest can have a downside for movements.

If governments are beset with multiple competing demands from different quarters of society, they may opt to respond with changes that satisfy the broadest grouping of claimants, which Tarrow notes can lead to policies built on the lowest-common denominator – not a recipe to please most movements.

In addition to general instability, other authors point to the presence of elite allies as another key determinant of movement success and impact (Schock 1999; Stearns and Almeida 2004). When there are allies who are sympathetic to a movement's demands, they can open the door to policy change, help to initiate legislation, and ward off opponents. When elite allies combine with favorable political opportunity structures, the environment becomes particularly favorable to movement claims (Franceschet 2004), a finding that Brayden G. King (2007: 15) finds also holds true for movements that target corporations instead of the government. Such allies are helpful when there is strong opposition to the proposed changes from some quarters of the government or when the policy changes involve lengthy, complex legislative process (Santoro and McGuire 1997). At the same time, Tarrow (2011: 218) points out that having elite allies can sometimes work against movements if they forfeit aggressive action and disruptive tactics to give their partners inside government room to operate. While such insider allies can help to advance a movement's agenda, allies do not always deliver and they do not always deliver the results that the movement would like. The student movement in Chile encountered this scenario when, in 2013, Michelle Bachelet was re-elected to the presidency and promised to enact many of the movement's core demands. The student movement scaled back its protests accordingly to give the new government space to push reforms forward. But in 2015, the protestors resumed their demonstrations out of frustration at the slow and incomplete progress of change. They discovered that, sometimes, elite allies are not enough to make sufficient difference.

Organizational structures are also highlighted as a key factor that separates successful from unsuccessful movements. In general, scholars have argued, movement organizations that are more formal in structure, bureaucratic, and professional have a better chance of accomplishing their goals (Gamson 1990; Cress and Snow 2000; Soule and King 2006). Moreover, groups that are relatively unified in identity and purpose are predicted to be more effective, as factional in-fighting can divert attention and energy inwards, away from pursuing policy goals (Frey et al. 1992). For these authors, more formal organizations are better equipped to interact with government elites and play a role in the lengthy and technical process of shaping legislation. Because, as chapter 3 discusses in more depth, formal organizations have an advantage when operating in institutionalized environments, they can be more effective in policy discussions. Not all scholars would agree with this assessment, however. Frances Fox Piven and Richard Cloward (1977) would argue the inverse, noting that movement groups that become more formal sacrifice their disruptive power and, in turn, their ability to demand more transformative policy changes.

Framing choices can also help movement groups to exert influence or, conversely, prevent them from achieving the success that they desire. For frames to be effective, they must resonate with the intended target audience. Brayden G. King (2007) argues that, in particular, they must resonate with a movement's potential allies, be they corporate executives or political elites. In this instance, movement organizations' prognostic frames would be the most relevant, since their proposal of how to address their grievances must also be congruent with what elite allies think is plausible, reasonable, and realistic. Framing can also undermine movement efforts, either because prognostic frames fail to resonate with the elite audience or when diagnostic, prognostic, and motivational frames are not entirely congruent with one another. The appeals that might energize a movement organization's members might turn off its elite allies, for example, or alienate members of the general public. The Irish Republican Army found this to be true when its commitment to armed struggle, which was popular with its support base, made it harder both to bargain with the British government and to appeal to the majority of Catholics in Northern Ireland who were sympathetic to the nationalist cause but turned off by the IRA's use of violence.

Finally, tactical choice is frequently invoked as a key factor that differentiates successful and unsuccessful movements. Most often, this discussion centers on whether movement groups use disruptive or violent tactics versus more contained and institutional choices; a related point is whether groups pursue radical or transformative goals that potentially up-end the status quo or more modest change. William Gamson (1990) found that violence was effective at furthering a group's aims, a finding that others have corroborated to varying extents. Lee Ann Banaszak (1996) notes that aggressive and confrontational tactics succeeded in her study of women's suffrage movements, and James Button (2015) likewise found violence can be effective at advancing movement goals under certain circumstances. Like other scholars, he does not claim that violence is always a successful strategy but, instead, that it must be matched to the particular context in which a movement finds itself. He points out that violence is most likely to work in a movement group's favor if it is adopted in combination with other strategies, when violence is not severe enough to undermine public or elite sympathy toward the movement, when violence is not too frequent or severe enough to disrupt or threaten other social actors, when the movement's aims are specific and limited, and when power holders have sufficient resources to meet movement demands. But not everyone agrees that violence is a potentially useful strategy. Paul Schumaker (1975) argues that non-militant approaches have a positive effect, though he acknowledges that the effect is weak and not universal. Supporters of institutionalized and contained tactics also note that such approaches are more likely to be effective when movement organizations are seeking complex policy changes (Santoro and McGuire 1997). Looking more specifically at protest against corporations, Forrest Briscoe, Abhinav Gupta, and Mark S. Anner (2015) argue that movements are more likely to see greater diffusion of desirable practices when they use persuasive tactics, as opposed to disruptive tactics, especially when the target being persuaded is prominent or well regarded by others.

While political opportunity structures, organizational forms, frames, and tactics are the most commonly invoked independent variables used to explain variations in movement success, other scholars have proposed more movement-specific possibilities as well. Muzammil M. Hussain and Philip N. Howard (2013) argue, for instance, that in the Arab Spring uprisings, the information infrastructure, primarily the use of mobile phones, became a key ingredient that separated successful outcomes from mobilizations that ended poorly for the activists; they conclude that countries that lack the necessary digital infrastructure are less likely to experience popular movements for democracy. Kiyoteru Tsutsui and Hwa Ji Shin (2008), in turn, argue that, for Korean residents living in Japan, a variation of the transnational boomerang strategy discussed in chapter 4, not violence, was most effective at furthering a human rights agenda; for them, movements that were able to harness both top-down pressure from international organizations and bottom-up local pressure were able to achieve the most gains. This pincer-like move, however, was also contingent on having a favorable opportunity structure both domestically and internationally, such as strong global human rights norms and integration of the domestic political arena into the international one.

From Variables to Pathways and Processes

For most scholars, no single variable magically accounts for the difference between social movement success and failure. Instead, political opportunity structures typically combine with other considerations like framing or tactical choice. Such combinations underscore the argument that a group's strategy must match its organizational aptitudes and its operating environment in order to have any chance at success; a mismatch would make it difficult to have any meaningful impact (Szymanski 2003). However, even with this fluid relationship between variables and outcomes, this idea of outcomes can still feel rather static with its suggestion that particular "recipes" of variables can produce positive movement outcomes. A more dynamic approach moves away from these variables and focuses instead on the different pathways and processes by which movements are likely to influence outcomes, using methodological techniques like Qualitative Comparative Analysis (QCA), which is the focus of this chapter's methods spotlight. This shift in focus from variables to processes also makes it possible to consider not just how different variables and contexts might combine but also how targets can react in different ways to similar conditions as well as how the choices of movement actors, targets, and other relevant groups combine with each other to produce variable effects.

One way in which movement organizations can influence change is by serving as informational shortcuts for lawmakers. According to this perspective, people in positions of power and influence have little time and limited ability to inform themselves about the range of policy choices in front of them. Given these restrictions, lawmakers will use shortcuts like the signals that social movements send to understand the public's preferences and act accordingly (Giugni 1998; Burstein 1999; Burstein and Linton 2002). Because lawmakers presumably want to choose policies that the public favors, social movements provide government officials with one measure of what the public wants. By demonstrating en masse, Polish voters, for

Methods Spotlight: Qualitative Comparative Analysis (QCA)

QCA is a method pioneered by sociologist Charles Ragin (1987, 2008) that attempts to bridge large-N quantitative techniques and small-N qualitative techniques by offering an approach that allows researchers to combine detailed knowledge of individual cases with the ability to identify larger patterns and dynamics across those cases. As such, QCA is sometimes described as a "medium-N" method (Wagemann 2014). In their study of corporate responsiveness to social protest, for example, Marc Dixon, Andrew W. Martin, and Michael Nau (2016) used QCA to analyze 31 campaigns – far more than can be adequately described and analyzed using purely qualitative methods and too few for standard statistical tests; likewise, in her study of tactics used by teachers' unions to respond to unfavorable legislation, Amanda Pullum (2016) used QCA to analyze 15 campaigns. Charles Ragin suggests that QCA is particularly useful for analyzing from 5 to 50 cases.

QCA focuses on the different causal pathways by which variables (also known as "conditions") might combine to produce an outcome of interest. Because causality can be complex, there is no presumption that there is one and only one pathway that leads to the outcome; instead, QCA makes it possible to explore whether there are different "recipes" or combinations of conditions that can produce the outcome (Wagemann 2014). To use a frivolous example, you can use many different recipes to produce a chocolate chip cookie; it does not ultimately matter whether you use wheat flour or gluten-free flour, or whether you use white sugar or a combination of white and brown sugar – ultimately, many different recipes will give you chocolate chip cookies. QCA, which draws on the mathematical logic of set theory, also allows researchers to identify causal conditions that might be necessary or sufficient for producing the outcome in question. While chocolate chip cookies may not require a particular kind of sugar (and some may be made with sugar substitutes), we might agree that chocolate chips are the one necessary ingredient; without them, the end result cannot be called a chocolate chip cookie.

A researcher performing QCA identifies an outcome of interest and a set of relevant cases that include instances where the outcome is present as well as instances where it is absent. Based on these cases and relevant theoretical literatures, the researcher identifies the causal conditions that might influence the outcome of interest. This is one way that QCA allows for qualitative exploration of cases; without this case-specific knowledge, a researcher will not be able to proceed with the classification of cases that the method requires. The next step is to construct a "truth table" in which cases are sorted by the different causal recipes that they exhibit. An example will clarify this step. Let us imagine I am interested in understanding the conditions under which my fairly disobedient dog will shake hands. Having observed my dog on 40 occasions, I have identified three conditions that might be particularly important factors in successful hand-shaking: whether I offer a treat, whether he has a large audience, and whether he is feeling playful. With these three conditions, my truth table will have eight rows that, combined, will represent all possible combinations of my conditions (in the table, 1 = condition present, and 0 = condition absent).

I additionally sort my observed cases according to these combinations: in six cases, none of the conditions were present, and my dog did not shake hands; in five cases,

Treat offered	Audience present	Feels playful	Shakes hands (# of cases)	Does not shake hands (# of cases)
0	0	0	0	6
1	0	0	5	0
0	1	0	0	4
0	0	1	0	4
1	1	0	6	0
1	0	1	4	0
0	1	1	5	0
1	1	1	6	0

I offered a treat and my dog did shake hands, etc. With the truth table, I can then use specialized software that uses Boolean algebra to further analyze this table and identify specific causal pathways that might lead to the outcome of interest. With this truth table, for example, the software identifies two distinct causal pathways that lead to my dog shaking hands: he will shake EITHER when a treat is offered OR when there is both a large audience and he is feeling playful at the same time. These alternative pathways will produce the same outcome, but no other combination, it seems, will induce my dog to shake hands. With these alternative recipes, I can then go back to my cases and explore the relevant causal sequences further and think about how these pathways increase our knowledge of both the underlying theory and the chosen cases.

Explore this Method

The example given above is highly simplified; QCA with real data often involves cases that do not neatly fit, or that contradict each other. As a result, before getting hands-on with data and QCA tools, it is useful to read more about some of the specific techniques involved for constructing, simplifying, and analyzing truth tables. In addition, QCA can involve so-called "crisp sets," in which cases are coded as 1 or 0, or "fuzzy-sets" in which cases can be evaluated in a more nuanced way. Nicholas Legewie (2013) has a nice introduction to QCA techniques at www.quali-tative-research.net/index.php/fqs/article/view/1961/3594. To analyze truth tables, it is helpful to have access to software that can handle QCA techniques. If you have access to statistical software like Stata or R, there are specialized commands that work within these programs that support QCA, like the "fuzzy" command in Stata and the QCATools package in R. The COMPASS research network, which connects researchers interested in this method, lists a number of other software tools that can be used for QCA (www.compasss.org/software.htm#QCA3), which include stand-alone programs that can run on Windows, Mac, and Linux operating systems.

example, sent a sharp and clear message to the ruling party that their support for the anti-abortion measure would result in falling public approval and perhaps a tough re-election battle in a few years. This mechanism can also work in autocratic societies, though not as strongly. Absent electoral competition, political elites do not have to worry about winning votes, but they also do not gratuitously want to choose policies that have little public support. All else being equal, they would rather pass laws that have public support and, in turn, require less coercion to enforce. For issues that are of central importance to authoritarian regimes, rulers may disregard unpopularity to pick policies that shore up their hold on power, but given that even strong authoritarian states have limited resources to expend, they too would prioritize policies that have some public legitimacy (or at least not active opposition) over those that might give rise to popular challenges to their power.

Given this causal pathway, the factors that would be most likely to play to a movement's advantage would, therefore, include anything that enhances its capacity to send clear and unequivocal messages to those in power. Size of protest, for example, can be a useful way to show widespread public support, which might make movements prioritize mobilization and tactics that have broad appeal and low barriers for participation. As Paul Burstein and April Linton (2002: 386) write, "when an organization makes demands of elected officials, the officials want to know what the organization wants, and how meeting its demands will affect the officials' electoral prospects. Does the organization have many members or few? Can it mobilize them to vote? Will their decisions about how to vote be affected by what they hear from the organization?" Large displays of collective preferences can sway undecided officials to back the issues the movement cares about.

Another combination of variables, however, can achieve similar results. Because the public does not care equally about all issues, movements that are able to signal the intensity of their interest might be able to sway lawmakers, who calculate that they are more likely to be punished electorally by the smaller group that is deeply invested in an issue, compared to the larger group that might be indifferent. Many so-called "NIMBY" ("not in my backyard") movements have this dynamic. Such movements spring up to oppose the proposed site for a controversial project – a landfill, a nuclear power plant, a halfway house for convicted felons – and frame their opposition not to the project itself but to its location.

If the residents of the proposed neighborhood band together and are vocal about their opposition, it might override the fact that the rest of the community has no objections to that site. Calculating the electoral consequences of pushing forward versus relocating the project to a less hostile neighborhood, government officials may well conclude that, even though the larger population might back the location, they are far less invested than the individuals of the neighborhood; officials might not be rewarded by the majority for backing the project site, but they are much more certain to be punished by the minority. Given such calculations of salience, officials may decide that relocation is the less risky political option. With this logic at play, movements may instead opt for smaller displays of high-cost protest to signal their resolve and commitment to the cause, rather than larger displays of low-cost protest. The pathway remains the same, but, given different contextual factors, movements might opt to prioritize different strategies and tactics.

Movements can also do more than simply create signals for lawmakers; they can also present themselves as assets that can help officials further their own goals by offering public support, mobilizing their activist base, providing symbolic and sometimes tangible resources. In this mediation model, Edwin Amenta and his co-authors (2010: 298) write: "[for] a movement to be influential, state actors need to see it as potentially facilitating or disrupting their own goals – augmenting or cementing new electoral coalitions, gaining in public opinion, increasing the support of the missions of government bureaus." Paul Burstein and April Linton add that officials must also consider whether "the organization can provide resources – money, campaign workers, access to media – that can help the elected officials win re-election" (Burstein and Linton 2002: 386). Labor unions, for example, can mobilize their members, provide outreach, generate media coverage, and more in support of candidates who back their positions on workers' rights, minimum wage laws, or free trade deals. Members of the Religious Right can offer the same for politicians whose positions on social issues such as abortion, same-sex marriage, abstinence-only sex education, and other salient policies match their own (Leege 1992).

A more indirect way to affect outcomes is to sway the opinion of the public through movement activities in order to influence how power holders behave. This approach recognizes that most officials will not go against the wishes of the majority (even in authoritarian countries, as long as the issue in question has little bearing on the government's hold on power). By influencing how the majority of people think or behave, or the values that they hold, or the salience they assign to issues, movements can change the incentives that govern lawmakers' choices. This pathway is more likely to be used by movements that have a distinct disadvantage in terms of numbers, organize around salient issues in which their stance differs from that of the majority, or face other constraints that make it hard for them to appeal directly to officials in charge. The movement opposed to capital punishment, for example, had had little impact in appealing directly to lawmakers; the number of activists is relatively small and the majority of the American public does not agree with their stance (table 8.1).

Gallup provides data on attitudes to capital punishment going back to 1936 and, apart from a short period in the late 1960s, more people have favored the death penalty than opposed it. And, unlike the NIMBY example above, the death penalty is salient to more people who tend to have stronger opinions about whether the government has the right to execute certain criminals. Given their numbers, current public opinion, and the salience of the issue, it would be unlikely for this movement to be able to move lawmakers' position through protest signaling alone. Instead, changing public opinions about the death penalty might be a more effective use of organizational resources and activist energies. This suggests that tactics that focus more on public education, awareness, and outreach, or efforts to shape public discourse and norms through framing work, might have more impact than either contained or disruptive protests in public sites. Here again, the specific tactics and strategies that can make a difference are contingent on the particular pathway by which movements think they are best able to make change, and the context and preferences of other actors that have a say on the issue.

A completely different mechanism to sway officials has less to do with persuasion and more to do with direct force and disrupting the status quo. The logic here is that, for some issues that may be more marginal, persuasion and signaling will do little to bring concerns to the forefront and place them on the political agenda; in such circumstances, movements may decide that destabilizing the status quo and forcing political elites to deal with the crisis may be the best option (Soule and Olzak 2004). Because social movements tend to have less social, institutional, and political power compared to government officials (or corporations or most other targets), they

Table 8.1 Historical attitudes toward capital punishment in the United States

Year	Percent favor	Percent oppose	No opinion
2015	61	37	2
2014	63	33	4
2013	60	35	5
2012	63	32	6
2011	61	35	4
2010	64	29	6
2009	65	31	5
2008	64	30	5
2007	69	27	4
2006	67	28	5
2005	64	30	6
2004	64	31	5
2003	64	32	4
2002	70	25	5
2001	68	26	6
2000	67	28	5

Source: Gallup: www.gallup.com/poll/1606/death-penalty.aspx.

cannot bargain in the same way that other groups occupying more privileged spaces might. With an unequal playing field, so to speak, the only way to increase bargaining power is to protest and disrupt business as usual (Piven and Cloward 1977; Burstein et al. 1995). This is also the principle that Saul Alinsky advocates in *Rules for Radicals* (1971: 127) when he recommends that movements "go outside of the experience of the enemy" to keep them off-balance and uncertain. Such a strategy can have real drawbacks, including the possibility of a backlash severe enough to make the new status quo more restrictive and harsh than before the movement took action. Still, in cases where the issues get little public traction and little official support, some movements may decide that this is the best route to being heard. In such cases, the choices that might enable large protests, or sustained protests, or credibility with lawmakers and the general public might be set aside in favor of more controversial and polarizing choices that promote transgressive methods.

The above discussion suggests that, rather than a fixed and static set of variables that potentially affect movement outcomes, what is instead required is a focus on how context, strategies, and the potential pathways by which movements hope to influence decision makers all interact. Moreover, the calculations that movements make are also influenced by what they have tried in the past and what other actors may do as well. Movements that opted for large, peaceful displays to influence policy makers directly may decide, based on prior results, to shift to small displays of high-cost activism, or switch to a different form of pressure entirely. These calculations are also influenced by their assessments of how other actors – including governments, countermovements, and the general public – might react. If the discursive opportunity structure is open and the public seems primed for a different way of framing an issue, that avenue might be prioritized over, say, disruption. In sum, a movement's ability to have an impact is highly contingent on a number of factors and calculations, which makes it impossible to formulate a standard "recipe" for influence, but that also opens up a range of strategic options that movements can adjust as their circumstances require.

Looking Beyond the Movement

In addition to internal effects and external effects on policy, norms, and discourse, social movements can also have larger consequences that shape macro-social processes such as the spread of democracy around the world, the development of civic virtues and social capital, and even the growth of a global civil society. In none of these areas are the effects of social protest clear-cut or unambiguously positive (or negative). Rather, social protest adds complexity to the political and social dynamics that are already in motion.

Social Movements and Democratization

There are more democracies in the world today than there were 100 years ago; this is not a particularly insightful claim given that there are also more countries now than a century prior. But democracies are more widespread and more people live under democratic regimes than in previous decades (figure 8.2). This spread of democracy is also accompanied by a spread of social movements and protest. This is no coincidence; in many parts of the world, including sub-Saharan Africa, Eastern Europe, Latin America, and

Southeast Asia, the emergence of budding democracies was facilitated by widespread popular protest that swept away old authoritarian structures and ushered in more responsive political systems (Bratton and van de Walle 1997; Schock 2004). As a result, these fledgling democracies "are arriving already equipped with habits and experience of mobilization for collective action" (Goldstone 2004: 337). Not only do people have more familiarity with protest as a way of achieving radical change, but this experience also spills over into the institutional arena where parties and other formal actors frequently have organizations and memberships that overlap with movement groups. Such an overlap becomes even more explicit when movements evolve into political parties that operate within the institutional arena while still retaining the broad membership support and mobilizing potential from their movement past. South Africa's African National Congress, for example, transitioned from being a social movement to a governing party, as did Robert Mugabe's Zimbabwe African National Union – Patriotic Front party, Hamas in the Gaza Strip, and Evo Morales' Movement for Socialism in Bolivia. Such transitions from movements into political parties are not limited to new or transitional democracies; movements can become parties in places where democratic institutions and norms are well established. The environmental movement spawned the Green Party in Germany and other European countries, and nationalist movements of both progressive and conservative bents have produced associated political parties in various places, including Wales (Plaid Cymru), India (the BJP), Belgium (Vlaams Belang), and Canada (Parti Québécois). In Spain, the anti-austerity *indignados* movement spawned Podemos, a political party that currently holds the third-largest block of seats in the Spanish parliament. In both developed and developing democracies, movements that overlap with or become political parties can deliver memberships that are civically engaged, familiar with advocacy, and committed to participatory norms – all attributes that can produce robust and vigorous democratic institutions and habits.

The relationship between protest and democratization goes the other way as well: not only can social movements help usher in democracy, but democratic governments in turn also increase opportunities for social mobilization and protest. Jack Goldstone (2004: 342) argues that this mutually reinforcing relationship stems from the fact that "*both* democratization *and* social movements built on the same basic principle, that ordinary people are

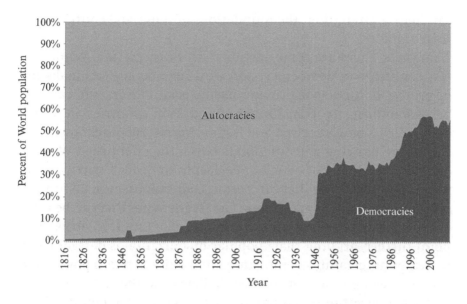

Source: Polity IV: www.systemicpeace.org/polityproject.html.

Figure 8.2 *Population living under democratic regimes, 1816–2015*

politically worth consultation. Both protests and normal election-eering seek to influence the decisions of representative bodies by presenting to the public and to those bodies the degree of popular support behind particular goals." As a result, new democracies are likely to experience particularly high levels of protest and social mobilization, as engaged actors carry on using a political tool that is well suited for the more open political environment and easy institutional access of democracies, and that also has demonstrated power as an instrument of social change. The net result, Goldstone argues, is the creation of a "movement world" in which social movements become increasingly normalized and a routine part of political expression (2004: 335).

This development has much to recommend it. Democracies allow for more free expression and a role for citizens in matters of governance. And when social movements and direct action are considered a standard part of politics, rather than something unconventional and threatening, Pippa Norris (2006) argues, they can supplement traditional channels for citizen involvement and, in turn, make participation broader, more inclusive, and more democratic. With more people feeling like they have a stake in the system and have the power to affect meaningful change, Norris argues that protest can help to strengthen the foundations of states and contribute to their stability.

However, there are some caveats to this rosy picture. While protest can usher in democracy, and while democracy can make use of protest to further legitimate itself, social movements can also be destabilizing to transitional societies or countries in which democracy is newly arrived and fragile. Norris (2006) acknowledges this point, drawing a distinction between the established Western democracies, many of which have deeply embedded participatory norms and principles that can permit contentious, even disruptive, politics, without fear of collapse, and fragile states that can be more easily up-ended by disruption. Adrienne LeBas (2011: 15) drives this point further, arguing that "popular mobilization is destabilizing. It creates uncertainty over incumbents' ability to retain power, and it may open up space for further challenges to the status quo. But increased uncertainty has ambiguous effects on democratization." Moreover, she argues, in societies that have extensive experiences with protest, the nature of how disputes get resolved can change by developing institutional practices and norms that encourage conflict escalation rather than compromise and negotiation.

Such dynamics are not present everywhere, but when they coincide with social cleavages based on ethnicity, language, religious, or other deep divides, the combination of newly established democracy and a reliance on non-institutional means to voice grievances can be explosive. LeBas (2011) notes that, in such polities, political parties are often diverse coalitions that are held together by reinforcing exclusionary identities that create sharp dividing lines between who belongs to a group or community and who is excluded. But such identity-building measures can be polarizing and heighten conflicts between those who are part of the in-group and those who are part of the out-group. In itself, this may not be particularly destabilizing; however, if these dynamics coincide with increasing democratization without tangible policy outcomes, the results can be explosive. Jack Goldstone (2004: 345) points out that the US Civil Rights movement started out using largely non-violent tactics, but when legislation gave blacks voting rights and widespread access to political institutions and "it became clear that even those victories in gaining institutionalized recognition were not going to yield much immediate economic benefit or relief," the amount of violence spiked – a pattern he also discerns in the labor movement. As a result, newly arrived democratic institutions in combination with social protest can usher in periods of intense violence, which can undermine fragile states; if those democratic institutions do not immediately bring long-anticipated benefits to the population (which they often do not), and protest is normalized as an effective and quick way to get demands heard, and such movement organizations are formed along exclusionary lines, then the results can be quite damaging indeed, and perhaps – as in cases like Rwanda – even genocidal.

Such extreme outcomes may not be common, but they caution us to consider the ambiguous ways in which democracy and social movements might be connected outside the European core that was Charles Tilly's primary focus. While many laud the ability of movements to strengthen participation in civil society, to increase political engagement, to provide greater citizen feedback and input into the legislative process, and, in general, to complement democratic politics (Meyer and Tarrow 1998: 7; Goldstone 2004: 343; Norris 2006), we should also not lose sight of the fact that such complementarities might also hinge on the strength of democratic institutions themselves and the overall stability of society. The ability to mobilize and engage in social protest can be a net benefit for citizens, but it is not always and forever so around the world.

Moreover, many social movements that attract considerable contemporary attention, such as the anti-globalization movement, OWS, or the *indignados* – are themselves skeptical of conventional democratic institutions and practices, holding them partially responsible for the rise of political and economic elites who are disconnected from the lives of ordinary citizens. While such social movement groups themselves frequently operate according to radical democratic and egalitarian norms, their movement culture simultaneously tends to hold established democratic institutions at arm's length out of concern for their perceived corruption and fallibility. The resulting tension that can exist between such movements and existing political institutions is yet to be resolved; it is somewhat unclear what this critique of democracy by radical democratic movements will ultimately yield.

Social Movements and Globalization

Globalization and the increasing interconnectedness of societies have facilitated the spread of protest around the world and made it more transnational in nature (Bandy and Smith 2005; della Porta and

Tarrow 2005; Tarrow 2005). They have done so by making it easier, faster, and cheaper to connect sites across borders. Communications networks, ease of travel, and other ways in which the world is more tied together make it possible for movement actors to share ideas and strategies, coordinate protests, meet each other, and learn from other activists. But globalization has also facilitated transnational movements by becoming their target as well (Batliwala 2002). As globalization's leading agents – multinational corporations and global capital, international organizations, supranational entities – have come to be seen as increasingly remote, disconnected from the lives of ordinary people, and unaccountable, their activities have spawned transnational movements in response.

The World Social Forum, for example, brings together civil society organizations and social movement actors from all over the world as an explicit counterpart to the World Economic Forum. The latter meeting brings together influential business and political elites to discuss pressing global issues; these attendees are perceived by the World Social Forum attendees as apologists for the neoliberal economic order that they feel has been detrimental to ordinary people. The World Social Forum offers such activists a space to meet, share ideas, and consider how to build a more equitable and democratic global society. In turn, such contacts – both face-to-face and mediated by technology – help to generate social capital, new cosmopolitan identities, collective action frames, and discursive possibilities (Smith 1998). Over time, some argue, these transnational interactions and transnational spaces in which movement actors can meet have begun to constitute a global civil society. As Jackie Smith argues about this transnational arena, "It strengthens the global public sphere by mobilizing this disenfranchised public into discussions of global issues, thereby democratizing the global political process. It provides information channels and opportunities for transnational dialogue and learning that contribute to the realization of commonalities in experiences of global problems and to the emergence of transnational identities" (1998: 102). This transnational civil society, its advocates argue, can act as a "third force" to counterbalance the interests of states and corporations in the global arena, much as domestic civil society creates autonomous space in which citizens can interact and organize voluntary groups based on a plethora of interests. As a third force, a transnational civil society can be a way to put pressure on political actors, as Matthew Evangelista (1999) claimed occurred when transnational groups of scientists organized collective action around issues like nuclear weapons testing and missile defense and, in turn, helped to shape the global environment in ways that facilitated the end of the Cold War. While such movements may not be able to mobilize economic clout or military might, their ability to shape international norms and discourse has given them power to act as potential moral agents that also bring issue expertise and a claim to political legitimacy to their actions (Higgott et al. 2000). In so doing, they can broaden the scope of who can influence global policy, making it more inclusive (Florini 1999: 105).

While this all might sound appealing and represent forward progress for democracy, transparency, and giving ordinary people more of a role in global politics, there are some limitations to this view of a global civil society. Srilatha Batliwala (2002: 397) argues, for example, that the emerging transnational publics that have been created from social movement and non-government organizations are not necessarily democratic and transparent in themselves. She argues that "global civil society is a microcosm, in many ways, of the imbalances of power, resources, and access that characterize the world at large." These imbalances give more clout and space to those movement groups and actors from the developed world, which can marginalize voices from the Global South. Consequently, questions emerge about the representativeness of this emerging transnational space and the internal hierarchies that might develop between more- and less-powerful groups. This is a concern that is not particularly new, but one that requires close attention if the democratic promise of social movements and the moral and ethical possibilities of global civil society are to be realized.

Concluding Summary

Social movements are important features in modern politics – particularly in democracies, but also in non-democratic states. This chapter explored the extent to which their importance rests on their success: do people engage in popular protest because they believe it to be an effective way to bring about desired social and political change? As this discussion has highlighted, "success" is an overpacked idea, and to understand the impact that movements can have, it is important to disaggregate the concept in several ways: to think critically about what types of success matter, how much success matters, and even when and where we look for

evidence of success. While most of the research on movement outcomes has focused on policy outcomes, this discussion has made
the case that movements can have multiple non-policy impacts
as well, some of which – like strengthening collective identity
or generating desirable emotions – can be intangible. The challenge overall for studies of movement outcomes is untangling the
thorny issue of causality, since movements are but one of many
actors seeking to influence existing social, political, and economic
arrangements. Ultimately, there is no magic formula for movements seeking to influence the world around them, but dynamic
strategies must take into consideration the pathways by which
movements seek change, the external context in which they operate, the choices that they make about mobilization, organization,
tactics, and frames, and the choices of other actors – all of which
combine to influence the outcomes of movement activities.

Taking a step back, we can also point to the way in which movements are influential more broadly, in terms both of advancing
democratization around the world and of helping to generate a
transnational civil society. In both cases, social movements can play
a positive role, but their impacts are not unequivocally positive.
Social movements, like most political phenomena, can generate
both intended and unintended consequences, and their influence
can generate hope, peace, stability, and a more just world – but
these are not automatic outcomes. For those who want to make
the world a better place, social movements can be powerful instru-
ments to help realize these visions, as long as we attend to their
limitations and trade-offs along the way.

Questions for Discussion

1 Why is it difficult to determine what counts as movement
  success? Why might it be overly limiting to look primarily at
  whether a movement is able to achieve its stated policy goals as
  the main measure of its influence?

2 How can political opportunity, organizational structure, framing, and tactical choice influence a movement's likelihood of
  success? If you were a social movement actor, what combination
  of variables would you conclude are most likely to bring about
  desired change?

3 How do movements that act as informational shortcuts differ from movements that present themselves as helpful assets to lawmakers, or those that seek to sway public opinion, or those that disrupt the status quo? What might induce movements to prioritize one of these persuasive pathways over the others?

4 Why might social movements and protest activity be both beneficial and potentially detrimental to democratic governance and the power of ordinary citizens over time?

Additional Readings

Burstein, Paul, and April Linton. 2002. "The Impact of Political Parties, Interest Groups, and Social Movement Organizations on Public Policy: Some Recent Evidence and Theoretical Concerns." *Social Forces*, 81(2): 381–408. Takes a closer look at the impact that movements can have specifically on policy outcomes.

Giugni, Marco. 1998. "Was it Worth the Effort? The Outcomes and Consequences of Social Movements." *Annual Review of Sociology*, 24: 371–93. Provides a good overview of some of the challenges in assessing movement outcomes.

Smith, Jackie. 1998. "Global Civil Society? Transnational Social Movement Organizations and Social Capital." *American Behavioral Scientist*, 42(1): 93–107. Examines the impact of social movements on global civil society, and its implications.

CHAPTER 9

The Future

Objectives

- To examine how contemporary protests reinforce as well as challenge ideas about how social movements operate.
- To identify some of the forces that may reshape protest politics in the future.

Introduction

After a particularly acrimonious and controversy-filled campaign, Donald Trump was sworn in as the 45th President of the United States on January 20, 2017. He was greeted almost immediately by protests around the country from people who viewed his election – and his policy promises – as deeply alarming and who wished to express their worry and their opposition to his agenda. Most of these inauguration-day protests unfolded without much incident, although in Washington, DC, over 200 people were arrested after anti-fascist groups began to smash windows, set a limousine on fire, and threw rocks at police; in Seattle, one protestor wound up in critical condition after being shot in the stomach during clashes between supporters and opponents of the new administration. But, even with these confrontations, these protests were merely a warm-up for the major demonstrations scheduled for the following day when hundreds of thousands of people gathered in the capital as part of the Women's March on Washington while many more protested in sister demonstrations across the world in support of women's rights and other progressive issues, including environmental justice, support for immigrants and refugees, and combating racism. Los Angeles hosted the single biggest gathering with an estimated 750,000 people taking part. In Chicago, the crowds grew so big that they filled up the planned route; what was supposed to be a march turned instead into a rally. Protests happened in smaller, rural areas as well. Grand Marais, Minnesota – population

1,351 – had 97 people turn out to protest, while tiny Adak, Alaska – population 326 – had a march with 10 people. People outside the United States got in on the action too, with protests spread across all seven continents, including 100,000 people in London, 50,000 in Toronto, and even a small protest of 30 people at a research station in Antarctica. People in authoritarian regimes protested quietly, taking pictures of solidarity walks in Moscow or knitting circles in Beijing and posting them on social media to link their efforts to the larger worldwide protest. While crowd counts are not exact, a tally of these protests compiled by Jeremy Pressman from the University of Connecticut and Erica Chenowith from the University of Denver (2017) estimates the total number of participants in this one day of action to be over 4 million people in the United States alone – involving more than 1 out of every 100 people in the country – making it the single largest protest in US history.

While the Women's March generated considerable media coverage, it was not the only protest to make January headlines. Every day of the following week, demonstrations were organized over a number of issues, ranging from the new administration's nominees for cabinet-level posts to executive orders reviving controversial projects like the Dakota Access Pipeline, to restrictions on the National Park Service from communicating directly with the public through social media, to a directive barring scientists at the US Department of Agriculture from releasing taxpayer-funded research to the public. One week after the Women's March, mass protests again unfolded across the country in response to an executive order temporarily banning citizens of seven Muslim-majority countries from entering the United States – an order that initially also seemed to include individuals holding valid visas and even green card holders with permanent resident status in the United States. Crowds quickly gathered at international airports across the country as well as in front of the White House and in other public spaces to denounce the policy and express solidarity with immigrants and refugees.

Although protest is as much a part of democratic politics as casting a ballot or writing a letter to an elected official, this continuous barrage of protests, combined with the scale and scope of demonstrations, has led some observers to wonder whether we might be witnessing a change in the way politics is practiced in the United States, or, at the very least, seeing a shift in the role that protest plays in political life. Opinion pieces wonder whether this upsurge in grassroots activism signals an end to political apathy, while a headline in the *Washington Post* asks "Is this a new era of perpetual protest?" For every breathless editorial, however, there are skeptics to be found: those who see the current crop of protests not as a break with tradition, but as a continuation, or even possibly just a short-term phenomenon – a temporary uptick in outrage sparked by an unpopular and unrepentant new President. While it is too early to make a definitive diagnosis on what these current protests might signify, there is evidence of both change and stability in protest dynamics – some things seem familiar based on the theories and patterns discussed in earlier chapters of this book, while other features of contemporary protest suggest innovations that over time could reshape how social movements go about their activities or attempt to effect change.

Protest Continuities?

Analysis of the Women's March on Washington underscores how much of its planning, operations, execution, and aftermath conform to many of the ideas previously discussed in this book. It got its start on social media when, in the days following the election, several individuals around the country proposed a national march in response to Trump's victory and then, in response to an outpouring of enthusiasm for the idea, united their efforts. This consolidated effort soon took organizational form, complete with national co-chairs, official partner organizations like Planned Parenthood and the National Resources Defense Council, a set of core principles, and a website that sought to make it easier for supporters to find out about the protest and reduce the costs of attending. The group's website, for example, offered an official app for participants to get real-time updates during the march; advice for people with physical disabilities on how to navigate accessibility issues once there, and find transportation to Washington, DC; tips for parents planning to protest with their children; help finding accommodation; and even a portal for buying public transportation tickets to avoid lines at transit stations in the city. In all of these ways, the formal organization sought to reduce the transaction costs of participation and tip the cost–benefit calculation in favor of taking part in the march. The organization also sought to raise funds to defray logistical costs, offered training in nonviolence

Photo credit: Adeet Deshmukh, www.adeetdeshmukh.com and
https://www.instagram.com/adeet77 (Creative Commons license).

Figure 9.1 *Protestors at the Women's March on Washington, DC*

and bystander intervention, and collected expertise on legal matters that it could share with participants. In all of these activities,
the organization was able to act in ways that helped to make the
collective action problem less onerous and to increase the likelihood that a wide range of people would mobilize and turn up. In
this, the Women's March organization was joined by a number of
other formal organizations in its partner and sponsor list, including labor unions, professional organizations, and a wide variety of
non-profits, all of which helped spread awareness and information
through their membership networks and encouraged their own
supporters to take part.

While formal organizations were vital in planning the march,
informal, horizontal networks connecting individuals also played
an important role in both recruiting participants and building
movement identity. Social media connected individuals across
space, encouraging them to share personal stories of their reasons for attending and helping to foster a sense of shared community. Facebook groups like Pantsuit Nation, which started as a

community of Hillary Clinton's supporters, generated hundreds of discussions in which women could describe why they planned to participate, ask questions, air concerns, and support one another. After the march was over, these same sites provided space to share photos and anecdotes of the protests, discuss next steps, and process the emotions that participants felt, both positive and negative. Just as Alison Dahl Crossley (2015) found that online networks helped to nourish offline networks, build community, and aid recruitment for future action, so too did online social movement networks contribute to the Women's March.

As well as exemplifying the importance of organizations and networks in helping to recruit and mobilize people, the Women's March also included a diversity of organizations working with each other, often cooperatively and collaboratively, but also in ways that highlighted the tensions and conflicts that can occur in broad coalitions and among like-minded activists. Participants asserted unity in multiple ways, from wearing pink knitted "pussy hats" to singing protest songs, to wearing shirts proclaiming themselves nasty women, a reference to an offhand remark made by Donald Trump about Hilary Clinton in the final presidential debate. These displays not only made the case that the sea of protestors were part of a common cause, but also reinforced a sense of shared identity. They also helped to create a playful air about the protest, which enhanced the sense of pleasure, even euphoria, that many participants reported as they took part in the day's events and processed their participation afterwards.

The organizers of the Women's March also made inclusivity a priority from a fairly early point, recognizing that the protest should reflect diverse backgrounds and interests and appeal to a wide range of participants. Indeed, the protestors who showed up around the world highlighted a number of concerns based on their protest signs – protecting reproductive rights, decrying sexual assault, calling for human rights, prompting action on climate change, promoting anti-racism, supporting the Black Lives Matter campaign, calling attention to the new administration's conflicts of interest, and more. At least one sign at the Washington protest simply proclaimed: "Too many demands to fit on one poster." But even with a broad and inclusive intent, both of people and of causes, the march prompted some uncomfortable discussions on social and mainstream media about whom it represented. For some activists of color, the march raised fears about the historic marginalization of non-white women's voices in the feminist movement and invited questions about the extent to which intersectionality would be a priority of those taking part in the protest. Fears that their voices would be drowned out, their sacrifices in prior protest and advocacy work overlooked, and their concerns pushed to the side led to some withdrawing their participation. Others urged white women to talk less and listen more to people of color, and to show solidarity with marginalized groups by showing up at protests against police brutality and related matters with as much enthusiasm and energy as they displayed at the Women's March. These suggestions were themselves met with varied responses, including defensiveness and withdrawal on the part of some supporters. Separate from the internal tensions over intersectionality, disputes also arose over the diversity of views represented at the march and whether feminists with pro-life views would be welcome at a march in which the majority of participants identified as pro-choice, and in which Planned Parenthood, NARAL Pro-Choice America, and other supporters of reproductive freedoms were official partners. Although a pro-life feminist group was initially listed, and then removed, as an official event sponsor, some pro-life activists decided to march anyway and stand by their point of view. These different rifts and tensions underscore the point that, despite assertions of unity, social movements are never really unified actors, and that groups and individuals within such campaigns can have a range of relationships with each other, including connections that are occasionally combative and dissenting.

The Women's March drew on a very familiar and contained part of the protest repertoire: the peaceful protest. While the event featured plenty of humorous signs and props (figure 9.1), this was not a protest that made much effort to innovate tactically. It followed existing rules of assembly, filled out permits and forms, registered parade routes, and did not seek to blur the lines between contained and transgressive protest in any way. In part, this tactical choice helps to explain the police response to the protests and how little confrontation there was with law enforcement. In contrast to the previous day, when a much smaller contingent of anti-fascist protestors clashed with police, not a single arrest was made in Washington, DC during the march; there were no arrests at the protests in New York, Los Angeles, or Chicago. Given the size of the crowds present, this is a remarkable fact. But given earlier discussions about situational policing, the lack of arrests can be explained in part by the non-threatening and relatively orderly nature of the tactic – one that would be familiar and comfortable to officials. The demographics of these protests also may have played a role in the police response; the prominent participation of middle-class, white women – not a group traditionally viewed as big threats to law and order – could have lessened the concerns that police at the event might have otherwise had given the size of the crowds. The presence of older people and children would have mitigated police anxieties in similar ways.

The Women's March also illustrates how movement activity can spur further action and mobilization, by both sympathetic groups and adversaries, which collectively can contribute to a larger protest cycle. In the wake of the protest, for example, scientists announced their own march on Washington to protest restrictions on scientific research, cuts to funding, and what supporters see as the politicizing of science, especially on matters related to climate change. The Women's March also inspired the organization of a National Pride March on Washington to defend gains made by LGBTQ activists, such as marriage equality, and to demand action on other issues of concern to the community. Like the Women's March, both of these events are framed in opposition to the policies and priorities of the new administration.

But the Women's March has also influenced groups that see the Trump government as an ally as well. Although the anti-abortion March for Life Campaign existed for years before the Women's March, its annual protest less than one week after the Women's March invited participants and observers to make comparisons between the two. In a piece for the *Independent Journal Review*, a strongly conservative online publication, Antonia Okafor wrote about attending both the Women's March and the March for Life and then posted a series of pictures inviting readers to draw their own conclusions about each event. The pictures of diversity at the March for Life, for example, featured women carrying signs identifying themselves as Muslim, feminist, and pro-life; the comparison for the Women's March, by contrast, included photos of protestors tearing up pro-life signs. The March for Life was depicted as featuring positive, uplifting, and loving messages, contrasted with signs from the Women's March that featured profanities and graphic depictions of sex organs. Even the featured speakers at both events were compared, with the juxtaposition of Vice President Mike Pence looking grave with a photo of singer Miley Cyrus sticking out her tongue. Even though the March for Life did not form in response to the Women's March, the latter became a point of reference for those seeking to promote their own oppositional cause and to emphasize their relative worthiness, unity, numbers, and commitment.

One of the most important ways in which the Women's March is like many other social movements that have come before it is that its success or overall impact is not clear-cut and requires careful parsing. Some commentators worried that, given the diversity of issues and lack of a focused, narrow policy agenda, this march would result in feel-good energy and little tangible action; others argued that, even absent tangible action right away, the march would inspire people to more concrete follow-up actions that would start the process of change. Still others pointed to the general feelings of goodwill and solidarity that many (though not all) participants gained from marching; that building of identity and community and feeling less alone in alienating political times were themselves seen as positive outcomes. Still others pointed to statements from administration spokespeople and Donald Trump's tweets that questioned the point or size of the march as evidence that the protest was getting under the new President's skin, and that in itself should be a sign of success. And, of course, there were voices that dismissed the march as pointless, or perhaps even counterproductive. All these different interpretations merely underscore that, as for most social protests, trying to parse out the effectiveness of the Women's March is neither straightforward nor uncontested.

Protest Innovations?

The above discussion highlights a number of ways in which the Women's March demonstrates similarities with protests that have come before. It may have been the largest protest in US history, but, in some key respects, it features dynamics and patterns that are familiar to scholars of social movements. So what, if anything, is new or different about protest now and in the future? Here, it may be more useful to think in terms of innovations – some more significant than others – that can potentially change the way we think about or act in social movements over time – though, at present, none of these innovations represents a real break with past practice.

Blurring of Institutional and Non-Institutional Protest

While social movements and protest have made use of conventional political channels frequently, the surge of protests in the early days of 2017 suggests that the distinction between institutional and non-institutional forms of protest are getting blurrier than ever before and are not likely to become more distinct anytime soon. For example, following the Trump administration's initial immigration order, which barred citizens of Iran, Iraq, Sudan, Syria, Yemen, Libya, and Somalia from entering the country for 90 days, protestors carrying signs were accompanied by lawyers from groups such as the American Civil Liberties Union who worked on site at airports to render legal aid to affected travelers, while also filing court documents challenging the provision's constitutionality and having it temporarily suspended by the federal courts.

What is perhaps somewhat newer in this trend, however, is *who* is participating in institutional versus non-institutional spaces. When social movement organizations take part in institutional activities, the customary examples tend to involve a limited number of their members – usually leaders – operating within formal institutions. This might take the form of organizational experts testifying before the legislature, or a group's lawyers filing a legal suit, or charismatic leaders running for office. Many of the examples that come from recent mobilization, however, explicitly attempt to broaden the number of people involved in institutional processes. Capitalizing on the energy of the Women's March, for example, 500 women took part in a training session the following day to learn how to run for office. The group sponsoring the event – Emily's List – notes that nearly the same number were on a waiting list to get into the training. Other groups that train and encourage people to run for office have seen a similar surge of interest, including one group that focuses primarily on encouraging more scientists to run, in response to the Trump administration's stance on climate science. The crossover energy from events like the Women's March – and the discussions on social media before, during, and after – drive even more people to such opportunities.

The connection between institutional and non-institutional political action is further blurred when social movement organizing ideas are combined with institutional targets. The Indivisible Guide (indivisibleguide.com) blends these two pathways by combining the insider knowledge of legislative staffers who know what gets the attention of elected officials with mass mobilizing strategies. Drawing on the lessons from Tea Party activists, who were able to compel many Republican lawmakers to pay attention to their demands or face retribution at the polls, the progressive writers of the Indivisible Guide counsel putting pressure on elected officials by combining the conventional methods of institutional politics with some of the ethos of a social movement. They suggest, for example, that calls to congressional offices can be effective, but, in social movement fashion, these should be done as part of a coordinated, mass action. They advocate some tactics that are more akin to traditional protest, like showing up in a group at local events and engaging in more confrontational conversations, as well as tactics like taking part in a town hall meeting or visiting an elected official's district offices in person. Such strategies do not prioritize institutional or non-institutional venues, nor do they think of one as a substitute for the other; rather, this sort of protest approach sees institutional and non-institutional tactics as complementary, fluid, and interchangeable. This is hardly a novel perspective, but in the future, may become far more standard practice.

Media, Technology, and Participation

Another area of innovation involves the way in which technology and social media affect protest and communication. On one hand, technology has made protest easier. Online protest typically is seen as shallower than in-person or face-to-face actions, and therefore as easier to dismiss. But websites like dailyaction.org offer both the ease of online protest and the potential impact of real-world action. At this website, and others like it, potential activists sign up for a daily text message alert and input their home postal code. After that, they receive a text outlining a specific action to be taken and providing a phone number to call to learn more about the issue at stake. Subscribers also get automatically connected to their own elected officials to make the specified call. Similar services all purport to offer the combination of easy participation with actions that typically have more impact because they traditionally require more commitment and effort. Such tools make it possible to involve a wider swath of people in activism, especially institutional forms of action. However, as such tools become more widespread and used, it is unclear whether there will be a corresponding decline in impact.

In terms of media trends, the concerns over the spread of misleading clickbait articles, fake news, and self-imposed media bubbles in which only information that confirms one's worldviews is given credence are not new, but have reached a fever pitch in wake of the 2016 US presidential campaign. On one hand, this toxic mix of information can fuel the outrage machine, providing ongoing support for protest events of both the left and the right. But there is a potential downside for movements struggling to maintain enthusiasm amid such a heightened sense of constant crisis. When everything feels like a catastrophe, it can be hard for supporters to prioritize how they will react and where to spend their energies; rather than galvanizing support, over time it can wear it down, akin to the "compassion fatigue" experienced by those who work constantly to provide support and care to others. Rather than encouraging involvement, such fatigue can promote hopelessness, despair, and disengagement. Given that activist retention is already a challenge that movements must negotiate, alarmist social media and news might be a long-term double-edged sword for mobilization.

Evolving Corporate Role in Protest

One of the more interesting developments in recent waves of protest involves the role of corporations as simultaneous targets and allies of protest. Rather than corporations being targeted in the traditional ways in order to get them to change their behavior as an end in itself, increasingly corporations are being targeted as an intermediate step in order to exert pressure on a third target (Young and Schwartz 2014). In chapter 4, we saw that this strategy was used by Greenpeace in its campaign against LEGO in order to put pressure on Shell Oil and stop its Arctic drilling plans. Clearly, this approach is not new, but in the past several weeks, corporate targeting has become a more high-profile activity for protestors in the United States. In part, corporate targets might be seen as relatively vulnerable to concerted negative attention, compared to a newly elected administration in which one political party controls two of the three branches of the federal government. But these campaigns aimed at corporate targets are about not just threatening profits, but imploring them to act as better guardians of public values than current elected officials. Corporations, in a sense, have been increasingly cast as champions of moral virtue.

One such campaign is the Sleeping Giants twitter campaign,

which targets companies whose advertisements appear on the Breitbart.com website, a right-wing news source that has been criticized for supporting racist, homophobic, and xenophobic ideas. The campaign asks supporters to take screenshots of ads appearing on the Breitbart site and then send the images to the advertisers in question. In many cases, these advertisers might be unaware that their ads were appearing on the site at all, given how online ad buys frequently work. But, once notified, some companies have taken action to disassociate themselves from Breitbart. The Sleeping Giants twitter campaign claims that over 250 companies have pulled their ads from this site, including some major corporations like Kelloggs, Audi, and US Bank.

In addition to targeting corporations as proxy actors, recent protests have also seen more direct corporate activism, insofar as companies have engaged in social protest, both for principled reasons and to simultaneously improve their market position vis-à-vis possible rivals. In the middle of protests against the administration's temporary entry ban against selected Muslim-majority countries, for example, New York City taxi drivers implemented a boycott on taking people to and from JFK Airport to stand in solidarity with activists. In the middle of this stance, taxi rival Uber continued to accept fares to and from the airport, leading some of its critics to condemn the company for engaging in strikebreaking behavior and prioritizing its own profits ahead of human rights. With Uber on the defensive and trying to explain its actions, rival Lyft announced a $1 million donation to the American Civil Liberties Union in support of the organization's work in fighting against the immigration order and other examples of government overreach. In one movement, Lyft branded itself as aligned with progressive protestors and in stark contrast to a commercial rival. For their part, progressively minded users of these services took notice, as the hashtag #deleteuber started to circulate on social media, a move that rewards the company seen as morally aligned with those opposed to the immigration ban. Air BnB is another company poised to recoup goodwill and commercial benefit with a similar stance: by offering free accommodation to those turned away from the United States because of the entry ban, it creates signals about corporate values that it hopes will also be kind to the corporate bottom line.

Perhaps one of the most unusual instances of corporate targeting that has emerged in the past several weeks is the case of protests against corporations not as proxy targets but as official extensions of a government entity. Amid concerns about Donald Trump's conflicts of interest and lack of divestment from his many business ventures, activists have started to target these businesses as substitutes for action that would normally be directed at the White House itself. The website whitehouseinc.org, for example, connects callers to one of Trump's hotels, golf courses, or other properties that activists are encouraged to consider "satellite White Houses," where they can bring their policy concerns. The idea is to pester these corporate entities not because they are likely to get the messages back to the President, but because doing so distracts and disrupts them from their for-profit activities and, in turn, inflicts some potential pain on their owner. This tactic, of course, depends on some fairly specific circumstances that may not present themselves commonly, at least in places where the political norms mitigate against such intertwined corporate and political interests.

Conclusions: The Future of Protest?

The above discussion is necessarily rather speculative since it is hard to say with any degree of confidence whether the surge in protest in early 2017 signals some kind of fundamental shift in social movement dynamics; even if we focus our attention on just the United States, such pronouncements would be premature. While there are some interesting patterns and indications of some innovations in tactics, in targeting, and in technology, it is important to keep in mind that even for some of the major campaigns that are meant to be a bellwether for this change – like the Women's March on Washington – there is also plenty of evidence that maybe not much is different from earlier examples of protest. It is hard to deny that the amount of protest that has taken place in a very short space of time in the United States and elsewhere in the world feels somehow unprecedented in scale and scope, and perhaps – only time will tell – duration as well; while new presidential administrations have certainly faced protests in their early days, protests since January 20 seem at least an order of magnitude larger. But whether this means protest itself has fundamentally changed or social attitudes toward it have begun to transform seems an overly rushed judgment – partly because the circumstances surrounding the recent surge in activity are not generalizable across space or time, and partly because those circumstances that touched off recent protest waves are not permanent. This chapter has focused mostly on protests in the United States; while there have been transnational demonstrations in solidarity and campaigns focused on events in other countries, the wave of protests described here is not a geographically universal one. Moreover, the outpouring of activity in early 2017 fed off a bitterly contested election, one in which many people on both sides felt the stakes to be much higher than the mere transfer of political power: the struggle is cast by both supporters and opponents of the new administration as a Manichean struggle for the soul of a country and a particular type of world order. Under such circumstances, it is perhaps no wonder that protest seems to have taken on heightened importance. Such circumstances, though, are not meant to be permanent. Even if this surge of activism banishes political apathy, or turns into a perpetual protest motion machine, once the political context changes, so too will the amount, type, and focus of protest. At that point, society will discover a new equilibrium point that balances protest with other forms of political action.

Questions for Discussion

1 Do the seemingly constant protests in early 2017 seem to you to be an indication that the role or importance of protest has changed? What evidence would you provide to support your argument?

2 How do you think the media "outrage machine" that is built on fake news, clickbait, and informational bubbles will affect support for and participation in social movements over time? How concerned should social movement organizations be about possible "compassion fatigue," and how might they overcome it?

3 Some of the innovations and new dynamics described in this chapter seem dependent on the particular political context created by the election of Donald Trump to the presidency, and might not persist once that context changes. Other innovations might last over time. Which of the innovations described in this chapter strike you as having the potential to endure, and why?

Additional Readings

Given that this chapter attempts to look at the very present and
future of social protest and is, therefore, rather speculative, students interested in what lies ahead for social movements might
find it worthwhile to read some of the blogs written by social
movement researchers. These blogs present some of the most
recent ideas and research in the field.

Mobilizing Ideas (Center for the Study of Social Movements,
University of Notre Dame)
https://mobilizingideas.wordpress.com.

Politics Outdoors (David S. Meyer, Department of Sociology,
University of California, Irvine)
https://politicsoutdoors.com.

Social Movements Blog (The World Bank; note, posts here are from
policy analysts and non-profit leaders rather than academics)
http://blogs.worldbank.org/category/tags/social-movements.

Bibliography

Adam, Barry D. 2003. "The Defense of Marriage Act and American Exceptionalism: The 'Gay Marriage' Panic in the United States." *Journal of the History of Sexuality*, 12(2): 259–76.

Agnew, John. 2011. "Space and Place." Pp. 316–30 in *Handbook of Geographical Knowledge*, ed. John Agnew and David N. Livingstone. London: Sage.

Alimi, Eitan. 1999. "Mobilizing Under the Gun: Theorizing Political Opportunity Structures in a Highly Repressive Setting." *Mobilization*, 14(2): 219–37.

Alinsky, Saul. 1971. *Rules for Radicals: A Practical Primer for Realistic Radicals*. New York: Random House.

al Malky, Rania. 2007. "Blogging for Reform: The Case of Egypt." *Arab Media and Society*, 1: 1–31.

Almeida, Paul. 2003. "Opportunity, Organizations, and Threat-Induced Contention: Protest Waves in Authoritarian Settings." *American Journal of Sociology*, 109(2): 345–400.

Almond, Gabriel, and Sidney Verba. 1965. *The Civic Culture*. Boston: Little, Brown & Co.

Amenta, Edwin, Bruce G. Carruthers, and Yvonne Zylan. 1992. "A Hero for the Aged? The Townsend Movement, the Political Mediation Model, and US Old-Age Policy, 1934–1950." *American Journal of Sociology*, 98(2): 308–39.

Amenta, Edwin, and Michael P. Young. 1999. "Making an Impact: Conceptual and Methodological Implications of the Collective Goods Criterion." Pp. 22–41 in *How Social Movements Matter*, ed. Marco Giugni, Doug McAdam, and Charles Tilly. Minneapolis, MN: University of Minnesota Press.

Amenta, Edwin, Neal Caren, Elizabeth Chiarello, and Yang Su. 2010. "The Political Consequences of Social Movements." *Annual Review of Sociology*, 36: 287–307.

Anckar, Carsten. 2008. "On the Applicability of the Most Similar Systems Design and the Most Different Systems Design in

Comparative Research." *International Journal of Social Research Methodology*, 11(5): 389–401.

Anderson, Benedict. 2016. *Imagined Communities*. New York: Verso.

Anderson, Monica, and Paul Hitlin. 2016. "Social Media Conversations about Race." Pew Research Center, www.pewinternet.org/2016/08/15/social-media-conversations-about-race.

Andia, Tatiana. 2015. "The Inverse Boomerang Pattern: The Global Kaletra Campaign and Access to Antiretroviral Drugs in Colombia and Ecuador." *Studies in Comparative International Development*, 50(2): 203–27.

Andretta, Massimiliano, and Donatella della Porta. 2014. "Surveying Protestors: Why and How." Pp. 308–34 in *Methodological Practices in Social Movement Research*, ed. Donatella della Porta. Oxford: Oxford University Press.

Andrews, Kenneth T. 1997. "The Impacts of Social Movements on the Political Process: The Civil Rights Movement and Black Electoral Politics in Mississippi." *American Sociological Review*, 62(5): 800–19. 2002. "Movement–Countermovement Dynamics and the Emergence of New Institutions: The Case of 'White Flight' Schools in Mississippi." *Social Forces*, 80(3): 911–36.

Andrews, Kenneth T., and Sarah Gaby. 2015. "Local Protest and Federal Policy: The Impact of the Civil Rights Movement on the 1964 Civil Rights Act." *Sociological Forum*, 30(S1): 509–27.

Aouragh, Miriyam, and Anne Alexander. 2011. "The Egyptian Experience: Sense and Nonsense of the Internet Revolution." *International Journal of Communication*, 5: 1344–58.

Archer, John E. 2000. *Social Unrest and Popular Protest in England 1780–1840*. Cambridge: Cambridge University Press.

Arquilla, John, and David Ronfeldt. 2010. *Networks and Netwars*. Santa Monica, CA: RAND.

Ayoub, Philip M. 2010. "Repressing Protest: Threat and Weakness in the European Context, 1975–1989." *Mobilization*, 15(4): 465–88.

Ayoub, Philip M., Sophia J. Wallace, and Chris Zepeda-Millán. 2014. "Triangulation in Social Movement Research." Pp. 67–96 in *Methodological Practices in Social Movement Research*, ed. Donatella della Porta. Oxford: Oxford University Press.

Ayres, Jeffrey M. 1999. "From the Streets to the Internet: The Cyber-Diffusion of Contention." *The Annals of the American Academy of Political and Social Science*, 566(1): 132–43. 2002. "Transnational Political Processes and Contention Against the Global Economy." Pp. 191–206 in *Globalization and Resistance:*

Transnational Dimensions of Social Movements, ed. Jackie Smith and Hank Johnston. Lanham, MD: Rowman & Littlefield.

Aytaç, Selim Erden, Luis Schiumerini, and Susan Stokes. 2017. "Protests and Repression in New Democracies." *Perspectives on Politics*. 15(1): 62–82.

Baker, Bruce. 2010. *Security in Post-Conflict Africa: The Role of Non-State Policing*. New York: CRC Press.

Balliet, Daniel, Craig Parks, and Jeff Joireman. 2009. "Social Value Orientation and Cooperation in Social Dilemmas: A Meta-Analysis." *Group Processes and Intergroup Relations*, 12(4): 533–47.

Banaszak, Lee Ann. 1996. *Why Movements Succeed or Fail: Opportunity, Culture, and the Struggle for Woman Suffrage*. Princeton, NJ: Princeton University Press.

Bandy, Joe, and Jackie Smith, eds. 2005. *Coalitions across Borders: Transnational Protest and the Neoliberal Order*. Lanham, MD: Rowman & Littlefield.

Barkan, Steven E. 1979. "Strategic, Tactical and Organizational Dilemmas of the Protest Movement against Nuclear Power." *Social Problems*, 27(1): 19–37.

Baron, David P., and Daniel Diermeier. 2007. "Strategic Activism and Non-Market Strategy." *Journal of Economics and Management Strategy*, 16(3): 599–634.

Bartley, Tim, and Curtis Child. 2011. "Movements, Markets and Fields: The Effects of Anti-Sweatshop Campaigns on U.S. Firms, 1993–2000." *Social Forces*, 90(2): 425–51.
2014. "Shaming the Corporation: The Social Production of Targets and the Anti-Sweatshop Movement." *American Sociological Review*, 79(4): 653–79.

Batliwala, Srilatha. 2002. "Grassroots Movements as Transnational Actors: Implications for Global Civil Society." *Voluntas: International Journal of Voluntary and Nonprofit Organizations*, 13(4): 393–409.

Baumgartner, Frank R., and Christine Mahoney. 2005. "Social Movements, the Rise of New Issues, and the Public Agenda." Pp. 65–86 in *Routing the Opposition: Social Movements, Public Policy, and Democracy*, ed. David S. Meyer, Valerie Jenness, and Helen Ingram. Minneapolis, MN: University of Minnesota Press.

Baunach, Dawn Michelle. 2011. "Decomposing Trends in Attitudes Toward Gay Marriage, 1988–2006." *Social Science Quarterly*, 92(2): 346–63.

Bayor, Ronald H. 1988. "Roads to Racial Segregation: Atlanta in the Twentieth Century." *Journal of Urban History*, 15(1): 3–22.

Beamish, Thomas D., and Amy J. Luebbers. 2009. "Alliance Building across Social Movements: Bridging Difference in a Peace and Justice Coalition." *Social Problems*, 56(4): 647–76.

Beissinger, Mark, Amaney A. Jamal, and Kevin Mazur. 2015. "Explaining Divergent Revolutionary Coalitions: Regime Strategies and the Structuring of Participation in the Tunisian and Egyptian Revolutions." *Comparative Politics*, 48(1): 1–24.

Bellei, Cristián, and Cristian Cabalin. 2013. "Chilean Student Movements: Sustained Struggle to Transform a Market-Oriented Educational System." *Current Issues in Comparative Education*, 15(2): 108–23.

Benford, Robert D. 1993a. "Frame Disputes within the Nuclear Disarmament Movement." *Social Forces*, 71(3): 677–701.

   1993b. "'You Could Be the Hundredth Monkey': Collective Action Frames and Vocabularies of Motive within the Nuclear Disarmament Movement." *The Sociological Quarterly*, 34(2): 195–216.

   1997. "An Insider's Critique of the Social Movement Framing Perspective." *Sociological Inquiry*, 67(4): 409–30.

   2013. "Frame Disputes." Pp. 468–70 in *Blackwell Encyclopedia of Social & Political Movements*, ed. David A. Snow, Donatella della Porta, Bert Klandermans, and Doug McAdam. Hoboken, NJ: John Wiley and Sons.

Benford, Robert D., and David A. Snow. 2000. "Framing Processes and Social Movements: An Overview and Assessment." *Annual Review of Sociology*, 26: 611–39.

Benkler, Yochai. 2006. *The Wealth of Networks: How Social Production Transforms Markets and Freedom*. New Haven, CT: Yale University Press.

Bennett, W. Lance. 2003. "Communicating Global Activism: Strengths and Vulnerabilities of Networked Politics." *Information, Communication & Society*, 6(2): 143–68.

   2004. "Communicating Global Activism: Strengths and Vulnerabilities of Networked Politics." Pp. 109–28 in *Cyberprotest*, ed. Wim van de Donk, Brian D. Loader, Paul G. Nixon, and Dieter Rucht. London and New York: Routledge.

   2012 "The Personalization of Politics: Political Identity, Social Media, and Changing Patterns of Participation." *The Annals of the American Academy of Political and Social Science*, 644(1): 20–39.

Bennett, W. Lance, and Alexandra Segerberg. 2012. "The Logic of Connective Action: The Personalization of Contentious Politics." *Information, Communication, & Society*, 15(2): 739–68.

Bensusán, Graciela. 2016. "Organizing Workers in Argentina, Brazil, Chile, and Mexico: The Authoritarian-Corporatist Legacy and Old Institutional Designs in a New Context." *Theoretical Inquiries in Law*, 16(131): 131–61.

Berbrier, Mitch. 1998. "'Half the Battle': Cultural Resonance, Framing Processes, and Ethnic Affectations in Contemporary White Separatist Rhetoric." *Social Problems*, 45(4): 431–50.

Bernstein, Mary. 2003. "Nothing Ventured, Nothing Gained? Conceptualizing Social Movement 'Success' in the Lesbian and Gay Movement." *Sociological Perspectives*, 46(3): 353–79.

Bhardwaj, Ashutosh. 2015. "RSS Mouthpiece Defends Dadri Lynching: Vedas Order Killing of Sinners Who Kill Cows." *The Indian Express*, October 18. http://indianexpress.com/article/india/india-news-india/rss-mouthpiece-defends-dadri-vedas-order-killing-of-sinners-who-kill-cows.

Bird, Frederick B., and William Reimer. 1982. "A Sociological Analysis of New Religious and Para-religious Movements." *Journal for the Scientific Study of Religion*, 2l(1): 1–14.

Birthal, P. S., P. K. Joshi, D. S. Negri, and S. Agarwal. 2014. "Changing Sources of Growth in Indian Agriculture." IFPRI Discussion Paper 01325. International Food Policy Research Institute, New Delhi.

Blee, Kathleen, and Amy McDowell. 2012. "Social Movement Audiences." *Sociological Forum*, 27(1): 1–20.

Blee, Kathleen M., and Verta Taylor. 2002. "Semi-Structured Interviewing in Social Movement Research." Pp. 92–117 in *Methods of Social Movement Research*, ed. Bert Klandermans and Suzanne Staggenborg. Minneapolis, MN and London: University of Minnesota Press.

Blumer, Herbert. 1951. "The Field of Collective Behavior." Pp. 67–121 in *Principles of Sociology*, ed. Alfred McClung Lee. New York: Barnes & Noble.

——— 1971. "Social Problems as Collective Behavior." *Social Problems*, 18(3): 298–306.

Bob, Clifford. 2006. "'Dalit Rights are Human Rights': Caste Discrimination, International Activism, and the Construction of a New Human Rights Issue." *Human Rights Quarterly*, 29(1): 167–93.

Boggs, Carl. 1977. "Marxism, Prefigurative Communism and the Problem of Workers' Control." *Radical America*, 6: 99–122.

Bonilla, Frank. 1960. "The Student Federation of Chile: 50 Years of Political Activism." *Journal of Inter-American Studies*, 2(3): 311–34.

Boudreau, Vincent. 1996. "Northern Theory, Southern Protest: Opportunity Structure Analysis in Cross-National Perspective." *Mobilization*, 1(2): 174–89.

2005. "Precarious Regimes and Matchup Problems in the Explanation of Repressive Policy." Pp. 33–57 in *Repression and Mobilization*, ed. Christian Davenport, Hank Johnston, and Carol McClurg Mueller. Minneapolis, MN: University of Minnesota Press.

Bowers v. *Hardwick*, 478 US 186 (1986)(Burger, CJ, concurring).

Bratton, Michael, and Nicholas van de Walle. 1997. *Democratic Experiments in Africa: Regime Transitions in Comparative Perspective*. Cambridge: Cambridge University Press.

Briggs, John, Christopher Harrison, Angus McInnes, and David Vincent. 1996. *Crime and Punishment in England: An Introductory History*. London: University College London Press.

Briscoe, Forrest, Abhinav Gupta, and Mark S. Anner. 2015. "Social Activism and Practice Diffusion: How Activist Tactics Affect Non-Targeted Organizations." *Administrative Sciences Quarterly*, 60: 300–32.

Britt, Lory, and David Heise. 2000. "From Shame to Pride in Identity Politics." Pp. 252–68 in *Self, Identity, and Social Movements*, ed. Sheldon Stryker, Timothy J. Owens, and Robert W. White. Minneapolis, MN: University of Minnesota Press.

Buechler, Steven M. 2011. *Understanding Social Movements: Theories from the Classical Era to the Present*. Boulder, CO, and London: Paradigm.

Burstein, Paul. 1999. "Social Movements and Public Policy." Pp. 3–21 in *How Social Movements Matter*, ed. Marco Giugni, Doug McAdam, and Charles Tilly. Minneapolis, MN: University of Minnesota Press.

Burstein, Paul, Rachel Einwohner, and Jocelyn A. Hollander. 1995. "The Success of Political Movements: A Bargaining Perspective." Pp. 275–95 in *The Politics of Social Protest: Comparative Perspectives on States and Social Movements*, ed. J. Craig Jenkins and Bert Klandermans. Minneapolis, MN: University of Minnesota Press.

Burstein, Paul, and April Linton. 2002. "The Impact of Political Parties, Interest Groups, and Social Movement Organizations on Public Policy: Some Recent Evidence and Theoretical Concerns." *Social Forces*, 81(2): 381–408.

Button, James W. 2015. *Black Violence: Political Impact of the 1960s Riots*. Princeton, NJ: Princeton University Press.

Bystydzienski, Jill M., and Steven P. Schacht. 2001. *Forging Radical*

Alliances across Difference: Coalition Politics for the New Millennium.
London and Boulder, CO: Rowman & Littlefield.

Caiani, Manuela. 2014. "Social Network Analysis." Pp. 368–96 in
Methodological Practices in Social Movement Research, ed. Donatella
della Porta. Oxford: Oxford University Press.

Caren, Neal, Raj Andrew Ghosal, and Vanesa Ribas. 2011. "A Social
Movement Generation: Cohort and Period Trends in Protest
Attendance and Petition Signing." *American Sociological Review*,
76(1): 125–51.

Carroll, Glenn R., and Michael T. Hannan. 2000. *Demography of
Corporations and Industries*. Princeton, NJ: Princeton University
Press.

Casey, Nicholas. 2016. "Venezuelans Ransack Stores as Hunger Grips
the Nation." *New York Times*, 19 June, www.nytimes.com/2016/06/20/
world/americas/venezuelans-ransack-stores-as-hunger-stalks-
crumbling-nation.html?_r=0.

Castañeda, Ernesto. 2012. "The *Indignados* of Spain: A Precedent to
Occupy Wall Street." *Social Movement Studies*, 11(3–4): 309–19.

Castells, Manuel. 2012. *Networks of Outrage and Hope: Social Movements
in the Internet Age*. Cambridge, and Malden, MA: Polity.

Chang, Paul Y., and Alex S. Vitale. 2013. "Repressive Coverage in
an Authoritarian Context: Threat, Weakness, and Legitimacy
in South Korea's Democracy Movement." *Mobilization*, 18(1):
19–39.

Christensen, Henrik S. 2011. "Political Activities on the Internet:
Slacktivism or Political Participation by Other Means?" *First
Monday*, 16(2–7), http://firstmonday.org/ojs/index.php/fm/article/
view/3336/2767&quot%3B&gt%3B.

Clemens, Elisabeth S., and Debra C. Minkoff. 2004. "Beyond the Iron
Law: Rethinking the Place of Organizations in Social Movement
Research." Pp. 155–70 in *The Blackwell Companion to Social Movements*,
ed. David A. Snow, Sarah A. Soule, and Hanspeter Kriesi. Malden,
MA: Blackwell.

Clifford, Sadie. 2000. "The Daily Express' Reporting of Suffragette
Crime 1913." Sheffield Online Papers in Social Research, University
of Sheffield, https://www.sheffield.ac.uk/polopoly_fs/1.71450!/file/
clifford.pdf.

Coleman, Stephen. 2005. "Blogs and the New Politics of Listening."
Political Quarterly, 76(2): 272–80.

Collier, David. 2011. "Understanding Process Tracing." *PS: Political
Science & Politics*, 44(4): 823–30.

Constanza-Chock, Sasha. 2003. "Mapping the Repertoire of Electronic Contention." Pp. 173–91 in *Representing Resistance: Media, Civil Disobedience and the Global Justice Movement*, ed. Andrew Opel and Donnalyn Pompper. London: Praeger.

Cooper, Alice Holmes. 2002. "Media Framing and Social Movement Mobilization: German Peace Protests against INF Missiles, the Gulf War, and NATO Peace Enforcement in Bosnia." *European Journal of Political Research*, 41(1): 37–80.

Coy, Patrick G. and Timothy Hedeen. 2005. "A Stage Model of Social Movement Co-optation: Community Mediation in the United States." *The Sociological Quarterly*, 46(3): 405–35.

Crawford. Elizabeth, ed. 2013. *Campaigning for the Vote: Kate Parry Frye's Suffrage Diary*. London: Francis Boutle.

Cress, Daniel M., and David A. Snow. 1996. "Mobilization at the Margins: Resources, Benefactors, and the Viability of Homeless Social Movement Organizations." *American Sociological Review*, 61(6): 1089–109.

    2000. "The Outcome of Homeless Mobilization: The Influence of Organization, Disruption, Political Mediation, and Framing." *American Journal of Sociology*, 105(4): 1063–104.

Crossley, Alison Dahl. 2015. "Facebook Feminism: Social Media, Blogs, and New Technologies of Contemporary U.S. Feminism." *Mobilization*, 20(2): 253–68.

Cummings, Peter M. M. 2015. "Democracy and Student Discontent: Chilean Student Protest in the Post-Pinochet Era." *Journal of Politics in Latin America*, 7(3): 49–84.

Dahlberg, Lincoln. 2007. "The Internet, Deliberative Democracy, and Power: Radicalizing the Public Sphere." *International Journal of Media and Cultural Politics*, 3(1): 47–64.

Dahlgren, Peter. 2011. "The Public Sphere and the Net: Structure, Space, and Communication." Pp. 33–55 in *Mediated Politics: Communication in the Future of Democracy*, ed. W. Lance Bennett and Robert M. Entman. Cambridge: Cambridge University Press.

Dalton, Russell J., and Alix van Sickle. 2005. "The Resource, Structural, and Cultural Base of Protest." Working Paper, Center for the Study of Democracy, University of California, Irvine, https://escholarship.org/uc/item/3jx2b911.

Dauvergne, Peter, and Genevieve Lebaron. 2014. *Protest, Inc.: The Corporatization of Activism*. Cambridge, and Malden, MA: Polity.

Davenport, Christian. 1995. "Multi-Dimensional Threat Perception and State Repression: An Inquiry into Why States Apply

Negative Sanctions." *American Journal of Political Science*, 39(3): 683–713.

2007a. "State Repression and the Tyrannical Peace." *Journal of Peace Research*, 44(4): 485–504.

2007b. "State Repression and Political Order." *Annual Review of Political Science*, 10: 1–23.

2014. *How Social Movements Die: Repression and Demobilization of the Republic of New Africa*. New York: Cambridge University Press.

Davenport, Christian, and David A. Armstrong, II. 2004. "Democracy and the Violation of Human Rights: A Statistical Analysis from 1976–1996." *American Journal of Political Science*, 48(3): 538–54.

Davenport, Christian, Sarah A. Soule, and David A. Armstrong, II. 2011. "Protesting While Black? The Differential Policing of American Activism, 1960–1990." *American Sociological Review*, 76(1): 152–78.

Davies, Christian. 2016. "Poland's Abortion Ban Proposal Near Collapse After Mass Protests." *The Guardian*, October 5, https:// www.theguardian.com/world/2016/oct/05/polish-government-performs-u-turn-on-total-abortion-ban.

Davis, Diane. 1999. "The Power of Distance: Rethinking Social Movements in Latin America." *Theory and Society*, 24(4): 589–643.

Deckman, Melissa. 2012. "Of Mama Grizzlies and Politics: Women and the Tea Party." Pp. 171–92 in *Steep: The Precipitous Rise of the Tea Party*, ed. Lawrence Rosenthal and Christine Trost. Berkeley, CA: University of California Press.

DeLaet, Debra L., and Rachel Paine Caulfield. 2009. "Gay Marriage as a Religious Right: Reframing the Legal Debate over Gay Marriage in the United States." *Polity*, 40(3): 297–320.

della Porta, Donatella. 1999. "Protest, Protestors, and Protest Policing: Public Discourses in Italy and Germany from the 1960s to the 1980s." Pp. 66–96 in *How Movements Matter*, ed. Marco Giugni, Doug McAdam, and Charles Tilly. Minneapolis, MN: University of Minnesota Press.

2014a. "Social Movement Studies and Methodological Pluralism: An Introduction." Pp. 1–20 in *Methodological Practices in Social Movement Research,* ed. Donatella della Porta. Oxford: Oxford University Press.

2014b. "In-Depth Interviews." Pp. 228–61 in *Methodological Practices in Social Movement Research*, ed. Donatella della Porta. Oxford: Oxford University Press.

della Porta, Donatella, and Mario Diani. 1999. *Social Movements: An Introduction*. Malden, MA, and London: Blackwell.

della Porta, Donatella, and Hanspeter Kriesi. 1999. "Social Movements in a Globalizing World: An Introduction." Pp. 3–22 in *Social Movements in a Globalizing World*, ed. Donatella della Porta, Hanspeter Kriesi, and Dieter Rucht. Basingstoke, UK: Macmillan.

della Porta, Donatella, and Lorenzo Mosca. 2005. "Global-Net for Global Movements? A Network of Networks for a Movement of Movements." *Journal of Public Policy*, 25(1): 165–90.

della Porta, Donatella, and Herbert Reiter. 1986. "The Policing of Protest in Western Democracies." Pp. 1–32 in *Policing Protest: The Control of Mass Demonstrations in Western Democracies*, ed. Donatella della Porta and Herbert Reiter. Minneapolis, MN: University of Minnesota Press.

2006. "The Policing of Transnational Protest: A Conclusion." Pp. 175–89 in *The Policing of Transnational Protest*, ed. Donatella della Porta, Abbey Peterson, and Herbert Reiter. Aldershot, UK, and Burlington, VT: Ashgate.

della Porta, Donatella, and Sidney Tarrow, eds. 2005. *Transnational Protest and Global Activism*. Lanham, MD: Rowan & Littlefield.

2012. "Interactive Diffusion: The Coevolution of Police and Protest Behavior with an Application to Transnational Contention." *Comparative Political Studies*, 45(1): 119–53.

Desai, Manisha. 2002. "Multiple Mediations: The State and the Women's Movements in India." Pp. 66–84 in *Social Movements: Identity, Culture, and the State*, ed. David S. Meyer, Nancy Whittier, and Belinda Robnett. Oxford, and New York: Oxford University Press.

Diani, Mario. 1997. "Social Movements and Social Capital: A Network Perspective on Movement Outcomes." *Mobilization*, 2(2): 129–47.

2002. "Network Analysis." Pp. 173–200 in *Methods of Social Movement Research*, ed. Bert Klandermans and Suzanne Staggenborg. Minneapolis, MN, and London: University of Minnesota Press.

2003a. "'Leaders' or Brokers? Positions and Influence in Social Movement Networks." Pp. 105–22 in *Social Movements and Networks: Relational Approaches to Collective Action*, ed. Mario Diani and Doug McAdam. Oxford: Oxford University Press.

2003b. "Introduction: Social Movements, Contentious Actions, and Social Networks." Pp. 1–19 in *Social Movements and Networks: Relational Approaches to Collective Action*, ed. Mario Diani and Doug McAdam. Oxford: Oxford University Press.

2004. "Networks and Participation." Pp.339–59 in *The Blackwell Companion to Social Movements*, ed. David A. Snow, Sarah A. Soule, and Hanspeter Kriesi. Malden, MA, and Oxford: Blackwell.

Dimond, Jill P., Michaelanne Dye, Daphne LaRose, and Amy S. Bruckman. 2013. "Hollaback! The Role of Collective Storytelling Online in a Social Movement Organization." In *Proceedings of Association of Computing Machinery Conference on Computer Supported Cooperative Work (CSCW'13), San Antonio, February 23–27*: 477–90.

Dishman, Chris. 2005. "The Leaderless Nexus: When Crime and Terror Converge." *Studies in Conflict & Terrorism*, 28(3): 237–52.

Dixon, Marc, Andrew W. Martin, and Michael Nau. 2016. "Social Protest and Corporate Change: Brand Visibility, Third-Party Influence, and the Responsiveness of Corporations to Activist Campaigns." *Mobilization*, 21(1): 65–82.

Dorf, Michael C., and Sidney Tarrow. 2014. "Strange Bedfellows: How an Anticipatory Countermovement Brought Same-Sex Marriage into the Public Arena." *Law & Social Inquiry*, 39(2): 449–73.

Drezner, Daniel W., and Henry Farrell. 2004. "Web of Influence." *Foreign Policy*, 145: 32–40.

Dubuisson-Quellier, Sophie. 2013. "A Market Mediation Strategy: How Social Movements Seek to Change Firms' Practices by Promoting New Principles of Product Valuation." *Organization Studies*, 34(5–6): 1–21.

Earl, Jennifer. 2011. "Political Repression: Iron Fists, Velvet Gloves, and Diffuse Control." *Annual Review of Sociology*, 37: 261–84.

Earl, Jennifer, Heather McKee Hurwitz, Analicia Mejia Mesinas, Margaret Tolan, and Ashley Arlotti. 2013. "This Protest will be Tweeted: Twitter and Protest Policing during the Pittsburgh G20." *Information, Communication & Society*, 16(4): 459–78.

Earl, Jennifer and Katrina Kimport. 2008. "The Targets of Online Protest: State and Private Targets of Four Online Protest Tactics." *Information, Communication & Society*, 11(4): 449–72.

Earl, Jennifer, and Sarah A. Soule. 2006. "Seeing Blue: A Police-Centered Explanation of Protest Policing." *Mobilization*, 11(2): 145–64.

Earl, Jennifer, Sarah A. Soule, and John D. McCarthy. 2003. "Protest under Fire? Explaining the Policing of Protest." *American Sociological Review*, 68(4): 581–606.

Edgerton, William. 1961. "The Strikes in Ramses III's Twenty-Ninth Year." *Journal of Near Eastern Studies*, 10(3): 137–45.

Edwards, Gemma. 2014. *Social Movements and Protest*. Cambridge: Cambridge University Press.

Eisenstein, Elizabeth L. 1979. *The Printing Press as an Agent of Change: Communications and Cultural Transformations in Early-Modern Europe*, vols. I and II. Cambridge and New York: Cambridge University Press.

Eisinger, Peter. 1973. "The Conditions of Protest Behavior in American Cities." *American Political Science Review*, 67(1): 11–28.

El-Nawaway, Mohammed, and Sahar Kamis. 2013. *Egyptian Revolution 2.0: Political Blogging, Civic Engagement, and Citizen Journalism*. New York: Palgrave Macmillan.

Ellis, Stephen. 2011. "The Genesis of the ANC's Armed Struggle in South Africa 1948–1961." *Journal of Southern African Studies*, 37(4): 657–76.

Eltantawy, Nahed, and Julie B. Wiest. 2011. "Social Media in the Egyptian Revolution: Reconsidering Resource Mobilization Theory." *International Journal of Communication*, 5: 1207–24.

Emirbayer, Mustafa, and Jeff Goodwin. 1994. "Network Analysis, Culture, and the Problem of Agency." *American Journal of Sociology*, 99(6): 1411–54.

Enders, Walter, and Xuejan Su. 2007. "Rational Terrorists and Optimal Network Structure." *Journal of Conflict Resolution*, 51(1): 33–57.

Ennis, James G. 1987. "Fields of Action: Structure in Movements' Tactical Repertoire." *Sociological Forum*, 2(3): 520–33.

Entman, Robert M. 1993. "Framing: Toward Clarification of a Fractured Paradigm." *Journal of Communication*, 43(3): 51–8.

Epstein, Barbara. 1991. *Political Protest and Cultural Revolution: Nonviolent Direct Action in the 1970s and 1980s*. Berkeley, CA: University of California Press.

Eren, Colleen. 2015. "The Right Anti-Death Penalty Movement? Framing Abolitionism for the Twenty-First Century." *New Politics*, 15(2): 95–100.

Escobar, Arturo, and Sonia E. Alvarez, eds. 1992. *The Making of Social Movements in Latin America: Identity, Strategy, and Democracy*. Boulder, CO: Westview.

Evangelista, Matthew. 1999. *Unarmed Forces: The Transnational Movement to End the Cold War*. Ithaca, NY: Cornell University Press.

Evans, John H. 1997. "Multi-Organizational Fields and Social Movement Organization Frame Content: The Religious Pro-Choice Movement." *Sociological Inquiry*, 67(4): 451–69.

Faris, Davis. 2008. "Revolutions without Revolutionaries? Network Theory, Facebook, and the Egyptian Blogosphere." *Arab Media & Society*, 6: 1–11.

Fein, Helen. 1995. "More Murder in the Middle – Life-Integrity Violations and Democracy in the World, 1987." *Human Rights Quarterly*, 17(1): 170–91.

Fernandez, Raquel, and Dani Rodrik. 1991. "Resistance to Reform: Status Quo Bias in the Presence of Individual-Specific Uncertainty." *The American Economic Review*, 81(5): 1146–55.

Ferree, Myra Max. 1992. "The Political Context of Rationality: Rational Choice Theory and Resource Mobilization." Pp. 29–52 in *Frontiers in Social Movement Theory*, ed. Aldon D. Morris and Carol McClurg Mueller. New Haven, CT: Yale University Press.
      2005. "Soft Repression: Ridicule, Stigma, and Silencing in Gender-Based Movements." Pp. 138–55 in *Repression and Mobilization*, ed. Christian Davenport, Hank Johnston, and Carol McClurg Mueller. Minneapolis, MN and London: University of Minnesota Press.

Florini, Ann, ed. 1999. *The Third Force: The Rise of Transnational Civil Society*. Tokyo and Washington, DC: Japan Center for International Change and Carnegie Endowment for International Peace.

Franceschet, Susan. 2004. "Explaining Social Movement Outcomes: Collective Action Frames and Strategic Choices in First- and Second-Wave Feminism in Chile." *Comparative Political Studies*, 37(5): 499–530.

Freeman, Jo. 1979. "Resource Mobilization and Strategy: A Model for Analyzing Social Movement Organization Actions." Pp. 167–89 in *The Dynamics of Social Movements: Resource Mobilization, Social Control, and Tactics*, ed. Mayer N. Zald and John D. McCarthy. Cambridge, MA: Winthrop.

Frey, R. Scott, Thomas Dietz, and Linda Kalof. 1992. "Characteristics of Successful American Protest Groups: Another Look at Gamson's *Strategy of Social Protest*." *American Journal of Sociology*, 98(2): 368–87.

Friedman, Debra, and Doug McAdam. 1992. "Collective Identity and Activism: Networks, Choices, and the Life of a Social Movement." Pp. 156–73 in *Frontiers in Social Movement Theory*, ed. Aldon D. Morris and Carol McClurg Mueller. New Haven, CT: Yale University Press.

Gale, Richard P. 1986. "Social Movements and the State: The Environmental Movement, Countermovement, and Government Agencies." *Sociological Perspectives*, 29(2): 202–40.

Gamson, Joshua. 1989. "Silence, Death, and the Invisible Enemy:

AIDS Activism and Social Movement 'Newness.'" *Social Problems*, 36(4): 351–67.

Gamson, William A. 1990. *Strategy of Social Protest*. Belmont, CA: Wadsworth.

1995. "Constructing Social Protest." Pp. 85–106 in *Social Movements and Culture*, ed. Hank Johnston and Bert Klandermans. Minneapolis, MN: University of Minnesota Press.

Gamson, William A., and David S. Meyer. 1996. "Framing Political Opportunity." Pp. 275–90 in *Comparative Perspectives on Social Movements: Political Opportunities, Mobilizing Structures, and Cultural Framings*, ed. Doug McAdam, John D. McCarthy, and Mayer N. Zald. Cambridge: Cambridge University Press.

Gamson, William A., and Andre Modigliani. 1989. "Media Discourse and Public Opinion on Nuclear Power: A Constructionist Approach." *American Journal of Sociology*, 95(1): 1–37.

Gamson, William W., and Gadi Wolfsfeld. 1993. "Movements and Media as Interacting Systems." *Annals of the American Academy of Political and Social Science*, 528: 114–25.

Geertz, Clifford. 1973. *The Interpretation of Cultures*. New York: Basic Books.

Gellner, Ernest. 2009. *Nations and Nationalism*, 2nd edn. Ithaca, NY: Cornell University Press.

George, Alexander L., and Andrew Bennett. 2005. *Case Studies and Theory Development in the Social Sciences*. Cambridge, MA: MIT Press.

Gerhards, Jürgen, and Dieter Rucht. 1992. "Mesomobilization: Organizing and Framing in Two Protest Campaigns in West Germany." *American Journal of Sociology*, 98(2): 555–95.

Gerlach, Luther, and Virginia H. Hine. 1970. *People, Power, Change: Movements of Social Transformation*. Indianapolis, IN: Bobbs-Merrill.

Ghannam, Jeffrey. 2011. "Social Media in the Arab World: Leading up to the Uprisings of 2011." Report to Center for International Media Assistance, National Endowment for Democracy, Washington, DC.

Gieryn, Thomas F. 2000. "A Space for Place in Sociology." *Annual Review of Sociology*, 26: 463–96.

Gillham, Patrick F. 2011. "Securitizing America: Strategic Incapacitation and the Policing of Protest since the 11 September 2001 Terrorist Attacks." *Sociology Compass*, 5(7): 636–52.

Gillham, Patrick F., Bob Edwards, and John A. Noakes. 2013. "Strategic Incapacitation and the Policing of Occupy Wall Street Protests in New York City, 2011." *Policing and Society*, 23(1): 81–102.

Gillham, Patrick F., and John A. Noakes. 2007. "'More than a March in a Circle': Transgressive Protests and the Limits of Negotiated Management." *Mobilization*, 12(4): 341–57.

Giugni, Marco. 1998. "Was it Worth the Effort? The Outcomes and Consequences of Social Movements." *Annual Review of Sociology*, 24: 371–93.

1999. "How Social Movements Matter: Past Research, Present Problems, Future Developments." Pp. xiii–xxxiv in *How Social Movements Matter*, ed. Marco Giugni, Doug McAdam, and Charles Tilly. Minneapolis: University of Minnesota Press.

2007. "Useless Protest? A Time-Series Analysis of the Policy Outcomes of Ecology, Antinuclear, and Peace Movements in the United States, 1977–1995." *Mobilization*, 12: 53–77.

Giugni, Marco, and Sakura Yamasaki. 2009. "The Policy Impact of Social Movements: A Replication Through Qualitative Comparative Analysis." *Mobilization*, 14(4): 467–84.

Goffman, Erving. 1974. *Frame Analysis*. Cambridge, MA: Harvard University Press.

Goldstone, Jack A. 1980. "The Weakness of Organization: A New Look at Gamson's *The Strategy of Social Protest*." *American Journal of Sociology*, 85: 1017–42.

ed. 2003. *States, Parties, and Social Movements*. New York: Cambridge.

2004. "More Social Movements or Fewer? Beyond Political Opportunity Structures to Relational Fields." *Theory and Society*, 33(3–4): 333–65.

Goldstone, Jack A., and Charles Tilly. 2001. "Threat (and Opportunity): Popular Action and State Response in the Dynamics of Contentious Action." Pp. 179–94 in Ronald R. Aminzade, Jack A. Goldstone, Doug McAdam, et al., *Silence and Voice in the Study of Contentious Politics*. Cambridge: Cambridge University Press.

González-Bailón, Sandra, Javier Borge-Holthoefer, Alejandro Rivero, and Yamir Moreno. 2011. "The Dynamics of Protest Recruitment Through an Online Network." *Scientific Reports*, 1: 197, www.nature.com/articles/srep00197?message-global=remove&WT.ec_id=EXTERNAL&WT.mc_id=SR1205CECOMPLISI.

Goodwin, Jeff, and James M. Jasper. 1999. "Caught in a Winding, Snarling Vine: The Structural Bias of Political Process Theory." *Sociological Forum*, 14(1): 27–54.

Goodwin, Jeff, James M. Jasper, and Francesca Polletta. 2001. *Passionate Politics: Emotions and Social Movements*. Chicago: University of Chicago Press.

Goodwin, Jeff, and Steven Pfaff. 2001. "Emotion Work in High-Risk Social Movements: Managing Fear in the U.S. and East German Civil Rights Movement." Pp. 282–302 in *Passionate Politics: Emotions and Social Movements*, ed. Jeff Goodwin, James M. Jasper, and Francesca Polletta. Chicago: University of Chicago Press.

Gould, Deborah B. 2004. "Passionate Political Processes: Bringing Emotion Back Into the Study of Social Movements." Pp. 155–75 in *Rethinking Social Movement Studies: Structure, Meaning, Emotion*, ed. Jeff Goodwin and James M. Jasper. Lanham, MD: Rowman & Littlefield.

Graeber, David. 2013. *The Democracy Project: A History, a Crisis, a Movement*. New York: Spiegel and Grau.

Granovetter, Mark S. 1973. "The Strength of Weak Ties." *American Journal of Sociology*, 78(6): 1360–80.

Grassroots Solutions. 2013. "'Conversation Campaign' Creates Path to Victory," www.grassrootssolutions.com/wp-content/up loads/2013/05/Conversation_Campaign_Sreates_Path_To_Victory_ MN_Marriage.pdf.

Gray, Barbara, Jill M. Purdy, and Shahzad Ansari. 2015. "From Interactions to Institutions: Microprocesses of Framing and Mechanisms for the Structuring of Institutional Fields." *Academy of Management Review*, 40(1): 115–43.

Guenther, Katja M. 2009. "The Impact of Emotional Opportunities on the Emotion Cultures of Feminist Organizations." *Gender and Society*, 23(3): 337–62.

Gupta, Devashree. 2007. "Selective Engagement and its Consequences for Social Movement Organizations: Lessons from British Policy in Northern Ireland." *Comparative Politics*, 39(3): 331–51.

2008a. "Nationalism across Borders: Transnational Nationalist Advocacy in the European Union." *Comparative European Politics*, 6(1): 61–80.

2008b. "Militant Flanks and Moderate Centers: The Struggle for Power and Influence in Nationalist Movements." Unpublished doctoral dissertation. Cornell University, Ithaca, NY.

2009. "The Power of Incremental Outcomes: How Small Victories and Defeats Affect Social Movement Organizations." *Mobilization*, 14(4): 417–32.

2014. "The Limits of Radicalization: Escalation and Restraint in the South African Liberation Movement." Pp. 137–66 in *Dynamics of Political Violence*, ed. Lorenzo Bosi, Chares Demetriou, and Stefan Malthaner. London and New York: Routledge.

Gurr, Ted. 1970. *Why Men Rebel.* Princeton, NJ: Princeton University Press.

Haas, Tanni. 2005. "From 'Public Journalism' to the 'Public's Journalism?' Rhetoric and Reality in the Discourse on Weblogs." *Journalism Studies*, 6(3): 387–96.

Haenfler, Ross, Brett Johnson, and Ellis Jones. 2012. "Lifestyle Movements: Exploring the Intersection of Lifestyle and Social Movements." *Social Movement Studies*, 11(1): 1–20.

Haines, Herbert H. 1984. "Black Radicalization and the Funding of Civil Rights: 1957–1970." *Social Forces*, 32(1): 31–43.

1988. *Black Radicals and the Civil Rights Mainstream, 1954–1970.* Knoxville, TN: University of Tennessee Press.

1996. *Against Capital Punishment: The Anti-Death Penalty Movement in America 1972–1994.* Oxford: Oxford University Press.

Hammond, John L. 2015. "The Anarchism of Occupy Wall Street." *Science & Society*, 79(2): 288–313.

Harlow, Summer. 2011. "Social Media and Social Movements: Facebook and an Online Guatemalan Justice Movement that Moved Offline." *New Media & Society*, 14(2): 225–43.

Harmes, Adam. 2006. "Neoliberalism and Multilevel Governance." *Review of International Political Economy*, 13(5): 725–49.

Harris, C. Frederick. 2014. "The Rise of Respectability Politics." *Dissent*, 61(1): 33–7.

Hathaway, Will, and David S. Meyer. 1993–4. "Competition and Cooperation in Social Movement Coalitions: Lobbying for Peace in the 1980s." *Berkeley Journal of Sociology*, 38: 157–83.

Hennessey, Thomas. 1998. *Dividing Ireland: World War One and Partition.* Abingdon, UK, and New York: Routledge.

Hess, David, and Brian Martin. 2006. "Repression, Backfire, and the Theory of Transformative Events." *Mobilization*, 11(2): 249–67.

Higginbotham, Evelyn Brooks. 1994. *Righteous Discontent: The Women's Movement in the Black Baptist Church, 1880–1920.* Cambridge, MA: Harvard University Press.

Higgott, Richard, Geoffrey Underhill, and Andreas Bieler. 2000. *Non-State Actors and Authority in the Global System.* New York: Routledge.

Hindman, Matthew. 2008. "What is the Online Public Sphere Good For?" Pp. 268–88 in *The Hyperlinked Society*, ed. Joe Turow and Lokman Tsui. Ann Arbor, MI: University of Michigan Press.

Hofheinz, Albrecht. 2005. "The Internet in the Arab World: Playground for Political Liberalization." *International Politics and Society*, 3(1): 78–96.

Hooghe, Liesbet, and Gary Marks. 2003. "Unraveling the Central State, but How? Types of Multi-Level Governance." *American Political Science Review*, 97(2): 233–43.

hooks, bell. 1994. *Outlaw Culture: Resisting Representations*. New York and London: Routledge.

Howard, Philip N. 2010. *The Digital Origins of Dictatorship and Democracy*. New York: Oxford University Press.

Huff, Connor, and Dominika Kruszewska. 2016. "Banners, Barricades, and Bombs: The Tactical Choices of Social Movements and Public Opinion." *Comparative Political Studies*, 49(13): 1774–808.

Hull, Kathleen E. 2001. "The Political Limits of the Rights Frame: The Case of Same-Sex Marriage in Hawaii." *Sociological Perspectives*, 44(2): 207–32.

Hunt, Scott A., and Robert D. Benford. 2004. "Collective Identity, Solidarity, and Commitment." Pp. 433–60 in *The Blackwell Companion to Social Movements*, ed. David A. Snow, Sarah A. Soule, and Hanspeter Kriesi. Oxford: Blackwell.

Hunt, Scott A., Robert D. Benford, and David A. Snow. 1994. "Identity Fields: Framing Processes and the Social Construction of Movement Identities." Pp. 185–208 in *New Social Movements: From Ideology to Identity*, ed. Enrique Laraña, Hank Johnston, and Joseph R. Gusfield. Philadelphia: Temple University Press.

Hussain, Muzammil M., and Philip N. Howard. 2013. "What Best Explains Successful Protest Cascades? ICTs and the Fuzzy Causes of the Arab Spring." *International Studies Review*, 15(1): 48–66.

Hutter, Swen. 2014. "Protest Event Analysis and its Offspring." Pp. 335–67 in *Methodological Practices in Social Movement Research*, ed. Donatella della Porta. Oxford: Oxford University Press.

Imig, Doug, and Sidney Tarrow. 1999. "The Europeanization of Movements? A New Approach to Transnational Contention." Pp. 112–33 in *Social Movements in a Globalizing World*, ed. Donatella della Porta, Hanspeter Kriesi, and Dieter Rucht. Basingstoke, UK: Macmillan.

Inglehart, Ronald. 1990. *Culture Shift in Advanced Industrial Society*. Princeton, NJ: Princeton University Press.

Iyengar, Shanto. 1991. *Is Anyone Responsible? How Television Frames Political Issues*. Chicago: University of Chicago Press.

Jaime-Jiménez, Oscar, and Fernando Reinares. 1986. "The Policing of Mass Demonstrations in Spain: From Dictatorship to Democracy." Pp. 166–87 in *Policing Protest: The Control of Mass Demonstrations in*

Western Democracies, ed. Donatella della Porta and Herbert Reiter. Minneapolis, MN: University of Minnesota Press.

Jasper, James M. 1997. *The Art of Moral Protest: Culture, Biography, and Creativity in Social Movements*. Chicago: University of Chicago Press. 2010a. "The Innovation Dilemma: Some Risks of Creativity in Strategic Agency." Pp. 91–113 in *The Dark Side of Creativity*, ed. David H. Cropley, Arthur J. Cropley, James C. Kaufman, and Mark A. Runco. Cambridge and New York: Cambridge University Press. 2010b. "Cultural Approaches in the Sociology of Social Movements." Pp. 59–110 in *Handbook of Social Movements Across Disciplines*, ed. Bert Klandermans and Conny Roggeband. New York: Springer. 2014. *Protest: A Cultural Introduction to Social Movements*. Cambridge, and Malden, MA: Polity.

Jasper, James M., and Jane Poulsen. 1993. "Fighting Back: Vulnerabilities, Blunders, and Countermobilization by the Targets in Three Animal Rights Campaigns." *Social Forces*, 8(4): 639–57.

Jefferson, Tony, and Roger Grimshaw. 1984. *Controlling the Constable: Police Accountability in England and Wales*. London: Frederick Muller.

Jemmott, III, John B., Loretta S. Jemmott, and Geoffrey T. Fong. 2010. "Efficacy of a Theory-Based Abstinence-Only Intervention over 24 Months: A Randomized Controlled Trial with Young Adolescents." *Archives of Pediatric Adolescent Medicine*, 164(2): 152–19.

Jenkins, J. Craig. 1998. "Channeling Social Protest: Foundation Patronage of Contemporary Social Movements." Pp. 20–35 in *Private Action and the Public Good*, ed. Walter W. Powell and Elisabeth S. Clemens. New Haven, CT: Yale University Press.

Jenkins, J. Craig, and Craig M. Eckert. 1986. "Channeling Black Insurgency: Elite Patronage and Professional Social Movement Organizations in the Development of the Black Movement." *American Sociological Review*, 51(6): 812–29.

Jenkins, J. Craig, and Charles Perrow. 1977. "Insurgency of the Powerless: Farm Workers' Movements 1946–1972." *American Sociological Review*, 42(2): 249–68.

Johnson, Erik W., and Scott Frickel. 2011. "Ecological Threat and the Founding of U.S. National Environmental Movement Organizations, 1962–1998." *Social Forces*, 58(3): 305–29.

Johnston, Hank A. 2005. "Talking the Walk: Speech Acts and Resistance in Authoritarian Regimes." Pp. 108–137 in *Repression and*

Mobilization, ed. Christian Davenport, Hank Johnston, and Carol McClurg Mueller. Minneapolis: University of Minnesota Press.

2011. *States and Social Movements*. Cambridge, and Malden, MA: Polity.

2014. *What is a Social Movement?* Cambridge, and Malden, MA: Polity.

Johnston, Hank A., and Carol McClurg Mueller. 2001. "Unobtrusive Practices of Contention in Leninist Regimes." *Sociological Perspectives* 44: 351–76.

Joppke, Christian. 1993. *Mobilizing Against Nuclear Energy: A Comparison of Germany and the United States.* Berkeley, CA: University of California Press.

Juris, Jeffrey S. 2008. "Performing Politics: Image, Embodiment, and Affective Solidarity during Anti-Corporate Globalization Protests." *Ethnography*, 9(1): 61–97.

Karakasdou, Anastasia. 1993. "Politicizing Culture: Negating Ethnic Identity in Greek Macedonia." *Journal of Modern Greek Studies*, 11(1): 1–28.

Katzenstein, Mary Fainsod. 1998. *Faithful and Fearless: Moving Feminist Protest Inside the Church and Military*. Princeton, NJ: Princeton University Press.

Keck, Margaret, and Kathryn Sikkink. 1998. *Activists Beyond Borders: Advocacy Networks in International Politics*. Ithaca, NY: Cornell University Press.

Kelling, George L., and James Q. Wilson. 2015. "Broken Windows." Pp. 455–67 in *Critical Issues in Policing: Contemporary Readings*, ed. Roger G. Dunham and Geoffrey P. Alpert. Long Grove, IL: Waveland Press.

Keogh, Stacy. 2013. "The Survival of Religious Peace Movements: When Mobilization Increases and Political Opportunity Decreases." *Social Compass*, 60(4): 561–78.

Khan, Surina. 2009. "Tying the Not: How the Right Succeeded in Passing Proposition 8." *The Public Eye*, 24(1), www.publiceye.org/magazine/v23n4/proposition_8.html.

King, Brayden G. 2007. "A Social Movement Perspective of Stakeholder Collective Action and Influence." *Business and Society*, 47(1): 21–49.

King, Brayden G., Marie Cornwall, and Eric C. Dahlin. 2005. "Winning Woman Suffrage One Step at a time: Social Movements and the Logic of the Legislative Process." *Social Forces*, 83(3): 1211–34.

Kitschelt, Herbert. 1986. "Political Opportunity Structures and Political Protest: Anti-Nuclear Movements in Four Democracies." *British Journal of Political Science*, 16(1): 57–85.

1993. "Social Movements, Political Parties, and Democratic Theory." *The Annals of the American Academy of Political and Social Science*, 528: 13–29.

Kitts, James. 2000. "Mobilizing in Black Boxes: Social Networks and Participation in Social Movement Organizations." *Mobilization*, 5(2): 241–57.

Klandermans, Bert. 1984. "Mobilization and Participation: Social-Psychological Expansions of Resource Mobilization Theory." *American Sociological Review*, 48(5): 583–600.

1992. "The Social Construction of Protest and Multiorganizational Fields." Pp. 185–208 in *New Social Movements: From Ideology to Identity*, ed. Enrique Larana, Hank Johnston, and Joseph R. Gusfield. Philadelphia: Temple University Press.

1997. *The Social Psychology of Protest*. Cambridge, MA: Blackwell.

Klandermans, Bert, and Dirk Oegema. 1987. "Potentials, Networks, Motivations, and Barriers: Steps Towards Participation in Social Movements." *American Sociological Review*, 52(4): 519–31.

1994. "Why Social Movement Sympathizers Don't Participate: Erosion and Nonconversion of Support." *American Sociological Review*, 59(5): 703–22.

Klandermans, Bert, and Jackie Smith. 2002. "Survey Research: A Case for Comparative Design." Pp. 3–31 in *Methods of Social Movement Research*, ed. Bert Klandermans and Suzanne Staggenborg. Minneapolis, MN, and London: University of Minnesota Press.

Klandermans, Bert, and Suzanne Staggenborg, eds. 2002. *Methods of Social Movement Research*. Minneapolis, MN, and London: University of Minnesota Press.

Klandermans, Bert, Suzanne Staggenborg, and Sidney Tarrow. 2002. "Conclusion: Blending Methods and Building Theories in Social Movement Research." Pp. 314–50 in *Methods of Social Movement Research*, ed. Bert Klandermans and Suzanne Staggenborg. Minneapolis, MN, and London: University of Minnesota Press.

Kohler, Pamela K., Lisa E. Manhart, and William E. Lafferty. 2008. "Abstinence-Only and Comprehensive Sex Education and the Initiation of Sexual Activity and Teen Pregnancy." *Journal of Adolescent Health*, 42(2): 344–51.

Koopmans, Ruud. 1997. "Dynamics of Repression and Mobilization:

The German Extreme Right in the 1990s." *Mobilization*, 2(2): 149–64.

Koopmans, Ruud, and Dieter Rucht. 2002. "Protest Event Analysis." P. 231 in *Methods of Social Movement Research*, ed. Bert Klandermans and Suzanne Staggenborg. Minneapolis, MN, and London: University of Minnesota Press.

Koopmans, Ruud, and Paul Statham. 1999. "Ethnic and Civic Conceptions of Nationhood and the Differential Success of the Extreme Right in Germany and Italy." Pp. 225–51 in *How Social Movements Matter*, ed. Marco Giugni, Doug McAdam, and Charles Tilly. Minneapolis, MN: University of Minnesota Press.

Kornhauser, William. 1959. *The Politics of a Mass Society*. New York: Free Press.

Kricheli, Ruth, Yair Livne, and Beatriz Magaloni. 2011. "Taking to the Streets: Theory and Evidence on Protests under Authoritarianism." Paper presented at American Political Science Association Annual Conference, September 2–5, 2010, Washington, DC, https://papers.ssrn.com/sol3/papers.cfm?abstract_id=1642040.

Kriesi, Hanspeter. 1996. "The Organizational Structure of New Social Movements in a Political Context." Pp. 152–84 in *Comparative Perspectives on Social Movements: Political Opportunities, Mobilizing Structures, and Cultural Framings*, ed. Doug McAdam, John D. McCarthy, and Mayer N. Zald. Cambridge and New York: Cambridge University Press.

Kydd, Andrew H., and Barbara F. Walter. 2006. "The Strategies of Terrorism." *International Security*, 31(1): 49–80.

Lagerkvist, Johan, and Tim Rühling. 2016. "The Mobilization of Memory and Tradition: Hong Kong's Umbrella Movement and Beijing's 1989 Tiananmen Movement." *Contemporary Chinese Political Economy and Strategic Relations*, 2(2): 735–74.

Larrabure, Manuel, and Carlos Tochia. 2015. "The 2011 Chilean Student Movement and the Struggle for a New Left." *Latin American Perspectives*, 42(5): 248–68.

Leander, Anna. 2004. "Wars and the Un-Making of States: Taking Tilly Seriously in the Contemporary World." Pp. 69–80 in *Contemporary Security Analysis and Copenhagen Peace Research*, ed. Stefano Guzzini and Dietrich Jung. London and New York: Routledge.

LeBas, Adrienne. 2011. *From Protest to Parties: Party-Building and Democratization in Africa*. Oxford: Oxford University Press.

Le Bon, Gustave. [1895] 2001. *The Crowd: A Study of the Popular Mind*. Mineola, NY: Dover.

Lee, Yu-Hao, and Gary Hsieh. 2013. "Does Slacktivism Hurt Activism? The Effects of Moral Balancing and Consistency in Online Activism." Pp. 811–20 in *Proceedings of the SIGCHI Conference on Human Factors in Computing Systems*. New York: ACM.

Leege, David C. 1992. "Coalitions, Cues, Strategic Politics, and the Staying Power of the Religious Right, or Why Political Scientists Ought to Pay Attention to Cultural Politics." *PS: Political Science and Politics*, 25(2): 198–204.

Legewie, Nicolas. 2013. "An Introduction to Applied Data Analysis with Qualitative Comparative Analysis (QCA)." *Forum: Qualitative Social Research*, 14(3), www.qualitative-research.net/index.php/fqs/article/view/1961/3594.

Lelieveldt, Herman. 2014. "Lobbying Government or Corporations? A Comparative Case Study of Old and New Tactics to Improve Factory Farming in the Netherlands." Paper presented at the ECPR General Conference, September 3–6, Glasgow, UK.

Li, Xiang. 2013. "Hacktivism and the First Amendment: Drawing the Line between Cyber Protests and Crime." *Harvard Journal of Law and Technology*, 27(1): 302–30.

Lichbach, Mark Irving. 1987. "Deterrence or Escalation? The Puzzle of Aggregate Studies of Repression and Dissent." *Journal of Conflict Resolution*, 31(2): 266–9.

Lim, Merlyna. 2012. "Clicks, Cabs, and Coffee Houses: Social Media and Oppositional Movements in Egypt, 2004–2011." *Journal of Communication*, 62(2): 231–48.

2013. "Framing Bouazizi: 'White Lies,' Hybrid Network, and Collective/Connective Action in the 2010–11 Tunisian Uprising." *Journalism*, 14(7): 921–41.

Lindbeck, Assar, and Dennis J. Snower. 2001. "Insiders versus Outsiders." *The Journal of Economic Perspectives*, 15(1): 165–88.

Lindekilde, Lasse. 2014. "Discourse and Frame Analysis: In-Depth Analysis of Qualitative Data in Social Movement Research." Pp. 195–227 in *Methodological Practices in Social Movement Research*, ed. Donatella della Porta. Oxford: Oxford University Press.

Lo, Clarence Y. H. 1982. "Countermovements and Conservative Movements in the Contemporary U.S." *Annual Review of Sociology*, 8: 107–34.

Luders, Joseph. 2006. "The Economics of Movement Success: Business Responses to Civil Rights Mobilization." *American Journal of Sociology*, 111(4): 963–98.

Lyman, Rich, and Joanna Berendt. 2016. "Poland Steps Back from Stricter Anti-Abortion Law." *New York Times*, October 6, www.nytimes.com/2016/10/07/world/europe/poland-abortion-law-protests.html.

Maeckelburgh, Marianne. 2011. "Doing is Believing: Prefiguration as a Strategic Practice in the Alterglobalization Movement." *Social Movement Studies*, 10(1): 1–20.

Maguire, Edward R. 2015. "New Directions in Protest Policing." *St. Louis University Law Review*, 35: 67–108.

Maheshwari, Sapna. 2016. "How Fake News Goes Viral: A Case Study." *The New York Times*, November 20, https://www.nytimes.com/2016/11/20/business/media/how-fake-news-spreads.html.

Mallya, Ganeshchandra, Vimal Mishra, Dev Niyogi, Shivam Tripathi, and Rao S. Govindaraju. 2016. "Trends and Variability of Droughts over the Indian Monsoon Region." *Weather and Climate Extremes*, 12: 43–68.

Maloney, William A., Grant Jordan, and Andrew M. McLaughlin. 1994. "Interest Groups and Public Policy: The Insider/Outsider Model Revisited." *Journal of Public Policy*, 14(1): 17–38.

Marenin, Otwin. 2014. "Styles of Policing and Economic Development in African States." *Public Administration and Development*, 34(3): 149–61.

Marks, Gary and Doug McAdam. 1999. "On the Relationship of Political Opportunities to the Form of Collective Action: The Case of the European Union." Pp. 97–111 in *Social Movements in a Globalizing World*, ed. Donatella della Porta, Hanspeter Kriesi, and Dieter Rucht. Basingstoke, UK: Macmillan.

Marston, Sallie. 2003. "Mobilizing Geography: Locating Space in Social Movement Theory." *Mobilization*, 8(2): 227–33.

Marwell, Gerald, and Pamela Oliver. 1993. *The Critical Mass in Collective Action*. Cambridge: Cambridge University Press.

Marx, Gary. 1979. "External Efforts to Damage or Facilitate Social Movements: Some Patterns, Explanations, Outcomes, and Complications." Pp. 94–125 in *The Dynamics of Social Movements*, ed. Mayer Zald and John McCarthy. Cambridge, MA: Winthrop.

Matsuzawa, Setsuko. 2011. "Horizontal Dynamics in Transnational Activism: The Case of Nu River Anti-Dam Activism in China." *Mobilization*, 16(3): 369–87.

McAdam, Doug. 1982. *Political Process and the Development of Black Insurgency, 1930–1970*. Chicago: University of Chicago Press.

1983. "Tactical Innovation and the Pace of Insurgency." *American Sociological Review*, 48(6): 735–54.

1986. "Recruitment to High-Risk Activism: The Case of Freedom Summer." *American Journal of Sociology*, 92(1): 64–90.

1990. *Freedom Summer*. Oxford: Oxford University Press.

1995. "'Initiator' and 'Spin-Off' Movements: Diffusion Processes in Protest Cycles." Pp. 217–39 in *Repertoires and Cycles of Collective Action*, ed. Mark Traugott. Durham, NC: Duke University Press.

1996. "The Framing Function of Movement Tactics: Strategic Dramaturgy in the American Civil Rights Movement." Pp. 338–55 in *Comparative Perspectives on Social Movements: Political Opportunities, Mobilizing Structures, and Cultural Framings*, ed. Doug McAdam, John D. McCarthy, and Mayer N. Zald. New York: Cambridge University Press.

1999. "The Biographical Impact of Activism." Pp. 119–46 in *How Social Movements Matter*, ed. Marco Giugni, Doug McAdam, and Charles Tilly. Minneapolis, MN: University of Minnesota Press.

2004. "Revisiting the U.S. Civil Rights Movement: Toward A More Synthetic Understanding of the Origin of Contention." Pp. 201–32 in *Rethinking Social Movement Studies: Structure, Meaning, Emotion*, ed. Jeff Goodwin and James M. Jasper. Lanham, MD: Rowman & Littlefield.

McAdam, Doug, and Ronnelle Paulsen. 1993. "Specifying the Relationship between Social Ties and Activism." *The American Journal of Sociology*, 99(3): 640–67.

McAdam, Doug, Charles Tilly, and Sidney Tarrow. 2001. *Dynamics of Contention*. Cambridge and New York: Cambridge University Press.

McCammon, Holly J. 2003. "'Out of the Parlors and into the Streets': The Changing Tactical Repertoire of the U.S. Women's Suffrage Movements." *Social Forces*, 81(3): 787–818.

McCammon, Holly J., Courtney Sanders Muse, Harmony D. Newman, and Teresa M. Terrell (2007). "Movement Framing and Discursive Opportunity Structures: The Political Successes of the U.S. Women's Jury Movement." *American Sociological Review*, 72(5): 725–49.

McCarthy, John D., and Mayer N. Zald. 1973. *The Trend of Social Movements in America: Professionalization and Resource Mobilization*. Morristown, NJ: General Learning Press.

1977. "Resource Mobilization and Social Movements: A Partial Theory." *American Journal of Sociology*, 82(6): 1212–41.

McDonnell, Mary-Hunter, and Brayden King. 2013. "Keeping Up Appearances: Reputational Threat and Impression Management after Social Movement Boycotts." *Administrative Science Quarterly*, 58(3): 387–419.

McGee, Marcus J., and Karen Kampwirth. 2015. "The Co-optation of LGBT Movements in Mexico and Nicaragua: Modernizing Clientelism?" *Latin American Politics and Society*, 57(4): 51–73.

McPhail, Clark. 1991. *The Myth of the Madding Crowd*. New York: A. de Gruyter.

McPhail, Clark, David Schwingruber, and John McCarthy. 1986. "Policing Protest in the United States: 1960–1995." Pp. 49–69 in *Policing Protest: The Control of Mass Demonstrations in Western Democracies*, ed. Donatella della Porta and Herbert Reiter. Minneapolis, MN: University of Minnesota Press.

McVeigh, Rory, Daniel J. Myers, and David Sikkink. 2004. "Corn, Klansmen, and Coolidge: Structure and Framing in Social Movements." *Social Forces*, 83(2): 653–90.

McVeigh, Rory, Michael R. Welch, and Thoroddur Bjarnson. 2003. "Hate Crime Reporting as a Successful Social Movement Outcome." *American Sociological Review*, 68(6): 843–67.

Melucci, Alberto. 1995. "The Process of Collective Identity." Pp. 41–63 in *Social Movements and Culture*, ed. Hank Johnston and Bert Klandermans. Minneapolis: University of Minnesota Press.

1996. *Challenging Codes*. Cambridge: Cambridge University Press.

Meng, Bingchun. 2011. "From Steamed Bun to Grass Mud Horse: E Gao as Alternative Political Discourse on the Chinese Internet." *Global Media and Communications*, 7(1): 33–51.

Merton, Robert K. 1972. "Insiders and Outsiders: A Chapter in the Sociology of Knowledge." *American Journal of Sociology*, 78(1): 9–47.

Meyer, David S. 2003. "Political Opportunity and Nested Institutions." *Social Movement Studies*, 2(1): 17–35.

2004. "Protest and Political Opportunities." *Annual Review of Sociology*, 30: 125–45.

Meyer, David S. and Debra C. Minkoff. 2004. "Conceptualizing Political Opportunity." *Social Forces*, 82(4): 1457–92.

Meyer, David S., and Suzanne Staggenborg. 1996. "Movements, Countermovements, and the Structure of Political Opportunity." *The American Journal of Sociology*, 101(6): 1628–60.

Meyer, David S., and Sidney Tarrow. 1998. "A Movement Society: Contentious Politics for a New Century." Pp. 1–28 in *The Social*

Movement Society: Contentious Politics for a New Century. Oxford, and Lanham, MD: Rowman & Littlefield.

Meyer, David S., and Nancy Whittier. 1994. "Social Movement Spillover." *Social Problems*, 41(2): 277–98.

Meyer, Megan. 2004. "Organizational Identity, Political Contexts, and SMO Action: Explaining the Tactical Choices Made by Peace Organizations in Israel, Northern Ireland, and South Africa." *Social Movement Studies*, 3(2): 167–97.

Milkman, Ruth, Stephanie Luce, and Penny Lewis. 2013. *Changing the Subject: A Bottom-Up Account of Occupy Wall Street in New York City.* Joseph F. Murphy Institute for Worker Education and Labor Studies, City University of New York, https://media.sps.cuny.edu/filestore/1/5/7/1_a05051d2117901d/1571_92f562221b8041e.pdf.

Minkoff, Debra C. 1994. "From Service Provision to Institutional Advocacy: The Shifting Legitimacy of Organizational Forms." *Social Forces*, 72(4): 943–69.

1995. *Organizing for Equality: The Evolution of Women's and Racial Ethnic Organizations in America, 1955–1985.* New Brunswick, NJ: Rutgers University Press.

1997. "The Sequencing of Social Movements." *American Sociological Review*, 62(5): 779–99.

1999. "Bending with the Wind: Strategic Change and Adaptation by Women's and Racial Minority Organizations." *American Journal of Sociology*, 104(6): 1666–703.

Minkoff, Debra C., and John D. McCarthy. 2005. "Reinvigorating the Study of Organizational Processes in Social Movements." *Mobilization*, 10(2): 289–308.

Mische, Ann. 2002. "Cross-Talk in Movements: Reconceiving the Culture-Network Link." Pp. 258–80 in *Social Movements and Networks: Relational Approaches to Collective Action*, ed. Mario Diani and Doug McAdam. Oxford: Oxford University Press.

2008. *Partisan Publics: Communication and Contention across Brazilian Youth Activist Networks.* Princeton, NJ: Princeton University Press.

2011. "Relational Sociology, Culture, and Agency." Pp. 80–97 in *Sage Handbook of Social Network Analysis*, ed. John Scott and Peter Carrington. London and Thousand Oaks, CA: Sage.

Mitchell, Amy, Jeffrey Gottfried, Michael Barthel, and Elisa Shearer. 2016. "Pathways to News." Pew Research Center, www.journalism.org/2016/07/07/pathways-to-news.

Moghadam, Valentine M. 2013. *Globalization and Social Movements:*

Islamism, Feminism, and the Global Justice Movement. Lanham, MD: Rowman & Littlefield.

Moore, Will H. 2000. "The Repression of Dissent: A Substitution Model of Government Coercion." *Journal of Conflict Resolution*, 44(1): 107–27.

Morris, Aldon. 1996. "The Black Church in the Civil Rights Movement: The SCLC as the Decentralized, Radical Arm of the Black Church." Pp. 29–46 in *Disruptive Religion: The Force of Faith in Social Movement Activism*, ed. Christian Smith. New York and Abingdon, UK: Routledge.

Morrow, James D. 1999. "The Strategic Setting of Choices: Signaling, Commitment, and Negotiation in International Politics." Pp. 77–114 in *Strategic Choice and International Relations*, ed. David A. Lake and Robert Powell. Princeton, NJ: Princeton University Press.

Moscowitz, Leigh. 2013. *The Battle over Marriage: Gay Rights Activism through the Media*. Chicago: University of Illinois Press.

Mottl, Tahi L. 1980. "The Analysis of Countermovements." *Social Problems*, 27(5): 620–35.

Munson, Ziad W. 2002. *The Making of Pro-Life Activists: How Social Mobilization Works*. Chicago: University of Chicago Press.

Myers, Daniel J. 1997. "Racial Rioting in the 1960s: An Event History Analysis of Local Conditions." *American Sociological Review* 62(1): 94–112.

Narula, Smita. 1999. *Broken People: Caste Violence Against India's "Untouchables."* New York: Human Rights Watch.

Navsarjan. n.d. "Minimum Wage Implementation Campaign," http://navsarjan.org/programmes/minimum-wage-implementation-campaign.

Nepstad, Sharon Erickson. 2004. "Persistent Resistance: Commitment and Community in the Plowshares Movement." *Social Problems*, 51(1): 43–60.

2008. *Religion and War Resistance in the Plowshares Movement*. Cambridge and New York: Cambridge University Press.

Neuhouser, Kevin. 2008. "I am the Man and Woman in this House: Brazilian *Jeito* and the Strategic Framing of Motherhood in a Poor, Urban Community." Pp. 141–65 in *Social Movements, Protest and Contention: Identity Work in Social Movements*, ed. Jo Reger, Rachel L. Einwohner, and Daniel J. Myers. Minneapolis, MN: University of Minnesota Press.

Newport, Frank. 2010. "Tea Party Supporters Overlap Republican

Base." Gallup, July 2, www.gallup.com/poll/141098/tea-party-sup-porters-overlap-republican-base.aspx.

Noakes, John A., and Patrick F. Gillham. 2007. "Police and Protestor Innovation since Seattle." *Mobilization*, 12(4): 335–40.

Noakes, John A., Brian Klocke, and Patrick F. Gillham. 2005. "Whose Streets? Police and Protestor Struggles over Space in Washington, DC, 29–30 September 2001." *Policing and Society*, 15(3): 235–54.

Noonan, Rita K. 1995. "Women against the State: Political Opportunities and Collective Action Frames in Chile's Transition to Democracy." *Sociological Forum*, 10(1): 81–111.

Norris, Pippa. 2006. "Political Protest in Fragile States." Paper presented at the International Political Science Association World Congress, July 9–13, Fukuoka, Japan, https://www.hks.harvard.edu/fs/pnorris/Acrobat/IPSA%202006%20Political%20Action%20in%20Fragile%20States.pdf.

Oberschall, Anthony. 1995. *Social Movements: Ideologies, Interests, and Identities.* New Brunswick, NJ, and London: Transaction.

Oliver, Pamela E. 1980. "Rewards and Punishments as Selective Incentives for Collective Action: Theoretical Investigations." *American Journal of Sociology*, 85(6): 1356–75.

1989. "Bringing the Crowd Back In: The Nonorganizational Elements of Social Movements." *Research in Social Movements, Conflicts, and Change*, 11: 1–30.

Oliver, Pamela E., and Daniel J. Myers. 2002. "The Coevolution of Social Movements." *Mobilization*, 8(1): 1–24.

Olson, Mancur. 2002. *The Logic of Collective Action.* Cambridge, MA, and London: Harvard University Press.

Olzak, Susan, Maya Beasley, and Johan Olivier. 2002. "The Impact of State Reforms on Protest against Apartheid in South Africa." *Mobilization*, 8(1): 27–50.

Olzak, Susan, and Emily Ryo. 2007. "Organizational Diversity, Vitality and Outcomes in the Civil Rights Movement." *Social Forces*, 85(4): 1561–91.

Opp, Karl-Dieter. 2009. *Theories of Political Protest and Social Movements: A Multidisciplinary Introduction, Critique, and Synthesis.* Abingdon, UK, and New York: Routledge.

Ortiz, Isabel, Sara Burke, Mohamed Berrada, and Hernán Cortés. 2013. "World Protests 2006–2013." Working Paper, Initiative for Policy Dialogue, Friedrich Ebert Foundation, New York, www.cadtm.org/IMG/pdf/World_Protests_2006–2013-Final-2.pdf.

Pallas, Christopher L. 2016. "Inverting the Boomerang: Examining the Legitimacy and North–South–North Campaigns in Transnational Advocacy." *Global Networks*, doi: 10.1111/glob.12129.

Pan, Po-Lin, Juan Meng, and Shuhua Zhou. 2010. "Morality or Equality? Ideological Framing in News Coverage of Gay Marriage Legitimization." *The Social Science Journal*, 47(3): 630–45.

Passy, Florence. 1999. "Supranational Political Opportunities as a Channel of Globalization of Political Conflicts: The Case of the Rights of Indigenous Peoples." Pp. 148–69 in *Social Movements in a Globalizing World*, ed. Donatella della Porta, Hanspeter Kriesi, and Dieter Rucht. Basingstoke, UK: Palgrave Macmillan.

  2003. "Social Networks Matter. But How?" Pp. 21–48 in *Social Movement and Networks: Relational Approaches to Collective Action*, ed. Mario Diani and Doug McAdams. Oxford: Oxford University Press.

Pastor, Jr., Manuel, Chris Brenner, and Martha Matsuoka. 2009. *This Could Be the Start of Something Big: How Social Movements for Regional Equity are Reshaping Metropolitan America*. Ithaca, NY: Cornell University Press.

Pew Research Center. 2007. "Where People Get Their News," www.pewglobal.org/2007/10/04/chapter-7-where-people-get-their-news.

  2009. "Majority Continues to Support Civil Unions," www.pewforum.org/2009/10/09/majority-continues-to-support-civil-unions.

  2012. "Growing Public Support for Same-Sex Marriage," www.people-press.org/2012/02/07/growing-public-support-for-same-sex-marriage.

Pfeffer, Jeffrey, and Gerald R. Salancik. 1978. *The External Control of Organizations: A Resource Dependence Perspective*. New York: Harper and Row.

Pickerill, Jenny, and John Krinsky. 2012. "Why Does Occupy Matter?" *Social Movement Studies*, 11(3–4): 279–87.

Pini, Barbara, Kerry Brown, and Josephine Previte. 2004. "Politics and Identity in Cyberspace: A Case Study of Australian Women in Agriculture Online." Pp. 225–38 in *Cyberprotest*, ed. Wim van de Donk, Brian D. Loader, Paul G. Nixon, and Dieter Rucht. London and New York: Routledge.

Piven, Frances Fox, and Richard A. Cloward. 1974. *The Politics of Turmoil*. New York: Pantheon Books.

  1977. *Poor People's Movements: Why They Succeed, How They Fail*. New York: Pantheon.

Polletta, Francesca. 2002. *Freedom is an Endless Meeting: Democracy in American Social Movements*. Chicago: University of Chicago Press.

Pousadela, Inés M. 2012. "Student Protest, Social Mobilization and Political Representation in Chile." Paper presented at the International Political Science Association World Congress, July 8–12, Madrid, http://paperroom.ipsa.org/papers/paper_11698.pdf.

Poushter, Jacob. 2016. "Internet Access Growing Worldwide but Remains Higher in Advanced Economies." Pew Research Center, www.pewglobal.org/2016/02/22/internet-access-growing-world-wide-but-remains-higher-in-advanced-economies.

Pressman, Jeremy, and Erica Chenowith. 2017. "Crowd Estimates, 1–21–2017," https://docs.google.com/spreadsheets/d/1xa0iLqYKz8x9Yc_rfhtmSOJQ2EGgeUVjvV4A8LsIaxY/htmlview?sle=true.

Price, Vincent, Lilach Nir, and Joseph N. Capella. 2005. "Framing Public Discussion of Gay Civil Unions." *Public Opinion Quarterly*, 69(2): 179–212.

Przeworski, Adam, and Henry Teune. 1970. *The Logic of Comparative Social Inquiry*. New York: Wiley Interscience.

Pullum, Amanda. 2016. "Social Movements, Strategic Choice, and Recourse to the Polls." *Mobilization*, 21(2): 177–92.

Ragin, Charles C. 1987. *The Comparative Method*. Oakland, CA: University of California Press.

 2008. *Redesigning Social Inquiry: Fuzzy Sets and Beyond*. Chicago: University of Chicago Press.

Rahr, Sue, and Stephen K. Rice. 2015. "From Warriors to Guardians: Recommitting American Police Culture to Democratic Ideals." New Perspectives in Policing Bulletin. National Institute of Justice, Office of Justice Programs. Washington, DC: US Department of Justice.

Ramachandran, Vimala, and Taramani Naorem. 2013. "What it Means to be a Dalit or Tribal Child in Our Schools: A Synthesis of a Six-State Qualitative Study." *Economic and Political Weekly*, 48(44): 43–52.

Rand, Erin J. 2014. *Reclaiming Queer: Activist & Academic Rhetorics of Resistance*. Tuscaloosa, AL: University of Alabama Press.

Rasler, Karen. 1996. "Concessions, Repression, and Political Protest in the Iranian Revolution." *American Sociological Review*, 61(1): 132–52.

Redekop, Vern Neufeld, and Shirley Paré. 2010. *Beyond Control: A Mutual Respect Approach to Protest Crowd–Police Relations*. London and New York: Bloomsbury Academic.

Regan, Patrick M., and Errol A. Henderson. 2002. "Democracy,

Threats and Political Repression in Developing Countries: Are Democracies Internally Less Violent?" *Third World Quarterly*, 23(1): 119–36.

Reiter, Herbert, and Olivier Fillieule. 2006. "Formalizing the Informal: The EU Approach to Transnational Protest Policing." Pp. 145–73 in *The Policing of Transnational Protest*, ed. Donatella della Porta, Abbey Peterson, and Herbert Reiter. Aldershot, UK, and Burlington, VT: Ashgate.

Ritter, Daniel P. 2014. "Comparative Historical Analysis." Pp. 97–116 in *Methodological Practices in Social Movement Research*, ed. Donatella della Porta. Oxford: Oxford University Press.

Robertson, Graeme B. 2009. "Managing Society: Protest, Civil Society, and Regime in Putin's Russia." *Slavic Review*, 68(3): 528–47.

Rojas, Fabio. 2006. "Social Movement Tactics, Organizational Change and the Spread of African-American Studies." *Social Forces*, 84(4): 2147–66.

Roscigno, Vincent J., Julia Miller Cantzler, Salvatore J. Restive, and Joshua Guetzkow. 2015. "Legitimation, State Repression, and the Sioux Massacre at Wounded Knee." *Mobilization*, 20(1): 17–40.

Roscigno, Vincent T., and William F. Danaher. 2001. "Media and Mobilization: The Case of Radio and Southern Textile Worker Insurgency, 1929 to 1934." *American Sociological Review*, 66(1): 21–48.

Roudometof, Victor. 1996. "Nationalism and Identity Politics in the Balkans: Greece and the Macedonia Question." *Journal of Modern Greek Studies*, 14(2): 253–301.

Rucht, Dieter. 1988. "Themes, Logics, and Arenas of Social Movements: A Structural Approach." Pp. 305–21 in *From Structure to Action: Comparing Movement Participation across Cultures, International Social Movement Research*, vol. I, ed. Bert Klandermans, Hanspeter Kriesi, and Sidney Tarrow. Greenwich, CT: JAI Press.

1990. "Campaigns, Skirmishes, and Battles: Anti-Nuclear Movements in the USA, France, and West Germany." *Industrial Crisis Quarterly*, 4: 193–222.

1996. "The Organizational Structure of New Social Movements in a Political Context." Pp. 185–204 in *Comparative Perspectives on Social Movements: Political Opportunities, Mobilizing Structures, and Cultural Framings*, ed. Doug McAdam, John D. McCarthy, and Mayer N. Zald. Cambridge and New York: Cambridge University Press.

1999. "Linking Organization and Mobilization: Michel's Iron Law of Oligarchy Reconsidered." *Mobilization*. 4(2): 151–69.

2004. "Movement Allies, Adversaries, and Third Parties." Pp. 197–216 in *The Blackwell Companion to Social Movements*, ed. David A. Snow, Sarah A. Soule, and Hanspeter Kriesi. Malden, MA, and Oxford: Blackwell.

Rudy, Kathy. 2001. "Radical Feminism, Lesbian Separatism, and Queer Theory." *Feminist Studies*, 27(1): 190–222.

Rule, James. 1988. *Theories of Civil Violence*. Berkeley, CA: University of California Press.

Saad, Lydia. 2010. "Tea Partiers are Fairly Mainstream in their Demographics." Gallup, April 5, www.gallup.com/poll/127181/tea-partiers-fairly-mainstream-demographics.aspx.

Samuelson, William, and Richard Zeckhauser. 1988. "Status Quo Bias in Decision Making." *Journal of Risk and Uncertainty*, 1(1): 7–59.

Santoro, Wayne A., and Gail M. McGuire. 1997. "Social Movement Insiders: The Impact of Institutional Activists on Affirmative Action and Comparable Worth Policies." *Social Problems*, 44(4): 503–19.

Saunders, Clare. 2007. "Using Social Network Analysis to Explore Social Movements: A Relational Approach." *Social Movement Studies*, 6(3): 227–43.

Sauter, Molly. 2014. *The Coming Swarm: DDoS Actions, Hacktivism, and Civil Disobedience on the Internet*. New York and London: Bloomsbury Academic.

Sawyers, Traci M. and David S. Meyer. 1999. "Missed Opportunities: Social Movement Abeyance and Public Policy." *Social Problems*, 46(2): 187–206.

Scarritt, James R., Susan M. McMillan and Shaheen Mozaffar. 2001. "The Interaction between Democracy and Ethnopolitical Protest and Rebellion in Africa." *Comparative Political Studies*, 34(7): 800–27.

Schattschneider, E. E. 1963. *Politics, Pressure, and the Tariff*. Hamden, CT: Archon.

Scheufele, Dietram A. 1999. "Framing as a Theory of Media Effects." *Journal of Communications*, 49(1): 103–22.

Schmalz, Jeffrey. 1993. "In Hawaii, Step Toward Legalized Gay Marriage." *New York Times*, May 7.

Schneider, Nathan. 2013. *Thank You, Anarchy: Notes from the Occupy Apocalypse*. Berkeley, CA: University of California Press.

Schock, Kurt. 1999. "People Power and Political Opportunities: Social Movement Mobilization and Outcomes in the Philippines and Burma." *Social Problems*, 46(3): 355–75.

2004. *Unarmed Insurrections: People Power Movements in Non-Democracies.* Minneapolis, MN: University of Minnesota Press.

Schulz, Markus S. 1998. "Collective Action across Borders: Opportunity Structures, Network Capacities, and Communicative Praxis in the Age of Advanced Globalization." *Sociological Perspectives*, 41(3): 587–616.

Schumaker, Paul D. 1975. "Policy Responsiveness to Protest-Group Demands." *Journal of Politics*, 37(2): 488–521.

Schussman, Alan, and Sarah A. Soule. 2005. "Process and Protest: Accounting for Individual Protest Participation." *Social Forces*, 84(2): 1083–108.

Schwab, Klaus, and Xavier Sala-i-Martín. 2013. *The Global Competitiveness Report, 2013–2014.* Geneva: World Economic Forum, http://www3.weforum.org/docs/WEF_GlobalCompetitivenessReport_2013–14.pdf.

Seidman, Gay W. 2015. "Divestment Dynamics: Mobilizing, Shaming, and Changing the Rules." *Social Research*, 82(4): 1015–37.

Sewell, William. 2001. "Space in Contentious Politics." Pp. 51–89 in *Silence and Voice in the Study of Contentious Politics*, ed. Ronald R. Aminzade, Jack A. Goldstone, Doug McAdam, et al. Cambridge: Cambridge University Press.

Sherkat, Darren E. and T. Jean Blocker. 1994. "The Political Development of Sixties' Activists: Identifying the Influence of Class, Gender, and Socialization on Protest Participation." *Social Forces*, 72(3): 821–42.

Shigetomi, Shinichi. 2009. "Rethinking Theories on Social Movements and Development." Pp. 1–16 in *Protest and Social Movements in the Developing World*, ed. Shinichi Shigetomi and Kumiko Makino. Cheltenham, UK, and Northampton, MA: Edward Elgar.

Shindler, Colin. 2013. *A History of Modern Israel*, 2nd edn. New York: Cambridge University Press.

Sichynsky, Tanya. 2016. "These 10 Twitter Hashtags Changed the Way We Talk about Social Issues." *The Washington Post*, March 21, https://www.washingtonpost.com/news/the-switch/wp/2016/03/21/these-are-the-10-most-influential-hashtags-in-honor-of-twitters-birthday/?utm_term=.a26c80b46842.

Sikkink, Kathryn. 2005. "Patterns of Dynamic Multilevel Governance and the Insider–Outsider Coalition." Pp. 151–73 in *Transnational Protest and Global Activism*, ed. Donatella della Porta and Sidney Tarrow. Lanham, MD: Rowan & Littlefield.

Simmons, Erica. 2014. "Grievances Do Matter in Mobilization." *Theory and Society*, 43(5): 513–46.

Simone, AbdouMaliq. 2006. "Pirate Towns: Reworking Social and Symbolic Infrastructures in Johannesburg and Douala." *Urban Studies*, 43(2): 357–70.

Singer, Jane B. 2003. "Who Are These Guys? The Online Challenge to the Notion of Journalistic Professionalism." *Journalism*, 4(2): 139–63.

Skocpol, Theda, and Vanessa Williamson. 2012. *The Tea Party and the Remaking of Republican Conservatism*. Oxford and New York: Oxford University Press.

Small, Albion. 1897. "The Meaning of the Social Movement." *American Journal of Sociology*, 3(3): 340–54.

Smelser, Neil. 1962. *Theory of Collective Behavior*. New York: Free Press.

Smith, Jackie. 1998. "Global Civil Society? Transnational Social Movement Organizations and Social Capital." *American Behavioral Scientist*, 42(1): 93–107.

2001. "Globalizing Resistance: The Battle of Seattle and the Future of Social Movements." *Mobilization*, 6(1): 1–19.

2002. "Bridging Global Divides? Strategic Framing and Solidarity in Transnational Social Movement Organization." *International Sociology*, 17(4): 505–28.

Smith, Michelle. 2014. "Affect and Respectability Politics." *Theory & Event*, 17(3): Supplement.

Smith, Miriam. 2007. "Framing Same-Sex Marriage in Canada and the United States: Goodridge, Halpern and the National Boundaries of Political Discourse." *Social & Legal Studies*, 16(1): 5–26.

Smithey, Lee A. 2009. "Social Movement Strategy, Tactics, and Collective Identity." *Sociology Compass*, 3(4): 658–71.

Snow, David A., and Robert D. Benford. 1988. "Ideology, Frame Resonance, and Participant Mobilization." Pp. 197–218 in *International Social Movement Research*, vol. I, ed. Bert Klandermans, Hanspeter Kriesi, and Sidney Tarrow. Greenwich, CT: JAI Press.

1992. "Master Frames and Cycles of Protest." Pp. 133–55 in *Frontiers in Social Movement Theory*, ed. Aldon Morris and Carol McClurg Mueller. New Haven, CT, and London: Yale University Press.

2000 "Clarifying the Relationship between Framing and Ideology in the Study of Social Movements: A Comment on Oliver and Johnston." *Mobilization*, 5(1): 55–60.

Snow, David A., Robert D. Benford, Holly J. McCammon, Lyndi

Hewitt, and Scott Fitzgerald. 2014. "The Emergence, Development, and Future of the Framing Perspective: 25+ Years since 'Frame Alignment.'" *Mobilization*, 19(1): 23–45.

Snow, David A., Burke Rochford, Jr., Steven K. Worden, and Robert D. Benford. 1986. "Frame Alignment Processes, Micromobilization, and Movement Participation." *American Sociological Review*, 51(4): 464–81.

Snow, David A. and Sarah A. Soule. 2010. *A Primer on Social Movements*. New York and London: W. W. Norton.

Snow, David A., Louis A. Zurcher, Jr., and Sheldon Ekland-Olson. 1980. "Social Networks and Social Movements: A Microstructural Approach to Differential Recruitment." *American Sociological Association*, 45(5): 787–801.

Snyder, David, and William R. Kelly. 1979. "Strategies for Investigating Violence and Social Change: Illustrations from Analyses of Racial Disorders and Implications for Mobilization Research." Pp. 212–37 in *The Dynamics of Social Movements*, ed. Mayer N. Zald and John D. McCarthy. Cambridge, MA: Winthrop.

Somma, Nicolás M. 2012. "The Chilean Student Movement of 2011–2012: Challenging the Marketization of Education." *Interface: A Journal for and about Social Movements*, 4(2): 296–309.

Soule, Sarah A. 1997. "The Student Divestment Movement in the United States and Tactical Diffusion: The Shantytown Protest." *Social Forces*, 75(3): 855–82.

2009. *Contention and Corporate Social Responsibility*. New York: Cambridge University Press.

Soule, Sarah A., and Brayden G. King. 2006. "The Stages of the Policy Process and the Equal Rights Amendment, 1972–1982." *American Journal of Sociology*, 111(6): 1871–909.

Soule, Sarah A., and Susan Olzak. 2004. "When Do Movements Matter? The Politics of Contingency and the Equal Rights Amendment." *American Sociological Review*, 69(4): 473–97.

Staggenborg, Suzanne. 1986. "Coalition Work in the Pro-Choice Movement: Organizational and Environmental Opportunities and Obstacles." *Social Problems*, 33(5): 374–90.

1988. "The Consequences of Professionalization and Formalization in the Pro-Choice Movement." *American Sociological Review*, 53(4): 585–605.

1995. "Can Feminist Organizations Be Effective?" Pp. 339–55 in *Feminist Organizations: Harvest of the New Women's Movement*, ed. Myra Marx Ferree and Patricia Yancey Martin. Philadelphia: Temple University Press.

1998. "Social Movement Communities and Cycles of Protest: The Emergence and Maintenance of a Local Women's Movement." *Social Problems*, 45(2): 180–204.

2011. *Social Movements*. New York and Oxford: Oxford University Press.

Stanger-Hall, Kathrin F., and David W. Hall. 2011. "Abstinence-Only Education and Teen Pregnancy Rates: Why We Need Comprehensive Sex Education in the U.S." *PLoS One*, 6(10).

Stearns, Linda Brewster, and Paul D. Almeida. 2004. "The Formation of State Actor – Social Movement Coalitions and Favorable Policy Outcomes." *Social Problems*, 51(4): 478–504.

Steinberg, Marc W. 2002. "Toward a More Dialogic Analysis of Social Movements Culture." Pp. 208–25 in *Social Movements: Identity, Culture, and the State*, ed. David S. Meyer, Nancy Whittier, and Belinda Robnett. New York: Oxford University Press.

Stern, Charlotte. 1997. "The Evolution of Social-Movement Organizations: Niche Competition in Social Space." *European Sociological Review*, 15(1): 91–105.

Stelter, Brian. 2011. "Camps are Cleared, but '99 Percent' Still Occupies the Lexicon." *New York Times*, November 30, www.nytimes.com/2011/12/01/us/we-are-the-99-percent-joins-the-cultural-and-political-lexicon.html.

Steuter, Erin. 1992. "Women Against Feminism: An Examination of Feminist Social Movements and Anti-Feminist Countermovements." *Canadian Review of Sociology*, 29(3): 288–306.

Stillerman, Joel. 2002. "Space, Strategies, and Alliances in Mobilization: The 1960 Metalworkers' and Coal Miners' Strikes in Chile." *Mobilization*, 8(1): 65–85.

Stott, Clifford, Martin Scothern, and Hugo Gorringe. 2013. "Advances in Liaison Based Public Order Policing in England: Human Rights and Negotiating the Management of Protest?" *Policing*, 7(2): 210–25.

Strang, David, and Sarah A. Soule. 1998. "Diffusion in Organizations and Social Movements: From Hybrid Corn to Poison Pills." *Annual Review of Sociology*, 24: 265–90.

Stürmer, Stefan, and Bernd Simon. 2004. "Collective Action: Towards a Dual-Pathway Model." *European Review of Social Psychology*, 15(1): 59–99.

Stürmer, Stefan, Bernd Simon, Michael Loewy, and Heike Jörger.

2003. "The Dual-Pathway Model of Social Movement Participation: The Case of the Fat Acceptance Movement." *Social Psychology Quarterly*, 66(1): 71–82.

Suh, Doowon. 2014. "What Happens to Social Movements after Policy Success? Framing the Unintended Consequences and Changing Dynamics of the Korean Women's Movement." *Social Science Information*, 53(1): 3–34.

Sullivan, Christopher M., Cyanne E. Loyle, and Christian Davenport. 2012. "The Coercive Weight of the Past: Temporal Dependence and the Conflict–Repression Nexus in the Northern Ireland 'Troubles.'" *International Interactions*, 38(4): 426–42.

Swart, William J. 1995. "The League of Nations and the Irish Question: Master Frames, Cycles of Protest, and 'Master Frame Alignment.'" *The Sociological Quarterly*, 36(3): 465–81.

Szymanski, Ann-Marie E. 2003. *Pathways to Prohibition: Radicals, Moderates, and Social Movement Outcomes*. Durham, NC: Duke University Press.

Tang, Lijun, and Peidong Yang. 2011. "Symbolic Power and the Internet: The Power of a 'Horse.'" *Media, Culture, and Society*, 33(5): 675–91.

Tanner, Murray Scot. 2004. "China Rethinks Protest." *The Washington Quarterly*, 27(3): 137–56.

Tarrow, Sidney. 1995. "Bridging the Quantitative–Qualitative Divide in Political Science." *American Political Science Review*, 89(2): 471–4.

2004. "Paradigm Warriors: Regress and Progress in the Study of Contentious Politics." Pp. 39–46 in *Rethinking Social Movements: Structure, Meaning, and Emotion*, ed. Jeff Goodwin and James M. Jasper. Lanham, MD, and Oxford: Rowman & Littlefield.

2005. *The New Transnational Activism*. New York: Cambridge University Press.

2011. *Power in Movement: Social Movements and Contentious Politics*, 3rd edn. New York: Cambridge University Press.

2012. *Strangers at the Gates: Movements and States in Contentious Politics*. New York: Cambridge University Press.

Taylor, Lynne. 1996. "Food Riots Revisited." *Journal of Social History*, 30(2): 483–96.

Taylor, Verta. 1989. "Social Movement Continuity: The Women's Movement in Abeyance." *American Sociological Review*, 54(5): 761–75.

Taylor, Verta, Leila J. Rupp, and Joshua Gamson. 2005. "Performing Protest: Drag Shows as Tactical Repertoire of the Gay and Lesbian

Movement." *Research in Social Movements, Conflicts and Change*, 25: 105–38.

Thompson, E. P. 1971. "The Moral Economy of the English Crowd in the Eighteenth Century." *Past & Present*, 50: 76–136.

1992. "Rough Music Reconsidered." *Folklore*, 103(1): 3–26.

Thorat, S. K., and Joel Lee. 2008. "Dalits and the Right to Food: Discrimination and Exclusion in Food-Related Government Programmes." Pp. 442–64 in *Reforming Indian Agriculture: Towards Employment Generation and Poverty Reduction*, ed. Sankar Kumar Bhaumik. New Delhi and Thousand Oaks, CA: Sage.

Tilly, Charles. 1978. *From Mobilization to Revolution*. Reading, MA: Addison-Wesley.

1992. *Coercion, Capital and European States, A.D. 990–1992*. Cambridge, MA: Blackwell.

1995a. *Popular Contention in Great Britain, 1758–1834*. Cambridge, MA: Harvard University Press.

1995b. "Contentious Repertoires in Great Britain, 1758–1834." Pp. 15–42 in *Repertoires and Cycles of Collective Action*, ed. Marc Traughott. Durham, NC: Duke University Press.

1996. *Regimes and Repertoires*. Chicago: University of Chicago Press.

2000. "Spaces of Contention." *Mobilization*, 5(2): 135–59.

2002. *Stories, Identities, and Political Change*. Lanham, MD: Rowman & Littlefield.

2003. *The Politics of Collective Violence*. New York and Cambridge: Cambridge University Press.

2004. *Stories, Identities, and Political Change*. Lanham, MD: Rowman & Littlefield.

2008. *Contentious Performances*. New York: Cambridge University Press.

Tilly, Charles, and Sidney Tarrow. 2015. *Contentious Politics*. Oxford: Oxford University Press.

Tilly, Charles, and Lesley J. Wood. 2004. *Social Movements, 1768–2004*. Boulder, CO, and London: Paradigm.

Touraine, Alain. 1971. *The Post-Industrial Society*. New York: Random House.

Tsutsui, Kiyoteru, and Hwa Ji Shin. 2008. "Global Norms, Local Activism, and Social Movement Outcomes: Global Human Rights and Resident Koreans in Japan." *Social Problems*, 55(3): 391–418.

Turner, Ralph H., and Lewis M. Killian. 1987. *Collective Behavior*. Englewood Cliffs, NJ: Prentice-Hall.

Uitermark, Justus, and Walter Nicholls. 2014. "From Politicization to Policing: The Rise and Decline of New Social Movements in Amsterdam and Paris." *Antipode*, 46(3): 970–91.

United Nations. 1980. *Patterns of Urban and Rural Population Growth*. Department of International Economic and Social Affairs, Population Studies 68. New York.

USDA-FAS. 2014. "India's Agricultural Exports Climb to Record High." Foreign Agricultural Service, US Department of Agriculture, Washington, DC, www.fas.usda.gov/sites/default/files/2015–02/india_iatr_august_2014.pdf.

Vairel, Frédéric. 2011. "Protesting in Authoritarian Situations: Egypt and Morocco in Comparative Perspective." Pp. 27–42 in *Social Movements, Mobilization, and Contestation in the Middle East and North Africa*, ed. Joel Beinin and Frédéric Vairel. Stanford, CA: Stanford University Press.

Valiant, Gabriela Gonzalez, Juhi Tyagi, Idil Afife Akin, Fernanda Page Poma, Michael Schwartz, and Arnott van de Rijt. 2015. "A Field Experimental Study of Emergent Mobilization in Online Collective Action." *Mobilization*, 21(3): 281–303.

Van Cott, Donna Lee. 2005. *From Movements to Parties in Latin America: The Evolution of Ethnic Politics*. New York: Cambridge University Press.

van Dyke, Nella, Sarah A. Soule, and Verta A. Taylor. 2004. "The Targets of Social Movements: Beyond a Focus on the State." *Research in Social Movements, Conflicts and Change*, 25: 27–51.

Van Laer, Jeroen, and Peter Van Aelst. 2010. "Internet and Social Movement Action Repertoires: Opportunities and Limitations." *Information, Communication & Society*, 13(8): 1146–71.

van Spanje, Joost. 2010. "Contagious Parties: Anti-Immigration Parties and their Impact on Other Parties' Immigration Stances in Contemporary Western Europe." *Party Politics*, 16(5): 563–86.

Vasi, Ion Bogdan, and Brayden G. King. 2012. "Social Movements, Risk Perceptions, and Economic Outcomes: The Effect of Primary and Secondary Stakeholder Activism on Firms' Perceived Environmental Risk and Financial Performance." *American Sociological Review*, 77(4): 573–96.

Vitale, Alex S. 2007. "The Command and Control and Miami Models at the 2004 Republican National Convention: New Forms of Policing Protests." *Mobilization*, 12(4): 403–15.

von Bülow, Marisa, and Germán Bidegain Ponte. 2015. "It Takes Two to Tango: Students, Political Parties, and Protest in Chile

(2005–2013)." Pp. 179–94 in *Handbook of Social Movements across Latin America*, ed. Paul Almeida and Allen Cordero Ulate. New York and London: Springer.

Voss, Kim, and Rachel Sherman. 2000. "Breaking the Iron Law of Oligarchy: Union Revitalization in the American Labor Movement." *American Journal of Sociology*, 106(2): 303–49.

Waddington, David P. 2007. *Policing Public Disorder: Theory and Practice*. Cullompton, UK: Willan.

Wagemann, Claudius. 2014. "Qualitative Comparative Analysis (QCA): What It Is, What It Does, and How It Works." Pp. 43–66 in *Methodological Practices in Social Movement Research*, ed. Donatella della Porta. Oxford: Oxford University Press.

Walgrave, Stefaan, Dieter Rucht, and Peter Van Aelst. 2010. "New Activists or Old Leftists? The Demographics of Protestors." Pp. 78–97 in *The World Says No to War: Demonstrations Against the War on Iraq*, ed. Stefaan Walgrave and Dieter Rucht. Minneapolis, MN: University of Minnesota Press.

Walgrave, Stefaan, Ruud Wouters, and Pauline Ketelaars. 2016. "Response Problems in the Protest Survey Design: Evidence from Fifty-One Protest Events in Seven Countries." *Mobilization*, 21(1): 83–104.

Walker, Edward T. 2014. *Grassroots for Hire: Public Affairs Consultants in American Democracy*. Cambridge and New York: Cambridge University Press.

Walker, Edward T., Andrew W. Martin, and John D. McCarthy. 2008. "Confronting the State, the Corporation, and the Academy: The Influence of Institutional Targets on Social Movement Repertoires." *American Journal of Sociology*, 114(1): 35–76.

Walker, Edward T., and Christopher M. Rea. 2014. "The Political Mobilization of Firms and Industries." *Annual Review of Sociology*, 40: 281–304.

Walsh, Edward J. 1986. "The Role of Target Vulnerabilities in High-Technology Protest Movements: The Nuclear Establishment at Three Mile Island." *Sociological Forum*, 1(2): 199–218.

Wang, Dan J. and Sarah A. Soule. 2012. "Social Movement Organizational Collaboration: Networks of Learning and the Diffusion of Protest Tactics, 1960–1995." *American Journal of Sociology*, 117(6): 1674–722.

2016. "Tactical Innovation in Social Movements: The Effects of Peripheral and Multi-Issue Protest." *American Sociological Review*, 81(3): 517–48.

Wang, Dan J., and Alessandro Piazza. 2016. "The Use of Disruptive Tactics in Protest as a Trade-Off: The Role of Social Movement Claims." *Social Forces*, 94(4): 1675–710.

Warner, Cody, and John D. McCarthy. 2014. "Whatever Can Go Wrong Will: Situational Complexity and Public Order Policing." *Policing and Society*, 24(5): 566–87.

Warnick, Barbara. 2007. *Rhetoric Online*. New York: Peter Lang.

Warren, Deirdre M., and Katrina R. Bloch. 2014. "Framing Same-Sex Marriage: Media Constructions of California's Proposition 8." *The Social Science Journal*, 51(4): 503–13.

Wasserman, Stanley, and Katherine Faust. 1994. *Social Network Analysis: Methods and Applications*. Cambridge: Cambridge University Press.

Weber, Klaus, Hayagreeva Rao, and L. G. Thomas. 2009. "From Streets to Suites: How the Anti-Biotech Movement Affected German Pharmaceutical Firms." *American Sociological Review*, 74(1): 106–27.

Weiss, Robert Frank. 1963. "Defection from Social Movements and Subsequent Recruitment to New Movements." *Sociometry*, 26(1): 1–20.

Williamson, Vanessa, Theda Skocpol, and John Coggin. 2011. "The Tea Party and the Remaking of Republican Conservatism." *Perspectives on Politics*, 9(1): 25–43.

Wilson, Christopher, and Alexandra Dunn. 2011. "Digital Media in the Egyptian Revolution: Descriptive Analysis from the Tahrir Data Sets." *International Journal of Communication*, 5: 1248–72.

Wischmann, Lesley. 1987. "Dying on the Front Page: Kent State and the Pulitzer Prize." *Journal of Mass Media Ethics*, 2(2): 67–74.

Wood, Lesley J. 2004. "Breaking the Bank and Taking to the Streets: How Protestors Target Neoliberalism." *Journal of World-Systems Research*, 10(1): 69–89.

Yates, Luke. 2015. "Rethinking Prefiguration: Alternatives, Micropolitics and Goals in Social Movements." *Social Movement Studies*, 14(1): 1–21.

Young, Kevin and Michael Schwartz. 2014. "A Neglected Mechanism of Social Movement Political Influence: The Role of Anticorporate and Anti-Institutional Protest in Changing Government Policy." *Mobilization*, 19(3): 239–60.

Yue, Lori Qingyuan, Hayagreeva Rao, and Paul Ingram. 2013. "Information Spillovers from Protests against Corporations: A Tale of Wal-Mart and Target." *Administrative Science Quarterly*, 58(4): 669–701.

Zald, Mayer N. and Roberta Ash. 1966. "Social Movement Organizations: Growth, Decay, Change." *Social Forces*, 44(3): 327–41.

Zald, Mayer N., and John D. McCarthy. 1980. "Social Movement Industries: Competition and Cooperation among Movement Organizations." *Research in Social Movements, Conflicts and Change*, 3: 1–20.

Zald, Mayer N., and Bert Useem. 1987. "Movement and Countermovement Interaction: Mobilization, Tactics, and State Involvement." Pp. 247–71 in *Social Movements in an Organizational Society*, ed. Mayer N. Zald and John D. McCarthy. New Brunswick, NJ: Transaction.

Zhao, Dingxin. 1998. "Ecologies of Social Movements: Student Mobilization During the 1989 Prodemocracy Movement in Beijing." *American Journal of Sociology*, 103(6): 1493–529.

Zürn, Michael. 2010. "Global Governance as Multi-Level Governance." Pp. 80–99 in *Handbook on Multi-Level Governance*, ed. Henrik Enderlein, Sonja Wälti, and Michael Zürn. Cheltenham, UK and Northampton, MA: Edward Elgar.

Index